PENGUIN HANDBOOKS
THE KITCHEN GARDEN BOOK

Born in Nebraska, Stella Standard has lived
most of her life, with her husband, Paul, in
New York, where she delights in regaling
friends with her latest succulent creations.
She is one of the world's most honored culinary authors and has won three gold medals
at the Frankfurt International Cookbook Ex-
hibition. Among her twelve cookbooks are
*Our Daily Bread, The Art of Fruit Cookery,
Menus and Recipes for All Occasions,* and
Whole Grain Cookery.

Stringfellow Barr was born in Virginia in
1897 and educated at the University of Virginia, at Oxford, and at the universities of
Paris and Ghent. Long famous as an educator
and political scientist, he is also one of America's most expert and versatile gardeners—a
horticultural artist whose feats with hoe and
pruning hook were celebrated in all the universities where he taught.

The Kitchen Garden Book

VEGETABLES FROM SEED TO TABLE

by

Stringfellow Barr

and

Stella Standard

PENGUIN BOOKS

Penguin Books Ltd, Harmondsworth,
Middlesex, England
Penguin Books, 625 Madison Avenue,
New York, New York 10022, U.S.A.
Penguin Books Australia Ltd, Ringwood,
Victoria, Australia
Penguin Books Canada Ltd, 41 Steelcase Road West,
Markham, Ontario, Canada
Penguin Books (N.Z.) Ltd, 182–190 Wairau Road,
Auckland 10, New Zealand

First published in the United States of America by The Viking Press 1956
Published in Penguin Books 1977

LIBRARY OF CONGRESS CATALOGING IN PUBLICATION DATA
Barr, Stringfellow, 1897-
The kitchen garden book.
(Penguin handbooks)
Reprint of the 1956 ed. published by
The Viking Press, New York.
Bibliography: p.
Includes index.
1. Cookery (Vegetables)   2. Vegetable gardening.
I. Standard, Stella, joint author.   II. Title.
[TX801.B292 1977]   641.3′5   76-53768
ISBN 0 14 046.257 0 (pbk.)

Printed in the United States of America by
Offset Paperback Mfrs., Inc., Dallas, Pennsylvania
Set in Linotype Times Roman

If you want to be happy for an hour, get intoxicated; if you want to be happy for three days, get married; but if you want to be happy forever, become a gardener.

—An old English saying.

M. le Président H. de P———, s'addressant à trois des savants les plus distingués de l'école actuelle (MM. de Laplace, Chaptal et Berthollet) leur disait en 1812: "Je regarde la découverte d'un mets nouveau qui soutient notre appétit et prolonge nos jouissances comme un évènement bien plus intéressant que la découverte d'un étoile. On en voit toujours assez."
Brillat-Savarin, *Physiologie du Goût.*

President H. of P———, speaking to three of the most distinguished scientists of the present school (Messrs. de Laplace, Chaptal and Berthollet) told them in 1812: "I regard the discovery of a new dish that sustains our appetite and prolongs our enjoyment as a much more interesting event than the discovery of a star. One can always see enough stars."

Contents

CONTENTS

Publisher's Preface

THIS BOOK is a natural outcome of the simple realization that vegetables are grown primarily to be eaten; that the vegetable garden, the kitchen, and the table are but backgrounds for three successive stages in a single progressive process—that of feeding the inner man. If, as Mr. Barr points out in his introductory general instructions for gardening, which also constitute a charming essay on the joys of intelligent and methodical messing about with soil and seeds and succulents, there is spiritual, as well as physical, nourishment to be found in growing vegetables (and in creative cooking, too), that is one of life's bonuses, as are flowers, brilliant sunsets, and rainbows. From time immemorial man has tilled the soil in order to eat—and he still does, whether earnestly and professionally on expansive fields of farmland or, as an avocation in what may be called symbolic obeisance to the ancient necessity, in a kitchen garden ten feet square. Vegetables are for eating.

Yet once the symbolic gesture has been made, an age-old yearning often stirs within the amateur gardener; the plot which was ten feet square the first year becomes twice that size the second, encroaching on what before was lawn, and four times as large the third; the miracle of the multiplication of a few tiny seeds into pounds of harvest is so engaging, the vision of bushels and bushels of vegetables so enchanting, that the thing gets away from him. He composts avidly; he learns the special virtues of mulching and seizes eagerly on every shred of lawn clipping and every bit of excelsior in which wrapped things come to the house, that he may put them between the rows of his pretties. Not only do the boundaries of his garden push outward, but the pounds of food which he can grow in each square foot increase with the constant acceleration of the earth's burgeoning fertility. (What joy to see the soil which at first produced carrots the size of his little finger yielding roots as stout as the wrist of a blacksmith!)

Alas! Before he knows it, all is a chaos of surplus vegetables. In vain does he give his less garden-conscious neighbors snap beans, cucumbers, and cabbages, lug large grocery-bags full of onions, Boston lettuce, and sweet-corn-picked-that-morning-with-the-dew-on-it to his colleagues at the office, and long for the days of horses when he could surreptitiously feed the iceman's waiting nag a peck of assorted vitamin-rich treasures. Still the supply overwhelms him. And his secret certainty that his children's cheeks are redder, their vitality more obnoxious, and their marks in school better than when they were eating stale, inorganically grown store vegetables does little to mitigate his annoyance when the same boiled carrots, or the same fried summer squash, or the undiscouraged but eventually discouraging snap beans for dinner make him wonder why he ever started a garden, and he growls at his wife (who is after all but nobly coping), "Isn't there some other way to fix these blasted things?"

The answer, of course, is "yes," but many of even the best wives have not yet learned it. And that is why over five hundred ways to cook vegetables have been included in *The Kitchen Garden Book,* along with instructions for growing them. Thus the snap beans, which the gardener thought on Monday night had gone far beyond the point of diminishing returns, become on Tuesday night a hitherto untasted delicacy; for twenty-two days in succession he may eat the lowly spinach and have a different dish each day, and he will find that squash (which, in a good garden, has a way of saying, "Never too much!") may become the chief ingredient of soup, an excellent vegetable course to be eaten with the main part of the meal, or a delectable dessert.

If there is a freezer in the house, or if the goodwife is one who enjoys the bustle of the canning season, she will emulate the squirrel and store much of the summer's yield for the coming winter, but that is another story. There are limits to the size and range of any book. And because the field of freezing vegetables at home and pressure-cooker canning is a large one and is excellently covered by several books, as well as in pamphlets issued by the Department of Agriculture, this book does not attempt to enter it, save that it includes a few of Mrs. Standard's favorite old-time recipes for pickles, relishes, and so on—things which, happily, she could not bear to leave out.

ACKNOWLEDGMENTS

I OWE warm thanks for help in preparing the gardening section of this book to Mildred Johnson, Cary Peebles, Barbara Turlington, and Barbara Witt.

Baldwin Barr gave me constant critical encouragement.

James Barr furnished me with detailed criticism based on half a century of experience in vegetable gardening and on a shrewd reading of the experience of other gardeners.

I thank also those gardeners, too numerous to name, on every continent except Australia, who have shown me their gardens with loving pride and explained their many ingenious devices for meeting their widely varying problems.

I record here with gratitude that my grandfather, Frank Stringfellow, and my aunt, Jane Stuart Patton, taught me more than fifty years ago to grow my own food. Neither had any means of predicting that the industrialization of American agriculture, and specifically of truck farming, would lend a new and vital importance to home-grown vegetables.

Most of all I owe thanks to Robert O. Ballou, my editor at The Viking Press. First, his gentle obstinacy and his own infectious love of gardening conquered my refusal to undertake this task—on the grounds that I was too busy. As if any man should ever be too busy to share his gardening experience! Second, when a trip to Asia postponed for a year my completion of the manuscript, he patiently hoped I would enjoy Asia. I did, especially the vegetable gardens I examined there. Last, his own rich experience in growing vegetables made him no ordinary editor but a valuable critic.

STRINGFELLOW BARR

Charlottesville, Virginia

I WISH to express my gratitude to Miss Elise Roberts and Mr. R. A. Seelig, research experts of The United Fresh Fruit and Vegetable Association, Washington, D. C., for their friendly help and excellent technical material which I have used in the part of this book which pertains to cooking vegetables.

STELLA STANDARD

New York

1. GROWING VEGETABLES

by Stringfellow Barr

Come into the Garden

GARDENERS KNOW, better than most people, that everything man has came out of the earth. Therefore they respect earth, and ultimately love it. But if you have decided to make a garden, you must first remember that on the face of this earth there are many places with no soil and that a garden can be made only where there is soil. I am not thinking for the moment of those parts covered by rivers, by lakes, or by oceans, or of the vast deserts, or of stretches of solid rock. If you live in a city or a town, I am thinking of your back yard, which probably looks as if it were covered with soil. But the dirt in your back yard may not be soil at all. It probably was soil once. And you can make it soil again—provided you know what soil is.

Gardening is so much fun that a lot of people, when the miracle of spring comes around, rush to a seed store, come home laden with seeds, and start planting. Many of them never rush to a seed store again, because they find they "can't make things grow." Nobody ever made anything grow. A seed is a tiny high-powered bundle of determination to grow. All the gardener has to do is make sure to put it where a seed can grow. And his first problem is to put it in soil. The people whom spring beguiled into a seed store and could never beguile again—those people, those disappointed lovers, usually put the seed in dirt all right, but not in soil. The gardener's first task is to make sure he has some soil. And there are precious few people who could not transform the dirt in their back yard into soil if only they knew how.

Maybe you think that spring can be celebrated by planting seeds but not by changing dirt into soil, that it is not worth your while to make a garden if you have to make soil first. If you think that, you must not know how exciting a thing it is to change dirt into soil. So this book must first deal with how to make a good "garden spot."

For a vegetable seed to do what it wants most to do—produce a beautiful, healthy, bountiful plant—it not only needs good soil. It also

3

needs plenty of sunlight. So, in planning your garden, watch carefully which parts of your available space get a long day's sunlight. A high board fence may mean that part of your yard will do better for types of flowers that love shade than for the vegetables this book is about. Above all, watch out for trees and even big shrubs. Nothing is lovelier than a tree. I sometimes think that even vegetables must enjoy looking at a fine tree. But vegetables like to look at trees from a safe distance. Never plant them too near a tree. The tree will steal from them: it will steal the water they need to make food available to their tiny roots. It will steal the food itself. It will steal the sunlight they must have; and in the shade the vegetable's complexion will grow pale and sickly and it will never be happy or make you a good dish. Look at almost any vegetable garden that has a tree at one end of its rows, and you will notice that the plants in each row taper off from health to sickliness. So make sure your garden spot gets plenty of sunlight.

Finally, the vegetables you plant to grow must have water, and in the right amounts. The water they will like most is, for many reasons, rain. But in most parts of the United States, even where annual rainfall is adequate, the rain does not always fall when the vegetable needs it. Most vegetable gardens in towns are reasonably near a hydrant, and it will pay to buy even quite a long garden hose in order to be able to rescue them. If you live in the country, you may need to run a pipe from the house, from a spring, from a well, or from a brook. If you depend on buckets, you are likely to be too stingy with water when drought comes and sickness or even death stares each vegetable in the face. Remember, vegetables get just as thirsty as people. If no water is brought to thirsty people, the people walk to a place where they can find water. But vegetables are like babies: they cannot walk. They get only the water that comes to them—from the sky, or through the soil from a nearby pond or brook, or up from below by capillary attraction, or from you. Moreover, hungry people can eat, even when they have no water. A vegetable can neither eat nor drink without it: its nutrients are available to it only in solution. When it lacks water, therefore, it is both hungry and thirsty. In short, your garden spot should be where you can give it plenty of water with the least labor possible.

But vegetables, like babies and other people, can also have too much water: they can drown. This should not frighten you. Even the water you cannot control—such as long, heavy rains—will not hurt your vegetables if your garden spot is so situated and so handled that it drains well. Most vegetables will not grow in a marsh, or even in a spot that frequently looks like a marsh. If your garden spot slopes lightly, so the water will run gently off it—without taking your soil with it, as it will do if the slope is steep—you are safe. Even better than this surface drainage is the drainage that occurs underground when you have, or have made, deep crumbly soil. To get that kind of drainage, you want to make sure there is no "hardpan" under your topsoil. If you dig a hole or trench in your garden spot, you can easily find out whether there is hardpan. The subsoil will be packed tight and water will not sink into it readily.

In that case, if your garden spot is big enough, you can hire somebody with a subsoiler—a plow with a long sharp blade instead of a moldboard—to break up the subsoil so water will enter it. If your garden spot is too small to let a horse or tractor maneuver, you can do a lot by "trenching." That means digging a foot and a half to two feet all through the garden, and it is good hard work. But if your subsoil is now so hard that water puddles and stands on your garden spot, you will later bless the day you opened things up for the deep roots of your vegetables. I repeat, you cannot grow vegetables in a swamp, or even in a spot that often becomes swampy—although, even in low ground, you can do a lot by "hilling up" or by making raised beds; both will increase drainage where you need it most.

For a start, that takes care of three things your seed will need if it is to do what it already wants to do: good soil—and we will have to talk again about that—plenty of sunlight, and the right amounts of water, given when your vegetables are clearly asking for it. By now you may want to rush to the seed store, but I urge you to wait and think a little more about the home, the garden spot, you expect your seed to live and work in. I am convinced that the average amateur failure in gardening is a result of not preparing that home. We Americans are now a nation of city people, and indeed, our farmer ancestors often came from Europe's towns, with peasant traditions. Too many of us imagine that any place that gets dusty in dry weather and muddy in wet weather must be capable of raising a vegetable. This is nonsense. Anybody who spends good money to plant seed in the average piece of city earth, without first preparing that earth, is fooling himself, wasting money, time, and effort, and getting ready for a big disappointment.

There is a fourth thing you ought to consider in advance: climate. Considerations of climate will have a great deal to do with your choice of a garden spot, if your place is big enough to offer you a choice. If it is not, you might think about renting a small plot conveniently near where you live, if it is safe from human and animal intruders and a better spot than your yard. And, in any case, you will have to find such a place if you live in an apartment with no rights to ground outside it. But even if you are not choosing between spots, the climate where you live may dictate your choice of which vegetables to grow, or else what difficulties to watch out for if you insist on growing those which are not very well adapted to your climate.

Remember, climate, and particularly temperature, is an intensely local matter. It is not just a matter of whether you live in the North or in the South, or whether you live in the mountains or in a river valley or on a coast. Average temperature can vary unbelievably between two places ten miles apart, and not just because there may be a range of mountains between them either. On the contrary, two sides of the same hill may have quite different climatic conditions. Rutgers University has been experimenting with the "climatic" difference between air at the level of a man's head and air on the same spot at the level of his ankles or shins, since cold air sinks. Most vegetables are considerably more interested in how cold it is at shin level than they are in the temperature at chin level. Fruit trees are commonly planted a little way up a hillside because the cold air that might destroy their fruit in spring will flow away from them down the hill, almost as if it were water.

It will not do, therefore, merely to consult one of the maps that certain books, magazines, agricultural bulletins, and seed catalogues print, showing temperature belts, or one of the weather tables showing the date of the last probable frost in each state of the Union. Find out who the best gardeners are quite near you, preferably by watching whose gardens seem to do best, and then boldly ask their advice on when to plant, which things do best, which things need special attention, and what kind of attention. Whether you are a beginner or merely a newcomer to a community, most of them will be quick to help. Gardeners who love their gardens are usually only too eager to help other people make their own gardens to love. They will most likely be willing to look at your proposed garden spot or help you choose a good one. If you really mean to learn gardening, you would be smart to offer to help one of them with his work in return for some of his crop. There is no substitute for apprenticeship, and this is truer in gardening than in most skills.

Every locality has its own problems and its own opportunities, and therefore very specific advice is as likely to be wrong as right. You can get considerable suggestive help from books, although you may be surprised and discouraged by the number of quite good garden books that contradict one another. In the last analysis you should supplement that advice with the advice of people who live near you and have learned how to run a good garden in that precise climate, in those precise physical surroundings. Practice will do the rest.

By now you may be wondering whether gardening is not a lot of work. I cannot answer that one, because the word "work" means different things to different people. If you mean by work something disagreeable that requires a lot of effort to do but that you do anyhow, in order to get paid some money with which you can do things you really enjoy, I can only answer that gardening in order to make money, or even to save money, is hard work. Why add one more disagreeable job to the disagreeable jobs you probably do already during your "working" day? Better look at television and try to forget your misery. But if you mean by work doing something intelligent that involves both your mind and your body, and doing it for so sensible and primary a purpose as to grow your own and your family's food, then gardening is delightful and rewarding "work," perhaps unlike any work you did last week. As industrial society gets more complicated and specialized, a lot of people work only for money, which spoils the fun the work might otherwise furnish. A home vegetable garden can leave out the confusing element of money. You plant grains of corn, cultivate the cornstalk which the seed produces, harvest the ears when the silk gets brown, and eat delicious corn. The work of planting, cultivating, and harvesting is so plainly connected with eating good corn that it is interesting: we know why we are doing it. The physical exercise does us more good than shoving up dumbbells in our bedroom because it is out of doors, in fresh air and sunlight, and makes sense. Because of these things the gardener ends up by enjoying the work he does in his garden as much as the taste of fresh vegetables at his table. At that point it becomes as silly to ask him whether there isn't a lot of work in gardening as it is to ask a golfer or a tennis player whether his sport isn't a lot of work. In any case, you have to be pretty feeble physically to find a home vegetable garden beyond your strength or even disagreeably tiring. You are more likely to find it exhilarating and tranquilizing by turns.

Finally, gardening is something a whole family can do together— father, mother, and even quite small children—with no fear that unequal skill will spoil the fun. In a garden families learn to work well together in order that they may eat well together. That is why growing food has so often in history been considered a sacramental act. A home garden is a hobby, but it has dimensions and meaning which few hobbies possess.

Is it an expensive hobby? The answer is an emphatic no. Anybody who dares not make a garden for fear of what it might cost is either silly or desperately poor. Like every other hobby, gardening can be made to cost a good deal of money: through expensive—and often unnecessary—tools; through interesting but expensive experiments. But a good vegetable garden can be run very cheaply indeed. It is hard to name a human art that has not developed tools to help the artist practice his art well, and the art of gardening is no exception. But the basic tools are few and simple: a long shovel, a spade, a steel rake, a "draw" hoe, a trowel, and a ball of twine to stretch between two sticks when you want to run a straight row, will get you by. Before long you will be wanting a wheelbarrow, preferably of light metal, and a wheel cultivator, with attachments, if your garden is big enough to justify it. All these tools should be kept clean and dry when not in use. Tools of good quality turn out cheapest in the end. Experience will later tell you whether more elaborate tools can help you, if you have the money to buy them. But go easy at the start. Most beginners in any art tend to overequip themselves.

Note that I have seemed to imply that the vegetables you grow will be worth no money; that your garden will not yield a profit or even break even. I could give a rosier account by a little fancy bookkeeping. I could remind you of the high cost of fresh vegetables at your grocery. I could claim that if you were not spending money on seed, fertilizer, and tools for your garden, you would probably be spending even more on alternative recreations; that people who garden have fewer doctors' bills than those who kill time playing bridge or drinking highballs or watching television. But let's not kid ourselves. I am convinced that if the average amateur gardener charged wages for his time and rent for the land he gardened on, he would have a tough time proving his vegetables cost less than when he bought them at the store. If money is what he is after, he could generally earn more doing something else. And why not? American truck farming is a highly industrialized process. Why should a lonely gardener, working with simple tools, compete financially with a "food factory" employing high technical skill, buying supplies in bulk, following market analyses, and able to invest profitably in expensive machinery?

On the other hand, "wage economics" can be most deceptive. A neighbor of a friend of mine is a machinist with eight children. He and his children run a garden, and their "unpaid" labor enables them to live well where they would have a tough time making do if all they now eat had first to be bought from a grocer with cash the father had earned as a machinist. He could, of course, consult Adam Smith, "charge" wages for his own gardening labor and for each child's labor, and prove it didn't "pay" to make a garden. If the children then got hungry, they could read Adam Smith for consolation. If you want to translate all your waking activities into terms of wage-labor, don't garden. And when you dress each morning, don't forget to enter in your day-book the "money" you are making by serving as your own valet! Valets come high these days.

I just don't think money profit is the argument for having your own vegetable garden. I think there are two main arguments. First, gardening is an utterly delightful hobby with deep primary meanings for the human spirit. A garden is one of the best places I know for turning hideous worries into interesting problems. It heals the soul. Second, I think that, of all the practical problems we practical Americans have tackled, the one we now have the least success with is the production and distribution of really fresh fruit and vegetables with delicious flavor and high nutrition content. We have done magnificently on quantity production, and we are doing less and less well on quality. We made the fundamentally false assumption that food can be produced and distributed like automobiles, clothes, or building materials. This is nonsense. Food is alarmingly perishable. To meet that problem, we have tried canning; we have tried freezing; we have shipped "fresh" vegetables great distances in refrigerated cars; we pick fruit green so it will last longer before it starts to rot; and, above all, our plant breeders have developed strains that are decidedly inferior in flavor but that will "ship well" and have lots of "eye appeal" for customers. Unhappily, we do not eat with our eyes or even taste with them, and many a gorgeous vegetable or fruit turns out to be a snare and a delusion when it reaches the human palate, and another delusion when it reaches the human stomach. Most of our agricultural science is directed at increasing the size of our fruits and vegetables, regardless of what happens to their taste, and above all at increasing the number of days between the time they were picked and the time they begin to "spoil." In the process, our breeders spoil the taste and connive at spoiling the vitamin content. Meanwhile the American palate has become steadily less critical. Cows and horses and chickens are guided by their palates to the most nutritious food available. We are hoping our eyes will guide us. They won't.

The best chance a gourmet has of getting delicious fruits and vegetables is to raise them himself—and this is the best chance he has of keeping in good health too. Good home-grown vegetables, like good handmade furniture, are both aesthetically better and more practical in terms of use. These are the reasons that this book is addressed neither to truck farmers nor to restaurant keepers but to people who want to raise vegetables they cannot buy and then cook them in ways that will bring out priceless flavor.

It goes without saying that, just as the most brilliant cook can do only so much with stale and tasteless vegetables, so the most delicious vegetables any man ever grew can be quickly spoiled by bad, or even by merely unimaginative, cooking. The usual fate of the stale vegetables we now buy is to be overcooked. In short, they never had much life, they lost in shipping most of the life they had, and the cook then cooks all the life out of them.

First, then, gardening is a glorious hobby. Second, it may well be your only chance to eat first-class food. But there is a third argument: in really practical terms, not in bookkeeping mythology, it can "pay" well—as it does for my friend's machinist neighbor, who spends his leisure balancing his family's diet instead of balancing his budget with fictitious wage entries. A man or woman, even more a family, and most of all a large family, can in their spare time, as a glorious hobby, get by on a pay-envelope that would leave them in sore straits if they had no garden.

I have tried to suggest that if you are to make a garden a real home for the seeds you plant, you will need real soil, which you may have to make or improve; plenty of sunshine; the right amounts of water; an adjustment to your precise local climate; some work, although a delightful and purposeful kind of work; at least a few simple tools to work with; very little money. To do a bang-up job, I am personally convinced you will need one other thing. But I find it hard to talk about without running the risk of sounding sentimental and a little superstitious. Here goes, anyhow: you will need to love the plants you are growing. I am convinced that the famous "green thumb" that good gardeners are supposed to have is in part their awareness that plants are living creatures like ourselves. They do not respond to love in precisely the same way as children and house pets, but they do respond. Treat your plants with some of the loving care you now reserve for little children.

The modern Occidental idea of the Conquest of Nature has no place in a home garden. The movements of a gardener among his plants are not the movements of violence, of wrenching force. They are gentle, careful, patient, helpful, and perhaps a little slow. If you cannot love your plants, move among them as if you did, lest the root in the dark earth be torn, lest the stem be broken, the flower shattered, or the fruit bruised. You cannot force your plants to grow: you can only put food and drink within their reach, protect them from the insects that prey upon them, perhaps bind them gently up when they have fallen.

II

So much about vegetable gardens in general. Now let's start your own garden. If you live in a city, there may be little choice. But remember that the spot where you plant must have plenty of sun. You can build your own soil if you have to, and have fun doing it. But you cannot supply sunlight, except maybe by cutting a branch off a tree to let sunlight through or by taking down a board fence. If you live in a small town or in the open country and have a choice of sites, a good piece of ground is one that slopes just enough to drain easily. If it slopes south—or, better still, southeast—so much the better. Dig a hole a foot deep and see what kind of soil you have to deal with. Normally the top few inches will be much darker and much more crumbly than what lies below. This is your topsoil: it is dark because it contains "humus"—decayed vegetable matter. That means it is capable of feeding plants. The subsoil below it may contain minerals that plants can use, but it lacks the necessary humus. Put an ounce or two of each in a small container and find out from your County Agricultural Agent or from the Department of Agriculture in your state capital where to send them for free chemical analysis. The analysis you get will tell you particularly whether you need additions to the three chemical elements plants need most, nitrogen, phosphorus, and potassium, and also whether your soil is too acid and needs calcium. If it does, you should spread agricultural lime on it, not quicklime. Commercial fertilizers are available which combine nitrogen, phosphorus, and potassium in various proportions according to what your soil analysis calls for.

If you can't get your soil samples professionally tested, there are now on the market a number of inexpensive "soil kits," which are advertised in garden magazines. And if you don't want to buy or borrow one of these soil kits, you can test for mere acidity with a nickel's worth of blue litmus paper bought from a druggist. Roll a ball of moist soil four or five inches in diameter in your hands. Cut it in half, place a piece of blue litmus paper between the halves, and press the halves tightly together again. Do the same thing with a handful of your subsoil.

In twenty minutes, open the balls. If the litmus paper is still quite blue, your soil needs no lime. If the paper has turned more than slightly red, your soil is sour, or acid. It needs a sprinkling of lime—about one pound to every twenty square feet; that is, a space five feet long and four feet wide. Don't give it more. But test again next year, and repeat the dose if the litmus paper still turns more than slightly red. Each time you lime, you raise the "pH" ("p" for parts, "H" for hydrogen ion concentration) or active alkalinity, and you lower the active acidity.

This liming will enormously improve the texture of your soil. It will make available to your vegetables minerals which your soil may already contain in unavailable form. And if you use some calcium limestone and some magnesium limestone, you will be adding two minerals that most vegetables crave. These benefits justify repeated annual liming.

Finally, as to your requirements of nitrogen, phosphorus, and potassium, if you insist on chemicals and have had no professional soil analysis, you can scarcely go wrong on "5-10-5" fertilizer. The numbers mean that a hundred-pound sack contains five pounds of nitrogen, ten pounds of phosphoric acid, and five pounds of potash. It is a standard mixture for the vegetable garden.

If you are after quality vegetables for your own table, and are patient enough to use surer, safer methods of getting fertile soil, you can use the methods of what is called "organic" agriculture. That is, instead of buying concentrated chemical fertilizers in sacks, and specially hydrated lime, you can stick to plain ground limestone and to the products of plants and animals. If you can't buy plain ground limestone where you live, use plasterer's lime—"hot lime"—remembering you need only half as much. The products of plants and animals make safer fertilizer than chemicals because the factory products, if misused, can "burn" your plants; and they are surer because there is a great deal of evidence that merely adding the needed chemical elements will not produce the "living" soil without which you cannot get high-quality flavor and maximum nutrition. There is a ferocious war of words on between organic farmers and those who depend on chemicals. The case for organic gardening has made great progress: the proof is that more and more of its opponents have begun to argue that both methods are needed. The case would have progressed even faster if cranks had not overstated it.

The reason I practice organic gardening myself is that unless you are a good chemist with lots of agricultural experience, high-powered chemicals are easy to misuse, and I am convinced you will not find them necessary, once you have built true soil by organic methods. But I am not interested in denouncing chemicals in this book and they certainly bring the quick results we Americans like to get in everything we do, even sometimes at the expense of results that are also good. This book is concerned not with the quickest way to get an edible vegetable, but with the best way. And even if you insist on using chemical fertilizers, you will still need to build a live soil by organic methods.

Before we had automobiles in this country it was a fairly easy job to garden organically. We then raised an immense number of draft animals—horses, mules, and even oxen, to do the heavy work which tractors and other machines do now. That meant that most farms produced as a by-product an abundance of animal manure and animal urine. Even people who did not farm, but had their own home garden, often kept their own cow. The by-product of that operation too was animal manure. And even if a man had no animals of his own, he could buy plenty of horse manure from a livery stable—the equivalent of today's U-Drive-It. Horse and cow manure, and to some extent poultry manure, not chemicals in a sack bought from a factory, were the standard garden fertilizers. Nature's balance of plant-plus-animal was preserved. People plowed rotted stable manure into their gardens and kept the soil in good heart, able to produce fine, vigorous vegetables.

But now the car and truck have largely replaced the horse; and cows tend to be concentrated in dairies, whose managers frequently and understandably refuse to sell the manure from their herds. The livery stable is gone. And it is often hard for the gardener to buy any manure, at least at a price within his reach. Sometimes he buys manure that has been processed in a factory and is sold by the sack. It is cleaner to handle than the old stable manure was, but vegetables don't like that particular kind of cleanliness very much. More often, as I have said, the gardener buys chemical fertilizers. If you can buy a load of stable manure, buy it quick. There are ways to multiply its effect which too few American farmers have ever practiced but which the peasantry of Europe and of Asia have practiced for hundreds and even thousands of years. The method is to compost the manure with vegetable matter.

The basic rules for composting are extremely simple; the frills come with knack, and the knack with practice. Stake off a space of ground four feet wide, and at least four feet long—or as much longer as the abundance of compostable material will permit. Take a shovel and turn the topsoil upside down. If there is no topsoil, if the earth is subsoil from an excavated cellar, and has no dark-colored vegetable matter in it, no humus, get some good rich earth from somewhere if you can and sprinkle the whole rectangle with it. Then spread any kind of vegetable matter over it to a depth of six inches— grass clippings, weeds, fallen leaves, table refuse, house sweepings. Sprinkle it with the garden hose until it is thoroughly wet, but not soggy. If you use weeds, they are best when they have withered for twenty-four hours but before they are brittle-dry. Then cover the whole pile with a couple of inches of manure. Lightly sprinkle the whole pile with rich earth—only one-eighth of an inch; more than that may prevent your pile from heating as soon as it should. Sprinkle the whole pile either with ground limestone or, if you burn wood in your home, with wood-ash. Coal ash will not do. The lime or wood-ash is to prevent acids from forming that would also slow up the bacterial

action you are striving to get started. Now take the hose again and
sprinkle the manure, earth, and lime, again enough to wet it through
but not enough to make it soggy. Keep repeating these layers in the
same order until your pile is four feet high. The process is just like
building a layer cake. As you build the cake, slope the sides in slowly,
and leave a depression on top to catch valuable rain-water. In a few
days the pile will begin to heat inside, as if it were running a fever; it
really is running a kind of fever. Hundreds of millions of bacteria are
breaking up the material. What you have done has provided the conditions for a sort of speeded-up decay, a kind of fermenting process.
The temperature may rise inside the heap to 120° or 140°—as you
can test for yourself if you tie a small thermometer to a stick and
thrust it to the center. If the weather is cold, the pile may start to
"smoke"—that is, throw off vapor.

After six weeks the pile should have cooled down and be ready for
turning. Prepare the ground next it to receive it, by turning the topsoil over. Then, with a pitchfork, shift the material to the adjacent site,
making sure that all the material that was outside the pile now gets
inside, to take its turn at decaying. The pile is likely to heat again.
After some five weeks it should be ready to enter the topsoil of your
garden. And I really mean enter. In the first place, it is now ripe and
teeming with life, though most of the life is too small to see. All you
can see is a dark brown crumbly mass that has the sweet smell of
wood-earth. Of course it has; you have just imitated Nature's way of
making the wood-earth on the forest floor. The compost does not re-
motely suggest manure either in smell or looks.

But its goodness will deteriorate if you do not work it soon into your
garden. Sunshine is extremely hard on it, for sunshine kills bacteria.
So, when you spread the compost, spread only a few square feet, work
that in to a depth of three inches or so, spread some more, and so
forth. You will discover that your topsoil is shortly transformed by
this humus. It keeps heavy clay soils from baking and packing and
thereby lets the tiny roots of your vegetables get through to do their
proper work. If your topsoil is sandy, humus will give it bulk and hold
the moisture that would otherwise leach quickly down after each rain,
out of reach of your vegetables. These are mechanical effects. But
humus has chemical effects too. It contains nowhere near the quantities of chemical elements that commercial fertilizer contains, but it
contains them in better form for your plants. The chief value of humus,
however, lies neither in its mechanical effects nor in its chemical effects
but in the complicated biological processes it sets going in your soil,
in the enormous work force of minute animal life it turns loose to work
your garden for you. That work force includes not only the hundreds

of millions of bacteria that distinguish virgin soil from the cement-like, dead soil that many amateur gardeners doom good seed to lie in. It will shortly include a large population of earthworms; and earthworms, as we have known ever since Charles Darwin, breed astronomically, convert second-rate soil into priceless garden soil by passing it through their digestive tracts, and even in death fill the earth with their fertilizing bodies. Millions of them are sold annually to home gardeners for just these purposes. But if you get plenty of humus into your topsoil by continuous composting, you will quickly breed your own. Whereas, if you buy five hundred from a breeder and put them into what most people think is soil, they are likely to starve to death or move next door.

You would think that if what I have said here about the value of compost heaps is true, every gardener in the country would have one. For several reasons, they are still relatively rare. Or they are built carelessly and are only half efficient. Why?

Well, most of us are just plain too lazy. If that is your trouble, there is a lazy man's way of composting that your garden will still be enormously grateful for. Just make sure to pile all compostable material in one spot, preferably adding a little of your best soil from time to time. Try never to let it dry out. After a year it is well worth spading in. Fundamentally, the art of composting consists of getting vegetable waste and, if possible, animal waste with it to rot.

People also claim they cannot find the main ingredient, vegetable waste. I believe this is because people are unobservant. Almost every community is full of compostable waste. It depends on where you live. Every autumn in my town hundreds of people burn leaves in the street. The fires make a delicious smell. But heavens, the waste of fertility they represent! Trees are regular fertilizer factories. They send their roots down twenty, thirty, forty feet; they bring up priceless mineral plant-food, convert it into leaves, then kindly drop these leaves in autumn where any fool can collect them and compost them.

If you have no trees, and if your neighbor won't let you rake his garden in return for his leaf supply, you may be able to get leaves the lazy way: city trucks may be glad to dump some in your back yard and save a long haul to the city dump. Fortunately for the fertility of our country, although perhaps unfortunately for you, in many towns people, particularly florists, are queuing up for the city's leaf collections.

Grocery stores often pass on to the garbage collector loads of spoiled vegetables that you could persuade the stores to let you collect. Fruit dealers, and even fruit wholesalers, do the same. Food processers sometimes throw away valuable waste. Above all, you have your own garbage tin. Never let your garbage go to the city dump. It will compost beautifully—if, of course, you persuade whoever prepares your food to put tin cans, bottles, broken crockery, and even paper in another container. Only a handful of American cities have shown enough concern for the basic fertility of America to compost the city garbage and sell it to surrounding farmers. But at least you can keep your own household garbage out of the wasteful hands of a stupid municipal government.

Do you ever drive in the country? Notice those tall weeds on the roadside. With a sickle you could in a few minutes fill the trunk of your car—and every load would help. The leafier they are, the better: leaves break down more quickly than woody stalks do.

If you live in the country, every fence row will be a gold mine for your compost heap. And spoiled hay will be extremely valuable: "spoiled" only means it has started to compost itself without your help. Help it finish the job under better conditions.

People who have come to admit they can find the vegetable waste they need sometimes swear they cannot locate any manure. This is a more legitimate excuse. But if you cannot find any animal manure almost anything that comes from an animal will help. Your work force of bacteria will be able to break down just about any part of an animal except solid bone. If cattle or poultry is slaughtered in your town, or if fish are scaled and cleaned, find out where and ask for what is thrown away. Feathers, hair, wool are all valuable. But animal parts, even as remnants in your household garbage, offer disadvantages manure does not offer. They attract stray dogs or cats, so that you may have to place mesh wire around and over your compost. Until the heating process starts, they may create offensive odors, at least in warm weather. City sanitary officers may complain. As to flies, manure breeds them too. But a pile heats quickly, and then all these objections disappear. If your heap smells or breeds flies, it is probably too wet. If ants appear, it is probably too dry. The heating process cures all disorders and kills weed-seed and the bacteria in diseased plant refuse too. Finally, vegetable matter, properly composted, will heat whether there is any animal matter added or not; but it will not have as extraordinarily good effects on your garden soil.

It follows from what I have said that you should never, never throw away or burn any part of a plant. Stack weeds, leaves, and all in one convenient place near the garden to quarry when you compost.

There are several ways of speeding up the fermenting process of a compost heap. One is to add chemical "activators," and several are regularly advertised. The best practice is to omit them. Another is to chop fine all the material you put in the pile. A number of machines, driven either by small motor or by small gasoline engines, are advertised for this purpose. I use one and find it helps. I have one criticism. In my machine the material is chopped by blades on a revolving cylinder. The blades are the small triangular ones used on the cutter-bars of mowing machines. But several times I have gotten into trouble with weeds I had pulled up and wanted to chop fine, roots and all. Some of the weeds had big roots, and though I tried to shake all the soil out of the roots, enough had adhered to some to hold against the roots a little stone or pebble. That can raise merry Andrew with the blades. And though the blades are extremely cheap, changing them is a long and tedious performance.

Another speed-up consists in inoculating the heap with the very bacteria you want to develop as soon as possible. Cultures of these bacteria can be secured inexpensively from a non-profit laboratory in Spring Valley, New York, called Threefold Farm. Although I have never used them myself, I know people who have and who like them.

Although one person, with a pitchfork and either a hose or a watering can, can build a compost heap, a team of two can speed things up immensely. One man distributes the material while the other sprays it gently. Placing the material is work. Turning the heap after the first few weeks, when the mass is thoroughly moist and therefore heavy, is fairly hard work, which a frail person might find more strenuous than spading up his garden. But the work you do to make compost so transforms your garden soil that all later work of cultivating the soil is lessened.

Finally, if you happen to complete a composting process just when your garden is full of vegetables, you will of course be unable to get the compost underground conveniently. To decrease deterioration, keep it protected from the sun; keep it moist, though never soggy; and turn it occasionally. But always work it into your garden topsoil as soon as you get a good opportunity, even if you can do it only in part of your garden.

Unless your garden spot is already covered with at least a thin layer of real topsoil containing real humus, it is worth postponing your actual plantings for a whole year and devoting your entire gardening time and energy to making compost and creating soil with it. But once you have soil, and the season for planting approaches, you should have two things ready: the necessary seed and a complete plan of where you expect to plant it.

First, as to the seed. It pays to get good seed. Get catalogues from reputable nurseries and choose the items you want. Nobody, of course, can tell you which these will be: that choice depends on your tastes and the tastes of your family. But one word of caution: whenever you can, choose varieties recommended for home use, not for commercial use. Most of the best-flavored varieties do not ship well. But you want to eat your vegetables promptly on picking, not ship them. A second word of caution: if you think you "don't like" certain vegetables, it may be that you have never tasted them fresh. Some vegetables, like corn and asparagus, for example, deteriorate with alarming rapidity, once they are picked. In corn, the sugar starts turning to starch within a couple of hours. Asparagus turns bitter. And so it goes. So try planting a few vegetables you think you don't like. A third word of warning: seed produced in your own part of the country is a better bet, other things being equal, than seed produced under other climatic conditions.

Now make a diagram of your future garden. Vegetables are normally—though not always or everywhere—planted in straight rows, because they are more easily worked that way later on. If your garden slopes gently, be sure the rows do not follow the direction of the slope. If they do, hard rains will wash away your valuable topsoil. For instance, if the garden slopes south, run your rows east and west. Also, if it slopes south, plant your tall things like corn and pole-beans as much as possible along the northern edge of the garden, where they will not cut off valuable sunlight from the little fellows, such as lettuce or carrots.

How wide apart should your rows be? This depends on a number of factors. Some vegetables require more space than others, either because they shade more ground or because they leave less room for the gardener when he cultivates or harvests between rows, or because they have bigger appetites and should not be forced to compete for the food in nearby soil with other vegetables planted too close to them. The table on pages 98–99 will help you decide. But you should remember, when you use it, that the closer your plants grow, the richer the soil must be to furnish them enough to eat, and that if you have plenty of space you gain nothing by crowding. It is when your garden is really smaller than you need that you must enrich your soil, be ingenious in using its surface, "interplant" quick-growing vegetables between those that take time to grow, and watch your step when cultivating or harvesting between your overcrowded rows.

How much of each vegetable should you plant? That depends, of course, on how much you want to produce. That in turn obviously depends on the size of your household, on its members' tastes, and even on their tuckaway! And, of course, if you want to can or freeze a part of your produce—a worthy aim, but one this book does not deal with—you need heavier plantings. The amount you plant also depends on the fertility of your soil and on what kind of growing weather you get. But if you have plenty of space, err on the heavy side—with one proviso: don't use up all your available space in first plantings. Some vegetables can be planted every two weeks in early summer, so long as the last planting has time to "make" before frost. It is silly to have a debauch of delicious vegetables for a few weeks and then fall back on the grocer for tired and wilted produce just as late summer makes you feel tired and wilted too. Your best bet on how much to plant will be that experienced gardener down the street, after he has had a look at your soil and location. Again, the table on pages 98–99 may help you.

If the directions for planting and cultivating and fertilizing a certain vegetable are not included in this volume, don't worry. The United States Department of Agriculture and the Department of Agriculture in each state publish inexpensive bulletins dealing with individual vegetables and garden fruits. Send for a price list. But, in reading them, remember climate. Items that do brilliantly in some areas of America—or in Europe—may be very hard to grow where you live. I know that fact represents a challenge to some people. For my part, I like to have vegetables that are glad of a place in my garden, not quarrelsome about my climate or homesick for a distant land. I do all I can for their comfort, but I cannot control the climate. I want vegetables that will do all they can for me. The chances are that, wherever you live, there are some luscious vegetables that will be glad to join you. And, in making your judgments of climate, remember once more that you have a local climate that may not be typical of your state at all.

When planting time draws really near, and your diagram is ready, you have a decision to make. You can wait for a date that local gardeners consider safe from frost, remembering that some vegetables are hardier than others. Or you can gamble and plant a week or ten days ahead of safety: you may get away with it and enjoy eating fresh vegetables earlier. You will not have lost much in either seed or labor. You can also spend a little extra and buy plants that have already been started by a local nursery, instead of planting seed. Or you can start them yourself by building simple hotbeds and coldframes. Directions for building them can be obtained from the various departments of agriculture. Personally, if this were my first year with a garden, I would buy young plants where possible. In addition, I would gamble some seed on those things, like peas and lettuce, that dread hot weather; this would give me, if I won my gamble, a few extra days of cool weather to grow them in. But then, I live where hot weather is a gardening problem, and you may not. In any case, I must insist that prime quality is a more exciting goal than beating your neighbor by two days. In other words, I suggest watching the calendar observantly, without letting it get you fussed.

You cannot plant if your garden is too wet. Rains may hold you up. The soil should be moist and crumbly, not muddy, when you put your seed to bed. When the plants begin to come up, do your "thinning" promptly. That is, remove all the plants except those that are at the distances called for in your catalogue or seed-packet directions. In the case of some plants, such as lettuce, you can do this by stages. If your directions call for six-inch spacing, leave a plant every two or three inches. Then, when the plants you have left begin to crowd each other a little, you can eat every other immature lettuce and still reach your six-inch goal. The same goes for baby beets and carrots. The flavor and food value of immature vegetables amply repay the extra trouble of picking and preparing smaller units. The only point of thinning a row of vegetables is to make sure that every plant has ample room to eat, drink, get warm in the sunshine, and grow. If it can still do that, why snatch it—yet?

Once your plants are an inch or two high you will have another decision to make, and a very interesting one. Even the best garden soil—and yours may not be that yet—tends to form a crust after a hard rain has beaten the air out of it and a hot sun has baked it. That crust, in turn, makes it hard for the soil to drink up the next rainfall, and often forces much of that rain to run off uselessly to lower ground. To prevent this, gardeners cultivate the soil with a hoe or a wheel cultivator or, in the case of large gardens, with a tractor or horse. Finally a "dust mulch" results, which diminishes loss of water by evaporation.

There is, of course, a second and important reason for cultivating the soil: to eliminate weeds. The much abused weed is a curious fact in the gardener's life. Very few weeds are poisonous to eat; many would be excellent eating if we had sense enough to eat them and energy enough to breed up their edible parts to a rewarding size and quality—as we have already done with the weeds we now call vegetables. But we do not eat them. And they compete with our vegetables for food, drink, and sunshine, precisely as a tree too near the garden will do—or, for that matter, as vegetables do to each other when they are not properly thinned in the row. So out the weeds must come. Cultivating kills those between the rows. Those inside the row must be pulled up, provided the vegetables are still so small that the operation will not disturb their tiny roots. If that is no longer the case, better leave the weed in, like the biblical tares in the midst of the good wheat: rooting out the evil, whether plants or people, is always a little hard on their less evil neighbors. If you can no longer risk pulling up a weed in the row, cut it off at the surface. The root may go on stealing food and drink, but at least there will be nothing to steal sunlight.

But there is a magnificent substitute for cultivating a garden. This substitute is mulching. Mulching consists in spreading some sort of cover over the soil between the rows. In Hawaii pineapple-growers developed the custom of using a tough paper that comes in rolls like roofing-paper. I have tried it, and, quite aside from expense, do not care for it. More recently, believe it or not, spun-glass fiber, developed for insulating roofs, has been used. It has the advantage of lasting longer than paper. But the ideal material ought to be cheap and it ought to be composed of a vegetable matter that will feed the worms, bacteria, and other micro-organisms in the soil, so that it will eventually be incorporated into the soil itself along with the products of your compost heap. Fortunately, there are many such products. Peanut hulls, buckwheat hulls, tobacco stems, peat, straw are all sold for this purpose. Sawdust and wood shavings are also good, although most people claim you must add lime to counteract their tendency to make the soil too acid. In fact, weeds themselves are good, provided they are enough dried out not to strike root the next time it rains, a disaster that happened to me. Fallen leaves are good. Spoiled hay is excellent, although there is a risk of its containing mature weed-seeds to annoy you later. Grass clippings are excellent, provided they contain no seed.

In any event, mulching beats cultivating all hollow, for a number of reasons. Supposing it rains. You cannot cultivate till the soil dries out a little, particularly if your soil is basically a clay. If you do, you may do real damage. You may produce clods that feel as hard as bricks. So you wait. Just then you get sick or are called out of town or arc appallingly busy with your job. Hundreds of weeds immediately spring from the soil. Remember, for every time you planted the seed of some weed we call a vegetable, the wind planted ten quite indiscriminately. Now, just as you arc finally ready to cultivate, the right tool is missing. Or, worse still, it rains again, cats and dogs. If you had had a mulch spread all over your garden, from one to even four inches thick, none but the toughest-rooted weeds could have forced their way through it. Since the mulch would hold the moisture to the soil—which you would have cultivated once, carefully, just before mulching—even the big weeds would come up relatively easily. Moreover, you could weed immediately after a rain, or even during a rain, without disturbing or ruining your soil and without even getting your feet muddy.

It is best to remember that bare soil is in a highly abnormal and highly vulnerable condition. When soil is undisturbed by man, the first thing it does is cover itself modestly with trees, grass, shrubs, or something else, provided it gets enough rain to grow things. This growth protects soil from the wind that tears it and makes dustbowls, from the water that washes it into the rivers and finally into the sea. It also shelters the billions of bacteria that should be working in your topsoil for you, free of charge. But if you imitate Nature a hundred per cent in your garden, you will get weeds and even trees instead of vegetables. The gardener's art should consist in covering the soil with something that does not compete with his vegetables for food, drink, and sunshine, as weeds and trees emphatically would; and with something, if possible, that will actually feed the micro-organisms that make his soil a living thing, capable of supporting the most highly flavored vegetables to grace his table. That is precisely what a decaying mulch of some vegetable material, no longer itself trying to grow, does for the garden. That is why I say: cultivate once, to make sure your soil is open and airy, and then promptly mulch. Then, even if you go on vacation, the only weeds that greet your return will be perhaps a few in the row itself, where the mulch sometimes has to be thinner to avoid mildewing certain vegetables, plus a few weeds that scuffled their way through the mulch and can be easily removed.

Note that mulching is like composting—a lot of work at the start in order to avoid more and less fruitful work later on. Above all, it provides better conditions for producing the quality of food that this book is concerned with. If composting has inoculated your land well with bacteria, the bacteria will devour the underside of your mulch. That is, they will compost it for you. This continues to enrich the soil, even if you no longer build compost heaps yourself. You can help by adding more mulch on top as your billions of unpaid assistant gardeners compost earlier doses. In short, once your land has "live" topsoil, you don't have to keep composting, provided you keep mulching —and mulching takes a lot less work. Now, when you pull weeds or cut the lawn, you can drop the grass clippings or the weeds on top of your mulch and know they will be converted into life-giving humus when their turn comes.

If rainfall is generous, you need not bother about your vegetables' getting enough to drink. But if the ground begins to get dry it is time to use your hose. Turn the hose nozzle to a spray: your vegetables are no more anxious than you are to have a hard stream of water hit them in the face. Or get a metal attachment for your hose in the form of a whirling spray that you can leave to do its work, only shifting it now and then in order to get all parts of the garden thoroughly soaked. Better than any spray is a "soil soaker" canvas hose to attach to your regular garden hose. What you want is to get your soil moist nine or ten inches deep. Then do no more watering for at least a week. Daily light watering is bad for any garden. It wets only the top inch or so of soil, and that encourages the plants to send roots up into damp soil where they can feed best, rather than down deep where there is not enough water to dissolve the food they are after. They should be encouraged to develop deep roots. Besides, if the daily sprinkling ever stops for a bit and the sun bakes out the top inch, they have no way at all to eat or drink. I admit that if two inches of mulch cover that top inch of soil, the daily sprinkle is a little less harmful. But avoid it. A soaking once a week, whether by rainclouds or by the gardener, is what the plants really want. Finally, if your soil lies naked and unmulched, it is better to water your garden after the sun is down than while the sun is shining. If your soil has been properly mulched, you can water any time your plants look thirsty, even in hot sunshine.

When it comes time to harvest your vegetables and turn them over to the cook, remember several things. Most vegetables contain more flavor and more complete nourishment when they are young than when they are fully mature. Obviously, in the case of a vegetable like the green pea, you have to wait till the peas form in the pod. But even then, don't wait too long. Second, you and the cook are now in collaboration. Confer together. She has a natural interest in composing a table symphony, and this interest may lead her to want a combination of vegetables that your garden does not at that moment afford. This interest is one of the factors that have driven the American cook to the grocery store, where vegetables arrive from all over the country and where the combinations she is after are to a large extent independent of seasons. The American cook thereby increased her symphonic range, but the quality of each piece in the orchestra declined remarkably. If she is to use the produce of your garden, she must accept the seasons again, and accepting the seasons is never easy for people in an urban, industrial culture. Accepting the seasons has become slightly un-American.

On the other hand, if you, her collaborator, just harvest whatever you feel is ready, and she is not ready to use it, you will end up by eating stale vegetables just as you did when you bought from the grocer. But usually you will have a little leeway on each thing you harvest, and should be able to report to the kitchen what is ready, what can be left growing for a day or two, and what is about to pass its prime. The gardener-cook collaboration calls for a quite different form of cooperation from the cooperation of a market gardener who is willing to grow a thousand bushels of spinach if the commission agent will pay him enough money for him to make a profit by it, and of the agent who is willing to pay for the spinach if he can get enough grocers to pay enough for it, and of the grocers who will handle it if enough customers will buy it. By that system the spinach reaches the table out of season but a little tired. Happily—or unhappily—few of the customers are any longer able to tell the difference between tired spinach and real spinach.

But the home garden invites mutual planning between gardener and cook. It invites subtle cooperation between the gardener and his soil. And, once more, it involves accepting the seasons: the fresh vegetables are gifts of the earth, and gifts are given only when the giver is ready. Gardens teach patience.

Vegetables, like all other living creatures, are attacked by other creatures whose hunger they satisfy. In the jungle, a tiger will eat a man. In the garden, a cow or horse or goat or groundhog or rabbit will eat a vegetable. If vegetable-loving animals wander around where you live, you may have to fence. A four-foot rabbit-and-poultry fence of wire mesh, with the bottom wire sunk a little in the soil, is your best all-round protection. In the city you are unlikely to face this problem, but in a small town your garden may easily attract a sociable, and hungry, rabbit.

But men are attacked not only by tigers, but by insects and by animals too small to be seen without a microscope, like the microbes of tuberculosis. Vegetables are attacked by insects too. And, for hotly debated reasons, during my lifetime insects have become more and more of a problem for the gardener. When I was a boy I worked in a garden where the only insect problem we were concerned with was the "potato bug"—the Colorado beetle. We children cleaned them off the potato vines by hand. Today the average gardener engages in a kind of perpetual chemical warfare against dozens of garden pests, and the insecticide industry has swollen to gigantic proportions. Now and then there is an outcry about the amount of poison still left on the fruits and vegetables we buy. Now and then a new insecticide like DDT is greeted as the secret weapon that will finally make all insects wish they had never been born. And, alas, now and then the insects develop tolerances for our secret weapons.

What has gone wrong? Scientists are not agreed on the answer. But there is a lot of evidence that, for one thing, the soil we plant vegetables in has often been worked to death and is too poor to grow healthy plants; and, second, that insects prefer sickly vegetables to healthy ones—just as the germs of tuberculosis seem to thrive best in undernourished, weak men. According to this theory, insects are scavengers, cleaning out the unfit: they are a sure sign your soil is sick and cannot grow healthy plants capable of building healthy people. Therefore, says this theory, instead of trying to exterminate insects with spray-guns and saving your sickly vegetables to half-nourish weedy people, why not build proper soil capable of producing healthy plants less subject to insects? I believe this reasoning is basically sound, provided you also remember that cows and horses and rabbits prefer healthy plants to sick ones, and that, unlike customers in a grocery, they can tell the difference. I believe the evidence shows increasingly that the basis of good gardening is not a good spray-gun and good poison but good, live, healthy soil. But until you get that soil you may personally feel that you require emergency methods developed by chemical science, and I have therefore added under each vegetable separately discussed in this book data on insect enemies and control measures. But remember, no spray-gun is ever going to give you fine-flavored food unless you have created good soil to grow that food in.

I should myself despair of gardening without insecticides—which I do not use—were it not for two facts. In the first place I remember that, while insects eat plants, birds eat insects. And we do all we can to encourage birds around our garden. If it were not for birds, insects would have run man off this planet long ago. And man has often so changed his environment that birds do not flourish; when that happens, insects have a field day. So encourage birds. Your public library has books that suggest many ways of doing it. Encourage birds to come to your garden, and encourage them to nest in or around it. When the hungry fledglings arrive, their parents will turn into insecticides with wings.

My second reason for not despairing may strike you as lazy or Hindu or superstitious. I fail to see why I should go out of my mind to get every last insect out of my garden. Some of them, like bees, are of course essential to my garden's health—and, incidentally, poison sprays have worked havoc on the American bee population. We have to have bees to pollinate our plants. Insects that are merely trying to eat my vegetables before I can eat them seem to share my tastes, which is a bond between us—provided they do not get too numerous and eat more than their share. Trying to make sure that not a single harmful insect exists in my garden again poses the biblical problem of the tares and the wheat. My garden is a complex free society of vegetables, insects, worms, bacteria, birds, and I don't propose to squirt chemical poisons all over that society in order to rid myself of a small criminal element. I have evidence that the criminals will not take over so long as the society remains in blooming health. I judge that, in gardens at least, the best way to control evils is to promote good, not to fight them with other evils like poison sprays. As to a crusade to end evil, I am now past fifty and have seen a lot of crusades. If you prefer destructive measures against evil to constructive measures for free and joyful growth, the spray-gun is just what you have been longing for. You keep spraying, and I will keep composting —composting and mulching. We can still be friends, as witness the fact I have mentioned—that I report later on which poisons are supposed to prevent which bugs from eating which vegetables before you can eat them.

When a row of vegetables has finished producing or is not earning its keep, pull it out promptly and put it in the compost heap. If the heap is not ready for it at the moment, put it nearby so it may be added soon. This feeder heap, if kept moist, will do a little fermenting on its own before it ever gets added to the compost heap proper. That is all to the good. However, if any vegetable refuse is obviously diseased, better not let it lie around. Either put it inside a fermenting heap with a high enough temperature to sterilize it, or else, regretfully, burn it.

When you have eaten all the lettuce in a row, or when it is clear that the string beans in a row will produce little or nothing more and you have pulled up the vines, you will of course have a vacant row. If there are still enough weeks left before the kind of cold that will kill, plant again. But it will be better if you do not plant the same thing. All vegetables can be roughly classified as follows: roots, such as beets or carrots; leaves, such as cabbage or lettuce; and edible seeds, such as peas or beans. If you have just cleared a row of a "seed vegetable," it is a good plan to shift to a "leaf vegetable" or a "root vegetable." The reason for this rotation of crops is that each vegetable has its own food requirements, and the things it needs will become scarce in the soil if every succeeding vegetable customer orders the same dish on the menu. Moreover, some vegetables, such as legumes —for example, peas and beans—actually put fertility that leafy vegetables crave into the soil. Legumes take nitrogen from the air.

Now you can understand why it is so important to construct a scale drawing of your garden during the winter evenings before you order your seed. That diagram will enable you to record not only your first plantings in any given row, but any subsequent plantings in that row. The next spring you will know what each row last contained—and therefore what it is best not to start off with.

Succession crops, as they are called, are important; for some quick-growing vegetables they are important even in cold climates with short growing seasons. They enable you to raise really fresh food for a longer period of the year, to the great joy of both your palate and your digestive system. Some vegetables, of course, can be planted in spring and late summer only, because they simply will not thrive in intense midsummer heat. Others love the heat, provided they have plenty to drink.

When light frosts begin to come in the autumn, don't surrender too quickly to them. Late tomatoes can often be protected from a light frost with a blanket thrown over the stake to form a warm tepee. If they are not staked, you might pile light straw all over them to keep out the cold. In either case, if they freeze anyhow, they may still be saved if you keep them covered until they have thawed out. The reason for that is that if the sun thaws their juicy vines quickly the cells break —and then you are really through. Other vegetables, such as cabbage, may improve from a light frost. And some vegetables, notably such root vegetables as parsnips and turnips, will in parts of the country go happily straight through the winter and even improve their flavor with cold. Even when a wicked cold snap kills their foliage in mild climates, they will send up more, thereby providing you with fresh green food during just those months when it is scarcest. There are even leafy vegetables like "winter kale" and spinach that can stand lots of cold.

But eventually most of your garden will have succumbed to a "black frost"—that is, to a lovely white frost that will turn your plants almost black! Any such plants should of course make a beeline for the compost heap or the feeder heap beside it. Every scrap is valuable. Meanwhile, if you get hard freezes in winter where you live, it would be a good idea to fork your mulch into the soil, or even to get a plowman to plow it in—that is, unless the mulch is a heavy layer of sawdust or shavings, in which case leave it on top. Mulches like hay or straw will decompose and further increase the humus in your soil. And the exposed soil will get wet, freeze, and break—all of which will be good for it. In climates without hard freezes and with hot sunny days even in winter, I would leave any mulch on. It will drink up the winter rains and release them gradually into the soil; it will protect the valuable topsoil from hot sunshine; and of course the underside of the mulch will decay steadily and add humus to your soil too.

Whether you can grow winter vegetables will depend on how harsh a winter your area has. But kale and chard and turnip greens—the leafy tops of the turnip roots, for which the vegetable is usually grown —can survive short sharp freezes if the freezes are followed by thaws and some sunny days. Even when the foliage freezes, the root will put up fresh, delicious foliage if the weather relents. If you do not live too far north, or if you live near the sea, ask local gardeners what vegetables they can pull through. Even if they have not discovered it, they may be able to utilize kale, chard, turnips, and parsley. Plant a few in late summer on a bet and see. But, in addition to those, you may have several rows that cannot be plowed up for the excellent reason that some of the commonest vegetables live not just one season, but several seasons. Globe artichokes, for example, live three or four years. They die down in winter, but the roots can be protected fairly far north if you give them a heavy enough mulch. Asparagus, if properly cared for, may go on doing well for forty or fifty years. In planning your garden in the first place, you will have put the permanent or relatively permanent things conveniently together in one part.

In your planning there should be one further consideration I have not talked about. If you are, or become, an enthusiastic gardener, your vegetable garden will be a place you will often steal time to visit. It ought to be a beautiful place. In general, a well-planned vegetable garden, healthy and productive, develops a distinctive beauty that reflects its function. But sometimes even that function can have alternative expressions, and you should choose the solution that makes your garden attractive. We moderns are inclined to make a sharp distinction between the things we have for beauty, such as flower gardens, and the things we have for utility, such as vegetable gardens. We make a similar distinction between "serious" work and play. But genuinely serious work contains a kind of playfulness as one of its necessary dimensions, as genuinely delightful play often contains an element of real work. Certainly successful gardening is a combination of work and play. And a well-ordered vegetable garden is both useful and extremely beautiful. Its products both delight our palates and usefully strengthen our bodies. The gourmet-gardener gets pleasure from cultivating his garden, gets pleasure from contemplating his garden, gets pleasure from eating its fruits.

All this suggests that you may wish to grow a few rows of cutting flowers among your vegetables. They not only add to the beauty of the garden; but can follow your vegetables to the table, to delight your eye while the vegetables delight your palate. But whether you add flowers or not you will learn a dozen ways to make your rows of vegetables exhibit their own special beauty. That beauty will protect you from the folly of supposing that it is a disagreeable task to raise them, even though it is a pleasure to eat them. And your garden will become a place where you can withdraw from the folly that characterizes so much of human life around you. Our generation would have a very different attitude toward business, toward professional work, toward manual labor, toward political and economic problems alike, if we were what our forebears were—a generation of gardeners.

ARTICHOKES

(*Cynara Scolymus*)

The true artichoke is usually called globe artichoke or French artichoke or crown artichoke. It belongs to the same botanical family as the common thistle. Two other vegetables, which are no kin to it at all, are also called "artichokes" for no reason except that their flavor suggests the flavor of true artichoke. One of these is the so-called Chinese artichoke. People eat its root or "tuber." It is not especially choice. The other is the Jerusalem artichoke, a delicious and—in America—much neglected vegetable. It is discussed on page 57.

The globe artichoke is a large plant that may grow as high as six feet, so it needs space. It lives and bears for three or four years, although the tops die down in winter. These two facts suggest running a row of the plants in the "back" of your garden, maybe right next to your asparagus—"back" meaning where it will not shade lower plants, along the northern or western edge of your garden, depending on which way your rows run. Artichokes need at least two feet between plants, and should be four feet from the nearest row of other vegetables.

The globe artichoke has had a long history as food. Some authorities think it was first cultivated in Africa, and legend has it that Antony and Cleopatra loved to eat it. It was certainly grown in southern Asia before the Christian era. And when the great French explorer, Samuel Champlain, struck Cape Cod in 1605, he found it growing in the gardens of the Indians.

It is not an easy plant to raise, so if you are an inexperienced gardener you might skip it your first year. It hates cold, and will not live through a really cold winter without special protection—although one must confess that its fruit tastes better in cold climates than in the warm ones where it is easy to raise. It is a heavy feeder, so it likes good fertile soil and plenty of water to drink. If you do try it, probably six plants will be enough. They will not bear fruit the first year unless they are started indoors, either by your nurseryman or by you in a sunny window or a hotbed. It likes lots of lime in its soil bed. A generous dose of wood ashes, worked into the soil, would be welcome. If you live where there is seaweed, mulch your artichoke plants with it.

Although delicious to eat, the artichoke is not very nutritious. It does contain B and C vitamins.

29

When the tops die down in autumn, cut the plant off cleanly and of course add it to your compost heap or material to be composted. Then mulch the root deeply. Gardeners have raised artichokes as far north as Pennsylvania, for example, by putting inverted peck-size peach baskets over the root, covering the basket with a deep mulch, and not removing either till all danger of frost was past. Since the seed does not always breed true to form, people sometimes transplant the sprouts which old plants put up in spring. These sprouts, incidentally, can be cut and eaten like asparagus, although it is the flower bud that the artichoke is really raised for.

Insect diseases and pests are not much of a problem. If your soil is badly drained you might get crown rot—but then, as we have already agreed, none of your garden should ever be badly drained. Plant lice and aphids sometimes attack the undersides of the leaves. If they do, use nicotine dust on them.

Harvest your buds when they are immature, before they show any signs of opening. Epicures claim they taste better when picked in the evening. In any case, if they are not to go straight into the pot, better put them into the refrigerator to preserve their flavor. That recommendation holds good for many vegetables.

ASPARAGUS

(*Asparagus officinalis*)

Whether asparagus came from the Caucasus or Siberia or the coasts of Asia and Europe, it has been eaten in the Eastern Mediterranean area since before the Christian era.

It is not hard to raise, but growing it is a long-term operation, more like setting out a fruit orchard than like planting a row of tomato vines. It takes about three years for asparagus to bear heavily; then it can last your lifetime. So this almost permanent vegetable obviously belongs on the edge of your garden, where it will not get in the way of a plowman. Indeed, since it will grow higher than your head, it might as well go on that northern edge, even though its foliage is too fernlike to steal much sun from its lowlier neighbors.

Asparagus feeds and thrives best in well-limed, deeply prepared, fertile soil. It loves stable manure, compost, bone meal, wood-ash. If you must use chemical fertilizers, give asparagus 5-8-7—say, five pounds for two dozen plants. Your asparagus bed must be well drained, and asparagus needs less water than most vegetables. If your soil is heavy clay, it will be worth your time to work in some sand or

cinders or both to lighten it. Your asparagus will respond gratefully
if you give each plant each spring from three to five pounds of ground
limestone, magnesium base being even more valuable than calcium.
In exchange for these good things, asparagus will give you about
eight weeks of tender shoots, or "spears," every spring, rich in protein, and sweeter than you can imagine if you have never eaten it
fresh. It should go from ground to stove, and if it is inconvenient to
run madly with it all the way from the garden to the stove, at least put
it instantly into the refrigerator. Otherwise, rapid chemical changes
will occur that will make it taste just like what the grocers sell. Finally,
if you have never been keen about asparagus, remember that this
may easily mean you just don't like the bitter taste which asparagus
speedily acquires as soon as it is cut. Try some fresh from your own
garden.

In establishing your asparagus bed, try to buy roots rather than
seed. And don't pay good money for two-year-old roots, either. One-
year-old roots will do better. Insist on a good rustproof variety, such
as Martha Washington or Mary Washington. Two dozen plants should
provide abundantly for a small family, but it is worth the money to
buy double that and use only the two dozen finest specimens. If you
absolutely cannot find roots, you can grow from seed. It will be
cheaper in money, of course, but more expensive in patience. You can
sow the seed in a row in your garden and thin out the young plants to
three or four inches apart. The second spring you will have one-year-
old plants yourself without buying them. But whichever way you get
the plants, first dig a trench fifteen inches deep where you want your
row, as soon as the ground can be worked. Work compost or rotted
manure into the top three or four inches of earth in the bottom of the
trench. Fill the trench with a mixture of soil and compost until it is
only six inches deep. Then, every two feet, make a little mound of
earth and straddle an asparagus root on it, with its little fat finger-roots
spread down the sides of the mound. When the roots have all been
set on their mounds, cover them thinly with mixed soil and compost.
Every time the plant peeks out, give it a little more soil; by August
the trench will be filled to garden level. If there is more than one row,
run the rows at least three feet apart, and five if you can spare the
space. The closer you are forced to plant for lack of space, the more
heavily the plants will have to be fed later to get bumper crops of the
little juicy spears you are after.

I repeat, if you insist on commercial fertilizers, use 5-8-7 instead
of compost. If you get some over the "crowns," or asparagus roots,
you are likely to damage them—which you probably deserve anyhow,
for not using compost instead! If any of your plants seem weak, which

composting could have prevented, a little nitrate of soda will at least appear to cheer them up.

Having done all this work, you still won't cut any spears the first season, if you don't want to weaken your plants and lessen your later harvests. The second spring, if your plants have made at least three feet of growth the year before, you can cut for perhaps three weeks. If they have grown six feet, you might even cut for five weeks. The third season—that is, a little over two years from the day you set your roots out—you can cut for eight weeks. If the spears start coming up spindly, quit cutting. Now the plants will grow high and store energy in the roots. Only when they have been killed by autumn frost should you cut them down. All you do meanwhile is protect them from weed competition. Finally, remember that in cutting you must not through carelessness destroy neighboring spears that are not yet up high enough to see. Run the knife down vertically beside the spear you are after and then give it just enough of a twist to cut that particular spear and no other.

You may feel I have described some pretty hard work to get one vegetable. But few other vegetables require so little attention once they are established. And, whatever attention they got, they still would refuse to bear for the rest of your lifetime. Asparagus is simply a pronounced example of what this book has been saying about gardening in general—that careful preparation often keeps down labor overhead when things begin to happen.

I could have advised you to make even more extraordinary preparations, and other people probably will. They may tell you to sprinkle salt on your asparagus bed. Don't do it; it will stimulate growth the first year and then damage your bed permanently. They will tell you to plant the roots fifteen inches deep. Don't do it. This merely means the spears will be blanched instead of green. If you prefer them blanched, I can only urge you to try to recover from your error. Green spears are more nutritious and taste better, a fact more and more people are discovering. Six inches is quite deep enough. In fact, I know gardeners who have gotten excellent results with "flat culture" —that is, with no trenching at all. Some people will tell you to bury tin cans, wood, and other roughage deep under your beds to aerate the soil. Coal cinders and sand, plus some brush if you like, will do just as good a job.

The true labor story on asparagus is high cost of installation, low maintenance. So take time to make a deep and fertile home for your asparagus to live in.

Unlike some vegetables, asparagus does get things the matter with it. It gets rust, but if you buy roots of a good rust-resistant strain you should have no trouble. And if you build the good, live, bacterial soil this book describes, you will be even safer. Several types of beetles sometimes prove a nuisance. Dusting the plants with lime sometimes repels beetles. The larvae of some beetles can be simply shaken off the plant, and they are too sluggish to climb back up before they die. If you can arrange, as many country dwellers easily can, to run a chicken or two among your plants, it will be tough on beetles. This is as good a place as any to point out that a young chicken or turkey can be as handy a military ally for a gardener as a wild bird or toad or lizard. Unfortunately, there are a few vegetables—like tomatoes, for instance—against which they sometimes line up as enemies! If that problem can be met, they can help a lot. And their manure is, of course, very helpful.

BEANS

(*Phaseolus vulgaris*)

The bean family is enormous. Except for the excellent broad bean (*Vicia faba,* the Italian *fava,* the French *fève*), which originated in the Old World, beans originated in the two Americas, were cultivated here by the Indians, and have since been taken all over the world. Species like the Mexican *frijoles* are now one of the staple foods of the Hungry Half of the world's population. The bean seed is rich in proteins. Beans are extremely easy to raise, and therefore a good vegetable for amateur gardeners to learn on. They will grow well even in poor soil, although they like sandy loam better than heavy soils. They enjoy lime. They like potash, and hence wood ashes. They like phosphorus, and will therefore be grateful for bone meal or ground rock phosphate. You need not bother to feed them nitrogen because, like all legumes, they have machinery for getting it from the air and depositing it in the soil. For this reason farmers often grow various species merely as "cover crops" to plow under and enrich the land. Beans not only do not require nitrogen; too much of it stimulates vine growth at the expense of pods.

Beans cannot stand frost, but they can stand lots of heat if they have enough water. So they are not worth planting before all danger of frost has passed and the soil has warmed up a bit. Cold wet soil often rots the seed before it can sprout. They do not transplant well, so gardeners rarely start them indoors, although it can be done. Use a four-inch flower pot or veneer band and be careful not to disturb the root. A better plan is to wait for the weather beans really like, and

then soak the seed overnight before planting. This will speed up
sprouting by several days.

The gourmet's choice should be string beans, or "snaps," whether
green (the French *haricots verts*) or wax (*haricots blancs*), or some
of both. The delicious broad bean, which does so brilliantly in England and on the Continent, is hard to grow here, and beginners had
best beware. If its marvelous flavor inspires you with courage, remember that the broad bean is frightened of heat, not cold. It should be
planted early; then it may escape the aphis, the blister beetle, and the
enervating effect of hot weather. I have grown delicious broad beans
in New England, and have never succeeded in the South. Black Leaf
40 is used as a spray against beetles.

But broad beans, alas, are somewhat of a digression in this story.
The string bean rejoices in our climate. When you choose your seed,
choose one of the stringless varieties and save your cook a lot of work.
Then you must decide between bush beans or pole beans—that is,
whether to have your beans growing on low, erect bushes, or on vines
that require something to climb on. Even if you vote for pole beans,
you had better put in a first planting of bush beans too, since bush
beans take a week or ten days less to produce edible pods. After that,
the later pole beans will keep you supplied till frost kills the vines. On
the other hand, if you vote for bush beans, they will not keep bearing
till frost, and you should put in a new row every two or three weeks
until an estimated seven or eight weeks before first frost. If your soil
is a heavy clay, pole beans will prefer it. If you dislike stooping to
harvest, pole beans will save your dignity. But you must save theirs;
they must have something to climb on. You can either drive six-foot
poles beside each "hill" of seed, or you can plant in two parallel rows;
and lean the tops of every "square" of four poles together and tie
them, tepee-fashion, which is both handy and decorative. Or run the
plants on a length of chicken wire. As to your choice of location, remember that pole beans, unlike bush beans, are another "high" vegetable and belong toward that northern—or western—edge if they are
not to steal good southeastern sunlight from their humbler vegetable
friends. After weighing all these questions carefully, go on and plant
bush beans as I do, and keep young by stooping when you pick. Seriously, wiser people than I plant one row of bush beans because they
produce more quickly than pole beans and one row of pole beans because they keep producing straight through till frost, which your early
bush beans will not do. Finally, some people claim that pole beans are
less bothered by either beetles or blight than bush beans are.

If you did not mulch your garden, you will have to protect your
beans from the competition of weeds. And here is where once more

mulching turns out to be both a labor-saver and a bother-saver. For beans are shallow-rooted, and you had better not cultivate around them more than an inch deep or you will do damage. And you had better cultivate them in nice hot sunshine, whether you enjoy it or not. In the morning and evening, when any sane person would prefer to do his cultivating, the vines are more full of water, more brittle, and hence more easily broken. Mulchers, meanwhile, won't need to cultivate and can sit in a hammock and watch you trying not to damage either root or vine.

If you did not compost and like commercial fertilizers, watch out; it is easy to "burn" bean vines with commercial fertilizer. Compost never burned anything. Neither did lime or ground rock phosphate or bone meal, though an overdose of wood ashes can. Commercial fertilizers, put too close, also encourage blight.

There are several insects and diseases that afflict beans, but they are unlikely to afflict you if you have built a good live soil and don't hit a spell of cold, rainy weather. A fungous disease called anthracnose may leave some black spots on the pods or stems; but you should be able to get a good variety that is resistant to this fungus. Anyway, avoid walking among your vines when they are wet: you will tend to spread the spores. Bean rust is best met by rust-resistant varieties. Bacterial blight may put a few brown splotches on your leaves. Mosaic and bean weevil do exist. In general, a well-limed soil may cause you to see none of these things. And sprinkling lime on the foliage after it has formed its "true" leaves may protect you from the Mexican bean beetle, one of the most objectionable insects that ever got past the immigration authorities. It is small, tan, with eight black spots, lays tiny patches of yellow eggs, which hatch into globular, juicy, sluggish yellow larvae. Some people dust the grubs with rotenone. Whenever I pick beans, I squash every beetle or larva I see—and squashing larvae is a bit on the messy side—and I crush the egg-patches between my fingers with a smudging motion. If you shrink from this mopping-up operation, just stay with the lime or rotenone. I am sorry to report that the birds in my garden, while not positively siding with the beetles against me, show signs of neutralism. If you persistently love chemistry, use calcium arsenate dust, though even the people who sell it advise against using it after the pods form. They assume you are going to eat the pods, you see.

Which, by the way, leads me to remind you that snap beans can be eaten in three stages: the best stage, when the pod has developed small seeds, too small to cause bulges in it; the still good stage, when the pods have become too tough to make good eating but the beans have got big enough to be worth shelling, are still soft and moist, and can be eaten as "shell beans"; and the third-rate stage, when the plant has dried standing, the pod has become brittle, and "dry beans" can be hulled, to store away for winter food, to eat immediately, or to plant as seed next spring. The best stage is, for a gourmet, still the best. The best time to harvest for flavor is in the evening, and, if the cook is not quite ready, get them into the refrigerator quickly.

A final word of caution about harvesting. Bean vines or bushes are regrettably easy to pull up and even easier to dislocate in the root system even if they don't literally come out in your hand. So harvest gently; don't yank. A little practice will give you the knack of pulling them off the vine without any strain on the plant itself. Use that thumbnail. If that doesn't work, better use both hands.

I have purposely spoken of the problems, but remember one thing: the string bean is one of the easiest of all vegetables to grow, one of the most bountiful, provided you keep picking so that the vine will keep flowering and trying to make seed, one of the most delicious, one of the hardest to get fresh from a grocer. Providence sent the Mexican beetle to keep it from being too ridiculously easy.

If you insist on everything's being easy, and cannot handle the Mexican beetle, consider shifting to soybeans. They are, of course, of a quite different taste, but the newly developed sweet varieties are getting increasingly popular. Nothing could be easier to grow—or better for your garden soil—and apparently Mexican beetles don't relish them. Some people have abandoned them because they found them too hard to shell. But if you plunge the day's harvest of pods into boiling water for five minutes, you will find that the hulls come off readily and no harm has been done. They are well worth experimenting with. For centuries in China they have been a food staple like rice. A century and a half ago we introduced them in this country, but as a farm crop. The new varieties are winning their way to the table.

The lima, or sugar, bean (*Phaseolus lunatus,* variety *macrocarpus*) is about as sure a bet as the string bean in American gardens, except that its tropical origins and relatively slow rate of growth make the pole lima risky for the colder sections of our country. The bush, or "dwarf," lima grows faster and is more practical for the gardener who has a short growing season. If you fail even with the bush varieties to make it before frost, better substitute the graceful scarlet runners and pull them and shell them green.

The lima bean originated in either Peru or Brazil or Guatemala, we are not sure which. It likes heavily limed soil and needs magnesium as well as calcium in its liming. Unless the soil is loose and crumbly, limas have a harder time sprouting than the smaller string-bean seeds have. Soaking overnight for twelve hours before planting will make the seed sprout faster, but use very little water; don't more than half cover the seed. A windbreak to the north helps start them—say a shingle stuck in the earth. Except that they are even more dependent on sunshine, they need about what string beans need. They are best when shelled green, but, like string beans, they can be allowed to dry on the vine and kept for winter. The pods are never eaten. Lima beans are extremely nutritious: they contain protein, fat, carbohydrate, vitamins, and are really a first-class dietary substitute for meat.

BEETS

(Beta vulgaris, variety *crassa)*

The modern garden beet comes from Southern Europe, where it was grown for its edible leaves even before the Christian era. Not much was done to develop the root for eating before the sixteenth century. The beet family now grown by man includes the sugar beet, which supplies a third of the world's sugar; the mangel-wurzel, grown as feed for farm stock and poultry; chard, grown for its leaves and succulent leaf-stem; and the garden beet, grown primarily for its sweet, delicious root, but also for its leaves or "beet-tops," eaten as greens.

Beets are easy to raise, although they produce their finest flavor only where the summer is cool and the air not too dry. If your summers are hot, the problem is to get fast growth and to eat the beets young; otherwise they will get stringy and woody. Nearly any soil will grow them if it is well limed. It is worth getting lime into the soil as far down as a couple of feet. The soil beets like best is a light, sandy loam. Unless the soil is loose to a considerable depth, the longer-rooted varieties will do poorly, and you will do better with the globe-shaped type, or even the flattened-globe kind, even though some connoisseurs think the well-grown long type has finer flavor.

Beware of *unrotted* stabled manure: it will make your beets produce wonderful leaves but not very good roots. Compost is, of course, perfect.

Sow as soon as the frost is out of the ground. Since every beet "seed" is in reality a little packet of as many as eight seeds, sow thinly. Even so, the plants will tend to come up in little clumps. Thin to a couple of inches apart; then, as soon as the plants begin to crowd each other, pull up every other one and eat as greens—root, leaves, and all. Keep the rest hustling, and eat them well before they mature if you want their finest flavor. If there are gaps in your row when the beets have come up, transplant from your thinnings. Beets transplant very well indeed when young, provided you are careful of the little root and set it vertical, and not curled up, in a hole deep enough to accommodate it.

Since you can grow young beets in a few weeks, succession plantings are in order if you want to enjoy them fresh until frost. So plant some every two or three weeks until within a couple of months of your first killing frost.

If you give your beets the food they need to grow well, they will furnish carbohydrates and vitamins A, B, C, and G in their roots, and valuable vitamins and minerals in their leaves, plus an unforgettable flavor. If your garden is tiny, naturally beets will not be as useful to you as leafy vegetables like lettuce, for the simple reason that the beets you buy contain more of their original flavor and food value than does lettuce from a market. But this is only relative; if you have room for the root vegetables you will quickly recognize that freshness means something in their case too. And, of course, beet leaves definitely fall in the category of perishables.

Your first job is to feed the beets. They love potash, so wood ashes will help them. They love phosphorus, so bone meal or ground rock-phosphate will please them. It happens that they like one of the rarer minerals, boron, and sometimes develop unsightly black spots by way of protest if they don't get it. You can give them some easily by dissolving ¼ teaspoon Borax in a pail of water and dribbling it along the row in a stream the width of your little finger.

As to enemies, in good soil the beet is a healthy plant. Its foliage sometimes develops a fungous disease, which may be dusted with a mercury or copper compound. However, you might try just removing any leaves that show any sort of disease. The beetroot can readily spare them. Either bury them in a compost heap or destroy them. In any case, don't leave them near the growing beets. If you have long, hot summers, you may find that late plantings are not worth while; but deeply worked, well-composted soil, protected from sun and weed competition by a good mulch, may even then see you through, provided you eat the beetroot young.

BROCCOLI

(*Brassica oleracea,* variety *italica*)

Broccoli is a member of the cabbage family, along with Brussels sprouts, cauliflower, collard, kale, and kohlrabi. Roughly, it is a branching cauliflower with heads full of the same sort of little flower-buds, set on a plant that grows some four feet high. It was eaten by the Romans, but it was brought to its present perfection by modern Italian and Danish gardeners. Although Thomas Jefferson reported seeing it in the markets of Washington, Americans did not eat it much before the present century, during which it has become more and more popular.

Like its cousin, the cabbage, it needs good soil and plenty of sunlight; and, like cabbage, it needs cool growing weather, particularly cool nights. With these conditions, broccoli is not hard to grow. It wants lots of nitrogen to eat, as leafy vegetables always do, and it is thirsty. It needs plenty of lime in the soil and plenty of the humus which your compost heap can furnish it. Given this food and drink, it will supply you with a nutritious, high-vitamin vegetable of delicate flavor.

In the North, if you cannot buy young plants, you will do well to sow indoors and transplant as soon as the ground can be worked. In warm climates you can start it in the fall, let it winter through and produce in the spring before the hot weather comes. It will stand quite cold weather. Light frost actually improves the flavor of broccoli. Or, if it cannot handle your winters, buy started plants in the spring, give them lots of water, and hope to beat the arrival of hot weather. In any case, since broccoli is a big plant with a good appetite, give it room; two feet between plants in the row, three feet between rows.

Cultivate shallowly or you will injure the roots. Once more, that problem disappears if you mulch well, and broccoli loves mulch.

If starved of lime, broccoli develops "club root" and does poorly. Sometimes the plant stem develops blackleg and dies. This disease should not cause you much trouble, but you might set out a few extra plants just in case blackleg competes with your kitchen. It is wise, as indeed it is in the case of most vegetables, not to plant broccoli in the same spot two seasons running. Your broccoli's most frequent problem is likely to be cabbage worm, which rotenone dusting should handle. Or, when you set the plant out, fit around the stem a cardboard or tar-paper disk with a slot to let you fit it on. If it develops plant lice or aphids, spray with Black Leaf. Or, more simply, cut out the infested portion of the plant and either place it inside a heating compost pile or destroy. After the flower heads have formed, you will not be able to get aphids that are inside them, so get them early.

Harvest your broccoli when the flower heads have formed, but while the "florets" or tiny flowers that form each head are still tight buds. Broccoli is no exception to the general rule that vegetables contain both more flavor and more nourishment when they are immature. When you cut off a head, cut at least two to four inches below the head; otherwise too many side shoots will form near the cut. Keep cutting heads regularly as they reach the right stage for eating; otherwise the plant will stop producing them.

Broccoli is a great deal more perishable than head cabbage, and you will get the full flavor only if you cut just when it is needed or, if that is impracticable, put the freshly cut heads immediately in the refrigerator until the cook is ready for them. For the same reason, it is more worth growing than cabbage, because the supply at the grocer's is less likely to be still fit to eat.

If your summers are quite hot, you may find that collards are the only members of the cabbage tribe really glad to live in your garden. But before you admit that, give a southern garden fall plantings of broccoli and a slightly northern one forced plants in the spring. Collards are an excellent vegetable, but they are not broccoli, any more than head cabbage is broccoli.

BRUSSELS SPROUTS
(*Brassica oleracea,* variety *gemmifera*)

This member of the cabbage family is a tall plant, without branches, with large ruffled leaves. It produces miniature cabbage heads as buds, in the crotches of the leaves, buds about one or two inches in diameter. It has been grown in Europe for centuries, and for a good century in this country. It needs just about the same things its cousin, broccoli (page 38), needs in the way of soil, culture, and climate, and it has just about the same disease and pest problems. Since it does its best growing in cool weather, people plant it around June, so that the buds will come on when things cool off. Remove the lower leaves from the stem when the little buds, or "sprouts," begin to mature.

CABBAGE
(*Brassica oleracea,* variety *capitata, Linn*)

This is the common cabbage, in its many interesting varieties. In my judgment both Brussels sprouts and broccoli are more interesting members of the family, but the common cabbage is much more widely eaten. Cabbage, though perhaps not the headed types, was eaten in ancient times. Those types were probably developed in Europe, and a cabbage head may now weigh from two to fifty pounds. As food, the cabbage is rich in both minerals and vitamins, although the latter are naturally more plentiful in the green outer leaves than in the blanched inner ones. It comes in numerous varieties and combinations: early, midseason, late; smooth or crinkly; green or purplish red; heads round, conical, or a flattened globe.

If you are not a cabbage fan and do not much enjoy our European types, even when they are not grossly overcooked, you may find in the Chinese cabbage a special favorite. It is a member of the *Brassica* family which the Chinese have grown since before the Christian era, and it makes delicious eating. It takes a few days longer to mature than some of our early cabbages do, and it hates hot weather, but its culture is essentially the same we give the others.

The directions for growing broccoli (page 38) will work for cabbage. There is little to add. Be sure to try some of the looser-headed Savoy cabbage, particularly if you like to eat cabbage raw as cole slaw—although most people think you need head cabbage for cole slaw. Although cabbage will stand quite severe frost, don't leave it out until the ground actually freezes. Unlike its cousins, cabbage stores pretty well—which means, among other things, that if you have very little garden space you may want to skip it. The difference between store and home-grown cabbage is likely to be much less than the difference between store broccoli and the broccoli you can grow. If you do grow cabbage and want to store it for winter, cut it with plenty of stem.

For such a strong vegetable, and one that eats so heavily, cabbage develops a good many pests. A small black fly sometimes lays eggs on the stem just above the ground, and these eggs hatch into larvae known as cabbage maggots. They are usually laid a few days after plants are set out. Keep an eye out for them, and rub them off with your finger before they hatch. Otherwise the maggot will crawl down the stem, feed on the taproot, and kill the plant in short order. If you don't want to watch for the eggs, you might imitate those growers who make a small disk of tarpaper or some tough material, make a small hole in the center to fit a young cabbage stem, slice a diagonal with a knife from the center-hole to the edge of the disk, and slip the disk onto the cabbage stem: this sometimes prevents the black fly from completing its life cycle. Small white and yellow butterflies also lay eggs, theirs at the base of a leaf, and hatch out larvae in the form of well-camouflaged green "cabbage worms," which among them probably eat more cabbage than any other creature except man. The eggs are hard to find, but if you spot the green worm dust the plant well with rotenone. It is fatal to the worm and harmless to human beings.

One other green worm succumbs to the same treatment: the looper, so called because he loops his back as he inches along. In cool weather cabbage aphids or plant lice may cause trouble. If so, spray them with Black Leaf 40 during the heat of the day and try to get rid of them before the head starts to form. Some people have claimed to control the aphid pretty well merely by spraying the plant hard with a garden hose.

In the Southern states an insect sometimes called the Harlequin cabbage bug occasionally arrives, sucks the juices from the leaves, and, to add insult to injury, injects a poison that stunts the plant. You can usually pick it off with your hands, and rotenone helps too. This bug was probably sent to remind us Southerners that cabbages prefer cold climates anyhow! Seriously, this list of pests is not as much bother as I have made it sound. The most frequent of them, the green cabbage worm, never covers his tracks: he makes fine holes all over the leaves. And he cannot stand up to a good dusting with rotenone.

CARROTS

(*Daucus carota,* variety *sativa*)

Carrots were probably developed from the beautiful, if bothersome, weed called Queen Anne's Lace. Provided a few simple conditions are met, they are relatively easy to raise, highly nutritious, and delicious to eat. They like to grow in a deep, fertile soil, well limed with magnesium limestone. They need less lime than beets, but they are extremely dependent on what they do need. If the soil lacks humus, or its surface gets packed, or it is shallow on a hardpan base, the roots will be deformed, unsightly, and awkward for the cook to clean. Carrots are also extremely dependent on potash for good growth. They don't need much nitrogen. Some people claim a little boron helps; certainly an ounce of borax to sixteen quarts of water, dribbled along fifty to sixty feet of row, will do no harm. If you take a snobbish delight in high-colored carrots, and put an ounce of copper dust, dissolved in sixteen quarts of water, to a hundred feet of row, they will achieve a fine complexion. If your soil is not pulverized to a foot or more of depth, better plant one of the short varieties. The longer ones will grow crooked. The same thing applies if your soil is full of stones.

As a Southern gardener, I hate to keep admitting how many vegetables dislike excessive heat. Alas, carrots too prefer cool summers to grow in. Spring and fall are therefore better growing times in the South than midsummer. Your fall carrots will stand mild frosts, but dig them before the ground freezes. Probably most Southern gardens will produce the short, quick-growing varieties better than the longer-rooted sorts.

Unlike beets, carrots don't transplant well. So plant the seed where it will eventually grow, and don't bother to transplant seedlings.

Like beets, carrots can be deliciously sweet. The three varieties that have tested highest on sugar are Nantes, Touchon, and Hutchinson.

With proper soil conditions, you are unlikely to be bothered by insects or disease. To preserve this immunity, you had better not plant carrots in the same place more often than every fifth year. There is a rust fly that sometimes damages carrots, though only the early planting. Succession plantings can be made from the time the ground can be worked in spring until early August.

A good mulch will of course help protect your carrots from the competition of greedy weeds, but you should put it on after your carrots are up an inch or two, and then only after thoroughly breaking the crust of the soil between the rows. Unfortunately, carrots germinate very slowly, and weeds may be growing in the row by the time they are up. Also, it is sometimes hard to pull up the weeds without disturbing the roots of the seedling carrots. Some gardeners get around this by the following procedure. They sow the seed in the row, dribble water on it, then cover the row with a little ridge of fine material like sawdust or buckwheat hulls, both of which are first-class mulch material. When the carrot seedling starts peeking through, they skim off half the ridge, thereby dislocating the roots of any weeds that may have sprung up in it while the carrots were taking their time getting started.

In the spring planting you can speed the germination considerably by propping a plank on edge alongside the row on the northern or western side; it makes a little suntrap that forces the early growth. In the hot summer planting you can protect the seed and the young seedlings by a finely divided mulch like sawdust or sand.

Carrots conserve their flavor and food value perhaps better than any vegetable we have discussed so far, including beets; so, if you are crowded for space, remember that good lettuce is harder to buy than reasonably good carrots. Still, like every other vegetable, carrots taste best when fresh from the ground.

CAULIFLOWER

(*Brassica oleracea,* variety *botrytis*)

Cauliflower has been eaten in the Near East since before the Christian era, but it was probably not before the late Middle Ages that it was introduced into Europe. It is another member of the cabbage tribe. It develops a single head of "curd," which is an inflorescence of minute buds like those in the several heads that develop on a stalk of broccoli. This curd is surrounded by a rosette of long, slender, cabbage-like leaves.

Unhappily, although the culture of cabbage (page 40) is basically that of cauliflower too, cauliflower is fussier. What it really craves is a cool, moist climate. Too much heat leads it to head up too soon, before it is properly grown. Broccoli stands heat better. If you live where the summers are very hot, you can defend your cauliflower a little by giving them heavy waterings. Or you may find that the long-season type with purplish curd will grow where you cannot get by with the short-season type with white curd. Heavy mulching will also give partial protection. You may discover you can raise the quicker-growing variety by setting out plants as soon as all danger of frost is past, if your ground is fertile enough to force rapid growth before the long hot weeks come. It is even more likely that you may be able to plant in late summer and produce good cauliflower by late fall. If spring frost catches your plants when they are young, they may try to head up prematurely. If they do, they are not worth nursing; pull them up and give their space to another set of plants or to a more cooperative vegetable. As to frost in autumn, although cauliflower is not quite so hardy as cabbage, once it starts to mature its head light frost will do no harm.

Remember two things. Cauliflower is a heavy eater. Poor ground will not satisfy its hunger. It needs even better soil than cabbage. It is also one of the thirstiest vegetables, even though its soil must be well drained too. Lack of abundant moisture will stunt its growth, and no first-class cauliflower was ever grown slowly. In short, unless you can dig the soil deeply, work plenty of compost and lime into it, defend it from drying out, preferably with plenty of mulch, and drench it with a garden hose if the ground gets dry, you had better choose a less fussy guest for your garden than cauliflower. Remember too that although cauliflower will not keep its flavor as long as a carrot will, it does not wilt with the speed of broccoli or leafier vegetables. It requires even more room than cabbage, so if you are short of space don't sacrifice to it such things as that priceless supply of fresh, unwilted lettuce.

If you just will not mulch, cauliflower will resent your decision even more than most vegetables, and you will have to protect it from weeds by shallow cultivation, at the constant risk of disturbing its shallower roots. If you just will not compost, and cannot furnish your cauliflower with a substitute in the form of rotted manure worked well in, use a commercial fertilizer containing plenty of nitrogen. As usual, commercial fertilizers can do damage that compost or rotted stable manure cannot do. If your soil lacks boron, the curd of your cauliflower may show ugly brown spots. A half-teaspoonful of borax mixed with twelve quarts of water and sprinkled along the row where you set out your plants should prevent this.

When you come to harvest the heads, you may prefer them blanched. Just bring the leaves together over the head enough to shade it and tie them that way lightly—that is, once the head is fully developed. One to three weeks, depending on temperature, should whiten the curd.

Cauliflower is subject to the same pests and diseases as cabbage, and they can be treated by the same methods. But in the case of cauliflower, as in the case of broccoli—that many-headed cauliflower—aphids are unassailable once they work inside the inflorescence, or curd. So make sure to clean them out before the curd forms.

CELERY AND CELERIAC

(*Apium graveolens*)

Celery seems to have developed originally in the Mediterranean area, but it is now found in wet locations throughout Europe and all the way to the Himalayas. Europeans probably domesticated it first for medicinal purposes; then as an herb to season other foods; and finally as a vegetable to be eaten in its own right, raw or cooked. Until recently it was almost always blanched. The tall green stems were grown in a trench; when they reached the stage of good eating the gardener filled the trench with earth and banked it against the plant almost to the top, thereby depriving the celery of chlorophyll and forcing it to turn the desired white. As in the case of asparagus, many people now prefer the vitamin-rich green state to the bleached state, and a good deal of celery is now eaten green. If you have never eaten it green, try it. But try it in its own right; don't judge it by bleached standards! Certain varieties, such as Giant Pascal, are better adapted than others to producing unblanched celery.

Celery is somewhat hard to grow, particularly if you assume the extra task of blanching it. It was originally a marsh plant, and most of the commercial crop is grown now on marsh or peat soils, although only after they have been drained and aerated. But the crop is still a thirsty one. It needs plenty of water to do well, and it prefers to have the water supplied at ground level and not sprinkled on top of its foliage. It likes deep fertile soil and will respond magnificently to good compost. It is greedy; it will likely prove the heaviest eater in your garden except asparagus.

If you are a beginner, try buying the young plants. But you can also sow indoors or under glass and transplant, preferably when the plants are not more than three inches high. For fall celery, sow in a row in the garden and transplant. Since celery seed germinates more slowly than some of the weed seeds that are likely to be lying in the row ready to spring to annoying life, you can profitably use the old trick of forming an inch-high ridge of soil or fine mulch over the row of celery seed, waiting for the weeds to rear their ugly heads, and then gently skimming off the top half-inch with your hoe, thereby destroying the young weeds and allowing the slower-germinating celery to come through and do its stuff. Some people speed up celery seeds by keeping wet cloths over them until they sprout, preferably in a wooden flat.

When the stalks are big enough to be worth eating, use alternate stalks and let the others get full growth. When they are about a foot high, if you are determined to bleach, form a tube of tough paper, about four inches in diameter, around the stalk and tie, leaving the top leaves exposed. The plant will bleach in a week or a little more, depending on the variety. The old trick of planting in a trench is unnecessary work.

Your celery may develop blight, which will show as spots and holes in the foliage, although a deeply dug, loose soil, containing plenty of compost, plus adequate watering if drought strikes, plus plenty of ground limestone containing both calcium and magnesium, should protect you. If blight comes, you can spray every week or ten days with Bordeaux mixture, 5-5-50. If caterpillars bother your foliage, they can be easily picked off and destroyed. Other troubles are unlikely to come your way.

Celery's cousin, celeriac, is even simpler to raise and furnishes a fine turnip-like root with a good celery flavor. Europeans use it widely for soups, purées, and salads, and we ought to. You may find it will do better in your particular garden than celery will, and in many places you can get it only by growing it yourself.

CHARD

(Beta vulgaris, variety *cicla)*

Chard, or "Swiss chard," is the beet as Aristotle described it in the fourth century before Christ, and grows wild in the Mediterranean area and clear to southern Asia. Probably the garden beet was developed from this wild plant. Chard is a beet in which the root is small and not edible and in which the leaves are highly developed. Of course the leaves of a garden beet make delicious eating, but it cannot compete with the chard for edible leaves which really yield two "vegetables"— the fleshy main stem of the leaf, often cooked and served like asparagus; and the rest of the leaf, which is cooked and served like spinach. Chard is so easy to raise that it is hard to discuss! Sow it as soon as the ground can be worked. As soon as the leaves are long enough to be worth cutting, start cutting a few leaves from each plant. There will be more in a few days, and they will keep coming right through the summer, and in many climates right through the following winter. Chard is a necessity in any good mild-climate "winter garden." It likes cold weather, but, unlike the vegetables in the cabbage family, it doesn't get sulky under intense heat, provided it has enough to drink. If a hard frost kills it to the ground, a few warm bright days will bring out another set of delicious leaves. It will even furnish leaves into the second season for a few weeks before it bolts to seed and while your next season's planting of chard is getting ready to take over.

Chard is an exceedingly beautiful plant, and the variety known as rhubarb chard, which has reddish leaves with brilliant crimson stems instead of dark green leaves with white stems, is perhaps the most beautiful of all. Either variety has a right to grow in anybody's flower bed, if space is scarce where most of the vegetables are grown.

I have no experience of diseases in chard. Not that I haven't grown it. I have grown plenty and like the taste better than that of spinach. But mine has always refused to develop any trouble of any sort. I gather, however, that insects do sometimes attack it, and that rotenone dusting has proved the best counter-measure. I gather also that sometimes brown spots appear on the leaves, if the soil lacks magnesium limestone and some potash material like wood ashes. If you build good garden soil, you are unlikely to have to think about such unpleasant things; and I have grown completely healthy chard on soil I was by no means proud of.

COLLARDS
(*Brassica oleracea,* variety *acephala*)

Collards are another member of the cabbage family. They are a tall-growing kale, which may reach from one to four feet, depending on growing conditions, but their leaves are not curly or ruffled like kale leaves. They may also be roughly described as a cabbage that never forms a head—either the kind the true cabbage forms, or the special kinds that are formed by Brussels sprouts, broccoli, and cauliflower. Historically speaking, they are probably the kind of cabbage originally grown before the other species were developed. They are easier to grow and freer of disease than most of their cousins. In this country they are grown chiefly in the Southern states, where the hot summers are unfavorable to those fussy cousins—although the finest flavor is brought out by autumn frosts, even in the South.

Northern gardeners start them in late summer for a fall crop—or else they eat young cabbage plants, set too close to head, and call them collards. Southern gardeners either start them indoors early and set them out as soon as the ground can be worked, or else they sow in late summer for use during the fall and winter. As to soil and fertilizing, what was said about their cousin the broccoli (page 38) works for collards.

In climates where cabbages will head, most people prefer cabbage to collards. But if you like crisp, green romaine lettuce better than the tightly headed, bleached iceberg (which ships better); if you like crisp green celery better than the more usual bleached celery; in short, if you take your chlorophyll straight, you may find you like collards better than cabbage, and you may certainly like the loose-headed Savoy cabbage better than the more widely eaten tight-headed varieties (which ship better!). I may be prejudiced, but I think the taste of my whole generation of Americans has been perverted from those vegetables and those varieties of vegetables that taste best when brought fresh from a home garden, to those that keep best, stand transportation best, and therefore yield the grower the most cash—and, usually, yield the eater the least taste and the least nourishment. So most people prefer head cabbage and would get more nourishment from collards!

Collards not only bring more health to you, they have more health themselves than cabbage. That is, except for the green caterpillar that afflicts head cabbage too—and that can be eliminated by dusting with rotenone—they are wonderful medical risks. Finally, if they do

well you can keep whittling leaves from them for some time just as
you can with kale and chard. But you can't very successfully treat a
head of cabbage that way.

CORN

(*Zea mays,* variety *saccharata*)

Sweet corn—or garden corn, or sugar corn—is a special variety, developed from so-called field corn, and quite different from popcorn.
All three come originally from a plant that is technically one of the
grasses of the two American continents, a grass that was first domesticated for its valuable grain by Indians in the Andes and also in the
northern part of Central America and Mexico. This domesticated
corn reached the southern part of what is now the United States before
700 A. D. and the northeastern part about 1000 A. D. The Indians
planted it with a stick and often put a fish in each hill of three or four
grains, which worked well as fertilizer. They hoed competing weeds
with a primitive hoe. They sometimes converted the grains into hom-
iny by using wood-ash lye, or they ground the hardened grain by hand
to make corn meal for bread.

The Indians grew "Indian corn" only as food for human beings.
When the European colonists introduced the wheel, and hence the
cart, and better draft animals than dogs and llamas, they raised big
corn crops for draft animals and farm stock. The corn now produced
for cattle, hogs, and the few horses the gas motor has not replaced,
is very good as corn on the cob if picked young enough; but this field
corn never tastes as delectable as such varieties of sweet corn as
Golden Bantam. Sweet corn has been grown only since about 1800.
I believe it is safe to say that, eaten from the cob, it is the favorite
vegetable of most Americans. Unfortunately for all these fans, corn
probably loses flavor between plucking and cooking faster than any
other vegetable. Yet most Americans buy corn that is from one day to
several days old.

One of my friends insists that corn should not be plucked from the
stalk until the water is already boiling on the stove. Then, says this
pleasant fanatic, the gardener should pull it rapidly and should run,
not walk, to the kitchen. He should husk or "shuck" the corn while
running. Presumably, with the gardener operating at this speed, the
wind would clean the cornsilk off the cob very neatly! Seriously, corn
should never be plucked until the last possible moment before cooking. If there must be an interval, keep it in the refrigerator, unshucked,

until the cook is ready to plunge it into boiling water. Because of the general migration of Americans to the city, and because of our national myth that food is not a highly perishable article, most young Americans have never eaten genuine corn on the cob. They have merely gnawed starchy grains off of a cob—and even so, they still love it.

There are three reasons why you ought to raise sweet corn in your own garden, two of which I have mentioned. First, it is likely to be a family favorite. Second, you cannot possibly buy corn fit for an epicure to eat. Third, if your garden offers hot sunshine and you can water it well when dry weather comes, corn will prove one of the easiest vegetables to grow of any in your garden. Corn grows on a great variety of soils; stands, and even rejoices in, terrific heat, provided it has plenty to drink; and responds magnificently to feeding. It is sometimes abused by agricultural experts for leaving this continent's soil bare to erosion by rainfall; you can cure that objection with a good mulch. So grow your own corn, even if your garden is too tiny to harbor more than a dozen stalks.

If your soil has lots of compost in it, corn will love it. This vegetable is not one of the heavier users of lime, but neither will it grow on acid soil. It prefers a pH of from 5.6 to 6.8. It also likes adequate supplies of phosphorus and potash: the first can readily be supplied with bone meal or ground rock-phosphate and the second from wood ashes, preferably hardwood. It does not crave too much nitrogen. Corn is extremely nourishing food for human beings, and yellow corn supposedly has even more vitamins than the white-grained varieties.

Corn cannot stand frost, so do not plant until all danger of frost is past, unless you want to gamble a little seed on the chance of getting eating ears early. In the same way, you can risk a late planting that the autumn frost will probably catch but may not. By all means plant at least every two weeks, as any given planting will yield prime ears for only from seven to ten days. Before that the grains will be too small for the best eating, and after that the grains will be getting mealy and tough. Every given planting will do better in two or three short parallel rows than in one long row. Corn is pollinated better that way: pollen from one or more tassels is carried by wind to the tuft of silk that protrudes from the shucks of each growing cob or ear, and a particle of pollen must reach each strand to get a fully grained cob. In a single row there is less chance of thorough pollination, and parts of some cobs may have grains missing. Rows should be anywhere from two to four feet apart; single stalks, after thinning, should be at least six or eight inches apart in the row. Some people make little mounds of earth, or "hills," two to three feet apart in the row, and plant three to five grains in a hill. If you want corn early, and don't want to risk a late spring frost, you can soak seeds overnight, or sprout single stalks in four-inch pots or paper bands or veneer bands and transplant them. Be careful; the roots must not be the least bit disturbed.

Many stalks sprout one or more "suckers" from their bases, and some people cut these off. It is not necessary, but, if you prefer to get rid of them, do it when the suckers are only four inches high.

Corn cannot compete with weeds and grow good ears too. Cultivate regularly when the weeds are only a couple of inches high, if weather will permit. If they get a foot high, don't pull them up but cut them off at ground level, or you may disturb the roots of your corn and cut the yield sharply. Better still, mulch your crop well, so there will be few weeds and so those few can be eased out of nice moist earth without disturbing tender corn roots. Needless to say, don't meddle with the delicate cornsilk, where the pollination must occur. When the silk turns dark brown or black and the ear it grows on feels nice and plump, that particular ear is probably ready for the pot and will not stay prime for many days. If you are still uncertain, peel down one or two husks, or shucks, and press your thumbnail against a grain. If it's just right, it should almost squirt "milk" in your face. If it is getting a little bit old, it will be moist but it won't squirt. To harvest, grasp the stalk firmly just below the ear you want and twist the ear off with your other hand. If you try to wrench off the ear with only one hand, you may easily break the tender stalk and lose a second, still unripe ear. As soon as all the ears have been eaten from a given stalk, pull it up and add it to your compost. If you cannot pull it up without disturbing a neighboring stalk, cut it off at ground level.

If your garden soil was loosened deep in the spring, and if good compost was mixed with it, you are unlikely to be bothered with disease or insects. Some of the early yellow-grained types of corn are a bit subject to bacterial wilt; but some excellent hybrids have been produced that are highly resistant to wilt, and the seed is not much more expensive. You may also get corn smut, a fungous disease that develops a kind of gray swelling or boil on the ears or tassel. Unless you remove it promptly, it will eventually release a sort of black dust —the spores, which spread it about. Apparently, by spraying the ears with Bordeaux mixture just as they begin to form, you can prevent this corn smut from appearing. Some of your cobs are almost sure to contain a fat corn-ear worm apiece, right at the top of the ear. People fight this worm with two pints of arsenate of lead to one pint of hydrated lime, but I never could see that he ate many grains. As to the mess he makes, you can easily chop off the spoiled end of the cob—being sure to kill him in the process. Finally, there is the European corn-borer, which sometimes gets inside the stalk and causes bent or broken tassels. To combat him, dust the axil of the leaf, where it joins the stalk, with nicotine dust every five days. Or dust with rotenone.

You may have none of these troubles—except perhaps the corn-ear worm—if your soil is healthy and you remove stalks from your garden as fast as they finish bearing. But then, no garden plant should ever be left standing idle when it has done its work for you: vacated houses always attract squatters—in this case, insects, fungus, and bacteria. The whole business of garden pests has been much exaggerated because the inexperienced gardeners have grown sickly plants on sickly soil and fought a losing battle with chemical warfare, instead of building good live soil to start with. Plants are like people: billions of bacteria are waiting to assault those that are hungry, thirsty, or pallid from lack of sunlight. It is easier to supply food, drink, and sunlight than it is to try to murder billions of anything, even bacteria.

CUCUMBERS
(*Cucumis sativus*)

Botanically the cucumber is classified as a "fruit," along with its cousins, the melons, the squashes, and the pumpkins, and along also with the tomato, the eggplant, and the pepper. But in terms of our eating habits it is one of our vegetables. It probably originated in the Himalayas, but it had spread both east and west before the Christian era. Although it still grows wild in the East Indies, it has been cultivated for some 3000 years. It was cultivated as far west as France by the ninth century after Christ.

It is one of the less easy vegetables to grow, chiefly because it is attacked by so many insects and diseases; but these hurdles are by no means insurmountable, and the best way to find out how much of a problem they will be in your garden is to plant some cucumbers and take simple measures against their enemies.

Cucumbers like hot weather, deeply worked, fertile soil, plenty of circulating air about them, and low humidity. They hate cold, and a light frost can kill the vines. But if you meet the stipulated conditions a few vines may supply all the fresh cucumbers you will want to eat. They are generally planted only after all danger of frost is gone and after the soil has had time to warm up a bit. They can of course be started indoors and set out when the weather is right, but they are a lot harder to transplant than vegetables like tomato or cabbage. If you do try starting them indoors, plant them in pots, or bands, or berry-boxes, or inverted sods, and try not to disturb the roots when you move them to the garden. Or plant them in the garden but use the paper "hotcaps" that florists use to protect them, ventilating the plants whenever weather permits.

Cucumbers grow best in hills four feet apart each way, six or seven seeds to the hill, thinned out to one or two good plants, or to three or four if your garden is fertile. For the later, longer-running varieties, a vine can use four feet one way and six the other. Your neighbors may warn you not to plant them too near squash or melons for fear they will cross-fertilize and spoil flavors. This is mere folklore; scientists have tried in vain to persuade cucumbers to cross with their cousins. Your cucumber vines will be even more grateful than most vegetables for ample compost, or well-rotted manure, or a commercial fertilizer containing ample nitrogen—preferred in that order and worked into the soil in advance. They will also be even more grateful than most vegetables for a good mulch. In choosing varieties, don't try to make do with the small pickling-size sorts and depend on oversize fruits for eating. Plant pickling-size types if you want to put up little pickles, and slicing-size types if you want to eat fresh cucumber, raw or cooked; and in both cases pick fruit before it is fully mature. It tastes better when it has not fully matured, and, besides, as in the case of most plants, fruits maturing on the vine encourage the vine to quit producing. It naturally concludes it has done its job when its seed begins to ripen. And it does not share your ambition to please the cook or your own palate.

If you fail to mulch, remember that cucumber roots are shallow and watch out that you don't damage them when you use the hoe or the wheel cultivator. But it is worth your knowing that a good mulch is likely to give you both more cucumbers and better-formed cucumbers. Any disturbed condition of the vines may result in malformed cucumbers. Don't leave them on the vine, hoping they will shape up properly later on. They won't. Pull them off and add them to your compost. In addition to liking plenty of lime, cucumbers want nitrogen, either from rotted manure or from chemical fertilizer if you must use it. A few side-dressings of liquid fertilizer from time to time will encourage rapid growth, which is always desirable.

Now for possible troubles. Make sure the soil is nicely aerated, loose and crumbly. Make sure it contains plenty of magnesium limestone. Since circulation of air about your plants discourages mildew, it may be worth while to run your vines on an A-shaped trellis. If mildew gets you anyhow, dust with sulphur. If a spell of cool weather slows up growth, you run a risk of aphids: spray with nicotine sulphate or Black Leaf 40. In extremely dry weather red spiders sometimes irritate the leaves; try hosing off the vines with a fine spray in the early morning hours.

Your biggest nuisance is likely to be the cucumber beetle. It not only sucks the juice out of the foliage, but, in the process of shopping around between plants, spreads bacterial wilt. The bacteria of this disease plug up the water lanes in the stem. If that happens pull up the diseased plants and either burn them or get them inside a heating compost heap. Meanwhile get that striped beetle if you can. One way is to protect the plants while young with mosquito netting. The beetle does his worst work before the vine begins to run. For that reason some people plant a week later than they would ordinarily have to, just so the weather will be really warm and hustle the plant to the running stage before the beetles attack. Dusting the baby plants with rotenone or even lime sometimes helps. And don't plant cucumbers in the same spot more than once every four or five years. Some people also find that one melon vine growing in the hill with young cucumbers until they begin to run decoys the beetles. Then they pull the melon up and get rid of it. It is a pity that efforts to breed cucumber strains that will resist wilt and mildew have been pretty fruitless. Obviously cucumbers are among the more delicate vegetables. It does not follow that you will have trouble if you create the right conditions for them.

EGGPLANT

(*Solanum melongena,* variety *esculentum*)

The eggplant is a tropical perennial, which we grow as an annual. In short, since it fruits the first year, we do not mind that the next winter our temperate climate takes its tropical life. It is a bushy plant that produces two to six large plum-shaped fruits, weighing from one to five pounds each. The size of the bush, the size of the fruit, and the color of the fruit all vary according to variety. Fruits come in purple, yellow, white, or even striped. The plant is sometimes called Guinea squash. It was grown in Asia before the Christian era, when it was often called "mad apple." It was grown for ornament before the fruits were used for medicinal or food purposes, and is still worthy of your flowerbed, if you have such a thing and if your vegetable garden is already crowded. We Americans used it only for ornament until around 1900. Now most Americans know it only as a purple fruit in a grocery store. It is the same old story: most Europeans think the white variety tastes better than the purple, but American truck-growers grow the purple because that is what the customer expects to find when she shops.

Being tropical, eggplant grows better in our Southern states than it does farther north. In fact, the Northern gardener may not find it worth coaxing unless his family is very keen about it. And even so, since eggplant not only keeps well but, according to most tastes, actu-ally improves a little with keeping, the Northern gardener may prefer to buy it and grow something that is at its best when fresh.

Eggplant likes hot weather, so long as it can quench its thirst. But it wants to quench that at the roots, not from the air: it does not care for humidity. It hates cold wind, and frost just plain kills it. If you want it early, you had better buy plants from a reputable firm, because the seedlings ought to be grown in virgin soil, such as leaf-mold from the woods, mixed with sand. If they are grown in soil taken from a vegetable garden they are likely to develop wilt. They like lots of compost in the holes where they are set out. More than with most vegetables, it is desirable to shift their location in the garden from season to season, also to avoid wilt. They adore magnesium limestone in the soil. In no circumstances should the plants be set out until the soil is warm, partly because a late frost may kill them, and partly be-cause, even without frost, a cold soil will retard their growth and render them more subject to their enemies. Set the plants a good two to three feet apart.

Your best defense against verticillium wilt is the magnesium lime-stone plus a new place in the garden. Some gardeners won't plant eggplant in the same place a second time for as much as ten years. The bacteria wilt is a less constant menace, but there is no good cure for it. Better remove affected plants.

The flea-beetle is least likely to annoy you if you avoid planting early in cold soil. If you set your plants out late, this pest will do little harm. Precisely the same precaution should be used against the Colorado potato beetle. Afflict this enemy with rotenone dust too, and destroy the orange-colored eggs it lays on the undersides of the leaves; otherwise the eggs will hatch into very hungry grubs and de-vour the eggplant's foliage. In the South the same rotenone dust may be needed against the tortoise beetle. Finally, plant lice can best be destroyed with nicotine spray.

As in the case of most vegetables, the fruit should be eaten before it matures. It tastes better then, and, besides, it turns an unappetizing brown as it matures. If you have plenty of eggplants you can begin harvesting as soon as the fruit attains the size of a large egg. How much bigger it will grow before maturing depends on the variety.

HERBS

Although vegetables have been grown for thousands of years, our medieval ancestors in Europe rarely grew them. What they did grow was herbs. It was not until the Renaissance that the vegetable garden took its place beside the traditional herb garden. Today, worse luck, the vegetable garden has all but pushed out the herbs. Medieval man wanted herbs to flavor the meats he ate, to make salads or soups, and most of all to furnish him with medicines. "Herbal medicine" has not yet died out in Europe, although it has almost died in America.

However, the gourmet today wants herbs to season not only his meats but his vegetables. And although a heavy-handed cook can destroy the subtlest flavors of good vegetables by overseasoning them with herbs, the gourmet is right: herbs in moderation can bring out the flavors in a vegetable rather than destroy them.

Luckily, herbs are on the whole easier to grow than vegetables and much less vulnerable to diseases and pests. Moreover, although some herbs, such as dill and basil and summer savory, are annuals and must be replanted each year, there are others, such as parsley—used more often as a herb than as a vegetable today—that are biennial and so produce for at least two seasons. Indeed, in many parts of the United States parsley will go straight through the winter, especially if covered with leaves or otherwise protected during extremely cold spells. When it is killed to the roots, my parsley has often put out delicious fresh growth at the slightest excuse.

Most of the herbs mentioned in the recipes to be found later in this book are actually perennials that go gaily on for several years, sometimes for many: chives, fennel, marjoram, mint, rosemary, sorrel, tarragon, thyme; although thyme grows coarse after two or three years and is better replaced with a new planting, and marjoram and rosemary cannot stand extreme cold.

Some herbs—dill, for instance—are grown for their seeds; some, such as fennel, for their roots, as well as their leaves. But most herbs are grown for their leaves. The plant is usually cut off when it starts to flower, is then hung up to dry, and is finally enclosed in a paper bag and hung again until needed. Some herbs—tarragon, for example —are thought to yield their essential oil more willingly if the leaf is ground up or crumbled after it has been dried and before it is stored.

Dried and ground herb leaves can, however, be purchased at a store, and the chief excuses for growing herbs are, first, that in America, although not in Europe, they are outrageously expensive; and, second, that a tiny herb garden can be a charming addition to any vegetable garden and costs very little in labor. The important advantage in having your own herb garden is that, at least during the growing season, you can use fresh herbs instead of dried ones. A really good cook will tell you that many herbs are much finer fresh than cured: for example, basil, chives, dill, mint, parsley, rosemary, sorrel, tarragon.

Most herbs will flourish best on rich soil; many will do pretty well on any reasonably good soil, provided they get enough moisture, and provided drainage is good; but there are some that actually do best where the soil is not too rich: marjoram, rosemary, summer savory, tarragon, and thyme, for example.

Some herbs, such as chives and parsley, are quite hardy and can stand cold weather; but basil and thyme are afraid of it; mint is richer in essential oil if the weather is mild; and rosemary, which in a mild climate might live ten years, will winter-kill if too much cold hits it.

As in the case of vegetables, some herb seed germinates very slowly. This is true of parsley—so true, in fact, that I always soak my parsley seed in a saucer of water for twenty-four hours before I plant it, which speeds things up a lot. This can be done with all slow seed. Tarragon often fails to seed at all, but root cuttings are easy to propagate, and so are stem cuttings in the spring. Bay is really a tree, or, in some climates, at least a bush, and you may not have room for it. Even dill and rosemary are too big, for example, for planting in a window box. Consult your seed-catalogue or seed-packet directions if you are short of space in your garden, before you plan an herb garden.

If thrips attack your chives, scatter a few flakes of naphthalene among the fine green stems. If a small green worm gets after your fennel, dust your plants with rotenone. Wet weather may cause rust fungus in your mint bed, but I never found it a serious problem. In general, herbs have little to fear from either insects or disease.

JERUSALEM ARTICHOKES

(*Helianthus tuberosus*)

The Jerusalem artichoke, to begin with, is not an artichoke and does not come from Jerusalem. It is a species of sunflower, native to both North and South America, that develops delicious tubers on its roots. Some people believe that the "Jerusalem" in its name is a corruption of the Italian word for sunflower, *girasóle*.

It is excessively easy to raise. It will thrive on even quite poor soil, under nearly any climatic condition. It is rich in sugar and insulin. If you have never eaten Jerusalem artichoke, imagine a small, knotty potato that really does suggest the flavor of globe artichoke and is ever so much easier to grow in most places.

This plant grows not from seed but from tubers, just as Irish potatoes do. Plant the tubers ten inches apart in rows two and one-half to three feet apart. The smaller ones are as good "seed" as the bigger. If the tuber is quite long, you can cut it in half to make two plantings. You can start digging the vegetables up in September as soon as the small, pretty sunflower blossoms begin dying. Or you can leave them in the ground and dig them when you like—or until your soil gets too hard to dig in, if your winters are that cold. In that case, they should be dug and stored in a cool place until wanted.

Once established, Jerusalem artichokes will keep coming up from any stray tubers the digger may miss. For that reason many gardeners prefer not to plant them in the garden proper, but edge the northern border or plant them in a clump where they will screen the compost pile. Since the plants get to be six feet high, there is an additional reason for not wanting them where they will steal sunlight.

KALE

(*Brassica oleracea,* variety *acephela*)

Kale is close kin to collards, and lots of people prefer it to cabbage for the same reason they prefer collards to cabbage, romaine lettuce to iceberg lettuce, and green celery to bleached. Some people prefer it to its chief competitor, spinach, because they object to the coppery taste in spinach. Kale is collards with frills on. It is headless cabbage. It therefore keeps less well than cabbage, which means there is more difference between what you buy and what you can grow. Finally, it is the hardiest of all our vegetables and will grow right through winter fairly far north, will sprout new leaves when frost cuts it down, and can be protected against getting completely frozen to death by a good thick mulch. A light frost merely improves the flavor. All this Eskimo talk does not obscure the fact that it probably started its career as one of man's best friends in the Eastern Mediterranean area. In gardens where heat is a problem, this cool-weather plant will naturally grow best in early spring or late fall.

Kale likes plenty of lime and compost in its soil, and the soil well watered but also well drained. It likes the three main elements of commercial fertilizers: nitrogen, phosphate, and potash. It is responsive to liquid fertilizer applied from time to time, for, like cabbage, it is a heavy eater. And it will convert its food into more vitamins for you than cabbage will. It has more vitamins than any of the other garden "greens," and the way to get both the most vitamins and the finest flavor is to cut the leaves young, while they are still deliciously tender. Remember, more will keep coming. For the same reason, don't throw away the young plants that you pull up when you thin the row. They make wonderful eating.

Plant your kale in rows two to three feet apart, and thin the plants, while still small, to every twelve or fifteen inches. Or you can even broadcast the seed in a patch. You don't have to cover the seed with more than one-half to three-eighths of an inch of soil.

Theoretically kale is subject to the same pests and diseases as the rest of the cabbage family, discussed in this book under Broccoli (page 38)—alphabetically speaking, the first member of the family. But you are likely to find kale the strongest, healthiest member of the family, and you may be unable to find the slightest medical problem to worry about! It is robust, joyful, bountiful, delicious, nourishing. If your winters are not too hard, you will find kale one of man's greatest Green Protectors when frost has struck, when winter comes, and so little is really green. And that is precisely why there is no need to write much about it, and every need to grow it and enjoy it.

LEEKS

(*Allium porrum*)

Leeks belong to the onion family, which also includes onion, garlic, "Welsh onion"—which does not come from Wales—shallots, and chives. Whereas the ordinary onion has a round, hollow "leaf," the leaf of the leek is flat and solid; and whereas the onion's edible root is more or less spherical, the leek's root, or bulb, is cylindrical. The leek is believed to have started its vegetable career in southern Asia. It has been eaten since ancient times, and there is a tradition that it was the Roman emperor Nero's favorite vegetable. It is certainly fit for an emperor: it has a much milder and subtler taste than onion has, and many people find it easier to digest.

Leek is an extremely hardy vegetable, and, given the right condi-tions, it is not hard to grow. It likes its soil bed to be light, crumbly, rich, well limed, and well drained. It likes plenty of water for its roots to drink. But it is not finicky; any good garden loam can be properly prepared to grow leeks, provided there is abundant sunshine. Good loam may mean lots of compost worked into the soil. If compost is not available, the next best material is well-rotted manure. If there is no manure, leeks will grudgingly accept chemical fertilizer, applied as a liquid side-dressing at least three times during the growing season.

Plant your seed in a garden row early in the spring, or indoors in a flat in a sunny window, and when the little green hair-like plants are three inches high, thin out or set out one to two inches apart. When the plants are about as plump as straws, cut them back to half their height, set them every four to six inches in a shallow trench, and set them deep enough to bury half their remaining length. As the season goes on, and your leeks acquire more length, gradually fill the trench a little at a time, and, when the weather gets cool in the fall, ridge the soil around them a little every two weeks. The point of the trenching and ridging is, of course, to blanch the lower part of the leek. Similar treatment blanches asparagus and celery, but more and more people like their asparagus unblanched, and they are even beginning to prefer green celery to white. I have never eaten an unblanched leek, so I cannot indulge my usual prejudice against blanched food. But I have a friend in Connecticut who blanches neither celery nor leeks. Accordingly, he does not trench for leeks. Nor does he sow indoors and transplant. He sows in the garden and transplants only those he has to remove from the row in thinning.

Since the leek requires a long season of growth, early spring sowings will not yield good leeks for eating till fall. If your winters are mild, leeks will winter through in the garden for eating during the winter and even during the following spring. If your garden freezes up too hard for that, they can be lifted before the ground freezes and stored in a cellar like celery, with their roots in moist earth. Leeks keep well, and that fact may be an argument against growing them in your own garden if you need the space for more perishable vegetables. The argument for trying to find the space for them is that fewer people in America have learned to enjoy them than in Europe, so that in many places they are not for sale.

The transplanting I advise is a little nuisance. But you will gain back later the time it takes, for leeks require little nursing. In dry weather onion thrips sometimes attack them. Most gardeners find that they can keep thrips away by sprinkling naphthalene flakes along the row.

LETTUCE
(*Lactuca sativa*)

There is hardly a more rewarding plant in the home garden than lettuce. Amateurs, and even beginners, find it relatively easy to grow. Except for the hottest part of the summer, it can be planted to advantage every two weeks throughout the growing season. It usually develops few diseases and is easy to protect from pests. No grocer can compete with your garden for furnishing you fine flavor in lettuce. And some of the most delicious varieties are sold either not at all or very rarely.

Garden lettuce was probably first developed from wild lettuce in Asia Minor. There are now many types: tight-headed, with inside leaves blanched; looser-headed, green-leafed kinds; tall, crisp-leafed types. Which type you choose to grow is partly a matter of personal taste and partly a matter of climate. Hot weather, and particularly weather when even the nights are hot, forces lettuce to run to seed, or "bolt," producing a long stalk and a bitter taste, and makes it especially difficult to produce the tight-headed variety. As to taste, a warning: the taste of most Americans has been perverted. They have become accustomed to the so-called iceberg lettuce because the big growers in our Southwestern states find that sort "keeps best" and is therefore easier to ship; and hotels and restaurants share the growers' affection for it. It keeps everything but its flavor, and it never had much of that to keep. The looser, green-leafed varieties have finer flavor and more vitamin content, but they are hard to make money out of because they are highly perishable. They are just the thing for the home gardener. If you are an iceberg-lettuce addict, try growing both kinds until you have recovered from your vice.

It so happens that in most parts of the United States the highly flavored, highly nutritious, green-leafed types are also easier to grow than iceberg or than any other tight-headed sort. This is especially true in warm climates.

People have been devouring lettuce in the Mediterranean area since before the Christian era. The Romans grew several varieties. By the fifth century lettuce had reached the Chinese. But the early types were loose-leafed. It was not till the Middle Ages that the tight-headed sorts were developed. The Greek island of Cos, in the Aegean Sea, developed what we call romaine lettuce. There is even an "asparagus lettuce," not much grown in America, which is raised for its edible stem.

In order to avoid having hot summer weather force their lettuce to bolt, people in most sections either buy the plants in early spring or grow them in a flat in the window or in a hotbed, and transplant when all danger of frost is past. Or else they plant in late summer so the days, and especially the nights, will be cool by the time the lettuce starts heading. Very far south there are of course gardens that can grow lettuce in the winter months. The seedlings are set out when they are four to five inches tall, and sometimes the top halves of the leaves are pinched off so the young roots won't have to maintain so much "overhead" while they are getting started in their new home. Sometimes, also, seed is planted in protected coldframes and the seedlings are thinned to two inches apart and allowed to remain more or less dormant during the winter, so they will develop strong root-growth before they are set out in the garden. When that time comes they will use space up to two feet each way if they are the larger-headed types, but not more than a foot each way if they are the green-leafed unheaded varieties. In fact, six inches to the row will take care of romaine if the soil is good and you like to eat it young. Finally, if you sow during the open season, in the garden rows, and thin out, remember there is no waste. Even quite tiny plants are delicious eating.

All lettuce likes deeply worked, crumbly soil, with plenty of magnesium lime worked clear down. It also loves compost in the soil, or, if you have failed to compost, well-rotted manure. It does not crave potash, so don't waste wood ashes on it. If you can furnish it neither compost nor rotted manure, it will prefer to have you plow under a crop of some sort of legume, such as soy beans, the fall before, rather than have you fall back on chemicals. Nitrate of soda, for example, which some growers use for side-dressing, causes tip-burn.

Lettuce also likes a reasonable amount of water, provided the soil it lives in is well drained. But, like celery, it doesn't want its head wet. So don't sprinkle if dry weather hits you; get the water to the roots. Water on the leaves can cause various disorders like bottom rot, lettuce drop, gray mold, anthracnose, and mildew. Don't let these facts make you dread rainfall, provided your lettuce gets a reasonable share of sunlight!

You are unlikely to have any trouble from insects except maybe aphids on late lettuce in the fall. If you have them try nicotine dust or sprays, preferably on a hot day. If worms attack your leaves, dust with rotenone. If you find cutworms, leave poison bran around the plants overnight. If slugs bother your leaves, spread some lime on the ground around your plants. But you may grow lettuce and never see any of these pests or be troubled by any disease.

Pull your lettuce, if possible, in the early morning before hot sun strikes it, wash it, and put it promptly in the refrigerator. If it is a loose-leafed, non-heading type, you may discover that what you took to be one "head," or bunch of leaves, is really two or three plants. Let that teach you to do your thinning more carefully! And, of course, since thinnings are good to eat, you can thin in stages, just making sure that at any given stage every plant has enough room to develop rapidly and that you end up with plants far enough apart to reach near-maturity. Pulling up—carefuly, if there are neighboring plants —is better than cutting, because the root that cutting leaves in the soil has no earthly function except to use up the nourishment in your soil. Lettuce is not like kale or chard: it doesn't keep producing leaves to good advantage, although I have a friend who picks leaves off of Oak Leaf and Salad Bowl lettuce and succeeds in persuading his plants to go on working for him.

Finally, don't let people bully you into supposing that it is impossible to raise lettuce during the hottest season, even if you live where it gets really hot. Varieties have been produced that stand a lot of heat. As I write these words I have some lettuce in my garden that has just been through a freak heat wave during which we had temperatures above a hundred for days in succession. It is a variety called Slobolt. It did not enjoy that heat. Neither did I. But I stood it a little better for having fresh lettuce that could also take it. Needless to say, Slobolt is not a headed variety. But then, I don't like head lettuce. Whether my favorite lettuce, romaine, could have made it I frankly don't know; it is so much my favorite that I had eaten up all I had grown. But do experiment with heat-resistant varieties and see if you can't make small fortnightly plantings straight through the summer, even though the seed is harder to sprout in hot weather.

For hot weather, try Slobolt, Oak Leaf, or Salad Bowl. You can help them sprout despite heat by covering the row of newly planted seed with burlap or with wet sawdust and keeping it wet. Later, when the young lettuce has sprouted, you can shelter it from the over-friendly summer sun by stretching the burlap over the row like an awning, suspending it from upright sticks about eight or ten inches above the ground.

Two fine loose-headed varieties are White Boston and Big Boston. These lettuces have soft, loose, mellow heads, and the inner leaves are less blanched than those of iceberg lettuce. They are a nice change from romaine. They won't stand hot weather well, but few lettuces do.

If hot weather strikes your garden early, you can get a head start on it by planting your row of lettuce in the fall after frost. It will come up the first thing in the spring. Or if you can't win the race against hot weather that way, start your Big Boston, and your romaine too, in a hotbed or a sunny window and set them out right after the last frost in the spring. You might put some compost or well-rotted manure in each hole to help your side win.

Remember, lettuce is one of the vegetables that is at its absolute best for only a few days, so keep planting if you want the best.

OKRA

(*Hibiscus esculentus*)

The sooner the rest of the country finds out why Louisianans have always loved okra, the better for the country. But I am being unjust, at least to the other states in the Deep South. Okra is fairly widely eaten throughout the South. The rest of the country knows it chiefly as one of the ingredients in canned gumbo soup. Indeed, the plant itself is sometimes called gumbo. Other sections, however, will never share the enthusiasm of Louisianans till people learn to grow it. It does not hold its flavor well on the grocer's counter. If you have tried "store okra" and think you dislike the vegetable, try one or two plants in the garden and see if fresh okra doesn't change your mind. In any case, you have nothing to lose: it would add beauty to any flower bed.

Okra belongs to the hibiscus tribe. It is a tall, erect plant that will grow normally about a yard high but can grow much higher. It bears profusely a yellow blossom with a red center that will remind you of its cousin the mallow. The flowers are followed by the edible seed-pod, a long, slender, pointed, graceful pod.

Okra originated in the Nile Valley, or anyhow in Northeast Africa. It was used for centuries in Egypt before it spread, in the Christian era, to Asia and Europe. Europeans brought it to America in the seventeenth century and the French settlers of Louisiana took to it in a big way.

Okra likes a warm climate, so it is best in the Northern states to start it indoors for the first month in pots. The reason for pots is that it does not transplant too well and cannot conveniently be just dug up and moved outside. It will do well on even poor soils. It likes lots of hot sunshine, and it detests cold winds. So if you garden in a cool-climate area try to find a sheltered spot for it, whether among the vegetables or in a flower bed. It is greedy for compost, but will settle for rotted manure. Give it abundant lime in its soil bed. And if your garden soil is not well drained—which is a scandal—okra will be annoyed.

Okra is extremely sensitive to frost, so don't plant, or set out plants, until all danger of that catastrophe is over for the season. Your plants should stand from fifteen to thirty inches apart in the row, depending on the variety you choose. Since the plants bear abundantly, four or five plants are probably all you will want. But if you intend to plant enough to run more than one row, the rows should be eighteen inches to three feet apart, again depending on the variety.

If you furnish the conditions okra loves, you are unlikely to have trouble with diseases or insects. It is a lusty plant. If your plants get powdery mildew or fusarium wilt, either the seed-bed or the garden row was probably infected. Shift both next time. Spinach aphids may cause annoyance; just dust with lime containing 3 per cent nicotine. The corn-ear worm may nibble a bit. If you give your okra what it really needs, you may never have any problem at all.

Harvesting is extremely easy but extremely important. You want the seed pods when they are still immature if an epicure is to enjoy them: finger length, and not too thick through. Remove them at that time whether you want to eat them or whether you add them to your compost. If you split them and string them up, they will dry out for winter use. If they are left on the plant to mature, the plant will stop making new pods. One more trick is to shell them like beans. The unripe seeds of even a tough old pod make good eating. But collect pods every other day to keep your okra working for you. When it is the finger-length young pod you are after, eat it as soon as possible after you pluck it. Then you will find out why people are enthusiastic about okra. Let me repeat: this is one vegetable that has often been misjudged by people who have never eaten it fresh from the stalk. The pods turn tough quickly, once removed—and then the eater spots the mucilaginous, sticky quality of the pod as his reason for not enjoying it. Ridiculous! There is nothing wrong with food's being sticky, if Nature meant it to be sticky. Besides, the cook can cut the sticky taste by cooking the okra with tomatoes. The true epicure will find okra a taste worth cultivating if it doesn't hit him right the first time. Even if his garden is in the North, and he has to do his first month's okra-growing indoors, he will be wise to give this decorative vegetable a sheltered spot in his garden or among his flowers.

ONIONS
(*Allium cepa*)

The onion belongs to the lily family and probably is one of Persia's many gifts to the world, but its cultivation spread early to other lands. The farmers of ancient Egypt grew onions. In modern times the Spaniards brought the domestic onion to the New World, although the native Indians already ate a species of wild onion.

A large number of varieties of onion have been developed for various table uses. Besides the stock varieties of white onions, yellow onions, and red or brown onions, there are the so-called tree onion or scallion or Egyptian onion, really a native of North America, that develops little bulbs at the top of the stalk; the cibol or Welsh onion —which is a native of Siberia, not Wales!—grown for its leaves; the shallot, from western Asia; the multiplier onion, the bulb of which can be separated into parts, each of which makes a new bulb; and of course the dreadful little wild onion that curses our lawns and so often spoils the taste of cows' milk in spring.

Which variety you grow will depend on your family's taste and your cook's purposes. Some people think an onion is an onion. But the varieties differ enormously in taste—in sweetness, and in the strength of the "oniony" flavor. Other people have their favorite variety or varieties, without realizing that to the connoisseur the recipe dictates the choice.

Some of the most delicious types require a longer growing season than your garden may afford. Or at least your growing season may yield no onions of these types before fall. In that event, depending on where you live, you may be able to buy a variety like the Utah Sweet Spanish in the form of young onion plants which have been flown up from Texas for you to plant as soon as your garden has safely passed its last frost. Utah Sweet Spanish has a magnificent flavor and produces an enormous bulb. You may be able to buy Bermuda onion plants in the same way—although the Bermuda won't winter-keep as well as the Sweet Spanish.

In general, white varieties are milder and blander than the yellow types, but the yellows keep better. The red varieties tend to be sweeter than either, and to winter-keep poorly.

The various types of garden onion can be grown from seed, but it is cheap and a lot easier for the home gardener to buy a pint or a quart of onion "sets," small onions grown from seed, and then to grow what he wants from the sets. However, some gardeners prefer to plant seeds. They say that if you want to store onions for winter use, you will find that those grown from seed keep better than those grown from sets. Seeding is a fussy job. If you do it, you can plant the tiny black seed in flats indoors about six weeks before the ground can be worked in the spring; and, when the green "leaf" is about the size of spaghetti, you can trim it back a bit, trim the roots from the bulb half back, and plant in rows two feet apart, two inches apart in the row. Some people put them an inch apart and "eat out" alternate onions early as "spring onions" or "bunch onions." If you do that, watch out that you don't disturb the shallow-rooted onion when you remove its neighbor.

Planting sets as early as you can work your garden in the spring is a much simpler method, and should give you good eating by early August. Sets should be planted, neck up, and to the neck, in light, sandy soil; but push them only halfway into the earth if your garden has heavy soil. Remember, in planting sets, that those over five-eighths of an inch in diameter are likely to produce seedstalks and big necks, so pull out their seedstalks when the plants get to be six inches tall, and avoid this trouble—but watch out not to disturb the bulb's little roots when you pull. Smaller sets don't misbehave this way, and you needn't bother them.

The onion is a greedy eater and does not want weeds to compete with. If you have not mulched to smother them out, keep the onions well cultivated, but don't disturb their shallow roots. To avoid doing just that, you will have to pull up weeds in the row when they are very small, and you will have to do it gently. If by accident you let them get big, cut them off instead of pulling them. Loosened onion roots mean checked growth, and checked growth may prevent maturing to a proper size.

Onions like plenty of water within reach of their shallow roots. If the topsoil around them dries out, onion thrips punish them for the gardener's neglect. And remember, weeds steal water as well as plant foods. Onions like a "sweet" soil, so give them lime, worked well in. They love wood ashes. They need organic matter, so work in compost too, or at least well-rotted manure.

If you want to keep eating green bunch onions all through the season—and who wouldn't?—plant seed in the spring at several intervals to make onions for late-season eating. Light frost won't hurt onions. You can, of course, instead of eating your onions green, let them mature in the ground (the tops die when they reach that stage). Then dry them in a ventilated shady spot and store them in a dark, well-ventilated room, at a temperature of from 35° to 45°. But presumably it is green onions, not dried and stored onions, that justify your turning to your own garden rather than to your grocer. If, on the other hand, your cook shrieks for the tiny onions Italians use so much, you can grow them from seed by seeding quite thickly in a row. An onion of any size is delicious, and the cook knows whereof she shrieketh. She ought to be told, however, that late sowings of seed are more difficult to coax along than very early spring sowings.

Onions have troubles. Except in the Southern states, onion smut sometimes comes to annoy the gardener. It is a fungous disease that can often be prevented by wetting the seed when planted with a formaldehyde solution. Onion mildew is a tougher problem: remove the sick plants! Then there are insects: the onion thrip and the onion maggot. If your garden is mulched, the topsoil is likely to be moist enough to protect your onion from thrips. If you did let your topsoil dry out, and thrips did come, scatter naphthalene flakes along the row. It won't kill them, but it will drive them away pretty well. The maggot is the larva of a fly; it attacks the onion bulb and causes it to rot. People confront the maggot with 4-6-50 Bordeaux mixture, with perhaps a 2-per-cent emulsion of lubricating oil thoroughly mixed in.

Whether you grow eating onions or not, you ought to consider, for your cook's sake, two members of the onion family that are used for seasoning—chives and garlic. Chives can be grown best from plants, not seeds. Their threadlike leaves are so valuable as seasoning that, when frost comes, it will be worth taking them up and transplanting to a pot in the kitchen to furnish seasoning during the winter months. Garlic may be grown readily from either seed or "cloves" ("buds")— the small sections of the garlic bulb. When the tops are ripe, pull the plant and allow the bulbs to dry in the sun.

PARSNIPS

(*Pastinaca sativa*)

Parsnips are a deliciously sweet vegetable which by incorrect harvesting can be given a quite unpleasantly bitter taste. Many persons who are sure they "don't like parsnips" might be delighted if they ever ate a nice one. Parsnips probably originated in the Mediterranean area. In any case, the ancient Greeks and Romans ate the roots of wild parsnips, and by the sixteenth century parsnips were being widely cultivated in northern Europe. They were introduced into Virginia eleven years before the Pilgrim Fathers hove to off Plymouth, and even the Indians took to cultivating parsnips. This edible root is full of starch, which frosty weather converts to sugar.

Parsnips are easy to raise if you prepare a proper place for them to live. They like their soil deep, rich, loose, moist but well drained. If you are unwilling to work the soil a foot or a foot and a half deep, and to remove any stones or other hard objects, you are likely to get curved, branched, or otherwise deformed roots and had better not fool with parsnips. Professional exhibitors have grown roots three or four feet long by pulverizing the bed very deep and filling it with plenty of nutrient. If you can't or won't pulverize deep, plant a short, chunky type of parsnip that doesn't want to go deep, just as I advise in the case of carrots. Because the roots don't like to battle their way down, a sandy loam is easier to grow parsnips in than a heavy clay. But this is true of most vegetables, not just those we produce for edible roots; so, if your soil is heavy, you need in any case to work in cinders and lots of compost to make it loose and crumbly. Parsnips are a special case in that they need their soil worked deeper than many shallow-rooted vegetables do. If you can get a horse or tractor into your garden, a "subsoiler" plow can loosen your soil very deep and, of course, without reversing the position of fertile topsoil and relatively barren subsoil. Finally, in addition to plenty of humus, parsnips like lime, also worked in.

Parsnips need three or four months to mature their roots, so plant your seeds as early as the ground can be worked. Like carrot seeds, they germinate slowly, which always means that quick-germinating weeds may steal their growing space before they can claim it. As with carrots, you can break up this racket by drawing an inch-high ridge of earth over the newly planted parsnip seed. Then, as soon as the weeds capture the ridge, you can scrape off half the ridge and the lusty young weeds with it. Before the weeds can stage their counter-counter-attack, the parsnips will be through. This is complicated to put into words and extremely easy to put into practice. An alternate method is to mix radish seed with your parsnip seed. The radish seed will come up very quickly and serve to mark clearly where the still dormant parsnip seeds are. Then you can keep the row clear of weeds till the parsnips show. Any radishes that are not in the way of your parsnip plants can be left till the right moment and eaten. When you are through all this business, you want, in any case, to come out with parsnips three to six inches apart in rows eighteen inches apart; distances, as usual, depend on type—and also on how much food there is in your soil for each plant to eat! None of that food ought to go to weeds, and I repeat for the nth time that the best defense against weeds is mulch in the spring, laid on cultivated ground with no crust and after the vegetables are too high to be smothered by it, rather than a hoe wielded during the hot summer months or even a wheel-hoe pushed in the same heat. But I've already given my reasons for this elsewhere.

Parsnips have no serious diseases or insect enemies, if grown under favorable conditions. Your next and last problem is, therefore, harvesting. They will taste better if left in the ground till after frost has turned their starch to sugar. You can dig those you need whenever, during the cold months, you need them—provided of course that you live where the ground does not freeze too hard in winter to permit digging. Most people think they taste better if left in the ground until spring. But there is a risk to that for the epicure: once they start to make their second season's growth, they change back from being sweet to tasting somewhat bitter. All of them should be dug and stored before that happens—or you will wonder why people claim to like parsnips! But before you wave parsnips aside, you would be wise to reflect, at least if your climate permits you to dig them throughout the winter, that fresh winter vegetables are not too numerous.

PEAS

(*Pisum sativum,* variety *arvense*)

Peas probably originated in Central Asia and were in all likelihood further developed in the Near East and in North Africa. They were grown in Egypt before the Christian era. The ancient Greeks and Romans grew them widely. The Swiss "lake dwellers," while still only in their Bronze Age, apparently grew them. But it seems that not until the Middle Ages did people eat them while the pods were still green. By 1500 the sugary green, or garden, pea was being grown, particularly in France, and has been popular ever since.

Peas are an easy vegetable to raise in cool weather and an extremely hard one to raise where the weather is hot, especially where the nights are hot. Succession planting is therefore practicable in New England, for example, whereas in the Southern states many people never attempt more than a single, early planting. This may be one reason so many people in the South eat "black-eyed peas," which are really beans and not true peas at all. What peas really enjoy is cool nights and bright, cool days.

Peas not only hate heat; they hate drought; although, as in the case of celery, they prefer to have the soil at their feet drenched rather than sprinkled. They like plenty of lime in their soil. They don't need much nitrogen, and sometimes object to it by producing pods without any peas inside them! They like lots of humus, so give them plenty of compost.

Most people think the smooth pea is less delicious than the wrinkled pea, and plant the smooth pea once in the spring merely because it is earlier. Personally, I like the taste of the smooth pea better anyhow. Many gardeners also make an early planting of dwarf peas rather than the high-growing vine peas, because they come in faster, even though they bear fewer pods than the high-growing vine types and stop bearing sooner. The vine varieties need more space, of course. They also offer their pods where they can be harvested without stooping. Finally, many Americans are discovering the *mange-tout* peas of Europe: varieties such as melting sugar and dwarf gray sugar, which are plucked young when the seeds are quite immature and are eaten, like string beans, pod and all. They are delicious.

The tall vine types require support of some kind—a fence, a wire trellis, a pole-wire-and-string trellis, or very twiggy brush stuck in the ground beside them. The dwarf varieties can do without support, but I find a low support makes them easier to handle. In the case of both types, you can save on supports by planting your peas in a double row only six inches apart with the support or trellis erected between, and by allowing both rows to use it. If you do that, and if you plant a second double row, better leave two and a half to three feet between the two double-row-and-trellis arrangements. If that sounds like giving up too much space to peas, remember you can grow a quick crop of lettuce between the rows.

As soon as the vines have quit bearing, pull and remove them. Many people prefer chicken-wire trellis because they can hold that over a hot fire and burn the dry vines out. Then they store the chicken wire for further use. Burning pea-vine is wasteful nonsense, since the roots store up nitrogen, as any legume roots will. Your vines should be composted. The only excuse for burning is a disease of the vines that you are afraid you can't eliminate in a hot compost heap in time to keep it from spreading. The vine is valuable enough to justify the fuss of pulling it loose from its trellis and composting it.

The seed is usually thinned to three inches apart in the row for dwarf varieties and to four inches for tall vine types. If you want to get an early start, which is particularly important where a hot season looms ahead, soak the peas in a flat dish after spreading them only one pea deep and after putting in only enough water to submerge half of each pea. But just as soon as the little sprouts show, you must plant quickly, or your seed may rot. If this sounds fussy, consider that it may mean eating peas a week earlier. In any case, the seed should be in the ground, soaked or unsoaked, as soon as you can work the ground in the spring. Peas will be very grateful for mulch.

With proper conditions peas develop few diseases or insect pests. Before the warm days come the pea aphid, or "pea louse," sometimes damages the young plants. Spray or dust with nicotine. In warm, humid weather, powdery mildew sometimes causes trouble. Refuse lying around makes this problem more likely to occur; pea vines want ventilation. If it does occur, spray with Bordeaux mixture or dust with sulphur. If your vines develop root rot, don't plant in the same spot again for a few years. If a weevil enters the pod and destroys the peas in it, you probably got infected seed. Cutworms and slugs can be got at by leaving poisoned bran mash near the vines for a few nights. If birds eat your seed before it sprouts, you can generally keep them away by leaving a few lengths of small rope around. The birds mistake them for snakes and keep out. Once your peas are up, though, remove the "snakes." For remember, you want birds in your garden to clean it of insects. Just before you harvest, you may be able to use a few of those "snakes" again: blackbirds and starlings sometimes harvest the ripe peas for themselves and have a talent for doing it the day before you intend to do it. If your garden is unfenced and if rabbits live around you, they will be glad to learn there are unfenced peas about. But they will be glad to learn of other unfenced vegetables too. If you think all this sounds grim, I can only say that lots of people have grown peas without encountering a single one of these troubles. I have, myself.

When the pods start filling out, watch them. Peas are one vegetable your grocer cannot compete on, provided you pick promptly as soon as the pods have filled out. A little earlier, and your peas will be wastefully small and hardly worth shelling. A little later, and you might as well let your grocer do his worst. When you pluck the pods, be careful not to pull up the delicate vines or even to loosen their roots. Don't shell the peas until just before cooking or they will dry out and lose their flavor. And, if the cook is not ready to practice her art, get them into the refrigerator quick. Peas are like corn: their sugar turns to starch if they lie around between plucking and cooking. As to picking time, the pods usually turn a lighter green when they are ready for you to harvest; but you can double-check by opening a typical pod and examining the peas inside. You will end up by being as good an expert as one of those starlings, who have never once shown the slightest disrespect for my garden, who eat enormous quantities of harmful insects, and—I still dislike them!

PEPPERS

(*Capsicum frutescens*)

This is the edible garden pepper and has nothing whatever to do with the shaker or grinder that sits beside the salt cellar on your dinner table. The edible fruits of this plant are generally eaten green before they ripen to yellow or red or dark purple. But there is also a "sweet" red pepper that is eaten ripe. The family also includes such hot peppers as the chili, the cayenne, and the tabasco. The pepper that fills your shaker comes from a tropical shrub of quite another family. It was the "hot" type of garden pepper that led the Spanish explorers of America, when they first discovered it, to call it "pepper."

The garden pepper feels happiest in moist, light, warm soil, not too rich. Too much nitrogen in the soil does to it what it does to many plants: encourages it to produce lots of foliage instead of the fruit you want. If your soil is sandy loam, your chances are better. If it is heavy clay, you may run to foliage instead of peppers. If it is poorly drained, your peppers are unlikely to be handsome, shapely ones. Peppers also like plenty of ground limestone, and limestone containing magnesium—also plenty of phosphorus, which means bone meal or ground rock-phosphate. If your seed catalogues don't tell you which variety will flourish best in your locality, better check with an experienced local gardener or with your local florist. Different climates dictate different varieties.

You probably don't need more than three or four plants, since peppers are things most people prefer to eat occasionally, not as a staple. Better get plants from your florist or nurseryman if you can. If you want to grow these plants from seed yourself, you should sow in the hotbed about ten weeks before the last frost, and take no chances on frost either: peppers can't take it. When seedlings are two inches tall, transplant them to flats two inches apart. They should be five or six inches tall before they are transplanted a second time, this time to the garden, where they belong one to two feet apart in rows two to three feet apart, depending on how good a soil you have built. Cultivate as you would eggplant (page 54).

If the foliage is attacked by disease, spray with Bordeaux mixture. Missing foliage means sunburned fruit, and sunburned fruit is blamed for bringing on fruit rot. If aphids appear, spray or dust with nicotine. And if the pepper maggot gets into the fruit, dust repeatedly with talc. But you are unlikely to have trouble with either blights or insect pests if you have loose, well-drained, well-composted soil, with an ample supply of magnesium limestone for your pepper plants to feed on. Also, next season, plant your pepper plants in a different place.

For a good harvest, keep cutting off your fruit—when it is a little immature for the best flavor. When the first frost threatens, gather all your fruit, no matter what size it is, and store in a cool place where the air is not too dry. People have kept peppers till Christmas that way.

POTATOES

(*Solanum tuberosum*)

This is the white or "Irish" potato—although it reached Ireland very late in its history. The sweet potato is discussed in this book under "S." They are no kin. The Irish potato is a cousin of the tomato, the eggplant, and the pepper. The sweet potato belongs to the morning-glory family. The Irish potato is a native of the South Andes and was cultivated by the Incas. It was taken to Spain around 1700 and later to Italy, to Austria, to Germany, and to the British Isles. European colonists took it to North America.

For a good while most Europeans considered it food for farm stock, not for human beings. It was denounced from Scottish pulpits as unfit for a Christian table since it was not mentioned in the Bible; and at the very same time other clergyman proclaimed that it was the forbidden fruit mentioned in the book of Genesis. On the other hand, Frederick the Great gave orders to plant it widely in Prussia and furthermore specified carefully that it should be planted in the dark of the moon and harvested at Michaelmas! A little later the French epicure Auguste Parmentier, in order to persuade the skeptical French that potatoes were a good idea, persuaded Queen Marie Antoinette to attend a royal ball wearing a wreath of potato blossoms in her hair. Either that remarkable wreath or something else convinced the French: potatoes are now a favorite French dish—including potatoes *parmentière*. Maybe someday a queen of some country will wear some corn silk in her hair and persuade the people of northern Europe that our favorite vegetable is a delicacy and not just feed for livestock. Some of the southern Europeans need no persuading.

There are a great many types of Irish potato, ranging in color from white to red, varying in length, some slender, some chunky. The varieties are adapted not only to different kitchen uses and to different tastes, but to different localities, and no sound advice can be given as to which variety to plant without knowing what place and climate are being talked about. This is one vegetable about which it is extremely important to consult local gardeners. Finally, some varieties are for early harvesting and some for late.

One might as well admit now that, since potatoes keep extremely well if they are in the dark and the temperature is not too high, there is less excuse for giving them space in a home garden than there is for leafy vegetables or even for seed vegetables such as peas and beans. Incidentally, they take up considerable space. Finally, they are subject to more diseases than many of the vegetables discussed in this book. So you may decide to skip potatoes and give your grocer a hand with his private financial problems. On the other hand, new potatoes, freshly dug from your own garden, are pretty wonderful eating; and besides, you can go French on potatoes and serve delicious tiny ones that no American grocer would bother with.

Potatoes like plenty of humus in the soil and will consequently be very grateful for compost. If you have no compost, then turning under some such "cover crop" as fall-planted rye or spring-planted soy beans, or even just a good crop of weeds, will help. You might even dig in some fallen leaves in the autumn. Potatoes also love potash, which means they will be grateful for wood ashes from your stove or fireplace if you are a lucky enough gardener to have wood ashes. Unlike most vegetables, they don't need much lime; in fact, an overdose of lime will encourage them to develop scabs on their skins, which don't in the least interfere with their taste or their value as nourishment but which look unappetizing when they are served. They like well-drained, well-aerated, crumbly soil, and they even disapprove of a hard subsoil. If your subsoil is impermeable, fork into it as deeply as possible and break it up. Potatoes are heavy drinkers, so, if rainfall fails, give the ground they are in a good drenching once a week. Although potatoes hate frost, like all the members of their family, they prefer a temperate climate to a hot one. Nevertheless varieties have been developed, such as Chippewa, that stand heat very well provided you don't let them get thirsty. In return for furnishing your potatoes these conditions to grow in, they will give you plenty of starch, a little sugar, 2 per cent protein, and even a fraction of 1 per cent fat.

The potato is of course planted for its tuber, which is not a root at all but the tip of a rhizome. Although potatoes can be planted from seed, they won't breed true to variety that way. Consequently, they are planted from the tuber itself. Take a normal-sized potato and cut it into pieces, making sure that each piece contains at least two good "eyes," or buds. Each eye should sprout a plant. Most people think this yields better results than planting very small potatoes, some of which will be on any potato vine when it is dug. You ought to plant these potato slices at least a month before the date on which people in your section can reasonably expect their last frost. If your soil is heavy clay, don't plant more than a couple of inches deep. If it is light, sandy soil, plant at least three inches deep. Plant the slices of potato six to eight inches apart in rows eighteen inches apart. Contrary to popular belief, they don't need to be "hilled up."

When I was a boy my grandfather, in common with many gardeners of his generation, grew potatoes in a "lazy bed." He plowed a furrow eight or ten inches deep, covered the bottom of the furrow lightly with straw, laid his potato cuttings on the straw to sprout there, and then covered them with straw to the top of the trench. The potato sent down roots into the earth below the furrow, but developed its tubers not under the earth but in the straw that filled the trench. When the plants had finished "making," instead of digging dirty potatoes out of the earth at the risk of slicing some of them in two accidentally, you merely removed the straw and picked the new potatoes off the vine, clean and whole. I have never tried this out myself, partly because I rarely have room in my gardens for potato-growing, I am so anxious to grow vegetables that will not keep well as potatoes will; and it is forty or fifty years since I have seen potatoes in a lazy bed. But there is a lot to be said for the method.

If you have no compost and didn't prepare the ground by getting plenty of vegetable matter into it, work in some rotted cow manure. Horse manure tends to produce scabs. There is one excuse for hilling up temporarily, and that is the same reason people make ridges over plantings of carrot seed. The plants sprout in the hilled soil, you peel off half the hill with a hoe, and you thereby destroy the weeds that would be growing close to your potato vines without disturbing the vines. When the plants have emerged a couple of inches, spread on a mulch at least two inches thick. Sawdust would be particularly good; any tendency it has to make the soil acid should not hurt potatoes.

Of the diseases potato is subject to, "late blight," which attacks the leaves, is your likeliest enemy. Spray weekly with Bordeaux mixture 5-5-50.

Of insects that annoy potatoes, you are likeliest to find the Colorado potato beetle—the one the Russians claimed we dropped on the East German potato fields! Heaven knows who dropped them on us Americans, but they have been with us for a good while. Add lead arsenate to your Bordeaux mixture or dust with rotenone. Bordeaux mixture should also control flea beetle and leaf hopper. In the case of potato aphids, spray with Black Leaf 40. White grubs and wire worms should not bother you if you harvest your potatoes as soon as they are mature—that is, as soon as the potato vines begin to wither.

RADISHES
(*Raphanus sativus*)

The Pharaohs of ancient Egypt loved radishes, and so did the ancient Greeks. I find that even now, when spring comes, people are more likely to rush out and plant radishes than they are to plant any other seed. People who have failed generally at gardening have succeeded with radishes more often than with any other thing. For myself, I consider that the chief use of the radish is to mark the rows in which I have planted the seed of vegetables more worth planting. The radish comes up very quickly and warns off plows and hoes until the slow things have time to appear.

Plant the seed as early as you can stir the soil. If the soil is poor, or if the young roots lack moisture, they will grow slowly; and, as in the case of other edible roots, too slow growth produces woody, pithy roots—as too much heat will, too. In the case of radishes, slow growth also makes the root too peppery. The varieties used for spring planting grow fast; those used for summer planting usually take ten or twenty days longer to mature—say forty-five in all. The type used for late summer planting, in order to get roots for winter storage, take around sixty days to make. If temperatures in your neighborhood never drop below 20° above zero, you can grow radishes all winter. Or you can grow them indoors in a sunny window, in which case you may want to use sand instead of earth, supplemented by a little liquid fertilizer.

Most insects don't bother about radishes, except for occasional plant lice, which Black Leaf 40 can handle. As for diseases, radishes are exceedingly healthy.

SPINACH
(*Spinacia oleracea*)

Spinach is probably a gift of Southwest Asia and did not spread to Europe and the Far East until after Greek and Roman times. Now it is grown in most parts of the planet, wherever climate permits.

Spinach likes cool weather. It is therefore grown in our Southern states chiefly during the winter, and in most other areas in spring or fall. People who want to eat spinach during the hot summer weather usually grow New Zealand "spinach," which is not really a spinach at all but which loves hot weather and tastes like spinach if the cook knows her business. It is a native of New Zealand and Australia. It has several virtues: it collects less sand in its foliage, washes more easily, and is a great deal easier to grow than real spinach is. You can speed up its germination a lot by soaking the seeds two or three days before planting. Unlike real spinach, which stands cold magnificently, New Zealand spinach hates frost. It has two final advantages: whereas real spinach is pulled up or cut at the ground when harvested, you can whittle leaves off New Zealand spinach for weeks, just as you can whittle leaves off of Swiss chard or kale; and, second, unlike real spinach, it has no serious pests whatever. It is worth trying some to see whether you like it as much as real spinach, so you can have something that is at least called spinach and can be made to taste like spinach during those hot weeks.

Spinach likes plenty of nitrogen—as most leafy vegetables do—and will therefore be grateful for the humus supplied by good compost. It will also be very happy if you plant it where a legume, such as peas or beans, grew before. It likes mildly acid soil—say a pH of 6.0 to 6.7. If you give spinach the conditions it wants to grow in, it will give you many more vitamins than most vegetables, and some iron thrown in for good measure.

Since real spinach is extremely hardy, plant the seed just as soon as you can work the ground. Seed should be planted an inch apart in rows twelve inches apart. When the plants begin to crowd each other, thin out to three to six inches apart and eat the delicious young thinnings. Remember, don't try to eat a few leaves off the plant at a time, but remove the whole plant.

Spinach has several diseases, but spraying leaves that you are about to eat is not too good an idea. Some people prevent "damping off" by treating the seed before planting it with red copper oxide. Aphids can be controlled with nicotine dust. Nobody has invented a good way of controlling the spinach flea beetle. The same is true of the leaf miner: better remove and burn the affected leaves. With well-prepared soil and good growing conditions, you may see no disease or pest at all.

SQUASH

(*Cucurbita maxima*)

The word "squash" is a corrupted, abbreviated, American Indian name. The squash is an edible member of the gourd family and kin to the melon—with which it fortunately will not cross-fertilize in your garden. True, it will cross with one species of pumpkin—*cucurbita moschata*, the so-called "cheese" group. There are bush squashes and running-vine squashes. There are winter squashes and summer squashes. However, the winter squash is the true squash, and summer squash is actually a species of pumpkin (*cucurbita pepo*). Both sorts came originally from North and South America.

Squash likes rotted manure in the hill—but it prefers compost if you have some. Incidentally, there shouldn't really be a hill if your soil is light and sandy. Such soil, when hilled up, dries out too rapidly. On the other hand, in a heavy clay, a rounded hill, some six inches deep, will help. The soil in the hill should be crumbly and not the kind that packs. Though it should be well drained and well aerated, it should also be moist. Squash drinks hard when it starts fruiting. If your soil is clay, sand in the hill will be a welcome addition to the humus which compost or rotted manure provides. The hill should also contain plenty of lime.

Squash hates frost and delights in heat. It wants all three of the main fertilizing elements of the garden: nitrogen, phosphorus, and potash. Unless you insist on buying these in the form of commercial fertilizer, good compost plus meal or ground rock-phosphate plus a good dose of wood ashes should make your squash quite happy.

Don't plant squash seed until all danger of frost is past. If you want to get an early start, the seed can be started in four-inch pots, one to a pot, or in veneer bands. But the squash is a delicate vegetable to transplant; the roots must not be disturbed; so the earth in your pot or band should be moist enough to stay put when the frost is gone and you set out the plant in your garden.

If your garden is small, better not attempt the winter varieties with their long vines—unless you have a fence corner you don't want to use anyhow. Even in that case, remember that some species of squash grow so heavy that they cannot be grown on a vine that climbs without a net to support them. In a small garden, use a small or "bush" squash. Even the bushes will need from six to ten square feet, depending on the variety. Plant a small-fruited type, since the very big fruits are more than a family can eat at a sitting, and since once the fruit is opened, it dries out and becomes less palatable.

But if you feel that you have room for the winter-keeping types, investigate buttercup, butternut, acorn, table queen, and of course Hubbard. If it's to be Hubbard, choose a type that bears fruit the right size for your household. There are types for just about any size you may need.

I think the two summer squashes most worth growing are the early white bush scallop, which Southerners call cymling and which some people call pattypan; and the Italian variety called zucchini. They are quite different in appearance and flavor, but both are delicious.

Several insects enjoy squash as much as I do, but I have never had much trouble with them. I admit that I am not disturbed if an insect eats a small portion of a vegetable I intend to eat later. All you have to do, after all, is cut out the affected portion. Squash bugs are easy to catch: if you lay out a piece of plank on some small stones near the squash, they will accommodatingly crawl under the plank before dawn and you can readily collect them and destroy them. The cucumber beetle succumbs readily to dusting with lead arsenate or with rotenone. The squash-borer does worse than slightly deface the fruit; he bores into the stem of the bush or vine and may destroy it. Black Leaf 40 should handle him, although I much prefer a less chemical method: just "layer" the branches of the bush or vine by piling a little moist earth on the places where they fork. They will immediately put out roots there, and then when the squash-borer attacks the main stem the vine has other resources to draw on. Could anything be simpler?

Summer squash such as white bush scallop should be harvested very young, when it is not more than four to six inches in diameter and is still greenish rather than yellowish in color. The skin ought to be so soft that you can shove your fingernail through it without difficulty. Later on, the skin gets so tough that it ought not to be cooked for eating, and the seeds get big and tough too. Whether you are dealing with vine squash or bush squash, don't let any of the fruit mature. If you can't eat it yourself and if none of your neighbors want to eat it, chop it up and throw it in your compostable material. If you leave it on the vine to mature, the vine will get complacent, will think it has done its stuff for the season, and will quit flowering and fruiting. Pick 'em young, and keep your vines guessing. With any type of squash, if you think the night promises frost, harvest all the fruit and store it. Be careful not to bruise it and, if possible, keep it where the temperature does not rise above 50°.

SWEET POTATOES
(*Impomoea batatas*)

Sweet potato is no kin whatever to the Irish potato, but belongs to the same family as the common morning-glory. Like the morning-glory, it develops long, trailing vines, and it therefore takes up a good deal of room in a small garden. Since it keeps well, it may not be worth the space it demands. If you want to grow it but wonder about yielding all that space, you may solve the problem by running the vines on a garden fence or even letting them drape down from a window box, at least a foot deep and kept well watered. Both the leaf and flower are highly ornamental.

The sweet potato is, of course, grown for its roots, which are not true tubers as in the case of the Irish potato, but do look like tubers. It is probably the tropical world's most popular vegetable, and it even ranks seventh among food plants grown in the United States. It is a native of tropical America and may well have been cultivated in America longer than any other vegetable. The Indians also ate the wild sweet potato. The Spaniards took the sweet potato to Spain quite early, and from there it spread over southern Europe. Then European navigators spread it during the sixteenth and seventeenth centuries to the Far East, where Europeans later "discovered" it after they had forgotten that other Europeans had first found it in America. It is still important to the Far East: in Japan it is the biggest crop after rice, and is used by the Japanese as a source of alcohol, as a source of starch, as cattle feed, and of course as food for human beings.

In the United States it is grown chiefly in the Southern states, particularly the moist varieties which Southerners incorrectly call "yams." True yams are a tropical plant grown almost nowhere in our country outside Florida. Northerners generally prefer the drier, mealy type of sweet potato.

Sweet potatoes love hot weather and hate cold. They resent even light frost. But with proper soil treatment they can be grown in Northern gardens. They like sandy loam better than heavy soil, but they do not beg for rich soil, provided it is dug deep and made loose and airy. They prefer to have even the subsoil well broken up.

They will consent to grow in sweet, or limed, soil, but they show their resentment by developing various ground diseases that mar the appearance of their "tubers." In sour, or acid, soils they tend to escape these diseases. They want humus, so they will be grateful for compost or even well-rotted manure.

In return for these attentions you will harvest a vegetable as nutritious as any in the garden, and one of high sugar content. It is 18 per cent starch, 8 per cent other carbohydrates, 2 per cent protein, and is rich in vitamins, iron, and calcium. The dark yellow and reddish-orange types are also rich in carotene. It is perhaps the cook's business and not mine, but for heaven's sake learn to eat the skin along with the insides—and the same goes for Irish potatoes.

The sweet potato is not grown from seed; it is grown by planting the tubers. Each tuber sends up a series of sprouts that develop root structures and can be drawn out and transplanted from a hotbed or coldframe and set in your garden as soon as frost is past. You need the early start: the sweet potato requires a long season. But since you need only three to four plants to produce quite a number of potatoes, it is worth scouting ahead of time for plants at the nursery, ready to set out when the time comes. Set them fifteen inches apart in rows two and a half to three feet apart.

In order to keep down weeds, most gardeners cultivate sweet potatoes. But to do that the vines have to be moved out of the way, and to move the vines you have to tear them loose from the soil wherever they have struck new roots, which they do often. This in turn sometimes decreases the yield at harvest time. As a matter of fact, any damage to the vine tends to do just that. The answer is clear. Smothering the weeds out with a good mulch of from two to four inches is the proper way to grow sweet potatoes. Then the earth will remain nice and moist, which will discourage wire worms around harvest time.

Besides wire worms, the goldbug sometimes chews at sweet potato vines, but it hates rotenone dust. In the South the sweet-potato weevil feeds on the leaves, lays eggs on the stem, and hatches out larvae that start to work on the tubers. Gardeners use arsenical sprays to control the weevil.

Diseases are more likely than insects to prove an annoyance. Careless use of chemical fertilizers—which you don't need anyhow, if you have built a good organic soil—sometimes causes stem rot. Failure to plant in different parts of the garden in successive years will expose you to black rot, as will infected seed-tubers at planting time. If the soil lacks organic matter, which your compost should have provided, or if your topsoil contains too much of the lime most other vegetables insist on, then your plants may develop sweet-potato pox. But a good soil, covered with good mulch, and a properly rotated crop, will most likely protect you from all these terrifying enemies.

Unfortunately, sweet potatoes do not produce throughout the season. It will be only during the last few weeks before frost that your tubers will be making. They need all the time they can get, so don't dig them until the tender tips of the vines have been touched by the first frost. Then dig from the side, not from above. And dig carefully; bruised tubers are hard to keep. If they do get bruised you may repair the damage by dipping them, before storing, in a solution of four ounces of borax to five quarts of water. As soon as you dig them, expose them to the sun for a few days; or, if there is no sun, try to find a place where the temperature is around 75° to 80°. This toughens the skin and protects the potato from decay. Then store them in a cool place—at, say, around 50° to 60°. They are harder to store than Irish potatoes, so handle them carefully. Or use your garden space for a leafy vegetable that produces throughout the season, and let the grocer supply you with whatever sweet potatoes you want to eat!

TOMATOES
(*Lycopersicon esculentum*)

Botanically a fruit, the garden tomato is one of the world's most popular table vegetables. Like the Irish potato, the tomato is a gift of tropical America, probably of either Peru or Mexico. Like the potato, the tomato was not readily accepted by Europeans. But whereas Europeans merely scorned the potato as cattle food, they feared the tomato, clear into the nineteenth century, as a poison. This "poisonous," if ornamental, fruit was known as "gold apple" or as "love apple."

The garden tomato is now grown in many varieties. In size it varies from that of a currant to that of a small pumpkin. In shape it may resemble a cherry, a pear, a plum, a heart, or an apple. In color it may be white, yellow, pink, or red. In taste it may be tart, sweet, or insipid. Its habit may be to produce its fruit early or late. In this country the Rutgers variety is becoming a favorite for general home use. It is very juicy, deep red, weighing three or four fruits to the pound. But the home gardener should try out other varieties for special uses, such as the lovely little "cherry" tomato for hors d'oeuvre or salad, or the little yellow "pear" for pickling. If he insists on extra-early types, he must be prepared for inferior flavor. If he or other members of his family suffer indigestion from the acidity of tomatoes, he should try some yellow variety like Jubilee, which is less acid than the commoner red types.

The tomato is among the easiest of vegetables for the beginner to grow, provided it has abundant sunshine and all the water it wants. It is also among the most valuable foods, since it contains many of the protective elements that are usually found only in fruit. It prefers to grow in sandy loam, but it will make do in heavy soil if the soil is properly prepared. It likes its soil well drained, and well aerated, thoroughly worked and loose. It wants the subsoil opened up for it.

The tomato likes pulverized magnesium limestone worked deep into the soil, though it can tolerate acid soil if it has to. It will be grateful for humus, so use that compost. It will be grateful for bone meal or ground rock-phosphate; but go easy on nitrogen or it will produce magnificent vines and very little fruit.

You will probably need about three plants for every tomato-eater in your household, and you will probably do well to set out plants about three times, to get successive crops clear through till frost kills them. If you can buy plants of the varieties you choose to grow, they come cheap. Otherwise, it is simple to grow them from seed in a cold-frame or sunny window. Start the seed four weeks before the probable date of your last spring frost. Make sure the soil is moist enough to cling to the roots before you take them up and transplant them. When you transplant, put plenty of water in the hole first, and water the plant daily for a while. Remember that this is a tropical plant, so don't set it out till it is really safe from frost. Give the plants room: two to six feet apart, depending on the variety, in rows three feet apart.

Your vines will produce if you let them sprawl. But they will be far better off, and less subject to blight, if you stake them up. You can either tie each plant to a single stake, or you can run your rows double and bring the tops of every four stakes together like a tepee, and tie them there. In either case, when you tie your plant to the stake always use soft twine or strips of rag—or buy some "Twistems"; tomato vines have very soft, juicy—or "succulent"—stems and want the gentlest of treatment.

Few vegetables respond more gratefully to mulching. A good mulch, two inches deep, may even double your crop. But, in the case of tomatoes, there is an extra reason for mulching vines that are not staked: the fruit is less likely to rot on the vine.

Gardeners argue about whether to pinch out, or clip out, the new runners that sprout in the crotch of each vine-branch. I take them out. I do not claim that it gives me more pounds of fruit to eat, but I think it improves the quality of the fruit that does grow. And it certainly makes the vine more manageable in a small garden.

The tomato has some diseases. Your best protection against wilt is to grow a wilt-resistant variety. If black spots develop on a vine's main stem near the ground, either set it deep enough in the ground to cover them with soil or remove the plant—and put it deep in your rotting compost pile or else burn it.

If blossom-end rot develops, pick the infected fruit, compost it, or burn it. For blight, apply magnesium sulphate at the rate of one ounce to every three square yards. So-called streak disease is sometimes caused by tobacco-smokers' handling the vines. So don't sit among your vines while smoking Havana cigars—and don't transplant seedlings after smoking, without first washing your hands.

If your vines make too slow a growth early in the season, the Colorado potato beetle may bother them. Dust with rotenone—or, better, give them such a fertile spot to grow in that they become lusty even while young. Gardeners whose tomatoes are worried by fruit worm sometimes grow a few stalks of corn among their vines. The worms like corn silk better than they do tomato vines. Finally, cutworms may be poisoned in the usual way—by leaving poisoned bran mash overnight under the vines.

This list of gardening sorrows should not alarm you. A good garden, capable of producing joyous plants, will most likely escape them all; or it will take them, if they do appear, in its stride.

The epicure lets his tomatoes ripen on the vine, not on the back porch—although they will, of course, turn red there too. The tomatoes you buy in the store were probably picked green so they would keep while shipping. You have no excuse for allowing the habits of commerce to rob you of the full flavor of vine-ripened fruit. If your vines were granted ample space, you may get from fifteen to twenty-five pounds of delicious fruit from a vine. If you cheated on space, you may get only one-third of that, and less good fruit. So be generous when you set your vines out; then the vines can be generous to you. All through the middle and late summer they will happily feed you. But when that awful thing frost finally threatens, you had better clean the vines of fruit, whether ripe or green, big or small. They will keep well in a place where the temperature runs around 45°. They will ripen best where it is around 70°, and where the light is dim. Those that were nearly ripe when picked will naturally ripen best.

Finally, I strongly urge you, when you come to decide on what varieties you want to plant, to investigate the new hybrids. They yield better and they appear to be much more resistant to blight.

TURNIPS

(*Brassica rapa*)

This member of the cabbage family is grown primarily for its edible root, although its foliage or "turnip tops" make an excellent dish of greens. Turnips have been cultivated since before the Christian era, both in Europe and in Asia. They were introduced into North America as early as 1609 and were spread rapidly by both the colonists and the Indians.

Turnips, in common with the rest of the cabbage family, hate hot weather, particularly hot nights, and they show their hatred by growing slowly and developing a root that is both stringy and unpleasantly strong in taste. But in areas with hot summers and mild winters they make a magnificent addition to the winter garden. They want lots of humus. If they lack lime in the soil, they protest by producing a scarred root. They don't want too much nitrogen, but, since they love potash, they will be grateful for wood ashes. They also like phosphorus, so give them ground rock-phosphate or bone meal.

Plant your turnip seed in rows twelve to eighteen inches apart and, when the plants are four to six inches high, thin them out to from seven to nine inches apart. Eat the thinnings as cooked greens; they are delicious.

You are unlikely to find any serious pests on your turnips, or any sign of disease. This is a hardy vegetable. If aphids mess up the leaves, better spray them with Black Leaf 40.

No epicure lets his turnip root get big. Many turnips sold in our groceries are too big for good eating, and for this reason many persons with delicate palates decide they don't like turnips. Before making that decision, try harvesting them from your own garden when the roots are only two to three inches across. You may be surprised. And if you have never eaten turnip greens, you may be surprised that such large, hairy leaves can yield such a delicious dish. If your garden lies too far north for your turnips to weather through the winter, gather them before a hard frost strikes them, cut off the tops, not too close, eat the tops, and store the roots in a place where the temperature is as near 32° as possible. Turnips store quite well, which would be an argument for getting yours from a grocer, were it not for two things. First, you can harvest yours when the roots are younger than those you are likely to find for sale, and therefore more delicious. Second, if your garden is not too far north, turnips will furnish you fresher greens than any you are likely to buy—and in winter, at that, when greens are precious both for pleasure and for health. For these two reasons they are well worth the space they need. As for attention, they require almost none.

That is about all there is to say about turnips—till the cook takes over. Some vegetables are fun to eat and fun to talk about. Some are lots of fun to talk about but make indifferent eating. Turnips are fun to eat, but I have never found them what is sometimes called a conversation piece.

And Now Once More

Now THAT you have read this far, what I have said about the culture of the vegetables just discussed invites certain generalizations, even at the risk of repetition.

The beginner must have noted that certain vegetables are easier to raise than others, other things being equal. String beans, corn, lettuce, squash, and tomatoes are notably easy. So are Jerusalem artichokes, beets, carrots, chard, collards, kale, and turnips. Asparagus takes more trouble to get started, particularly if you decide to trench it. Broad beans are just about the only vegetable I have discussed that is bothered by our climate. Cucumber sometimes proves awfully vulnerable to pests.

Some vegetables dislike cold: globe artichokes, beans, lima beans, cucumbers, eggplant, okra, peppers, New Zealand spinach, squash, sweet potatoes. But this merely means a shorter growing season in rugged climates and, in my own judgment, finer flavor. Some adore heat: beans, lima beans, corn, cucumber, okra, squash, sweet potatoes, tomatoes. Others frankly dislike heat, especially hot nights: beets, broccoli, Brussels sprouts, cabbage, carrots, cauliflower, kale, lettuce, peas, Irish potatoes, spinach, turnips. In this last list the cabbage family and the edible roots are conspicuous.

But note that while these preferences tend to dictate the areas for commercial truck farming, they need not intimidate the home gardener.

You will have observed that practically all vegetables do better if the soil is deeply worked and loose, or "friable." But some especially dislike tight, shallow soil: beets, carrots, parsnips are conspicuous examples. Tight soil and an impenetrable hardpan tend to deform their roots.

Some vegetables are "gross feeders" and need lots to eat. Such are asparagus, broccoli, Brussels sprouts, cabbage, carrots, cauliflower, celery, kale, okra. Some will grow on poor soil: for example, Jerusalem artichokes, beans, and chard get by on thin rations.

87

For a number of reasons nearly all vegetables thrive best in soil that has been well limed. First, if your soil is acid they will need the calcium or the magnesium in the lime. Second, liming tends to lighten and aerate soil, so that it will not easily pack. Third, and perhaps most important, lime acts to release nutrients in the soil that would not otherwise be available. The food is already in the cupboard, but lime unlocks the cupboard door. One pound to twenty square feet, per season, should suffice if the litmus paper turns red. Scatter it evenly, and rake it into the top three inches of soil.

For the leafy vegetables, nitrogen is needed. Good compost will help supply it. Legumes such as beans collect it, and bean and pea vines are especially useful in the compost heap. Others crave phosphorus, and for them bone meal is a wonderful and completely safe fertilizer; also ground rock-phosphate. Some vegetables, such as carrots and chard, crave potash more than others do. Bone meal furnishes that too. So do ashes, especially wood ashes, and most especially hardwood ashes. But avoid concentrated doses: remember, our forefathers made lye from wood ashes. It is not true that coal ash is worthless as fertilizer, although its chief use is to "lighten" the soil and make it crumbly.

A few vegetables are perennials. Globe artichoke, if not winter-killed, will last three or four years. Asparagus will last a lifetime. Some are biennial and will stay alive two years—beets, for example. But they are eaten the first year, when they develop their root, not during the second, when they produce their flower and seed. For the perennials, our problem is merely to find a permanent bed, a little out of the way of a possible plow or harrow.

If your garden spot is very small, you may be bothered by the variations this book suggests in the distances to leave between rows and the distances to leave between plants in the row. If you read other books, and if you read the directions on seed packets, you may get even more different recommendations. Consult pages 98–99 on spacing; but there are four variable factors that modify any advice on distances. First, all other things being equal, the more your vegetables shield the ground, the better they will do, and this fact suggests close planting. But since a good mulch will shield it just as well, the mulcher can ignore this first point. Second, space between rows makes it easier to cultivate the rows, to tend them, and to harvest them; how big a space depends partly on your personal size and partly on your work habits. Also, a mulch cuts cultivation to a minimum. Third, many vegetables forage for food with their roots for a considerable distance, and for water too. Unless your ground is quite fertile, closely planted vegetables will compete for the same food supply and will not do well. You then have the choice of wider spacing or building up your garden's fertility. Fourth, some vegetables are bulky and, if they lack space, they may shade their neighbors and thereby steal the sunlight their neighbors are depending on. This, incidentally, is a good point at which to observe that beginners are often chicken-hearted about removing vegetables that have "volunteered"—that is, come up in the wrong part of the garden from stray seeds. Be ruthless with these. If you can't transplant the vegetable to a row of its own kind, pull it up and compost it. No matter how handsome a vegetable your volunteer may be—and volunteers have a perverse tendency to do better than others of their kind just because they know they are uninvited guests and had better be on their best behavior—show no mercy; an out-of-place vegetable can be a frightful nuisance.

Making allowance for the problems raised by these four points, you can follow the usual directions. If you plan to plant your rows of corn three feet apart, note that what you are really doing is allowing any given row of corn eighteen inches on each side of the row. If you plan to plant two rows of kale two feet apart, then you are really planning to give each kale plant one foot on each side of the row it grows in. Therefore, on the same measurements, if you run a row of kale alongside a row of corn, they would be one foot plus eighteen inches apart, or two and a half feet apart. To this observation, I should add that a "catch crop" of some quick-growing vegetable like radish or lettuce can sometimes be grown between two rows of bigger, slow-growing vegetables, and be harvested and eaten before it has time to get in the way of its big neighbors.

Some of the vegetables in this book transplant easily and well: chard will, and so will its cousin, the beet. But carrots won't. All the cabbage family will, and so will lettuce. But beans and corn and squash can be transplanted only if you plant in a container and shift the whole block of earth, which must be kept compact by moistening. Their roots simply must not be disturbed. With lettuce it sometimes helps to clip off half the length of the leaves when you transplant, in order to cut down on overhead until the plant builds a new root structure. All transplanting can be facilitated by a final good sprinkling and by shading the plant from sunlight for several days. And whenever you transplant, make the hole big enough for the root to assume its natural posture. No plant wants to be jammed in bed, curled up in a tight hole.

Most vegetables should be harvested before they are mature: they not only are more tender then, but they taste better and they contain more vitamins. This is true of leaf vegetables such as lettuce and cabbage. It is true of root vegetables such as carrots and beets. It is true of seed vegetables such as peas and beans and okra. It is true of "fruit" vegetables such as squash and eggplant. As I have already said, corn should have reached the stage where the grain is a reasonable size and squirts its milk when punched with your thumbnail. Tomatoes should be allowed to ripen on the vine. Note that most of the vegetables I have mentioned are not harvested by the commercial grower until after they have passed their prime. He is after price, and therefore after size and quantity. But your chief reason for growing vegetables yourself is that you are after quality. Hence, harvest early.

Early harvesting accomplishes one more thing. The more most vegetables, at least those that furnish you with seed or fruit, are deprived early of what they have borne, the longer they will bear. If you permit them to make good seed, they will have fulfilled their dearest ambition and will quit forming further seed. A vegetable's ambition is to "increase and multiply." Keep your vegetables striving. Better harvest beans and compost them than leave them on the vine too long.

But what you harvest, to be really prime, should also have grown rapidly, not slowly. It should have grown regularly, not in fits and starts. If a dry season retards growth, for example, the vegetable is weakened, and insects are likely to detect its weakness before you do, and attack. If your soil is poor and lacks vegetable matter, your vegetables will "make" only very slowly, and many of them will acquire toughness and oldness and stringiness from their prolonged struggle to grow up. Composting will ensure rapid, healthy growth, a minimum of disease and pests, a maximum of flavor, and a maximum of nourishment. So keep 'em hustling.

Insects prey on some vegetables more than on others. The cabbage family, for example, is relatively vulnerable. So are string beans. But lettuce and tomatoes and corn and root vegetables rarely attract real armies of insects. Many excellent gardeners never spray. They count on birds and toads to prey on the insects, and on good soil to make their vegetables hale and hearty. And if a few bugs insist on sharing the feast, they don't pout. If insects hit you hard, it is almost certain that your soil is poor and needs humus. That means composting.

It means composting and it means mulching. Many garden manuals advise mulching when they give cultural directions for almost any vegetable. But few bother to explain the enormous role mulching can play. Next to composting, mulching is the Great Neglected Art of the American gardener. Now, the point of composting is to introduce humus or vegetable matter into the topsoil, and along with it a few hundred million or even billion bacteria. If you want to avoid a "rotten" garden, then make sure you have rotting topsoil. To say that your soil should be rotting is to say that there should be countless micro-organisms attacking vegetable matter in it and ready to attack any vegetable matter that falls on it or is placed on it. Drop a dead weed or even a piece of cloth on soil of that sort and it begins to rot. Drop the same weed or cloth on an inorganic soil which lacks humus and bacteria, and it may lie there for months, just as it would on a slab of concrete.

This gives us a cue. If you compost for two or three years, depending on the sort of "soil" you start with, you can acquire a rotting soil, an organic, live soil. Now, if you spread from two to four inches of mulch on that soil—sawdust, grass clippings, spoiled hay, buckwheat hulls, tobacco stems, seaweed, peat, or what not—the bacteria and earthworms in your soil will attack its bottom layer and rapidly devour it, so that you will have to replace it. But replacing mulch is easier work than building more compost piles. As a matter of fact, composting was merely a quick way of getting the soil thoroughly inoculated with the microbes it needs. You could have done it more slowly by mulching alone, provided you kept the mulch wet enough to allow bacteria a chance. All you want, in the last analysis, is a soil that will promptly eat whatever vegetable waste you put on it, and then you want to keep it supplied with vegetable waste to eat. The name of that supply is mulch.

It is true that mulch does many other things for you, as we have seen. It keeps the soil from drying out when the wind blows, from eroding when downpours of rain flood it too suddenly. It keeps the sun from burning out the humus and bacteria in your topsoil. It makes it unnecessary to keep ploughing or hoeing, whether to clear out weeds or to create a "dust mulch" and delay evaporation of the precious water in the soil. By keeping the soil moist, it makes it easy to pull up those weeds which can be extracted without dislodging the roots of some nearby vegetable. But its chief virtue is to "feed" the live, and hence hungry, soil. That means feeding the billions of bacteria and the thousands of valuable earthworms that should be laborers in your garden—at zero wage! If your soil can live nicely on the mulch you give it to eat, then your vegetables can live nicely on the fattened soil that results.

Should you therefore stop making compost heaps? Well, once your soil is eating mulch hard and independently, you can quit building those layer cakes of vegetable matter and manure I have talked about. As for the weeds and lawn clippings and vegetable refuse you may accumulate, you can safely drop them on top of your carpet of mulch. If they are too big and messy, then drop them in the compost heap along with your kitchen garbage—since, in any case, you are not going to want to strew decaying garbage on top of the mulch between your rows of pretty vegetables, to draw flies and, sooner or later, a sanitary inspector. A little rich earth and adequate moisture will keep the stuff in your compost heap working. Any animal manure, or any parts of an animal that you can add to the mixture will be all to the good.

To the question, therefore, "How long must I keep up the hard labor of composting?" I would answer that you ought to keep it up until you have soil eager to devour any vegetable mulch you put on it. And this answer, of course, argues against the use of such manufactured mulches as spun glass or tough paper or anything else not easily rotted down—that is, eaten by the bacteria in a rich garden soil. To the requirement that mulch should be easily rotted down, I should want to add that it should be reasonably pleasant to walk on. For example, rotted stable manure makes a superb mulch, but it is a mess to walk on. Barley straw is very good, but it has barbs that can be annoying even through your stockings. Any straw risks catching fire from a cigarette butt. Flattened sides of old cartons are better than no mulch at all. In my own experience, sawdust is the most manageable mulch of all.

Most people will tell you that sawdust will sour, or acidify, the soil. Indeed, sawdust has traditionally been used to mulch certain plants that prefer an acid soil. But during recent years agricultural research workers have really gone to work on this problem in Alabama, Connecticut, Ohio, and Virginia. Their experiments convinced them that sawdust, either hardwood or softwood, either used as a mulch or mixed with the topsoil, for periods varying from one to twelve years, showed no appreciable effect on soil acidity. They also proved that even if the sawdust contained such "toxic" materials as tannin there were no harmful effects. Sawdust, especially fresh as distinguished from half-rotted sawdust, did render some of the nitrogen in the soil temporarily unavailable, but that is true of any mulch that is rotting on the surface and is an effect of bacterial action. A nitrogenous fertilizer such as ground blood can easily correct that. Even if sawdust did cause acidity, as ninety-nine out of a hundred gardeners believe, lime applied just before mulching would correct it, and lime is cheap and easy to spread—whereas it is by no means easy to find another material as ideal for mulching as sawdust. Unlike commercially sold peat or buckwheat hulls, it can often be had for the hauling. And even if you have to buy it, it comes cheap—provided it is bought by the cubic yard and not by weight, which can vary enormously according to moisture content. It is free of seeds, which is sometimes a problem with hay. Its fine particles can be more easily arranged around your plants than straw can. So by all means try to locate an abandoned pile of sawdust from a temporary roadside sawmill, and dig in. And replenish it as soon as there are signs your army of bacterial field workers are devouring it.

There is absolutely no doubt that sawdust breaks down less rapidly than many other vegetable materials—such, for example, as grass clippings. This objection, unlike the exploded objection about acidity, is a real one and worth your weighing. It amounts to admitting that sawdust will not feed your soil as rapidly as some other materials for mulching. But you should weigh against this two other considerations. First, if you have got your soil into a really "live" condition, it will eat up sawdust quicker than you think. Second, you can "work through" sawdust when you plant seed, for example, far better than through most mulches. For instance, a garden hoe, properly dragged, will open a furrow in the sawdust down to true earth. Seed planted on that earth, not necessarily under it, and covered to the normal depth, but in sawdust, not earth, is in a grand position to start life thriftily. Try to do that through straw, even chopped straw, and you will see how much handier sawdust is to "mold" to your work needs.

It is also objected that sawdust, at least if applied several inches deep, may not break down by spring, and that therefore it gets turned into the soil by the plow. Doing this for several years, it is argued, will produce a topsoil composed of unrotted sawdust seasoned with true soil! But this is true only if you plow under last year's mulch with a moldboard plow—the sort that turns the soil upside down. A disk harrow would condition your spring garden much better, because it would leave the topsoil where it belongs—on top. If you had hardpan underneath your topsoil, you should have broken that up with a subsoiler before you did anything else, the deeper the better. A subsoiler has a knifelike blade instead of the gracefully shaped moldboard. It breaks up the subsoil without hurling it on top of your live topsoil and spoiling your garden's fertility. If you weren't able to get a subsoiler, or your garden was too small to use one in it, you should have spaded it. Never turn under the topsoil in a good garden spot. Of course, if by sheer good luck you have rich topsoil that extends a foot or two below the surface, naturally you pay a minimum penalty for this crime. But many gardens can be simply ruined by it. The bacterial condition of the first six or seven inches of your topsoil, counting from the surface, is your prime asset in growing healthy, and hence delicious, food. Treat it reverently.

In short, if your garden soil is full of earthworms and soil bacteria, either because it is an old and fertile garden spot, or because you got it that way by composting, it will "eat" sawdust. My own garden ate one inch of it last winter. If you have the soil well tilled and crumbly, keeping it under sawdust will keep it crumbly and you won't have to plow it again—therefore there is no danger of working too much of last season's sawdust mulch into the ground. If, on the other hand, your soil is sterile clay, perhaps from a cellar excavation, and you have not yet had time to compost it to health, then it will not eat sawdust mulch. True, it will not eat any other mulch very readily, but it will handle grass clippings or chopped hay or even chopped straw better than sawdust, and you had better use them for a while until you get really good soil, even though they are less manageable material for the gardener. Finally, all choice of mulching material has to be reviewed in the light of these questions: Which are available in your neighborhood? What do they cost? Whether the material you use is or is not the sort that will decay on good soil and thereby feed it into being still better soil, it is worth spreading if it does nothing but shelter your soil from sun, wind, and too hard rain.

This part of the Kitchen Garden Book must end, and I must say I regret ending it. But gardeners, when they discuss gardening, must beware of garrulity. If I have been guilty, I ask pardon—but there was so much to talk about. Actually, I have exercised more self-control than may appear on the surface. I have tried to keep to the elements of gardening and to state them plainly. But two major hurdles, beside my personal inadequacies, confronted me. I have already spoken of the first one: gardening is of necessity an intensely local affair. For this reason it is often true that the more specific the advice you give, the more likely it is to mislead. That is one hurdle. The second is higher: modern agricultural science has made great strides, partly because it draws on physics and chemistry, and these two sciences have made great strides. But of course basically agriculture draws from biology, the science of life. And although modern biology has also made great progress, life remains a tremendous mystery. It is therefore not remarkable that there is a great number of interesting questions that agricultural science cannot answer. The fact is, the soil and the life processes that go on within it are often mysteries as dark as the burrow of an earthworm. So, even leaving aside the question of variations, the question of local soils and local climates, there is a great deal about an ordinary vegetable garden that not even the agricultural scientist yet knows, or that he knows only darkly and empirically. I know that many men dislike mystery and hope to abolish it some day. I suspect that most good gardeners are men who love knowledge without hating or fearing mystery.

Now that so many paranoids publicly discuss our chances of blowing up this fair Earth that was given us, or of rendering her too radio-active to support any life, or of perhaps turning our backs on her in a space ship bound for other, stranger planets, the humblest garden on our Earth assumes a new importance. It is at least a spot in space where man encounters the Earth, where man may love and nourish her, and she may love and nourish him. So—to your garden.

BIBLIOGRAPHICAL NOTE

THE LITERATURE on vegetable culture is vast. Much of it is too technical for the average gardener. Much of the rest was specifically written for commercial truck farmers and gives not too good advice for the home gardener.

The book that has proved most useful in my own gardening is *The Vegetable Encyclopedia and Gardener's Guide,* by Victor A. Tiedjens, a horticulturist at the New Jersey State Agricultural Experiment Station, Rutgers University, published by The Home Library, New York, 1943. It really is encyclopedic: it gives directions for cultivating over eighty vegetables, many of which have been neither eaten nor seen by the average reader; whereas *The Kitchen Garden Book* has deliberately restricted itself to the most popular vegetables, all of which will cooperate with a backyard gardener, even a beginner.

Professor Tiedjens also gives directions for nearly fifty herbs, many of them useless to the cook but delightful for other purposes.

A reference work that is more literally an encyclopedia is *Hortus Second,* compiled by L. H. Bailey and Ethel Zoe Bailey, and published by Macmillan, 1941. *The Wise Garden Encyclopedia,* edited by E. L. D. Seymour, William H. Wise & Co., 1951, is also useful.

But the books I think the home gardener, especially the beginner, needs most deal with what soil means; and fortunately some of the books on soil make really exciting reading. At the top of the list I place *An Agricultural Testament,* by Sir Albert Howard, Oxford, 1940. This book is the Bible of the true composters, and justly so. But a second book by Sir Albert, *The Soil and Health,* Devin-Adair, 1947, is also first-rate.

Nearly fifty years ago an American Sir Albert, F. H. King of the U. S. Department of Agriculture, traveled through China, Korea, and Japan, observing the traditional peasant agriculture of those countries. The story of that trip, *Farmers of Forty Centuries,* Rodale Press, Emmaus, Penn., 1948, is filled with wisdom.

The high doctrine on composting and humus can be found in *Bio-Dynamic Farming and Gardening,* by Ehrenfried Pfeiffer, published by the Anthroposophic Press, 211 Madison Avenue, New York, 1943. It was recently out of print, but a reprint has been announced.

There are a number of works on the humble but valuable earthworm, but the most exciting one I ever read was written by no other than the great Charles Darwin and called *The Formation of Vegetable*

Mould. Faber & Faber of London fortunately reprinted it in 1948. Whether you plan a garden or not, this book will excite you.

As a footnote to my expressed preference for a subsoiler or "chisel" plow over a moldboard plow, at least in any garden I expect to make, I mention two readable and highly controversial books. Both of them were written by Edward H. Faulkner and both were published by the University of Oklahoma Press. They are *Plowman's Folly,* 1943, and *Second Look,* 1951.

VEGETABLE-GROWING GUIDE

[When more than one method of planting may be used, the least usual is indicated thus: (√)]

	Plant in Garden as			When to Plant		Grown as[1]		Depth to plant	Space		Transplants well?
	Seeds	Started plants	Roots, bulbs, or rhizomes	As soon as ground can be worked	After last frost	Annual	Perennial		In row	Between rows	
Artichokes, globe	(√)	√			√		√	Seed ¼" Root	2'	4'	Yes
Asparagus	(√)		√	√			√	8"	2'	3'	Yes
Beans, snap	√				√	√		1"	3'	2'	No
Beans, lima	√				√	√		1"	8"	2½'	No
Beets	√			√		√		¼"	4"	2'	Yes
Broccoli	Late Crop	Early Crop		√		√		¼"	2'	3'	Yes
Brussels sprouts	√	√			√	√		¼"	2'	3'	Yes
Cabbage	Late Crop	Early Crop		√		√		¼"	2'	3'	Yes
Carrots	√			√		√		¼"	2"	12"	No
Cauliflower	Late Crop	Early Crop			√	√		¼"	2'	3'	Yes
Celeriac	Late Crop	Early Crop		√		√		¼"	6"	2'	Yes

Celery	✓ Late Crop	✓ Early Crop			✓	✓		¼″	8″	2′	Yes
Chard	✓			✓		✓		¼″	10″	2′	Yes
Chinese cabbage	✓ Late Crop	✓ Early Crop			✓	✓		¼″	3″	12″	Yes
Corn (sweet)	✓				✓	✓		1″	1′	2′	No
Cucumbers	✓				✓	✓		½″	4′	4′	No
Eggplants		✓			✓	✓		¼″	1′	2′	Yes
Jerusalem artichoke			✓	✓			✓	3″	10″	3′	No
Kale	(✓)	✓		✓		✓		¼″	1′	3′	Yes
Leeks	✓			✓		✓		¼″	2″	1′	Yes
Lettuce	✓	✓		✓		✓		¼″	6″	1′	Yes
Okra	(✓)	✓[2]			✓	✓		½″	1′–1½′	3′	No
Onions	✓	✓	✓	✓		✓		¼″	4″	1′	Yes
Parsnips	✓			✓		✓		¼″	3″	1′	No
Peas	✓			✓		✓		1″	4″	2′	No
Peppers		✓			✓	✓		¼″	1½′	2′	Yes
Potatoes			✓	✓		✓		3″	1′	2′	No
Radishes	✓			✓		✓		¼″	1″	1′	No
Spinach	✓			✓		✓		¼″	3″	20″	Yes
Squash	✓				✓	✓		1″	3′	4′	No
Sweet Potatoes		✓	(✓)	✓		✓		3″	18″	3′	Yes
Tomatoes	(✓)	✓			✓	✓		¼″	2′–3′	3′–4′	Yes
Turnips	✓			✓		✓		¼″	4″	2′	No

[1] Some vegetables, such as beet, cabbage, and carrot, are actually biennials, forming a plant the first year and seeds the second, but are grown in home and market gardens as annuals, and are so listed here.
[2] Plants should be grown in pots so as not to disturb roots when transplanting.

2. COOKING VEGETABLES

by Stella Standard

NOTE

Estimates of the number of servings have been given for each vegetable recipe. These can be only tentative because so much depends on the number of other dishes which comprise the meal, the amounts of the servings, and individual appetites.

ARTICHOKES

Artichokes have generally been considered a vegetable to serve on special occasions. At the height of their season they are now very plentiful and therefore quite inexpensive. But, although they are becoming more and more popular for our daily meals, there are only a few ways to cook them. If care is taken with their simple preparation they should be served as a separate course; they take a little time to eat, because each leaf must be plucked, dipped in sauce, and eaten with the fingers. In France and Italy the artichoke hearts (or bottoms) grow much larger and are often cooked and served without the leaves. Several American artichoke hearts would be required for each serving. Artichokes may be boiled in water, but they are much more delicious when cooked in white wine; the liquid should be served as their sauce.

ARTICHOKES VINAIGRETTE

artichokes (1 per person)
boiling salted water
white wine
olive oil

salt and pepper
lemon juice or vinegar
capers
Bahamian mustard (if available)

Wash the artichokes and remove any coarse, discolored outer leaves. Plunge them in boiling salted water and simmer for 5 minutes. Drain and stand them upside down. For 6 artichokes put ⅓ cup wine and ⅓ cup olive oil in the bottom of a heavy pot and stand the artichokes right side up close together in the pot. Sprinkle a little salt and pepper over the top, separate the leaves a little, and put 2 tablespoons olive oil and 2 tablespoons wine inside each artichoke. Cover tight and cook gently for 25 to 30 minutes, depending on their size. Turn the artichokes upside down in the pot to drain a little, then put them on serving plates. Have the seasonings ready to add to the liquid in the pot: the juice of 1 lemon, 2 tablespoons capers, 2 teaspoons mustard, and a little more oil and wine. Serve this sauce in a bowl for dipping the leaves. Both artichokes and sauce may be served cold.

STUFFED ARTICHOKES

artichokes (1 per person)
boiling salted water

minced green onions
crushed garlic in olive oil

STUFFING

grated cheese
buttered crumbs
ground ham
minced mushrooms

1 cup water, wine, or broth
⅓ cup melted butter
bacon (optional)

Prepare and parboil the artichokes as directed for Artichokes Vinaigrette. Mix any two or three of the suggested stuffing ingredients, separate the leaves, and put 2 or 3 tablespoons stuffing among the leaves of each. Put 1 cup liquid in the bottom of a pot. Fit the artichokes close together in the pot and steam them gently, covered, until they are tender—25 minutes for small ones and 30 to 35 minutes for the large. Lift them onto hot serving plates, add ⅓ cup melted butter to the liquid, if it is broth or wine, and serve it to dip the leaves in. If water is used in the cooking serve Hollandaise sauce with the artichokes. If desired, before cooking, a strip of bacon may be fastened around each artichoke for variation.

ARTICHOKES ITALIAN STYLE

artichokes (1 per person)
crushed garlic buds
olive oil
anchovy fillets

white wine
capers
grated Parmesan cheese

Prepare and parboil the artichokes as for Artichokes Vinaigrette. After they have been well drained, put them in a pot and stuff with crushed garlic buds, olive oil, and anchovy fillets. Use 1 bud and 2 tablespoons oil and 1 anchovy fillet for each artichoke. Put ⅔ cup white wine and ⅓ cup olive oil in the bottom of the pot, first spooning a little of each over the artichokes so they are well moistened with oil and wine. Cover tightly and cook gently for 25 to 35 minutes, depending on the size. Add capers and more oil and wine to the liquid in the pot and use it to dip the leaves in. Put the artichokes on serving plates and sprinkle Parmesan cheese over the top of each.

ARTICHOKE HEARTS WITH MUSHROOM SAUCE

12 or more artichokes	¾ cup sliced mushrooms
butter	2 teaspoons cornstarch
¼ cup consommé	½ cup cream
¼ cup white wine	¼ teaspoon nutmeg
salt and pepper	

Remove the leaves and chokes from the artichokes. Cut off a thin slice from each stem, and peel the stems, for they cook tender as quickly as the hearts. If the hearts are small prepare 2 or 3 of them for each serving. Roll them in butter over a low flame in a large heavy pot, then add the consommé and wine and a little salt and pepper. Cover and simmer gently about 18 minutes, until they are just tender. Do not cook them too long. Test them after 15 minutes. Meanwhile sauté the mushrooms in a little butter and when the hearts are done add the mushrooms. Blend the cornstarch with the cold cream, add the nutmeg, and pour it over the vegetables. Simmer, uncovered, until the sauce thickens. Serve on small plates as a separate vegetable course. The hearts may be sprinkled with chopped chives. Serves 6.

ASPARAGUS

Asparagus, to many people, is our most treasured vegetable and it should have the care in preparation it deserves. When the whole stalks are cooked they should never lie in water but should be tied, top and bottom, in bunches and stood up in the bottom of the double boiler. If the lower stalks are very tough, they may be broken off. Put 1½ cups water in the double-boiler bottom (after cooking, the liquid may be used in soup or in a sauce for the vegetable). Cover with the inverted top of the double boiler and steam until the tips are tender. If just the tender tips are needed for an asparagus pie or an omelet, they may be gently steamed in 2 tablespoons water and butter, covered tight. Asparagus lends itself to many garnishings, from a simple dressing of melted butter (many people's choice) to very rich sauces— Hollandaise, mayonnaise, vinaigrette, Mornay sauce, cream and almonds, cheese and ham. But the important thing is its initial preparation. Those who like it crisp cook it 15 minutes, while others prefer it very tender and cook it 5 to 7 minutes longer. Asparagus is one of the vegetables deserving a course of its own.

Most of these recipes specify a large 2½-pound bunch of asparagus, which will serve from 2 to 6 people, depending on the meal.

ASPARAGUS SOUP

2 lbs. asparagus	½ teaspoon nutmeg
8 cups veal or chicken broth	½ cup cream
3 tablespoons butter	2 egg yolks
2 tablespoons flour	*GARNISH*
salt and pepper	buttered toasted croutons

After the asparagus is well washed cut a ¼-inch slice from the end of each stalk and discard. Cut off the tender tips, 2 or 3 inches long, and reserve them. Cut the stalks in 1-inch lengths and crush them in the bottom of the soup kettle, add the broth, and simmer gently for 1 hour. Strain the soup, pressing the asparagus against the sieve, then discard the pulp. Brown the butter and flour and mix with a little of the soup, then combine it with the rest of the soup and the seasonings. Add the tips and simmer 15 minutes or until the tips are tender. Scald the cream and mix it with the egg yolks. Put the cream and yolks in a tureen and mix in the soup. Cover with buttered toasted croutons. Serves 6.

ASPARAGUS OMELET

MORNAY SAUCE	5 or 6 eggs
⅔ cup light cream	3 tablespoons cream
2 teaspoons cornstarch	salt and pepper
dash of nutmeg	3 tablespoons butter
salt and pepper	8 or 10 cooked asparagus tips
¼ cup grated Parmesan cheese	*GARNISH*
	grated Parmesan cheese

For the sauce, blend the cornstarch and cream in a saucepan, heat, stir in the seasonings and cheese, and cook until the sauce thickens. Beat the eggs, add the cream, salt, and pepper. Melt the butter in an omelet pan, coating the bottom and sides well. Cook the omelet until set, pushing back the edges so the uncooked part runs to the bottom. Add the asparagus tips to the hot sauce. Put half the sauce on the omelet, fold once, and slide it off onto a hot platter. Add the rest of the sauce to the top and sprinkle with a little more cheese. Serves 4.

ASPARAGUS ON TOAST

crisp toast
2½ lbs. asparagus (1 large bunch)

salt and pepper
melted butter

Prepare 1 slice good crisp toast per person and put the slices on a large platter. Boil the asparagus in 1½ cups water in a double boiler as directed on page 105. When it is done spoon 2 tablespoons asparagus water over each slice of toast. Lift the asparagus by the strings, hold it over the toast, snip the strings to remove them, and let the asparagus fall evenly over the toast. Salt and pepper it and pour melted butter over it, 2 tablespoons at least to each slice of toast. This toast is almost as good as the asparagus.

ASPARAGUS WITH SOUR CREAM
(Hungarian Style)

2½ lbs. asparagus, boiled
1 cup sour cream
salt and pepper

2 tablespoons lemon juice
½ cup fresh dry crumbs
3 tablespoons butter

When the asparagus has cooked, drain it very well. Put it in a shallow baking dish. Mix the sour cream, salt, pepper, and lemon juice, warm slightly, and pour over the asparagus. Brown the crumbs in butter and sprinkle them over the top of the cream. Bake in a hot oven 3 or 4 minutes.

ASPARAGUS ITALIAN STYLE

2½ lbs. asparagus, boiled
Italian bread (optional)
⅓ cup olive oil
2 buds garlic, crushed

salt and pepper
1 tablespoon lemon juice
grated Parmesan cheese

Cook the asparagus and drain it well. If you desire, toast Italian bread and dip it in the asparagus water, then lay it on a platter and cover it with the asparagus, or it may be put on individual serving plates. Heat the garlic in the olive oil and season it with salt, pepper, and lemon juice. Pour it over the asparagus and top with the cheese. Serve as a separate course.

ASPARAGUS WITH BROTH SAUCE

2½ lbs. asparagus
2 teaspoons cornstarch
juice of ½ lemon
1 pea-sized lump of beef extract
⅛ teaspoon nutmeg

½ teaspoon brown sugar
salt and pepper
GARNISH
browned crumbs or grated Parmesan cheese

Cook the asparagus as directed on page 105, in the double boiler with 1½ cups water. When the asparagus is cooked, save the water for the sauce. Blend the cornstarch in 2 tablespoons cold water, add it and all the other ingredients to the asparagus water and cook until it thickens. Have the asparagus on a hot platter and pour the sauce over it. Sprinkle the top with browned buttered crumbs or grated Parmesan cheese. Chopped parsley or green onions may be used instead of the other garnishes.

ASPARAGUS PIE

1 prebaked single-crust pie shell
2½ lbs. asparagus
2 tablespoons cornstarch
1½ cups light cream
½ cup asparagus water
¼ teaspoon nutmeg

salt and pepper
2 egg yolks
¼ cup grated Parmesan cheese
TOP
grated Parmesan cheese

Make quite a flaky rich pie crust. Cut the tender tips from the asparagus stalks, leaving them 4 inches long. Cook them until tender in very little water, ½ cup of which is to be used in the sauce. Mix the cornstarch with the cream, add the asparagus water and seasonings. Cook until it thickens; then add the egg yolks and cheese. Let cook until the cheese melts. Arrange half the asparagus on the crust like spokes of a wheel, then add half the sauce. Put the rest of the tips on the sauce the same way and cover with the rest of the sauce. Sprinkle with Parmesan cheese and run the pie under the broiler until it bubbles and browns a little. Serve hot.

ASPARAGUS WITH HARD-BOILED EGG
(Holland Style)

2½ lbs. asparagus, boiled
nutmeg
salt and pepper

quartered hard-boiled eggs
tureen of melted butter

Asparagus is served on the Continent as a separate course. The asparagus comes to the table on individual serving plates with 1 or 2 quarters of egg sprinkled with nutmeg, salt, and pepper. The egg is mashed with a fork and sprinkled over the asparagus, and melted butter is passed in a tureen.

ASPARAGUS WITH PROSCIUTTO

2½ lbs. asparagus
paper-thin slices of Italian ham
1 tablespoon cornstarch

1 cup light cream
⅓ cup grated Parmesan cheese

Tie the asparagus in bunches of 4 stalks and boil it as directed on page 105. When it is tender but not overcooked, wrap each bunch with a slice of ham, fastening it with toothpicks. Lay the bunches in a buttered shallow pan or, better, a baking dish. Blend the cornstarch with the cold cream, heat it, and mix in the cheese. Pour this sauce over the ham bundles and heat in a 375° oven until the sauce bubbles.

FRENCH-FRIED ASPARAGUS TIPS

2½ lbs. asparagus
butter
flour
salt and pepper

beaten egg
fine crumbs
deep oil or fat for frying

Cut the tips from the stalks in 2½- to 3-inch lengths. Put them in a covered pan with 2 or 3 tablespoons water and 2 tablespoons or more of butter, and steam 3 or 4 minutes, until they are about half tender. Season some flour with salt and pepper and roll the tips in it. Dip them in beaten egg, then roll them in crumbs. Fry in deep fat in a basket at 370° until they are a golden brown. Serve with a cutlet or with chicken.

ASPARAGUS AMANDINE

2½ lbs. asparagus, boiled   salt and pepper
¼ cup melted butter   1 tablespoon grated onion
½ cup sour cream   ⅓ cup browned chopped almonds

Put the freshly boiled, well-drained asparagus in a shallow baking dish. Mix the butter, sour cream, seasonings, and onion, and pour over the asparagus. Sprinkle the top with browned almonds. Run under the flame until the top browns a little. The cream may be omitted if desired. Asparagus is good dressed with butter and browned almonds or butter and ground ham.

ASPARAGUS VINAIGRETTE

cold boiled asparagus   1 tablespoon chopped pickles
salad greens   1 tablespoon minced chervil or
red pimento strips   tarragon
          SAUCE   2 tablespoons grated onion
1 cup French dressing   2 tablespoons chopped parsley
1 tablespoon capers   1 hard-boiled egg, sieved

Asparagus vinaigrette, when served cold, may replace a vegetable and salad. Arrange asparagus on individual plates and garnish with crisp salad greens. Watercress is very good for this. A strip or two of pimento may be added. Mix the dressing with the other ingredients and add 3 or 4 tablespoons of the sauce to each plate of asparagus.

OTHER USES FOR ASPARAGUS

Cold asparagus tips tossed with salad greens.

Asparagus, cold or hot, with mayonnaise or Hollandaise sauce.

Asparagus tips, cooked and added to egg noodles with crushed garlic and olive oil.

BEANS

String beans (green, snap, or wax), because of their delicate flavor, lend themselves well to many combinations: sautéed mushrooms, chestnuts, cheese, sauces, tomatoes, onions, green peppers, and various herbs—chervil, basil, thyme, chives, and parsley. To my taste, Frenching beans or cutting them in julienne sticks sacrifices their flavor, and if cooked a little too much they may become mushy and lose their crisp texture. Break off the tips and leave the beans whole, or, if they are large, cut them in half. If care is taken in their preparation they are one of the finest vegetables.

The lima bean, soy bean, cranberry bean, and the broad bean, to mention but a few of the numerous varieties of beans of meatier texture than the string bean, make epicurean dishes and may often take the place of meat because of their concentrated food value. The fresh young lima bean is one of the greatest gifts the earth yields. Cooked alone or with corn, peas, or carrots, or added to stews and soups, it may be counted upon to enrich any meal. Dried beans of different varieties furnish the main ingredients for dozens of fine casserole dishes, an excellent and delicious way to serve meals to growing children as well as to the most particular guest.

BEAN AND CURRY CONSOMMÉ

2 tablespoons butter	1 cup green peas
1 tablespoon curry powder	1 teaspoon basil
6 cups veal or chicken consommé	½ cup minced green onions
1 tablespoon light brown sugar	1 tomato, skinned, chopped, seeded
2 cups green beans	salt and pepper

Put the butter and curry powder in the top of a double boiler and let them cook over hot water 10 minutes. Add the consommé and sugar and let cook while the vegetables are being cooked. Cut the beans in ½-inch lengths and cook them in very little water. When they are tender add them and the liquid to the consommé. Do the same with the peas, cooking them with the basil. Add the other ingredients and let the soup stand 2 or 3 hours before it is served. Serve cold in summer and hot in winter. Serves 6 to 8.

GREEN-BEAN AND POTATO SOUP

2 cups green beans
salt and pepper
4 medium-sized potatoes, peeled
2 handfuls fresh dill, stemmed

2 tablespoons butter
1½ tablespoons flour
1 to 1½ cups heavy cream
3 tablespoons vinegar (or to taste)

Cut the beans in ¾-inch lengths and cook them in very little water until tender. Season with salt and pepper, but do not drain them. Cut the peeled potatoes in ¾-inch cubes, put them on to boil in 1 cup water, squeeze the dill, cut it up with scissors, and add to the potatoes. Cover and cook until the potatoes are just tender. Do not drain them, but combine them with the beans. The use of the water makes heavy cream necessary. Melt the butter, stir in the flour, and, when the mixture has cooked a little, slowly add the cream. Cook until it thickens a little, and then add to the vegetables. If the soup is too thick add a very little milk or light cream, but it should be the consistency of very heavy cream. Add vinegar to taste and serve. This is a delicious and unusual soup. Other green vegetables such as peas or lima beans may be used, but the rest of the soup is always the same. Serves 4.

BUTTERED STRING BEANS
(or String Beans with Bacon)

1½ lbs. string beans
⅓ cup diced onions
½ green pepper, diced

3 tablespoons butter or 2 strips bacon
salt and pepper
3 tablespoons cream

Clean and tip the beans and cut them in half if they are large. Put the butter or bacon cut in small pieces in the bottom of a heavy pot; then sauté the onion and green pepper gently in the pot for 3 or 4 minutes. Add the beans and ¼ cup water, cover tightly, and cook slowly about 15 minutes or until the beans are tender. The pressure cooker takes 2 to 2½ minutes. Salt and pepper the beans and add the cream. Serve hot. If you are not using a pressure cooker, watch that the beans do not burn. Hickory-smoked bacon flavors beans deliciously and is often cooked with them in the South. Serves 5 or 6.

STRING BEANS WITH SOUR CREAM AND DILL

1½ lbs. string beans	¾ cup heavy sour cream
1 onion, diced	handful of stemmed dill, chopped
1 green pepper, diced	¼ cup minced chives or green
3 tablespoons butter	onions

Cook the beans with the onion, pepper, and butter as directed in Buttered String Beans. Warm the sour cream with the dill. Mix with the cooked beans. Empty into a serving dish and sprinkle with the chives or onions. Serves 5 or 6.

ITALIAN GREEN BEANS

1 bud garlic, crushed	1½ lbs. beans
⅓ cup olive oil	1 teaspoon basil
1 small onion, diced	salt and pepper
1 green pepper, diced	⅓ cup grated Parmesan cheese

Put the garlic and olive oil in the bottom of a pot with the onion and green pepper. When they have cooked 2 minutes add the beans and the basil. If they are cooked in a regular pot, covered, 3 tablespoons water may be added. The beans must be watched to make sure that they do not burn. When they are done, season, empty into a serving dish, and sprinkle with the cheese. Serves 5 or 6.

STRING BEANS AND MUSHROOMS OR CHESTNUTS

½ lb. mushrooms	to recipe for Buttered String
2 or 3 tablespoons butter	Beans
1½ lbs. string beans, cut in 1-inch	¼ teaspoon nutmeg
lengths and cooked according	¼ cup cream

Bake the mushrooms 7 minutes in a 375° oven with the butter. Combine the cooked beans and mushrooms, add nutmeg and cream. Cooked halved fresh chestnuts may be substituted for the mushrooms. One cup sautéed green onions may be added to green beans after they are cooked. A large casserole of beans and 1 pound cooked mushrooms may be used to make a party dish. Put layers of mushrooms and beans and 2 cups of cream sauce in a baking dish, top with plenty of grated cheese, and bake until it bubbles and browns a little. Serves 6.

STRING BEANS AU GRATIN

1½ lbs. beans, cut in 1-inch
 lengths
1 onion, diced
1 green pepper, diced
3 tablespoons butter, or 2 strips
 bacon, diced
pinch of thyme or rosemary

milk
2 tablespoons cornstarch
1 cup light cream
salt and pepper
½ cup grated cheese, Cheddar or
 Parmesan

Cook the beans as directed in the recipe for Buttered String Beans, using the onion, pepper, either bacon or butter, and the herb. (When combining beans with other vegetables or with sauces, always cut them in 1-inch lengths or as directed.) Use the liquid in making the sauce; measure it and add enough milk to make ½ cup. Blend the cornstarch with the cream, add the milk mixture and seasoning, and cook gently until it thickens. Put half the cooked beans in a greased baking dish, add one-third of the sauce and the rest of the beans, and spread the rest of the sauce over the beans. Cover with the cheese and bake just long enough for the cheese to melt and brown a little in a 375° oven. Serves 5 or 6.

LAMB WITH BROAD BEANS, CRANBERRY BEANS, OR STRING BEANS

1½ lbs. neck of lamb
Kitchen Bouquet and honey
oil
1 cup diced onions
salt and pepper
2 teaspoons orégano

2 lbs. shelled broad or cranberry
 beans or 1 lb. string beans cut in
 ½-inch lengths
2 tablespoons lemon juice
½ cup tomato sauce

Have the lamb cut in big cubes and paint them with a mixture of Kitchen Bouquet and honey. Brown them over a brisk flame in some oil, then put them in a casserole. Sauté the onions in the pan the meat glazed in and then add them to the meat. Add seasonings, herbs, and ½ cup water, cover tightly, and braise gently for 30 minutes. Then add the beans, the lemon juice, and tomato sauce. Cover and finish cooking—another ½ hour or until the meat is tender. Serve with steaming brown rice cooked in consommé. Serves 4 as a vegetable, more as an hors d'oeuvre.

CRANBERRY BEANS

Cranberry beans—the meaty bean that is red-speckled—more often found in the markets dried, are very good fresh. They may be cooked the same ways as broad beans—stewed, dressed with butter or bacon, or creamed and made into soup. Cooked with oil, they are fine when tossed in a green salad mixed with fresh tarragon leaves.

FAVA OR BROAD-BEAN SOUP

2 lbs. broad beans	1 bay leaf
2 oz. salt pork or bacon	2 teaspoons basil
1 cup diced onions	1 qt. chicken consommé
1 white turnip, diced	½ cup light cream (optional)
1 stalk celery, thinly sliced	TOP
salt and pepper	grated Parmesan cheese

Shell the beans—choose young ones; they are the best. Dice the pork or bacon and fry it until it is crisp; scoop it out of the grease and reserve it to sprinkle over the soup when it is done. Sauté the onions in the grease until they are a little colored; then add the vegetables, salt, pepper, bay leaf, 1 cup water, and basil. Cook until the vegetables are tender, about 20 minutes. Do not drain. Take ½ cup beans out and purée the rest through a sieve or electric blender; then add the remaining beans and the consommé to the vegetable purée. If desired, add the cream. Add the crisp bacon or pork and sprinkle cheese over the top of each soup plate. This should be the consistency of cream. Serves 4.

STEWED BROAD BEANS

1 onion, diced	salt and pepper
¼ cup olive oil	½ teaspoon powdered fennel
2 lbs. broad beans, shelled	1 bud garlic, crushed (for serving cold)

Sauté the onion in olive oil a little, then add the beans and cook 2 or 3 minutes. Add ⅓ cup water, cover tightly, and simmer about 20 minutes or until the beans are tender. The pressure cooker takes from 6 to 9 minutes, depending on the age of the beans. Add the salt and pepper and fennel and serve hot. If the beans are to be served as an antipasto or tossed in a green salad, add the garlic to the olive oil and add the fennel after the beans are cold. More olive oil should be added if they are served cold. Serves 4.

BROAD BEANS IN CREAM

3 strips bacon or 1 of salt pork,   ½ cup cream
  diced   1 teaspoon cornstarch
1 onion, sliced   chopped parsley, green onions, or
2 lbs. broad beans, shelled   chives
salt and pepper

Fry out the bacon or fat pork and scoop out the crisp pieces and reserve for sprinkling over the top of the beans with the parsley or chives. Cook the onion in the grease for a few minutes over a gentle flame and proceed as directed in the recipe for Stewed Broad Beans. When the beans are done, blend the cream with the cornstarch, add, boil up the beans, empty into a serving dish, and garnish. Serves 4.

BUTTERED LIMA BEANS

¼ cup butter   ½ teaspoon honey
6 green onions, diced   1 teaspoon basil
2 lbs. lima beans, shelled   GARNISH
salt and pepper   chopped parsley or chives

Put the butter and onions in the bottom of the pot and sauté for 1 minute; then add the beans, 3 tablespoons water, and the other ingredients. Cover tightly and steam the beans tender. The pressure cooker takes 1 minute if the beans are young. Do not drain. Garnish with chopped parsley. For creamed lima beans, add ¼ to ⅓ cup heavy cream when the beans are done. Serves 4 to 6.

LIMA BEANS AND CORN

⅓ cup diced onions   1 cup cooked corn
1 small green pepper, sliced   salt and pepper
¼ cup butter   ⅓ cup cream
1½ lbs. lima beans, cooked as for
  Buttered Lima Beans

Sauté the onions and sliced green pepper in the butter until tender. Combine all the vegetables, seasoning, and cream. Heat and serve.

Lima beans are very good combined with baked small mushrooms and cream; also with halved boiled chestnuts, cream, and a dash of nutmeg. Serves 5 or 6.

LIMA-BEAN PURÉE WITH HAM

6 or 8 green onions, minced
3 or 4 tablespoons butter
2½ lbs. lima beans, shelled
salt and pepper
¼ teaspoon nutmeg
1 teaspoon basil

1 teaspoon honey or brown sugar
⅓ cup cream
1 tablespoon cornstarch
1 cup fluffy ground ham

GARNISH

chopped parsley or chives

Sauté the onions in butter 1 minute, add the shelled beans, and cook, covered, until tender with 3 tablespoons water, seasonings, basil, and honey. Mix the cream with the cornstarch, add the beans, mash or purée them, then add the ham. If 1 cup ham is too much, add it to suit your taste. The mixture should be fluffy. Bake for 5 to 7 minutes in a greased baking dish until the mixture is hot. Sprinkle with parsley or chives. This dish may be made also with soaked and cooked dried lima beans. Serves 4 to 6.

Note: Cream of Lima-Bean Soup may be made in the same way as Fresh Pea Soup (page 252).

LIMA-BEAN AND FRESH-PEA CASSEROLE

6 green onions, chopped
⅓ cup butter
2 lbs. lima beans, shelled
2 lbs. peas, shelled
rosemary or fresh dill

salt and pepper
1½ cups light cream
2½ tablespoons cornstarch
¾ cup grated cheese

Sauté the onions in the butter for 1 minute. Then add the beans and peas, ⅓ cup water, the herb, and salt and pepper. Cover tightly and steam until the vegetables are tender. Blend the cream with the cornstarch, add all the vegetable liquid, cook the sauce until it thickens. Add ¼ cup of the cheese to the sauce, season with salt and pepper, and mix with the vegetables. Put the vegetables in a greased casserole and sprinkle the top with the rest of the cheese. Bake until the dish is well heated and the cheese melts. A very good sauce for vegetables cooked this way may be made with half cream and half chicken consommé. To make this a big party dish, ½ pound mushrooms, baked in a little butter for 6 minutes, may be added to the sauce. Serves 7 or 8.

DRIED LIMA-BEAN CASSEROLE

1 lb. dried lima beans
3 strips salt pork or good bacon
1 cup diced onions
½ cup diced celery
1 green pepper, diced
2 buds garlic, crushed (optional)

⅔ cup ground ham (optional)
2 tomatoes, skinned, seeded, and chopped
3 tablespoons honey or light molasses
salt and pepper

Soak the beans in 3 cups of water overnight after they are washed. Do not drain, but see that there are 3 cups water on them and let them simmer ½ hour. Cut the pork or bacon in small pieces and fry it out, then scoop out the crisp pieces. Cook the onions, celery, and green pepper in the grease until they are almost tender. For variation, the garlic and ham may be added. Mix the tomatoes with the sautéed vegetables, add the honey and seasonings, and combine with the beans. Drain off some of the bean water if it seems too much and use it for basting the beans. Put the mixture in a greased baking dish and bake about 40 minutes. Do not bake too long, or the beans will become mushy. Just before removing the beans add the crisp bacon pieces to the top. A little hot heavy cream added to the top is another very good variation. Serves 8.

MINESTRONE

1 cup dried kidney beans
6 cups fresh water or broth
2 or 3 strips bacon or ham fat, cut in 1-inch lengths
2 big onions, diced
2 buds garlic, crushed
1 carrot, diced
1 stalk celery and leaves, cut fine
2 potatoes, diced
⅓ cup olive oil
salt and pepper

2 teaspoons basil
2 cups shredded cabbage
2 cups skinned, seeded, and chopped tomatoes
½ cup red wine
½ cup cooked or uncooked pasta or egg noodles
1 teaspoon grated lemon rind
handful chopped parsley
GARNISH
grated Parmesan cheese

Wash the beans (chick peas may be used) and soak in 2 cups water overnight. In the morning add the fresh water or broth. Fry out the bacon or ham fat and when it is browned scoop it out. Sauté the onions in the fat and add to the beans. Add the garlic. Simmer 1 hour. Put the carrot, celery, and potatoes in the olive oil, season, add basil, and cook a few minutes, then stir in the cabbage and chopped tomatoes. Stir them around well and after the beans have simmered with the onion 1 hour add these vegetables and simmer ½ hour more. Add the wine and cooked pasta—or uncooked pasta may be added and cooked another 15 minutes. The fine shell egg noodles are the best. Add the lemon rind and chopped parsley when the soup is done. This is best if it stands for 1 hour and is then reheated. Pass Parmesan cheese. This soup is traditionally thick, but it may be thinned out a little for serving as a soup course, if desired. Otherwise it is a complete meal. In Italy sautéed mushrooms, sliced zucchini, fava beans, sliced sausages, and sautéed eggplant are often added. Makes about 2 quarts of soup.

JAMAICA RICE AND "PEAS"

1¼ cups dried kidney beans
1 fresh coconut, grated, or ⅔ cup
   powdered coconut
2 strips bacon or salt pork, diced
1 big onion, diced
salt and pepper

2 buds garlic, crushed
1 teaspoon hot pepper sauce
1 tablespoon mixed herbs
1½ tablespoons brown sugar
2 cups brown rice, washed

Wash the beans and soak them in 4 cups water 12 hours. Do not drain but let them simmer 1 hour or more, until they are tender. Drain the water and pour it while it is hot over the grated fresh coconut, let it stand 5 minutes to make an infusion, then drain, squeezing the coconut hard to extract all the liquid. Discard the coconut. (If powdered coconut is used, just add it to the water.) If there are not 2¼ cups liquid, add water. Sauté the bacon or pork in the bottom of a heavy pot and when it is cooked a little add the onion and fry until it is a little colored. Then add all the other ingredients, including the rice and beans. Pour the coconut-bean water over all, cover tight, and cook over the lowest flame 45 minutes. This should be a little more moist than boiled rice; if it becomes dry add a very little boiling water. The Jamaicans call this dish "Rice and Peas," no matter whether they use beans, horse peas, or other legumes. If hot Jamaican pepper sauce is not available, a little chili sauce and cayenne may be used, or curry powder. Do not add too much condiment or the flavor of the coconut will be lost. This will serve 10 or more people and is excellent when left over and reheated.

KIDNEY BEANS WITH BURGUNDY

1 lb. kidney beans
2 big onions, diced
1 green pepper, diced
1 bud garlic, crushed
4 tablespoons bacon fat

½ teaspoon mustard
1 teaspoon chervil or tarragon
salt and pepper
1 cup Burgundy
4 strips bacon

Wash and soak the beans overnight in water 1 inch above the beans. Do not drain, but simmer them 1 hour with a little of the onion. Sauté the rest of the onion, the pepper, and the garlic in the bacon fat 2 or 3 minutes. When the beans have cooked 1 hour add the pepper, onions, garlic, mustard, herb, salt, pepper, and Burgundy. Add the bacon to the top. Cover and bake 2 hours. Add boiling water when necessary, as the beans must be kept moist. Little sautéed pork sausages may be buried in the beans if desired. Sour cream may be passed to serve with the beans. Serves 8 to 10.

CASSOULET OF BLACK OR WHITE BEANS

3 cups dried beans
2 big onions, diced
2 carrots, diced
5 whole cloves
salt and pepper
1 smoked pork butt
2 tablespoons oil

⅓ cup honey or molasses
6 thin slices pork fat or bacon
6 pork sausages
6 Czech, Hungarian, Italian, or
   Spanish spiced sausages
½ cup red wine
¼ cup rum

Wash the beans and soak them overnight in water enough to come 2 inches above the top of the beans. When ready to cook, do not drain them but put them in a big pot with the onions, carrots, 3 cups more water, cloves, 1 tablespoon salt and ½ teaspoon pepper. Cover and simmer them for 1½ hours. Meanwhile, wash the pork butt and simmer it ½ hour in 2 cups water. Reserve this water for basting the beans. When the beans have cooked, put the oil in the bottom of a big casserole, add half the beans, then the pork butt and the rest of the beans. Dribble the honey or molasses over the top, then add the slices of pork fat or bacon. Cover and bake slowly 4 or 5 hours, basting occasionally. Prick the sausages two or three times with a pin and sauté them a few minutes in a little fat or oil. Bury them in the beans ½ hour before the cassoulet is done and add the red wine. More salt

and pepper may be necessary, but taste the beans before you add it.
When the dish is done add the rum. This will serve 10 or 12 and is
a fine dish for a party or buffet supper.

BAKED PINK (PINTO) BEANS OR BROWN BEANS

1 lb. pinto or brown beans	1 cup tomato sauce
1 lb. chopped beef or 2 slices salt pork	1 tablespoon chili powder (optional) salt and pepper
1 cup chopped onions	3 tablespoons brown sugar
½ lb. mushrooms, sautéed	1 bud garlic, crushed (optional)

Wash the beans and soak them overnight in 3 cups water. Let them
simmer in the water until they are tender. If beef is used, sauté it a
little in some fat with the onions. (Beef, mushrooms, garlic, and chili
powder with pinto beans make a Mexican dish.) If the pork is used,
cut it in small pieces and sauté the onions with it. Mix all the ingredients you use with the beans after they have simmered until they are
tender, then put them in a bean pot or casserole and bake 40 minutes.
Beans should be moist, so when necessary add boiling water or hot
tomato juice to baste them. Serves 8.

PURÉED BEAN SOUP

baked beans—any kind	broth or milk	chopped parsley

Purée beans in an electric blender, or through a sieve, with broth
or milk to the right consistency, and add chopped parsley to the soup
plates. This is the most delicious bean soup if you bake your own
beans.

BEANS WITH CHEESE SAUCE

1 cup cream	2 cups baked beans
1 cup shredded Cheddar cheese	toast or mashed potatoes

Put the cream in the top of the double boiler and add the cheese.
Stir over hot water until the cheese is melted, then warm the beans in
the sauce. Serve over toast or mashed potatoes. Any of the foregoing
baked-bean recipes, or Boston baked beans, may be used. Serves 4
to 6.

FRENCH FLAGEOLET GREEN BEANS

½ lb. flageolet beans

6 strips hickory-smoked bacon

2 onions, diced

salt and pepper

2 teaspoons basil

1½ teaspoons honey

1 green pepper

2 buds garlic, crushed

⅓ cup olive oil

The little French light green beans have many uses. Wash them and soak them at least 6 hours in 2½ cups of water. Do not drain, but boil them gently for 10 minutes. Cut the bacon in 1-inch pieces, fry it until crisp, then add the bacon pieces to the beans. Sauté the onions until a little yellow in the fat, drain a little fat, and add the onions to the beans with the seasoning, basil, and honey. The bacon fat may be added to the beans later if they are dry. See that the beans begin baking with ⅔ cup liquid, and bake, covered, 1½ hours. Roast a whole green pepper in the oven 15 minutes or until it is tender. Skin and seed it. Cut the pepper in strips and marinate with the crushed garlic and olive oil. When the beans are done mix in the pepper, oil, and garlic. This may be eaten hot or cold. When cold, it is a fine hors d'oeuvre. It makes fine stuffing for Chard Rolls (page 178). The beans may be mixed with sour cream and served as an hors d'oeuvre or they may be tossed with a green salad. Serves 7 or 8 as hors d'oeuvre, and 5 as a vegetable.

BEETS

It is a good rule, when you are cooking beets for dishes other than soups, to scrub them well and boil them in not more than 2 cups water, so that the resulting fine red liquid may be used in sour-cream salad dressing or in aspic or a soufflé. Always leave 1-inch stems on the beets to prevent their bleeding. Beets may also be baked in their skins (see page 128), a fine way to preserve their full flavor. Beets mixed with sour cream, puréed beet soup, and beet soufflé provide dishes not only of fine flavor but of spectacular beauty, with colors ranging from deep creamy pinks to rich ruby reds. When the beets are young their stems and leaves make excellent greens and may be cooked like spinach or dandelion.

BEET AND ORANGE SOUP

2 lbs. beets
4½ cups lukewarm water
1 teaspoon salt
¼ teaspoon pepper
½ teaspoon thyme

1⅓ cups tomato purée (10½-oz. can)
1 cup strained orange juice
GARNISH
sour cream
minced green onions

Scrub the beets well but do not peel them. Grate the beets or slice them paper-thin. Add the water and simmer them 20 minutes. Strain and add the seasonings. Simmer the tomato purée 10 minutes very gently to remove the raw taste; then add it and the orange juice to the beet liquid. This soup may be served hot or cold. Add 2 tablespoons sour cream and 1 tablespoon minced green onions to each soup plate. Serves 6.

BEET AND DUCK OR GOOSE SOUP

BROTH
bones and skin of 1 duck or goose
1 onion, chopped
1 carrot, chopped
beef bones (if available)
2 tablespoons cornstarch
leftover gravy (if available)

1 bunch new beets
juice of 1 lime or lemon, strained
1 tablespoon brown sugar or honey
GARNISH
minced green onions
sour cream (optional)

Put the duck bones and skin, the chopped onion and carrot, and the beef bones in a pot with 2½ quarts water, and simmer for 2 hours. There should be 2 quarts of broth. Strain it and let it cool. Blend the cornstarch with a little cold broth to form a smooth paste, and thicken the rest of the broth with the mixture. Leftover gravy, which always gives richness to soup, may be added. Scrub the beets well, so that the water they cook in may be used. Cook them, whole and unpeeled, in 1¾ cups water until tender. If they are small they will take from 20 to 25 minutes. When they are tender, slip their skins with your hands. Strain the water and reserve it. Dice the beets and add them to the beet liquid with the lime or lemon juice and the sweetening. Add the beets and juice to the broth and let it stand an hour before heating it to serve. This is a very fine soup. Garnish with minced green onions and serve with a bowl of sour cream if desired. Serves 8 to 10.

BEET AND CHERRY SOUP

8 new beets
2 tablespoons chopped onions
1 teaspoon salt
1 cup pitted sour cherries
4 whole cloves

2 tablespoons honey
juice of 1 lime or lemon
GARNISH
sour cream

Scrub and grate or slice the beets very thin. Boil them gently 25 minutes with 5 cups water and the onion. Strain, but do not press the beets. Add the salt to the liquid. Simmer the cherries in 1 cup water with the cloves very gently for 8 or 10 minutes; add the honey and lime or lemon juice. Combine the cherries and their liquid with the beet juice. Chill and serve garnished with 1 or 2 tablespoons sour cream on each plate of soup. This is a delicious summer soup. Makes about 6 cups.

RUSSIAN OR POLISH BORSCHT

BROTH
cubed soup beef
bones
ham bone
1 cup chopped onions
2 carrots, chopped
salt, pepper, thyme

8 beets
1 cup shredded cabbage

3 potatoes, peeled and cut in large cubes
4 white onions, sliced
1 cup tomato purée
juice ½ lemon
2 tablespoons brown sugar
2 tablespoons cornstarch
GARNISH
sour cream
2 knackwurst, sliced and sautéed

Make the broth by simmering the ingredients with 10 cups water for 2 hours; then strain. Scrub the beets; do not peel them but grate or slice them paper-thin. Cook the beets in 4 cups water gently for 25 minutes; strain and add the liquid to the strained beef broth with the cabbage, the potatoes, the sliced onions, and the tomato purée. Simmer gently until the vegetables are done—about 30 minutes. Add the lemon juice and sugar. Blend the cornstarch with 3 tablespoons cold liquid, soup or water, and add. Serve hot and garnish each plate of soup with sour cream and two or three slices of knackwurst that have been browned in oil or butter. This hearty peasant soup provides a main dish for lunch or supper. Makes 2 to 2½ quarts soup.

CLEAR BEET SOUP WITH CUCUMBERS AND SOUR CREAM

2 or 3 bunches new beets
1 large Bermuda onion
6 cups lukewarm water
salt and pepper
juice of ½ lime
2 tablespoons brown sugar or honey

GARNISH
sour cream
thinly sliced cucumbers
chopped chives

Scrub the beets and slice or grate them without peeling them. Peel and slice the onion very thin. Put the beets and onion to cook with the lukewarm water and simmer for 25 minutes. Strain and add the seasonings, lime juice, and sweetening to the liquid. If you use honey, mix in 1 tablespoon and taste before adding more. Honey is sweeter than brown sugar. Chill and add the garnish to each soup plate—1 or 2 tablespoons sour cream, 3 slices cucumber, and a sprinkling of chopped chives. Makes about 6 cups.

PURÉED BEET SOUP

8 new beets
1 small onion, chopped
1¾ cups clear chicken consommé
   (optional)
½ teaspoon powdered cloves

salt and pepper
juice of 1 lemon
1 or 2 tablespoons honey
strained orange, grape, or grapefruit juice

Scrub the beets and simmer with 2 cups water and the onion until tender, about 20 minutes. Strain and reserve the juice the beets cooked in. Skin the beets and cut them fine. Either press them through a sieve with some of the beet juice, or, better, purée them in an electric blender, thinning to a proper consistency with the rest of the beet juice and the consommé. Add all the seasonings and, if it is necessary to thin the soup more, add some fruit juice. The soup is rather delicate in texture, so it should not be thinned too much. It is the most beautiful color. It is good served plain, but sour cream and chopped chives or green onions may be added to each soup plate. The soup is delicious too if you omit the onion and consommé and thin with an undiluted can of grape juice concentrate and grapefruit juice. Makes about 6 cups.

BEET ASPIC FOR SALAD

recipe for Puréed Beet Soup
gelatin

GARNISH
watercress
Beet-Juice Salad Dressing

For every cup of purée soak 1 teaspoon gelatin in the lemon juice or fruit juice for a few minutes. Heat the soup, add the gelatin, and stir until it is dissolved. Pour into a fancy mold and chill until set. Unmold on a large plate, garnish with watercress, and serve Beet-Juice Salad Dressing (page 131). This may also be made in small molds and used as garnishing for salad.

BEETS IN ORANGE SAUCE

2 bunches new beets
1 tablespoon vinegar (optional)
1 tablespoon grated orange rind
¾ cup orange juice
juice of ½ lime or lemon
1½ tablespoons cornstarch

salt and pepper
⅛ teaspoon powdered cloves or
    nutmeg
3 tablespoons butter
GARNISH
chopped chives

Scrub little new beets and cook them in 1½ cups water until they are tender. A tablespoon of vinegar may be added to the water when cooking beets, to retain their color. When they are tender, strain and reserve the water. Skin the beets. Put the orange rind and juice, cornstarch blended with the lime or lemon juice, salt, pepper, clove or nutmeg, and the butter in a saucepan and let it simmer until it thickens. Add ¼ cup of the strained beet juice to the sauce. Add a little brown sugar or honey to taste if the sauce needs it. Heat the beets in the sauce, empty the beets and sauce into a serving dish, and sprinkle with chopped chives. Large beets may be cooked and dressed this way, but slice them into the sauce. Serves 4.

BEETS IN POMEGRANATE SAUCE

8 new beets
½ cup pomegranate juice

1½ teaspoons cornstarch
1 tablespoon honey

Boil and skin the beets as directed for Beets in Orange Sauce. Peel a pomegranate and press the seeds against a sieve to extract the juice. Mix the juice with the honey and the cornstarch. Cook the juice until it thickens and heat the skinned beets in the sauce. This juice gives a delightful and different flavor to beets. Serves 4.

BEETS IN WINE SAUCE

8 new beets
½ cup red wine or ⅓ cup sweet vermouth
3 teaspoons cornstarch
salt and pepper

2 tablespoons butter
¼ teaspoon powdered cloves
GARNISH
chopped green onions or chives

Boil the beets as directed for Beets in Orange Sauce. Strain the beet water and use enough of it with the wine or vermouth to make 1 cup. Blend the cornstarch with this liquid; then combine it with the rest of the ingredients and cook until the sauce thickens. Skin the beets and heat them in the sauce. A little sweetening may be added to taste. Small beets should be left whole, and more than 8 may be cooked if needed; large beets should be sliced. A cup of sauce is sufficient for beets to serve 6.

BEETS IN CRANBERRY SAUCE

2 or 3 bunches small beets, boiled or baked
1½ cups cranberries

½ cup orange juice
¼ cup brown sugar or 3 tablespoons honey

Skin the cooked beets. Boil the cranberries in the orange juice until they are soft, then mash them through a sieve or purée them in the electric blender and sieve them to remove the skins. Add the sweetening to taste and heat the beets in the sauce and serve hot. This makes a nice change when served with turkey. Serves 6.

PICKLED BEETS

8 new beets, baked or boiled
¼ cup tarragon vinegar or sweet vermouth
salt and pepper
⅓ cup red wine

2 tablespoons honey or brown sugar
1 teaspoon powdered cloves
1 teaspoon cinnamon

Skin the cooked beets. Boil up the other ingredients together and pour them over the beets. Cool and chill. Serve with cold meats. Serves 4.

PURÉED BEETS WITH SOUR CREAM

2 bunches new beets
3 tablespoons butter
salt and pepper
2 or more tablespoons lemon juice
¼ teaspoon nutmeg or powdered
 cloves

2 tablespoons brown sugar or 1
 tablespoon honey
2 tablespoons fresh onion juice
¾ cup thick sour cream
TOP
chopped chives or green onions

Cook the scrubbed beets in 2 cups water until tender. Strain the liquid and skin and slice the beets. Mash the beets through a sieve, with 2 or 3 tablespoons liquid, if necessary, and mix with the next six ingredients. Put the purée in a baking dish, cover with sour cream, and heat 5 minutes in the oven. Sprinkle the top with chives or onions and serve. Serves 4 to 6.

BAKED BEETS

1 dozen new beets
butter

salt and pepper
¾ cup minced green onions

Choose young beets of uniform size, if possible, for baking. They are nicest if they aren't larger than golf balls, for then they will bake in 50 to 60 minutes. Leave an inch of stem on the beets and wash them well. Put them in a 350° oven for ½ hour; then turn the heat down to 325° so they won't dry out or burn. When they are tender, peel them and put them in a saucepan with plenty of melted butter, salt, pepper, and the onions. Heat and serve. Baking beets is an excellent way of keeping in all their flavor.

BOILED OR BAKED BEETS WITH SOUR CREAM

12 boiled or baked beets, whole or
 sliced, skinned
salt and pepper
1 tablespoon lemon juice
2 teaspoons brown sugar

1 cup sour cream
2 tablespoons butter
GARNISH
chopped chives or green onions

Reheat the beets in a saucepan with all the ingredients. These amounts are sufficient for 12 small beets. Empty them into a serving dish and sprinkle with chopped chives or onions.

GLAZED LONG BEETS

1 16-inch beet   salt and pepper
butter or chicken fat   *GARNISH*
1 tablespoon brown sugar or honey   chopped chives or green onions

Scrub the beet and cut it in 3 pieces but do not peel it. In 2 or 3 cups water, boil the thickest piece for 15 minutes, then add the middle piece, cook 10 minutes more, and add the slender end. Continue cooking until the beet is tender. In the pressure cooker the thick end of the beet takes 35 to 40 minutes. The cooker, of course, has to be opened twice to add the 2 smaller pieces. Peel the beet when it is tender and slice it in ½-inch slices. Put butter or fat in a skillet with the sweetening and glaze the beets a nice light brown. Season and sprinkle with chopped chives or onions. This will serve 6.

BEET SOUFFLÉ

8 new beets (3 scant cups diced)   4 egg whites, beaten until stiff
2 tablespoons honey   *SAUCE*
juice of 1 lemon   water from cooking beets
2 tablespoons fresh onion juice   ½ teaspoon cornstarch (optional)
½ teaspoon powdered cloves   dash of powdered cloves
salt and pepper   dash of salt
4 large egg yolks   honey to taste
¼ cup cornstarch   1 teaspoon lemon juice
⅓ cup fruit juice—orange, grape,
   or grapefruit juice

Scrub the beets and cook them in 2 cups water until they are tender. Drain and keep the liquid. Skin and dice them. Mash them through a sieve with the next five ingredients. Add the egg yolks. Blend the cornstarch with the fruit juices and add to the beets. All the ingredients except the egg whites may be puréed in the electric blender. Fold in the stiffly beaten whites last and pour into a well-greased 9-inch baking dish and bake at 350° about 30 minutes. The soufflé should be moist inside. For the sauce, thicken the beet juice with a little cornstarch, if desired, season with clove, salt, honey, and lemon juice, and heat. This may be passed separately. This handsome dish would be fine to serve 6 for luncheon, or, for dinner, goes well with almost any meat or poultry.

BEET-GREENS PUDDING

2 cups ground beet greens
3 tablespoons cornstarch
¼ cup light cream
3 green onions, ground
4 large egg yolks
1 tablespoon lemon juice
salt and pepper
4 egg whites, beaten until stiff
1 teaspoon basil or ½ teaspoon
  powdered cloves

2 tablespoons honey

SAUCE

½ to ¾ cup beet-greens juice
1 teaspoon cornstarch
cream
salt and pepper
1 tablespoon lemon juice
1 tablespoon honey
¼ cup Parmesan cheese
chopped green onions

The greens must be cut from very young new beets to make a good pudding. When they are ground, stems and leaves, press them against a sieve to extract ½ to ¾ cup juice, and reserve this for the sauce. Blend the cornstarch with the cream and mix all the ingredients with the ground greens and onions, folding in the stiffly beaten whites last. Pour into a greased baking dish ˉnd bake 25 minutes at 350°. For the sauce to serve over the pudu..ig, blend the cornstarch with the beet-greens juice and add cream to make 1 cup, seasoning, lemon juice, and honey. Cook until it thickens, add some chopped green onions, and serve in a sauce boat. Serves 4 to 6.

BEET SALAD

2 cups cooked diced or julienne
  beets
minced fresh tarragon
chopped green onions or chives
julienne sticks of tart apple
sliced oranges
grapefruit segments

shredded young cabbage
finely sliced celery hearts
salad greens
hard-boiled eggs
French dressing or Sour-Cream
  Mayonnaise

Lightly mix the beets with the tarragon and green onions or chives and any of the vegetables or fruits mentioned. Put on a bed of crisp greens. Sieve hard-boiled egg over the top. Dress with either salad dressing. The beet mixture may be put in a bowl and emptied in a form on a bed of greens. A well-known beet salad is a mixture of beets with onions and marinated herring cut in 1-inch lengths. This salad should be made fresh with a light touch or it is apt to be sticky. Many prefer the fish served separately.

Sour-Cream Mayonnaise for Beet Salad

2 eggs, beaten	1 tablespoon fresh onion juice
½ cup scalded milk	1 tablespoon brown sugar
1 teaspoon salt	2 tablespoons butter
1 teaspoon mustard	⅛ teaspoon pepper
⅓ cup lemon juice	1 cup sour cream

Put all the ingredients except the sour cream in the top of a double boiler and cook, stirring continuously, over simmering water until the mixture thickens and coats the spoon. Cool thoroughly and mix with sour cream. Store in a glass Mason jar in the refrigerator.

BEET-JUICE SALAD DRESSING

½ cup sour cream	1 tablespoon tarragon vinegar
¼ cup cold juice from cooked beets	salt and pepper
	1 teaspoon honey or brown sugar
1 tablespoon lemon juice	2 tablespoons olive oil

Mix all the ingredients for the dressing and toss with salad greens just before serving. Boston lettuce is not good with this. The greens must be crisp ones, such as chicory or romaine, for a cream dressing.

COLD BEETS IN SOUR CREAM

6 or 8 cooked small beets	2 teaspoons light brown sugar or 1 tablespoon honey
1 cup heavy sour cream	
1 tablespoon lemon juice	¼ cup chopped chives or green onions
salt and pepper	

Cool the beets and cut them in short julienne sticks or dice them. Mix all the other ingredients and let the sauce stand 1 hour in the refrigerator. Mix with the beets just before serving. Serve for summer suppers or for buffets.

CLEAR BEET ASPIC

8 new beets	gelatin
4 cups warm water	juice of 1 lemon, strained
6 whole cloves	orange, grapefruit, or grape juice,
2 tablespoons honey	strained
salt and pepper	½ cup white or red wine

Scrub the beets well but do not peel them. Grate them into the warm water, add the cloves, and simmer for 20 minutes. Strain without pressing the beets through the sieve so the liquid will be clear. Add honey and seasoning. Soak the gelatin in the lemon juice, using 1 teaspoon gelatin for every cup of liquid. If 6 cups of aspic are required, measure the beet liquid and add enough fruit juice to make 5½ cups—this will allow for the ½ cup of wine. Melt the soaked gelatin and lemon juice in the hot beet juice and, when it has cooled, add the wine. Pour into small greased molds, or into a large fancy mold or ring, and chill until set. Any amount of beet aspic may be made by increasing the amount of clear fruit juice. The small molds make good garnishes for salad or cold meat or fish platters. A fancy large mold or ring may be garnished with greens and served with dressing. A ring may be filled with a fruit or vegetable salad. Both this and the aspic made with Puréed Beet Soup (page 126) make beautiful dishes for buffet or summer entertaining.

BEET SAUCE FOR BOILED FISH

⅔ cup sour cream	2 tablespoons horseradish
salt and pepper	1 cup finely diced or mashed
1 tablespoon lemon juice	cooked beets

Mix the first four ingredients and add the beets just before serving. Otherwise, if allowed to stand, the beets will lose their color in the sour cream. This sauce may be served hot or cold over hot or cold fish.

BROCCOLI

Broccoli should be cooked standing up in the bottom of a double boiler, the way asparagus is, with the stems immersed in water; the flowerets will steam tender under the inverted double-boiler top. If no more water is added than is necessary, all of it may be reserved for sauce, soup, or part of the liquid for Broccoli Soufflé. Broccoli belongs to the more aristocratic branch of the cabbage family and is served with richer sauces. Perhaps the most popular way to serve it is with a Hollandaise sauce. Its flavor calls for a dash of lemon, egg, chopped ham, or cheese. Like asparagus, broccoli may be served cold with vinaigrette sauce. To prepare it, trim the coarse stalks and peel any thick stems up to the flowerets; then soak it 5 minutes in salted water. Split the thick stalks so they will cook more quickly. Rinse, drain, and tie in bunches; or if it is not to be served whole, slice it and cook quickly in salted water. Whole broccoli cooks in 15 to 18 minutes. If it is overcooked the color and taste become dull. When broccoli is young and fresh the buds are still closed.

CREAM OF BROCCOLI SOUP

2 cups cooked or uncooked
  chopped broccoli
¼ cup chopped onions
1 small green pepper, chopped
3 tablespoons butter
milk

¾ cup light cream
1 teaspoon curry powder
salt and pepper
  GARNISH
chopped green onions
sour cream

The soup may be made of leftover broccoli or fresh broccoli. Sauté the onion and pepper in the butter. If fresh uncooked broccoli is used, slice it fine and add it to the sautéed onions and green pepper, cover tight, and steam until all the vegetables are tender. One-half cup water may be added and used in the soup. Purée the vegetables; the electric blender is best for this. Thin with milk and the cream. Add the curry powder and seasonings. Garnish with green onions. The cream may be omitted and 1 or 2 tablespoons lemon juice added. Garnish each plate with 1 tablespoon sour cream. This is good hot or cold. Serves 4.

STEAMED BROCCOLI WITH CHEESE SAUCE

1 large bunch broccoli
salt and pepper
1 pea-sized lump beef extract
2 tablespoons grated onion

1 tablespoon cornstarch
¼ cup cream
⅓ cup grated cheese
juice of ½ lemon

Cook the broccoli standing up in the kettle with an inverted kettle that fits to cover it, if your double boiler is too small. Sprinkle salt and pepper over the broccoli and add 2 cups hot water. Cover and steam until it is tender, about 15 minutes or less. Lift the broccoli out and let it keep warm in the top kettle. Add the beef extract to the liquid in the pot and let it melt. Dissolve the cornstarch in 2 tablespoons cold water and stir it in. Add the other ingredients and cook gently until the sauce thickens. Lift the broccoli onto a platter and pour the sauce over it. More cheese may be sprinkled over the top. Parmesan cheese is a good cheese for broccoli. This recipe makes use of all the nourishment in the vegetable, as no water is drained off. Serves 4 to 6.

BROCCOLI WITH NUT SAUCE

1 large bunch broccoli
salt and pepper
⅓ cup dry crumbs

⅓ cup butter
⅓ cup browned, coarsely ground
cashew nuts, pecans, or walnuts

Salt and pepper the broccoli, steam it in very little water. Brown the crumbs in the butter. Drain the broccoli and put it on a hot platter. Mix the crumbs and nuts and sprinkle them over the broccoli. Add more melted butter if necessary. Serves 4 to 6.

BROCCOLI CASSEROLE

¼ cup chopped onions
1 green pepper, sliced
3 tablespoons butter
1 bunch broccoli

1⅓ cups light cream
3 tablespoons cornstarch
salt and pepper
⅔ cups shredded Cheddar cheese

Cook the onions and green pepper in the butter for 2 minutes. Slice the broccoli and add it and 1 cup water. Cover tight and cook until tender. Blend the cornstarch and cream in a saucepan and drain the vegetable water into it. Cook until this sauce thickens and season with salt and pepper. Put alternate layers of vegetables and sauce in a greased casserole, finishing with sauce. Cover with the cheese and bake in a hot oven until the cheese browns. Serves 6.

BROCCOLI LOAF

2 lbs. fresh broccoli or 3 cups
   cooked, chopped broccoli (or
   other vegetable)
¼ cup minced onions
2 tablespoons butter
2 tablespoons flour

⅓ cup grated cheese
2 eggs, beaten
1½ cups cooked brown rice
salt and pepper
1 teaspoon basil or tarragon

Any leftover green vegetable, or a mixture of vegetables, may be used for this loaf. Cauliflower may be used in it. If mashed potatoes are used, omit the rice. Two cups of breadcrumbs may be used instead of the rice. They must be fluffy and dry, not powdered. If fresh vegetables are used they should be coarsely chopped, cooked, then drained of the juice, which may go into a sauce for the loaf. Sauté the onions in the butter 2 or 3 minutes, add them to the vegetable, and stir in all the other ingredients. Bake in a greased loaf pan 30 minutes at 350°. To make this loaf a company dish, a fine sauce may be made with the vegetable liquid and ½ cup light cream, thickened with cornstarch or flour and seasoned with a dash of sherry, ½ cup cheese, or 1 cup sautéed mushrooms. Serves 6.

BROCCOLI OMELET

1 cup cooked chopped broccoli
6 eggs, beaten
1 tablespoon chopped parsley
salt and pepper
2 tablespoons grated onion

¼ cup cream
3 tablespoons butter
     GARNISH
olive oil
grated Parmesan cheese

Mix the first six ingredients together. Melt the butter in an omelet pan, coating the bottom and sides. Pour in the mixture and cook until it is nicely browned, lifting the edges so the uncooked part runs into the pan. When done and still moist on top, fold once and lift onto a hot platter. Pour a little olive oil on top and sprinkle liberally with cheese. This is a broccoli version of *frittata al verdi*. Serves 4 or 5.

BROCCOLI RING
(or Kale, Spinach, Chard, or Dandelion and Sorrel Ring)

1½ lbs. broccoli or other green vegetable

3 large green onions, minced

3 tablespoons butter

1 cup vegetable juice and light cream

salt and pepper

1 teaspoon chervil or tarragon

⅓ cup flour

3 egg yolks

½ lb. knackwurst, ground

3 egg whites, beaten until stiff

GARNISH

creamed seafood or vegetable

Slice the broccoli—or clean and cut up any leafy vegetable. After cleaning and removing the roots of the vegetable used there should be about 1 pound, 3 ounces. Sauté the onions in the butter, add the broccoli, cover tight, and steam till tender. (The pressure cooker takes but 30 seconds for spinach and 1 or 2 minutes for the broccoli or other greens.) A tablespoon or two of water may have to be added to the broccoli. When the vegetable has cooked press it a little to extract the liquid. Measure the liquid into a cup and fill with light cream. Purée the vegetable with the liquid. If an electric blender is used add the seasonings, flour, and egg yolks before puréeing; otherwise stir them in afterwards. Skin and grind the knackwurst; there should be 2 cups. Mix it with the vegetable and fold in the stiffly beaten whites of eggs. Pour into a very well greased ring and bake 30 minutes at 350°. Let it stand 2 minutes after it comes from the oven. Loosen all the edges with a knife, cover with an inverted round serving plate, and turn the ring over. If it breaks a little, build it up. Fill the center with creamed peas or any filling you choose. Creamed shrimp or crabmeat would make a complete main course for lunch or supper. Dandelion greens and a few sorrel leaves make a delicious ring. Serves 8.

BROCCOLI ITALIAN STYLE

1 large bunch broccoli

salt and pepper

2 buds garlic, crushed

½ cup olive oil

⅓ cup ground ham

⅓ cup grated Parmesan cheese

Season and steam the broccoli, drain it, and put it on a hot platter. Warm the garlic in the olive oil, add the ham, and spread it over the broccoli. Sprinkle the top with Parmesan cheese. Serves 4 to 6.

BROCCOLI WITH HOLLANDAISE SAUCE

1 large bunch broccoli   **salt and pepper**

Season and steam the broccoli until just tender. Meanwhile, make the sauce (see below). Drain the broccoli and put it on a hot platter. See that no water collects in the dish with it; if it does, drain it. Add the Hollandaise Sauce and serve immediately. If preferred, the sauce may be served in a sauceboat. This may be served as a separate course. Serves 4 to 6.

HOLLANDAISE SAUCE

½ cup butter   **5½ tablespoons hot water**
1 tablespoon lemon juice   **salt and pepper**
4 egg yolks, beaten

Put 3 tablespoons of the butter in the top of a double boiler with the lemon juice and beaten egg yolks. Cook over simmering water, beating continuously, until the sauce thickens, then add 3 more tablespoons butter and continue beating. When it is smooth add the rest of the butter, and when the butter is melted add the hot water. Beat until the sauce thickens again and season with salt and pepper.

BRUSSELS SPROUTS

One of the most attractive fall and winter vegetables is the little cabbage-shaped Brussels sprout. It cooks tender in 7 or 8 minutes in very little liquid. Small sprouts take less than a minute in the pressure cooker. Sprouts should never be cooked until they are soft, for their charm is their delicate but firm texture and pretty shape. Wash sprouts in lukewarm salted water, trim them, rinse in cold water, and drain. They combine well with cream and broth sauces, mushrooms, chestnuts, and cheese. They do not go as well with chicken or fish as they do with pork and other meats. When buying them, select compact, firm sprouts with bright green leaves.

BRUSSELS-SPROUT SOUP

1 qt. Brussels sprouts
6 or 8 cups rich veal or chicken
    consommé
2 tablespoons butter
2 tablespoons cornstarch

2 tablespoons lemon juice
¼ teaspoon nutmeg
1 teaspoon brown sugar or honey
GARNISH
grated Parmesan cheese

Wash and trim the sprouts. Remove the two or three good, big outer leaves of the sprouts and simmer them 10 minutes in the consommé, then mash them through a sieve. Cook the rest of the small sprouts in the butter and very little water—2 or 3 tablespoonfuls until they are just tender. Blend the cornstarch in 2 tablespoons cold consommé or water. Add to the soup and cook until it thickens. Add the sprouts and their liquid, lemon juice, seasoning, and honey. Serve hot, dipping three or four sprouts with soup into each plate, and sprinkle cheese over the top. Serves 6 or 8.

BUTTERED SPROUTS

1 qt. Brussels sprouts
2 spring onions, minced
3 tablespoons butter

salt and pepper
chopped parsley

Wash and trim the sprouts. Cook the onions and butter in the bottom of a heavy pot a few seconds, then add the sprouts and 2 or 3 tablespoons water. This will be sufficient water if some clings to the sprouts after washing them. Cover tight and steam gently until they are just tender. Sprouts may also be steamed over boiling water, but it will take a little longer. Season, empty into a hot serving dish, and sprinkle chopped parsley over them. Serves 4 to 6.

BRUSSELS SPROUTS WITH CHEESE

1 qt. Brussels sprouts
2 or 3 buds garlic, crushed
¼ cup olive oil

salt and pepper
½ cup grated Parmesan cheese

Wash and trim the sprouts. Put the garlic and olive oil in a heavy pan and after they have cooked a few seconds add the sprouts and mix them around in the oil so they are covered with it. Sprinkle with salt and pepper, add 3 tablespoons water and the cheese. Cover tight and bake in the oven about 10 minutes, or until the sprouts are tender. If they are done in a baking dish they may be served in it. Pass a bowl of cheese to add to the sprouts. Serves 4 to 6.

BRUSSELS SPROUTS CASSEROLE

1 qt. Brussels sprouts
3 tablespoons butter
2 spring onions, minced
light cream
salt and pepper

dash of nutmeg
3 tablespoons flour, or 2 table-
  spoons cornstarch, mixed with
  water
sliced Cheddar cheese

Cook the sprouts with the butter and onions as directed in the recipe for Buttered Sprouts. Drain the liquid into a cup and add enough light cream to make 1½ cups. Season with salt, pepper, and a dash of nutmeg. Heat, stir in flour or cornstarch, and cook until thick. Add the sprouts to the sauce, empty into a greased casserole, and cover with the cheese. Heat in a 375° oven until the cheese melts and browns a little. This may be doubled for serving a big party. Cook 15 small white onions and mix with the sprouts and sauce for variation. Cheese or buttered crumbs, or a combination of both, may top the casserole. Grate cheese to mix with crumbs. Cooked chestnuts or baked mushrooms in butter may also be used in this dish. Serves 6.

BRUSSELS SPROUTS WITH CHESTNUTS

1 qt. Brussels sprouts
2 tablespoons butter
2 tablespoons fresh onion juice
salt and pepper
beef broth

3 teaspoons cornstarch
15 cooked chestnuts, halved or
   quartered
¼ teaspoon nutmeg

Wash and trim the sprouts and cook in ½ cup water, butter, and onion juice. Season with salt and pepper. Add enough broth to the sprout liquid to make 1½ cups. Broth may be made (if necessary) with beef extract and boiling water. Blend the cornstarch with a little cold water or broth, add to the sauce, and cook till thickened. Season with nutmeg and salt and pepper. Add the chestnuts to the sauce and combine with the sprouts. Heat and serve. Sprouts and chestnuts may be bound together with cream sauce also, but this broth sauce is excellent. Serves 6.

BRUSSELS SPROUTS WITH POTATOES

1 qt. Brussels sprouts
⅓ cup butter
4 medium-sized potatoes

salt and pepper
paprika

Cook the sprouts with part of the butter as directed in the recipe for Buttered Sprouts. When they are done add the rest of the butter. Boil, skin, and rice the potatoes while hot. Season, mix as lightly as possible with the buttered sprouts, and empty into a serving dish. Sprinkle the top with paprika. If necessary, heat in the oven before serving, but this dish is better made at the last moment. Serves 8.

CABBAGE

Cabbage, that old standby, plebe among the vegetables, has been more in evidence on the dining tables of the peoples of the world than any other green vegetable, and has kept them well nourished. When this writer was growing up in the Middle West there was a Polish family whose young girls, one after another as they came of age, furnished our household with servants. We learned that in their family, whenever a youngster was ill, the mother sent him or her to the cellar to eat sauerkraut and drink its juice to .ure the ailments of childhood. The method seemed to work.

In the cookery of various countries this vegetable has often suffered at the hands of unimaginative cooks, and its reputation has suffered in consequence. There is no reason why this precious vegetable should not take its deserved place among the best of its companions of the garden. It must be redeemed by careful cooking: it must not be cooked in much water; it must not cook long; it must be crisp and of good color when it comes to the table. Any vegetable which is so good in its raw state requires only short cooking. Chinese or celery cabbage, elongated in shape and tender of leaf, may be treated in the same way as the other varieties. It is excellent buttered or creamed or raw in salads, and this is true also for Savoy cabbage, red cabbage, and the curly varieties. The head cabbage should take its rightful place among its cousins: kohlrabi, cauliflower, broccoli, collards, and Brussels sprouts.

POT AU FEU

4 lbs. brisket or bottom round of beef
split bones and marrow
2 tablespoons malt vinegar
bouquet garni: celery, thyme, bay leaf, basil, tied together
4 big onions, diced
1 small cabbage, finely shredded
1 large potato, diced
2 large skinned tomatoes, chopped
2 turnips, diced
2 parsnips, diced
2 carrots, diced
½ cup finely chopped celery
4 cloves
4 whole allspice
salt and pepper

Some like the rich brisket, and some prefer lean beef. If the meat is in one piece cut it in four large squares. Wash it. Put the meat, bones, 4 quarts cold water, and vinegar on to simmer slowly and when the liquid forms scum, skim it until it is all clear. Add the bouquet garni and all the finely cut vegetables and spices. Do not add the salt and pepper until the pot has simmered 1½ hours. In all, simmer very gently for 3½ hours, covered. When the soup is done, let it cool in the pot, then remove the meat and bones and put the soup in quart Mason jars. When it is entirely cooled put it in the refrigerator. Allow a cake of fat to form on top, and remove the fat. When heating to serve, mix the soup well and heat as much as is required at a time. It is better made the day before serving. Any leftover beef or fowl bones may be added while this soup is cooking. If it is too thick add more water.

CREAM OF CABBAGE SOUP

3 cups shredded new cabbage
3 tablespoons butter
1 bunch green onions, diced
2 cups hot water
1 tablespoon lemon juice
1 small potato, diced

2 cups hot chicken consommé
1 cup light cream, scalded
¼ teaspoon mace
salt and pepper
GARNISH
grated Parmesan cheese

Wash and drain the cabbage well before it is shredded very fine. Melt the butter in a heavy pot. Add the cabbage and onions. Stir the vegetables over a gentle fire a few minutes; then add the hot water, lemon juice, and potato. Cover and simmer 20 minutes. Add the hot consommé and hot cream. Season. The soup may also be sieved or puréed before the broth and cream are added. Garnish with cheese after it is served. Makes about 6 cups.

DOLMAS

cabbage, vine, or lettuce leaves
STUFFING NO. 1
1½ cups ground lamb or beef
¼ cup minced green onions
1 cup cooked brown rice or breadcrumbs
¼ cup olive oil
1 egg, beaten
salt and pepper
1 teaspoon orégano
a few minced mint leaves
¼ cup currants or raisins
¼ cup chopped parsley

½ teaspoon each cinnamon and
  allspice
1 tablespoon honey
1 teaspoon thyme
½ cup pine nuts (pignolias)
STUFFING NO. 2
1 slice steer or calf liver, ground
1 cup ground ham, beef, or lamb
selected seasonings from Stuffing
  No. 1

½ cup broth or water
¼ cup olive oil or butter

Real dolmas are always rolled in vine leaves. If you have no Syrian or Greek store nearby, they may be made of cabbage or lettuce leaves. These stuffings may also fill scooped-out tomatoes, cucumber boats, eggplants, or green peppers. Select big leaves from new, tender cabbage. Cover with boiling water and drain thoroughly after 5 minutes. They should be soft enough to roll. (Lettuce leaves should not be left in the water, just blanched, or they will be too soft.) The meat may be leftover or raw. If raw, brown it a moment in olive oil. Do the same with the green onions. Diced cooking onions may be used, in which case sauté them until just tender. Mix all the stuffing ingredients well and put the stuffing (amount according to size of leaves) on each leaf and roll the leaves, tucking in the ends as for a package. Lay the little rolls close together in a pot, so they will not unwrap, add ½ cup broth or water and ¼ cup olive oil or butter. The bottom of the pot may contain a bed of 1 cup shredded cabbage or leaves. Cover very tightly and cook very gently 1 hour. The dolmas may be served with sauce made of the liquid in the pot thickened with a little cornstarch—or with tomato sauce, yoghurt, or sour cream, mushroom sauce, or mustard sauce; or they may be served plain, either hot or cold. Little ones make delicious hors d'oeuvre served cold.

PORK OR ITALIAN SAUSAGE IN CABBAGE LEAVES

young cabbage leaves
boiling water
sausages
2 or 3 tablespoons oil
dry crumbs or corn meal

salt and pepper
1 tablespoon honey
1 teaspoon beef extract
2 shots Angostura bitters
½ cup sour cream

Blanch the cabbage leaves in boiling water until they are tender enough to roll, then drain well. Brown the sausages a little in the oil over a brisk fire. If the leaves are small use two for each roll. Sprinkle them with very little meal or crumbs, lay a sausage on each roll, and roll the leaves up like a package, tucking in the ends. Lay them close together in a heavy skillet or pot, sprinkle with salt and pepper and the honey. Melt the beef extract in ½ cup boiling water, add it with the bitters. Cover tight and simmer 40 or 45 minutes, turning the rolls once or twice. If the rolls are not tightly wrapped, they should be tied with a little white string. If the sauce becomes too thick add 2 or 3 tablespoons boiling water. When done the sauce should be almost like caramel. Lift the rolls to a hot platter, add the sour cream to the pot, and when it is hot and well mixed pour it over the rolls. This is a very fine dish.

BUTTERED CABBAGE

1 young cabbage   **salt and pepper**
butter   **paprika, basil, or marjoram**

Cut the cabbage in quarters or in eighths, depending on its size. Soak a few minutes in cold water until the leaves become crisp, then drain well. Melt 2 or 3 tablespoons butter in the bottom of a heavy pot and add the cabbage but no water; enough clings to the leaves. Add the seasonings, cover tight, and bring to a simmer over a medium flame. This will give the cabbage a chance to form enough steam to cook without burning. Cook until it is just tender, about 8 to 10 minutes, or less than 3 minutes in the pressure cooker. Never drain off the precious liquid. Either drink it, serve with the cabbage, put it into soup, or thicken it a little with ½ teaspoon cornstarch and serve with the vegetable. A little butter or cream or a little broth may be added to make more sauce.

CABBAGE WITH CHEESE SAUCE

recipe for Buttered Cabbage   **2 tablespoons flour or cornstarch**
              SAUCE   **salt and pepper**
cabbage liquid plus light cream to   **¼ teaspoon nutmeg or mace**
  make 1 cup
2 tablespoons butter   **½ cup grated cheese**

Drain off the liquid from the boiled cabbage, measure, and add cream to make 1 cup. If there is a quantity of cabbage more sauce may be required. Melt the butter in a saucepan and blend in the flour. Add the liquid gradually and cook until it thickens, then add the seasonings. (Or use cornstarch and blend it with the cream. It makes a more transparent sauce, but the flavor is the same.) Put the cabbage in a greased baking dish, add the sauce, and cover the top with the cheese. Heat in a 375° oven until the cheese melts and browns a little.

BAKED CABBAGE AND APPLES

1 small cabbage	salt and pepper
2 large tart apples	½ teaspoon powdered anise
½ cup fresh grapefruit juice	⅓ cup sour cream
3 tablespoons butter	

Select a young medium-to-small cabbage and shred on a disk shredder. Peel the apples and shred them. Mix with the cabbage. Do not salt before cooking or too much juice will form. Put the cabbage and apples in a greased 8-inch baking dish and add the grapefruit juice. Cover with a tight lid, or, lacking that, tie aluminum foil over the top. Bake 30 minutes in a 350° oven. Boil up the butter, seasonings, and cream and pour over the cabbage. This dish may be simmered in a heavy pot or pressure cooker; put in layers of cabbage and apple with ⅓ cup melted butter poured over the top, cover, and cook until tender. Season after it is done. McIntosh apples are good for this dish as they cook so quickly. Serves 4 to 6.

CORNED BEEF AND CABBAGE

corned brisket of beef	carrots (optional)
garlic buds, slivered	turnips (optional)
3 or 4 whole cloves	white onions (optional)
2 or 3 bay leaves	1 new cabbage, quartered
1 teaspoon pepper	*GARNISH*
2 onions, sliced	mustard sauce

Soak the meat 15 minutes in cold water, drain it, and stick garlic slivers in slits in it. Tie the meat with string so it will keep its shape. Put it in a big pot with cloves, bay leaves, and the pepper and sliced onions. Cover with lukewarm water and bring slowly to a boil. Boil very gently until a fork pierces the meat easily, from 3½ to 5 hours. Carrots, turnips, and onions may be added, as for New England Boiled Dinner, or you may use only cabbage. Taste the liquid and if it is too salty take a cup of it and add fresh water to boil the vegetables. If the liquid is not too salty add the carrots, turnips, and onions ½ hour before the meat is done, and the cabbage 15 minutes before. Cook white potatoes separately to serve with it. They may be boiled in their jackets or mashed.

NEW ENGLAND BOILED DINNER

6- or 7-lb. piece of ham
6 or 8 young carrots
6 or 8 young white turnips
6 or 8 white onions
6 or 8 potatoes, peeled

1 new cabbage, cut in sixths or
  eighths

GARNISH
mustard sauce

Soak the ham overnight. Bring it to a boil for 2 or 3 minutes, then drain. It must be freshened because all the vegetables cook with it. Simmer the ham 1 hour in fresh water. Heat the carrots, turnips, and onions in boiling water, drain, and add to the ham. After they have cooked 15 minutes heat the potatoes and cabbage the same way, add, and cook until the potatoes are just done. All the vegetables should be whole. This does not need salt. Lift the ham to a platter and put the well-drained vegetables around it. Serve with mustard sauce. Serves 6.

HAM AND CREAMED CABBAGE

1 ¾-inch slice tenderized ham
butter
1 head new cabbage
light cream

2½ tablespoons cornstarch
salt and pepper
grated cheese

Cook the ham, covered, in a little butter slowly 15 minutes. Then cut it in strips to facilitate serving. Coarsely shred the cabbage and steam it tender as directed in Buttered Cabbage. Drain off the liquid and add enough light cream to make 2 cups. Blend the cornstarch with the liquid, season with salt and pepper, and cook it until it thickens. Put half the cabbage in a greased baking dish, add the ham, the rest of the cabbage, and then add the cream sauce. Cover with plenty of grated cheese—Cheddar is good for this. Bake in a 375° oven until it is hot and the cheese browns a little. Serves 4 to 6.

CABBAGE SLAW WITH FRUIT

2 or 3 cups grated young cabbage
choice of:
  seedless grapes
  cantaloupe or melon balls
  sliced peaches
  julienne tart-apple sticks
  cherries, pitted

2 tablespoons honey
sour cream
¼ cup minced green onions
salt and pepper
lemon juice
powdered anise or fennel

Prepare the cabbage and fruit and have them cold. Do not combine until ready to serve. There isn't anything worse than a soppy, separated salad. As may be observed, cabbage is fine with almost any fruit—one or more may be used. Toss the fruit lightly with the cabbage. Dribble 2 tablespoons honey over it, and add the other ingredients to taste. One-half cup of sour cream or more may be needed, according to the amount you are making. Anise gives a delightful fragrance to this salad. This is a fine summer salad but is appropriate for any menu where cabbage salad is required.

WARM CABBAGE SALAD

2½ to 3 cups shredded or grated
  young cabbage
¼ cup minced green onions
¼ cup sour cream
1 tablespoon simple syrup
       SAUCE
2 eggs, beaten

½ cup very weak vinegar
1 teaspoon salt
1 teaspoon curry powder or turmeric (optional)
¼ teaspoon pepper
¼ teaspoon mustard (optional)
2 tablespoons butter

Mix the cabbage with the onions, cream, and syrup. Put all the ingredients for the sauce except the butter in the top of a double boiler. If curry powder is used, omit the mustard. Cook over boiling water until the sauce thickens, then stir in the butter until it melts. Pour hot over the cabbage and serve immediately. More cabbage may be used if required.

SAUERKRAUT

white firm fall cabbage   **salt**

Sauerkraut is made in the fall and winter because it requires mature cabbage and low temperatures. Shred the cabbage on a disk grater quite fine. Young green cabbage does not make good kraut. Put 2 cups cabbage in the bottom of an earthenware jar with a lid and sprinkle with salt. Repeat in this way until the jar is full. Then add water until it may be seen when the kraut is pressed with the back of a spoon. Cover and let stand in a cool—not too cold—place. In two or three days it will have fermented. Occasionally press it a little to be sure the water is almost to the top of the cabbage. Sauerkraut is an excellent food, rich in vitamins. The juice is a refreshing and healthful drink and is particularly good if mixed with tomato juice, half and half.

SAUERKRAUT WITH GRAPES

1½ lbs. sauerkraut   **½ cup boiling water**
⅓ cup diced onions   **1½ cups seedless grapes**
2 tablespoons butter

Wash the sauerkraut in cold water and drain. Sauté the onions in the butter 2 or 3 minutes; add the sauerkraut and the boiling water. Cover and cook gently for 12 minutes. Add the grapes and cook 1 more minute. This dish is fine served with game. Serves 4 to 6.

SAUERKRAUT WITH KNACKWURST OR SAUSAGES

1½ lbs. sauerkraut   **½ cup boiling water**
⅓ cup diced onions   **1 teaspoon powdered caraway or seeds**
2 tablespoons butter   **knackwurst or sausages**

Wash the sauerkraut, sauté the onions in the butter, and cook with the sauerkraut as directed in Sauerkraut with Grapes. Add the caraway. Boil the required number of knackwurst 10 minutes, drain, and lay on the cooked sauerkraut after it is emptied in a serving dish. If sausages are used, brown them and serve with the kraut. This makes a good supper dish served with mashed potatoes and a good mustard. Serves 4 to 6.

SHOULDER OF PORK WITH SAUERKRAUT
(Hungarian)

2 lbs. pork (boneless meat from shoulder)	2 tablespoons sweet Hungarian paprika
2 large onions	1½ cups sauerkraut
oil	sour cream
salt	

Cut the pork in good-sized cubes. Dice the onions fine and cook them in a little oil in a heavy pot until they are light yellow. Add a little salt and paprika. When they are well mixed add the pork. Simmer 10 minutes, stirring occasionally. Add ⅓ cup water, cover, and cook until the meat is tender. Cover the sauerkraut with cold water and drain. This is done to remove some of the sharpness, for this dish must be delicate. Add the sauerkraut to the meat and cook for 10 minutes, then add 1 cup sour cream and cook no more than 1 minute so that it is lightly mixed and heated. Serve immediately and pass more sour cream to add to the top of each serving. This is one of the finest goulashes. Serves 4 or 5.

SPARERIBS WITH SAUERKRAUT

3 lbs. fresh spareribs	salt and pepper
oil, honey, or brown sugar	1½ lbs. sauerkraut
1 cup ground onions	½ cup broth
1 cup ground carrots	1 teaspoon caraway powder or seeds

Cut the spareribs in 4-inch servings and brown them in hot oil and a dash of honey or brown sugar. Mix the ground vegetables and put half of them in the bottom of a roaster and season with salt and pepper. Lay on half the spareribs, then all the sauerkraut and the rest of the spareribs. Then cover with the rest of the ground vegetables. Add the broth mixed with the caraway. Cover tightly and bake 20 minutes in a 375° oven and 20 minutes at 325°. If this is done in a large casserole it may be served from it at the table. Mashed or boiled potatoes in their jackets are good to serve with rich and tart dishes. Serves 4 to 6.

SAUERKRAUT WITH RAISINS AND SOUR CREAM

2 lbs. sauerkraut
1 medium-sized onion, sliced thin
    and sautéed till tender
pinch of thyme

½ cup boiling water
⅓ cup raisins
1½ cups sour cream
paprika

Wash the sauerkraut in cold water and drain it well. Put it to cook with the onion, the thyme, and boiling water. Cover and simmer 5 minutes, add the raisins and cook 5 to 7 minutes more. Stir in ½ cup sour cream and empty into a hot serving dish. Warm 1 cup sour cream and add to the top, stirring a little but leaving the cream covering the top. Sprinkle with paprika and serve immediately. This is, to my taste, better served with goose than as a stuffing for the bird. Serves 7 or 8.

PICKLED CABBAGE

3 or 4 large cabbages, red or white
¾ to 1 cup salt
2 qts. wine vinegar
4 cups brown sugar

½ cup white mustard seed
2 red peppers, seeded and diced
1 oz. each, whole cloves, mace, all-
    spice, pepper, and celery seed

Shred the cabbage, mix the salt and water, cover the cabbage, and let stand 12 hours, then drain in a bag for 6 hours. The cabbage must be dry. Pack in Mason jars. Boil up the vinegar with all the spices and sugar. When it is cool fill the jars with the spiced vinegar and seal. If more vinegar is necessary, add a little to each jar after dividing the spiced vinegar evenly.

RED CABBAGE WITH RED WINE

1 red cabbage
2 tablespoons butter
1 big onion, diced
¼ cup sweet vermouth or claret
1 tablespoon honey or brown sugar

salt and pepper
3 or 4 tart apples, sliced
3 tablespoons butter
¼ teaspoon cinnamon
1 teaspoon cornstarch

Shred the cabbage coarsely, soak it briefly, and drain. Put the 2 tablespoons of butter and the onion in a heavy pot and sauté until the onion colors a little, then add the cabbage, the wine, honey or sugar, and salt and pepper. Cover and cook until the cabbage is just tender. This may be done in the pressure cooker and will take around 3 minutes. Peel the apples, sprinkle with cinnamon, and sauté them in 3 tablespoons butter until they are tender. Lightly mix with the cooked cabbage. Blend the cornstarch with a little wine, add it to the liquid in the cabbage and cook until it thickens. This is excellent served with duck, goose, or pork. If seedless grapes are used instead of apples, 1 cup may be added to the pot a minute before the cabbage is done; longer cooking makes the grapes limp. New white cabbage may be cooked as directed for Buttered Cabbage, and when done 1 cup seedless grapes may be added with a dash of honey and ¼ teaspoon or more of anise powder.

RED OR WHITE CABBAGE WITH CHESTNUTS

1 new cabbage, coarsely shredded
1 onion, diced
3 tablespoons butter
¼ cup sweet vermouth or red wine
1 tablespoon honey or brown sugar

½ lb. chestnuts, roasted
1 tablespoon cornstarch
½ cup cream
¼ teaspoon nutmeg
salt and pepper

Soak the cabbage briefly and drain. Sauté the onion in the butter a minute, add the cabbage, the wine, and the sweetening. Cover and cook until the cabbage is tender. Shell the chestnuts and cut them in half. Blend the cornstarch with the cream, add the seasonings, and blend with the liquid in the cabbage. Cook until it thickens like cream. Mix lightly with the cabbage and the chestnuts. This is fine with a goose dinner. One good-sized cabbage serves 8 or more.

CHINESE CABBAGE, CHINESE STYLE

1 Chinese (celery) cabbage
1 bud garlic, crushed
¼ cup soy or peanut oil
salt
1 tablespoon minced ginger root
1 tablespoon cornstarch

1 tablespoon sherry or vinegar
1 teaspoon soy sauce
GARNISH
julienne strips ham, shredded
   almonds, or minced green
   onions

Slice the cabbage thin and reserve the loose leaf ends. Put the solid half of the sliced leaves in a big frying pan or pot with the garlic and oil. Stir it 3 minutes over a gentle fire, then add the loose tender leaves, salt, and the ginger root. Cover and steam until it is tender. The Chinese fry their food in a large round-bottomed iron frying pan set on a metal collar to keep it from tipping. It is ideal for steaming, as there is so much space between the food and the lid. Blend the cornstarch with 3 tablespoons water, add the wine or vinegar and soy sauce. Stir this with the cabbage until it thickens and is well mixed. Do not cook the cabbage more than 3 or 4 minutes after it is covered. It must be crisp and fresh; this is the way the Chinese cook their vegetables. Serves 4 to 6 if served with other Chinese dishes.

CELERY CABBAGE AND POTATO SALAD

4 large potatoes
SAUCE
1½ tablespoons cornstarch
1 cup light cream
¼ cup wine vinegar
1 tablespoon brown sugar

1 teaspoon Bahamian mustard
salt and pepper

2 cups shredded celery cabbage
½ cup minced green onions

Boil the potatoes in their jackets, and meanwhile make the sauce. Blend the cornstarch with the cream, add the other ingredients, and cook over a gentle flame until it thickens, stirring continuously. Skin the potatoes and cube them. When both dressing and potatoes are lukewarm, mix them and then let them cool. A half-hour before serving, lightly combine the potatoes with the cabbage and onions. Serve cold. Serves 4 to 6.

CARROTS

The carrot is one of the principal vegetables in our gardens and in our markets. Rich in carotene, with more vitamin A than other vegetables, it is good for skin and eyes; but some people feel that the sweetish taste of cooked carrots is too affirmatively bland. This may easily be overcome by combining them with other foods of differing character: lemon and orange juice, tomatoes, onions, mint and other herbs; and by using them in soups, stews, sauces, and even with wines. Young, tender raw carrots cut in sticks are like candy; but, in cooking, this attractive crisp texture is lost, especially if the carrots are cooked too long. They must be cooked in the same way as other vegetables, in a minimum of water, and the liquid may be used in soups and in sauces to dress them. Only the big "cooking" carrots need be scraped, and sometimes they need only a scrubbing with a vegetable brush. Young new carrots never need scraping. In these days of expert care by shippers and vegetable and fruit markets, our produce comes in such good shape that there is no excuse for buying any vegetable that is not fresh or in top form. And there is little excuse for all the packaged and frozen short-cuts that we too often indulge in to save time at the expense of the complete joys of the table.

CARROT AND ORANGE SOUP

2 bunches young carrots
⅓ cup diced onions
3 tablespoons butter
salt and pepper
1 cup orange juice

dash of nutmeg
1 cup light cream
GARNISH
chopped mint or chives

Scrub the carrots, trim off the stems, and slice them thin. Sauté the onions until light yellow in the butter, add the carrots, salt and pepper, 1½ cups water, and orange juice. Cook until the carrots are tender, then mash them through a sieve with the liquid or purée in the electric blender. If the soup is thicker than cream, dilute with juice. Add the nutmeg and cream. Serve hot or cold, garnishing each plate with mint or chives. Makes over 1 quart of soup.

CARROT AND CHICKEN SOUP

1 bunch new carrots
½ cup diced onions
3 tablespoons butter
2 tablespoons lemon juice
salt and pepper
4 cups chicken consommé

4 tablespoons minced fresh tarragon or 2 teaspoons dried tarragon
1 cup cream (optional)
GARNISH
chives or green onions

Trim the carrots, scrub them, and slice them thin. Sauté the onions until just tender in the butter, add the carrots, the juice, salt, pepper, and ½ cup water, and cook until tender. This will take 2 minutes in the pressure cooker. Mash the carrots with the liquid through a sieve or purée in the electric blender. Mix with the consommé to the right thickness—about that of heavy cream—and add the herb. If this stands a few hours before serving, it tastes better. This may be served with or without the cream added, hot or cold. Garnish each soup plate with chopped chives or green onions. When measuring the quantities, always allow 2 cups or more for the vegetable mixture. For instance, this will make 6 cups of soup without the cream.

CARROT AND TOMATO SOUP

2 bunches new carrots
1 bunch green onions, minced
3 tablespoons butter
1 cup orange juice
1 tablespoon brown sugar

3½ cups tomatoes
salt and pepper
2 tablespoons lemon juice
GARNISH
sour cream

Trim and scrub the carrots and slice them thin. Sauté the onions in the butter 1 minute, add the carrots and orange juice, and simmer until tender. Mash through a sieve with the liquid, or purée in the electric blender. Add the sugar. Skin and slice the tomatoes, simmer a few minutes, then purée them. A large can of tomato purée may be used instead. Mix the tomato with the carrots, season with salt, pepper, and lemon juice. This may be served hot or cold. Garnish each soup plate with 1 tablespoon sour cream. Makes 6 or 7 cups.

BUTTERED CARROTS WITH HERBS

2 bunches new carrots
3 tablespoons butter
1 tablespoon lemon juice
salt and pepper

choice of herbs: minced tarragon,
mint, parsley, chervil, green onions, chives, basil

Trim and scrub the carrots. If they are very small, leave them whole; if not, cut them in two lengthwise. Put them in a heavy pot with the butter, juice, 2 or 3 tablespoons water, salt, and pepper. Cover tight and simmer gently until they are tender, about 10 or 12 minutes. The pressure cooker will take about 2 or 3 minutes. They must never be soft and limp. (They may also be steamed over boiling water, which takes somewhat longer, and seasoned and dressed with butter after they are cooked.) Put them in a hot serving dish, add more melted butter, and sprinkle liberally with several tablespoons of the chosen vegetable or herb. Serves 4 to 6.

CARROTS WITH LEMON OR ORANGE SAUCE

1 bunch new carrots
1 tablespoon lemon juice
salt and pepper
3 tablespoons butter
1 tablespoon cornstarch

3 or 4 tablespoons lemon juice or
⅓ cup orange juice
2 or 3 tablespoons honey
1 tablespoon chopped parsley

Cook the carrots with ⅓ cup water, 1 tablespoon lemon juice, seasonings, and butter, as directed for Buttered Carrots with Herbs. While the carrots are cooking blend the cornstarch with the lemon juice or orange juice, sweeten to taste with honey, and add this to the liquid the carrots cook in when they are done. Cook until the sauce thickens. If it is too thick, thin with a little additional orange juice; more lemon might make it too tart. Empty into a serving dish and sprinkle with parsley. Serves 3 or 4.

BRAISED LAMB WITH CARROTS

2½ lbs. breast or shoulder of lamb
1 bud garlic, crushed
⅓ cup olive oil
1 cup diced onions
1 green pepper, diced
salt and pepper
½ cup tomato sauce

1 cup broth
1 bunch new carrots
2 teaspoons orégano
2 tablespoons cornstarch
⅓ cup white wine
GARNISH
chopped parsley

Cut the lamb in servings. Put the garlic, oil, onions, and green pepper in the bottom of the pot or roaster the lamb is to be cooked in and let them simmer 1 minute; then add the lamb and cook 5 minutes over a gentle flame, stirring it frequently. Season with salt and pepper. Do not let it burn. Add the tomato sauce and broth, cover tight, and let the lamb roast at 325° for ½ hour. Trim, scrub, and cut the carrots in 1½-inch lengths. Let them boil up just to heat through, drain, and add to the lamb with the orégano. Let the dish cook slowly until the lamb is tender, perhaps 1 hour more. Blend the cornstarch with the wine, add it to the dish when it is done, and let the sauce thicken. Serve, sprinkling the top with chopped parsley. Serves 4.

CARROT MEAT LOAF

1 cup shredded raw carrot
1 cup shredded raw potato
1 lb. ground beef
1 slice beef liver, seared and ground
1 cup diced onions
fat or oil
1 cup sliced mushrooms
salt and pepper
½ teaspoon clove

1 teaspoon each, tarragon, thyme, and marjoram
⅓ cup corn meal or whole-wheat flour
½ cup tomato sauce or catsup
⅓ cup milk
2 egg yolks
2 egg whites, beaten until stiff
5 strips bacon

Mix the carrot, potato, beef, and liver. Sauté the onions in a little good fat or oil, sauté the mushrooms also, and mix them with all the other ingredients (except the bacon), folding in the stiffly beaten egg whites last. Line a greased baking dish with the bacon, mostly on the bottom, and add the mixture. Cover and bake ½ hour at 325° and another hour at 300°. This may be served from the dish or emptied on a chop plate. Brown the bacon and lay it on top. If much juice forms, a little tomato sauce may be added; thicken it with a little cornstarch and pour it over the top. This is a fine dish and may be sliced cold as well as served hot. Serves 6.

CARROTS BAKED WITH ROAST MEATS

roast pork or braised beef   sweet potatoes or white potatoes
1 bunch new carrots

When roasting meats—pork loin or braised short ribs of beef—30 to 45 minutes before the meat is done, boil up and drain whole scrubbed carrots and peeled potatoes (sweet potatoes for pork) and add them to the meat. The carrots will be browned, glazed, and delicious cooked this way. They may be added to rib roast of beef also, and to lamb.

CARROTS CURAÇAO

2 bunches new carrots	3 tablespoons butter, melted
grated rind 1 orange	salt and pepper
½ cup orange juice	butter
¼ cup light corn syrup	1 jigger curaçao

Trim, scrub, and shred the carrots. Mix the first six ingredients together and put in a baking dish. Add a few small bits of butter to the top and cover very tight. Bake at 325° 35 minutes. Do not add any water. When the carrots are done add a jigger of curaçao or any orange liqueur and serve immediately. Serves 6.

CARROTS BAKED WITH SHERRY

1 bunch new carrots	2 tablespoons honey
¼ cup melted butter	⅓ cup sherry
salt and pepper	

Trim, scrub, and shred the carrots on the finest disk shredder. Mix with the other ingredients, put them in a greased baking dish, and bake, covered, at 350° for 20 minutes. Uncover and bake 15 minutes more at 300°. Serves 4.

MASHED CARROTS

2 bunches new carrots
⅓ cup orange juice
2 tablespoons grated onion
salt and pepper

¼ cup butter
½ cup heavy cream
dash of nutmeg or mace
1 teaspoon grated orange rind

Scrub and trim the carrots, cut in thin slices, and steam in the orange juice. When they are tender, mash them with all the ingredients and serve immediately in a hot serving dish. Serves 4 to 6.

NEW CARROTS OR BEETS WITH POMEGRANATE SAUCE

1 pomegranate
1½ teaspoons cornstarch
honey to taste

1 bunch new carrots or beets,
cooked with butter

Mash the pomegranate seeds against a sieve to extract the juice. Blend ½ cup juice with 1½ teaspoons cornstarch and sweeten it to taste. Add this to the liquid the vegetable cooked in and cook until it thickens. Serves 3 or 4.

MASHED CARROTS AND WHITE TURNIPS OR PARSNIPS

1 bunch carrots
1 lb. white turnips or parsnips
⅓ cup melted butter

½ cup cream
salt and pepper
chopped parsley (optional)

Cook the carrots with butter, lemon juice, and water, as directed for Buttered Carrots with Herbs, omitting the herbs. Scrape or peel the turnips or parsnips and cook them the same way, separately. When they are done, mash the vegetables together with the butter, cream, and seasonings. Empty into a hot dish, dot the top with butter, and sprinkle with chopped parsley if desired. Serves 4 or 5.

CARROT RING

7 or 8 new carrots (2½ cups
  mashed carrots)
2 tablespoons lemon juice
1 teaspoon mustard
2 tablespoons grated onion
2 tablespoons chopped parsley
1½ teaspoons salt

½ teaspoon pepper
2 tablespoons flour
2 tablespoons melted butter
1 cup soft breadcrumbs
1 cup light cream, scalded
4 egg yolks, beaten
4 egg whites, beaten until stiff

Cook the carrots and mash them; use 2½ cups of the mashed vegetable. Add all the rest of the ingredients, folding in the stiffly beaten whites of eggs last. Pour into a well-greased and floured ring mold, set in a pan of water and bake 30 to 35 minutes at 350°, or until the ring is set. Let it stand 3 minutes when it comes from the oven, then cover with a chop plate and empty it out. If any sticks to the mold it may be spooned out and added to build up the ring. This may be filled with creamed or buttered vegetables or mushrooms, or creamed seafood or fowl. It makes a main dish for lunch or supper or a separate course for a dinner. Serves 6 to 8.

CARROTS WITH TOMATO DRESSING

8 or 10 new carrots
¼ cup chopped onions
3 tablespoons butter
salt and pepper
⅓ cup tomato juice

2 teaspoons cornstarch
⅓ cup cream
GARNISH
chopped parsley

Cut the carrots in half lengthwise or leave them whole if they are very small. Sauté the onions in the butter 1 minute, add the carrots, salt, pepper, and 3 tablespoons water. Cover and cook gently until the carrots are tender. Do not drain. Blend the tomato juice with the cornstarch and add the cream. Cook until the sauce thickens. Empty into a serving dish and sprinkle with chopped parsley. Serves 4 to 6.

CANDIED CARROTS

1 or 2 bunches young carrots
½ cup orange juice
grated rind 1 large navel orange

3 tablespoons butter
½ cup light corn syrup
dash of nutmeg or mace

Steam the carrots in the orange juice until almost tender. (The seasonings must be increased if you have over 8 or 10 carrots.) Lay the carrots in a shallow pan or dish with the liquid they cooked in, add the other ingredients, and cook until they are thick and syrupy. Serves 4 to 6.

CARROT AND APPLE CASSEROLE

8 young carrots, shredded
2 or 3 large tart apples, peeled and
   shredded
½ cup orange juice

grated rind 1 orange
½ cup melted butter
salt and pepper

Mix the carrots and apples and put them in a greased baking dish. Pour over them the orange juice and grated rind. Cover and bake 35 or 40 minutes at 325°. When they are done, season the melted butter with salt and pepper and pour over the dish. Serves 6 to 8.

FRESH CARROT RELISH

new carrots
orange-blossom honey

lime juice
chopped mint

Shred on a fine disk shredder a mound of sweet young carrots. Dribble honey over the top, letting it seep through, and the juice of ½ or 1 whole lime, depending on the amount of the carrots. Garnish with chopped mint.

CARROT AND ORANGE SOUFFLÉ

6 or 7 new carrots (2 cups mashed carrots)
2 tablespoons honey or light brown sugar
¼ teaspoon nutmeg or mace
salt and pepper
½ cup orange juice

4 green onions, minced, or ¼ cup diced onion
⅓ cup orange juice
juice of ½ lemon
4 tablespoons cornstarch
3 egg yolks, beaten
3 egg whites, beaten until stiff

Slice or shred the carrots and cook them with the honey or sugar, nutmeg, and seasonings, ½ cup orange juice, and the onions. Blend ⅓ cup orange juice in with the lemon juice and cornstarch and cook until thick. When the carrots are tender, mash them through a sieve or purée them in the electric blender with the cornstarch mixture and the egg yolks. Fold in the stiffly beaten egg whites last. Pour into a greased baking dish and bake 25 minutes at 350°. Serves 6.

STEAMED CARROT AND DATE PUDDING

1 cup light brown sugar
1 cup flour
1 teaspoon cinnamon
½ teaspoon ground cloves
1 cup shredded raw carrots
1 cup shredded raw potatoes

1 cup chopped dates
1 teaspoon vanilla
1 teaspoon baking soda, mixed in 2 tablespoons hot water
1 egg, plus 2 egg whites, beaten
3 tablespoons melted butter

Mix all the dry ingredients and toss the carrots, dates, and potatoes through them. Mix all the ingredients except the melted butter together. Empty into a well-greased melon mold to within an inch or so from the top to allow for expansion. Cover with melted butter, put on the lid, and boil in water 2½ hours. This is one of the finest light boiled puddings to serve for holidays. It may be emptied on a platter, and 3 tablespoons whisky or rum may be poured over it and blazed. Serve with your favorite brandy sauce. Serves 10 very well.

CAULIFLOWER

Literally and etymologically this vegetable is the flower of the cabbage family and lends itself to all the respectful treatment its position merits. When cauliflower is fresh its curd is closely packed, firm, and creamy white; and when cooked with care it has a delicate flavor. When cooking cauliflower, add 1 tablespoon vinegar or lemon juice and the same of sugar, and it will keep its whiteness. It may be cooked a very short time in the pressure cooker, or it may be steamed. Too long cooking darkens its color, and its flavor becomes strong. Some cooks prefer covering it with salted water, but I have a strong feeling against cooking any vegetable in a lot of water that must be drained and thrown away. Cauliflower makes beautiful dishes, is served as an appetizer, makes delicious soups, is served with a variety of sauces, and is fine in salads.

CREAM OF CAULIFLOWER SOUP

1 small head cauliflower	1 cup milk
¼ cup chopped onion	1 cup light cream
1 small potato, diced	¼ teaspoon nutmeg
3 tablespoons butter	*GARNISH*
salt and pepper	chopped parsley, chives, or green
2 cups chicken broth	onions

Break the cauliflower into small flowerets and chop the tenderest leaves and the core. Sauté the onion and potato in the butter until they are almost tender, add the cauliflower, salt, pepper, and 1 cup water. Cover and cook until the cauliflower is just tender. This takes 3 minutes in the pressure cooker. Reserve a dozen small flowerets and mash the liquid and the rest of the vegetables through a sieve, or purée in the electric blender. Thin with the broth, milk, and cream. Add the nutmeg and more salt and pepper if necessary. Garnish with the reserved flowerets and parsley, chives, or onions. Soup may be made with any leftover cauliflower, cooked in any way, puréed and thinned with milk or broth or both. Makes 6½ to 7 cups.

BUTTERED CAULIFLOWER

1 head cauliflower
salt and pepper
1 tablespoon lemon juice

melted butter or buttered crumbs
chopped tarragon, chervil, thyme,
summer savory, or basil

Cauliflower may be left whole or separated into flowerets. Wash it in cold salted water and drain. Chop the core and tenderest leaves and make a bed in a heavy pot to lay the cauliflower on. Sprinkle the flowerets with salt, pepper, and lemon juice. If you use a steamer, put the chopped leaves and core in the bottom with 1 cup boiling water, put the cauliflower in the top part, cover, and cook until the vegetable is barely tender. This is a perfect way to cook it when it is left whole; it may be tested and cooked exactly right. To steam it in a heavy pot, lay the cauliflower on the chopped leaves, add ½ cup water, cover tight, and cook until just tender. If you cook the vegetable in a pressure cooker, add no water, heat slowly so enough moisture will form to prevent burning, and, after the pressure is up, cook it only 1 or 1½ minutes. To serve cauliflower as a vegetable, buttered, after it is cooked dress it with melted butter or fried buttered crumbs. It may be sprinkled with any of the herbs mentioned; all are good with this vegetable.

Barely half-cooked cauliflower is fine for appetizers and salads. It is cooled then chilled before serving. If cauliflower is desired very crisp and almost raw for appetizers it is separated into flowerets, covered with boiling water for 10 minutes, drained and then this is repeated. Add lemon juice and vinegar to keep it gleaming white. Let cold water run over it and then chill it.

CAULIFLOWER PARMIGIANO

1 head cauliflower
2 buds garlic, crushed
⅓ cup olive oil

salt and pepper
grated Parmesan cheese

Break the cauliflower into small flowerets and steam until they are half cooked. Drain them well. Put the garlic and olive oil in a big skillet and briskly heat the cauliflower in the pan, stirring continuously, until it browns and cooks a little. Add more olive oil if necessary. Salt and pepper, empty into a serving dish, and sprinkle liberally with Parmesan cheese. This is good served with a veal cutlet and good red wine.

CAULIFLOWER WITH VARIOUS SAUCES

Note: To go with all these sauces, cook cauliflower as directed for Buttered Cauliflower.

MUSHROOM SAUCE

cauliflower liquid plus cream to
   make 1½ cups
2 tablespoons cornstarch
salt and pepper
¼ teaspoon nutmeg

1 cup mushrooms, sautéed
2 tablespoons butter

GARNISH
chopped chives or parsley

Use the drained cauliflower liquid in making the sauce. Blend the cornstarch with a little cream, then combine with the other ingredients. Cook until the sauce thickens and pour it over the cauliflower. Garnish the top with chives or parsley.

TOMATO SAUCE

¼ cup chopped onion
¼ cup chopped green pepper
cauliflower liquid plus tomato sauce
   to make ¾ cup

3 teaspoons cornstarch
⅓ cup sour cream

GARNISH
chopped chives or grated cheese

Mix the onion and green pepper with the cauliflower leaves before the vegetable is cooked, lay the cauliflower on this bed, and cook as directed. When it is done, drain the liquid, measure it and add the tomato sauce. (Very good tomato sauce comes in small cans.) Blend in the cornstarch, heat until the sauce thickens, and add sour cream. Pour over the vegetable and garnish.

SHRIMP SAUCE

½ lb. fresh shrimp
1 sliced onion
salt
cauliflower liquid, plus shrimp
   liquid, plus cream to make
   2 cups

2½ tablespoons cornstarch
salt and pepper

GARNISH
chopped chives or grated cheese

Wash the shrimp and steam them 4 minutes in ¼ cup water, with the onion and some salt. Let them cool in the liquid, drain and peel them, and add the liquid to the cauliflower liquid. Add enough cream to this to make 2 cups. Blend with the cornstarch and cook until the sauce thickens. Add the shrimp. Put the cauliflower on a round plate and surround it with the cooked leaves. Pour the sauce over it. Sprinkle the top with grated Parmesan or Gruyère cheese or with chopped chives. This is a fine luncheon or buffet supper dish.

LEMON CAPER SAUCE

cauliflower liquid
3 tablespoons butter
3 tablespoons lemon juice
1 tablespoon grated onion
salt and pepper

1 teaspoon turmeric
cornstarch
2 tablespoons capers

GARNISH

parsley or chives

When the cauliflower has been cooked, drain the liquid and add all the ingredients except the capers, measure, and blend in 1 teaspoon cornstarch to every ½ cup liquid. Heat the sauce until it thickens, add the capers, and pour it over the cauliflower. Garnish with chopped parsley or chives. This is attractive, as the turmeric makes the sauce yellow.

PASTA SAUCE

6 oz. tiny egg-noodle shells
cauliflower liquid plus cream to
　make 2 cups
1 tablespoon cornstarch
1 teaspoon curry powder (optional)

2 tablespoons grated onion
1 teaspoon grated lemon rind

GARNISH

grated Parmesan cheese

While the cauliflower is cooking, boil the noodle shells in salted water 4 or 5 minutes and drain them. When the vegetable is done, drain off the liquid for the sauce and mix the pasta with the cauliflower and put it in a baking dish or serving dish. Add enough cream to the liquid to make 2 cups and blend with the cornstarch, curry powder, onion, and lemon rind. Cook until the sauce thickens, then pour it over the pasta and cauliflower. Cover thickly with Parmesan cheese and brown in a hot oven.

HOT OR COLD CAULIFLOWER WITH HOLLANDAISE SAUCE OR OTHER SAUCES

A whole fine cooked cauliflower may be served cold or hot, with Hollandaise Sauce (page 137). Cold cooked cauliflower may also be served with cooked peas, string beans, carrots, and other vegetables. These should all be cooked separately, cooled, and chilled. Put the whole cauliflower in the center of a chop plate and place little piles of the other vegetables around it. Dress the vegetables with good homemade oil mayonnaise or aïoli sauce—the latter is mayonnaise with as much crushed garlic added as one can take. I have had 6 buds crushed in 1½ cups mayonnaise, and it is surprising how delicious it is. This is a dish from the South of France.

OIL MAYONNAISE

2 egg yolks
¾ teaspoon salt
1 teaspoon Bahamian mustard or
  ½ teaspoon dry mustard
1 teaspoon olive oil, plus 1 teaspoon water

1¼ cups good olive oil
lemon juice or vinegar
salt and pepper
½ teaspoon turmeric

Beat the egg yolks, salt, mustard, 1 teaspoon oil, and water for 1 minute—or, better, blend them in the electric blender. Add the oil (at room temperature) a little at a time at first. When the mayonnaise begins to thicken, add the oil more quickly. Thin with lemon juice or very mild vinegar to taste. Season. Lemon juice whitens the mayonnaise, and this may be rectified by adding the turmeric, which makes it a rich yellow.

CAULIFLOWER WITH AVOCADO DRESSING

1 head cauliflower, cooked and
  chilled
watercress or chicory
½ cup oil mayonnaise

1 small ripe avocado, sieved
¼ cup sour cream
2 tablespoons fresh onion juice
3 drops Worcestershire sauce

Put the cauliflower on a chop plate and garnish the base with greens. Mix the other ingredients and pour the dressing over the top of the cauliflower. This dressing may also serve as a dip for chilled cauliflower flowerets as an appetizer. Curry-seasoned mayonnaise is also good as a cocktail dip for cauliflower.

CAULIFLOWER SALAD

1 small cauliflower, cooked and
   chilled
4 hard-boiled eggs, quartered
1 cup cooked lima beans
1 cup cooked peas
2 tablespoons capers

1 zucchini, cooked in garlic and
   olive oil and chilled and sliced
watercress or chicory
French dressing
mayonnaise

Separate the cauliflower into small flowerets. Toss the vegetables, eggs, and capers together and lay them on a bed of greens. Mix French dressing with oil mayonnaise so it is a thick creamy dressing and add. This salad may be made any required size.

PICKLED CAULIFLOWER

1 qt. vinegar
2 tablespoons mustard seed
1 cup sugar

8 whole cloves
4 sticks cinnamon
2 heads cauliflower

Simmer all the ingredients except the cauliflower together for 15 minutes. Wash the cauliflowers and cut away all the leaves. Break them into flowerets all the same size. Put them in a kettle of actively boiling water, turn the fire off, and let them stand 2 minutes. Drain and put the flowerets in Mason jars. Pour the syrup over the cauliflower, and seal. The syrup should be ready when the cauliflower is put into the jars.

CELERY AND CELERIAC

In recent years the green, tender, almost stringless Pascal celery has more or less replaced the coarse, large, light green and white varieties. There is almost no waste to good celery, for both the inner tender stalks and the outer large stalks and leaves may be braised, creamed, and made into soups. The outer stalks of Pascal celery are eaten raw and are used in many salads. Crisp celery is especially suitable in salads combined with foods of smooth texture such as shrimp, crab, lobster, poultry, and so on. A favorite appetizer for two or three generations has been stuffed celery.

Celeriac or celery knob is a root which has the flavor of celery in concentrated form. It may be peeled, sliced, and cooked tender, then dressed with butter; or it may be creamed. Celeriac is excellent added to celery soup, as it gives it a richer celery flavor. Celeriac cut in julienne sticks may be served as an appetizer or mixed in salads.

CRISP CELERY

fine, tender celery   ice water

Separate the stalks of celery and wash them well, removing any blemishes. A few of the tenderest leaves may be left on the stalks. Put the stalks in ice water which has some ice cubes in it. Let them stand in the refrigerator for at least 3 hours before serving. Drain well and serve ice-cold.

STUFFED CELERY

celery	ground cooked shrimp
cream cheese	ground lobster
sour cream	ground crabmeat
salt and pepper	anchovy paste
curry powder or mustard (optional)	Roquefort cheese
paprika	chopped chives
CHOICE OF ADDITIONS	chopped mint or tarragon
ground clams	

Prepare fine tender celery according to directions for Crisp Celery. Have the stuffing ready so the celery may be drained and filled just before serving. Make a smooth, fluffy paste with the cheese and sour cream and season it to taste, then blend in any of the additions. Fresh or canned seafood may be used. If ½ cup cream cheese is used, add at least ⅔ cup seafood. One-third cup Roquefort cheese may be sufficient for ½ cup cream cheese. If herbs are used, use only fresh herbs and stem them. Fill neatly with a knife or press the filling through a tube. After the celery is filled sprinkle the filling with paprika.

CELERY AND SHRIMP COCKTAIL

1½ cups sliced celery
½ lb. shrimp, cooked and diced
2 tablespoons chili sauce
½ cup oil mayonnaise

2 tablespoons lemon juice
¼ cup minced green onion
6 small avocado halves

Have the ingredients cold. Mix the cocktail lightly and fill the avocado halves. Serve as a first course or for a main luncheon dish. Other seafood may be used instead of shrimp. A fine main-dish salad may be made by peeling and slicing or dicing the avocado and mixing it with the celery and seafood and dressing. Serve on watercress or shredded lettuce.

CELERY SANDWICH

hearts and leaves of crisp celery
cream cheese
sour cream
mayonnaise

salt and pepper
curry powder or horseradish
whole-wheat bread
butter

Dice crisp celery, hearts and leaves, quite fine. Just before making the sandwiches, mix the cheese with a little sour cream and mayonnaise. Season to taste, butter whole-wheat bread, and spread. The sandwiches may be open, in which case the bread should be cut in small squares.

CELERY SOUP

1 bunch celery (4 or 5 cups sliced
celery)
1 celery knob, peeled and sliced
(optional)
1 large onion, diced
1 green pepper, diced
¼ cup good fat or butter
2 small potatoes, diced

1 carrot, diced
salt and pepper
1 teaspoon brown sugar
1 teaspoon chervil or savory
milk, cream, and chicken broth
GARNISH
minced green onions, parsley, or
chopped fresh mint

Clean the stalks, heart, and leaves of a good bunch of celery and slice it very fine. Unless it is cut fine the fibers prevent its being easily puréed. A celery knob, peeled and sliced, may be added for a richer celery flavor. Put with the onion and green pepper in a heavy pot with the fat or butter and sauté 2 or 3 minutes. Then add the carrot and potatoes, both finely diced, and sauté 2 minutes more over a gentle fire. Add the seasonings, sugar, herb, and 1 cup water, and simmer until the vegetables are very tender; or cook 4 or 5 minutes in the pressure cooker. Purée through a coarse sieve or in the electric blender, then dilute to a creamlike consistency with milk, light cream, and chicken broth. Add one of the garnishes to the top of each plate of soup. An excellent summer celery soup may be made without the broth, garnished with mint, and served cold. Makes 7 or 8 cups.

CELERY AND TOMATO SOUP

1 large bunch celery
3 onions, diced
2 carrots, diced
1 teaspoon beef extract
steak or roast-beef bones
salt and pepper
3 whole cloves
1 teaspoon each thyme, basil, and
tarragon

2 tablespoons cornstarch
1 15-oz. can tomato purée or
skinned, sliced tomatoes, strained
¼ cup white wine or 1 tablespoon
lemon juice or vinegar
1 tablespoon honey or brown sugar
GARNISH
sour cream or yoghurt

Clean and slice the celery thin, including the heart and the good leaves. Put the vegetables (not the tomato), beef extract, bones, seasonings, cloves, and herbs in a heavy soup kettle with enough water to be visible when the ingredients are pressed down with a spoon. Cover and simmer gently for an hour or more; or cook in the pressure cooker 40 to 45 minutes. When the vegetables are done, strain through a sieve, first removing the bones; or purée in the electric blender. Mix the cornstarch with a little of the tomato purée or strained tomatoes and add it and all the rest of the ingredients to the soup. (Mixing a little cold tomato purée with the cornstarch before adding it gives the soup a better, creamier consistency.) Simmer the soup 7 or 8 minutes. This makes 2 quarts of fine soup, and it is good hot or cold. Garnish with 1 tablespoon sour cream or yoghurt in each soup plate.

BUTTERED CELERY

1 small bunch Pascal celery
2 leeks or 4 or 5 green onions, minced
⅓ cup butter
salt and pepper
1 teaspoon cornstarch

⅓ cup stock
pinch of thyme or chervil

GARNISH

grated Parmesan cheese or chopped parsley

Wash the celery and cut the stalks and the tenderest leaves in 2-inch lengths. Sauté the leeks or onions in the butter 1 minute, then add the celery but no water. Stir it well, then cover and cook slowly 25 or 30 minutes, until the celery is tender. When it is half-cooked add salt and pepper. Stir it twice. Blend the cornstarch in the cold stock, add the herb, and stir it into the celery when it is done. When the sauce thickens pour into a hot serving dish and add a garnish to the top. Serves 4 to 6.

BRAISED CELERY WITH MUSTARD

4 cups sliced celery
4 tablespoons olive oil
2 tablespoons butter
salt and pepper

1 teaspoon fennel powder
1 teaspoon basil
⅓ cup heavy cream
1 tablespoon Bahamian mustard

Cut the celery in 1-inch lengths. Put all the ingredients except the cream and mustard in a heavy iron skillet. Put the skillet in a hot oven, uncovered, and bake at 400° for 10 minutes; then reduce the heat to 350° and cook 12 minutes more. Empty the celery into a hot serving dish. Put the cream and mustard in the skillet, heat and stir it, and when it is hot and mixed well pour it over the celery. This is delicious with game. Use tender Pascal celery. Serves 4.

BRAISED CELERY WITH CREAM AND NUTS

1 medium-sized bunch Pascal
   celery
juice of ½ lemon
1 cup beef (or chicken) consommé
pinch of marjoram or thyme
1 teaspoon simple syrup

salt and pepper
½ cup heavy cream
⅓ cup grated Cheddar cheese
¼ cup toasted chopped almonds or
   mixed nuts

Trim and cut celery into 1½- to 2-inch lengths. Wash and drain it and lay it in a shallow baking pan or casserole. Squeeze the lemon juice over it, add the consommé, herb, and syrup, and cook in the oven or on the stove slowly for 30 minutes. Drain and reduce the sauce to ½ cup in a saucepan, then add the seasoning, cream, and cheese. When the cheese is melted pour the sauce over the celery and sprinkle the top with the nuts. Serves 4.

CREAMED CELERY AU GRATIN

⅔ cup minced leeks or ½ cup
   diced onions
4 tablespoons butter
4 cups sliced celery
salt and pepper
celery liquid plus light cream to
   make 1½ cups

2 tablespoons cornstarch
1 teaspoon curry powder or ½ teaspoon chervil or basil
1 teaspoon turmeric
½ to ⅔ cup grated Cheddar cheese

Sauté the leeks or onions in the butter 2 minutes, then add the celery. Add ⅓ cup water, salt and pepper, cover tight, and cook until the celery is tender. (If you are using a pressure cooker add just 3 tablespoons water and cook 2 minutes. Reduce the pressure immediately so the celery will not cook too long.) Transfer to a fireproof serving dish. Measure the juice and add enough cream to make 1½ cups liquid. Blend the cornstarch in a little cold cream and add. Add the curry powder and turmeric, cook until the sauce thickens, and pour the sauce over the celery. Add the cheese to the top and brown in a very hot oven a few minutes. Serves 4 to 6.

CREAMED CELERY AND ONIONS

recipe for Creamed Celery au Gratin

12 or 14 little white onions

Peel and cook the onions separately with very little water. Mix the water with the celery water and cream to make the sauce, and add the onions to the celery. This will serve 8 and is an excellent combination.

CREAMED CELERY WITH VEGETABLES

recipe for Creamed Celery au Gratin
1 lb. fresh mushrooms, or ½ lb. cooked chestnuts, or ½ lb. cooked

okra, or 2 cups corn cut from ears, or 2 cups fresh cooked peas or lima beans, or 1 lb. sliced cooked celery knob

It can readily be seen that celery enhances, and is enhanced by, a variety of vegetables. To combine it with mushrooms, bake the mushrooms 10 minutes in butter, combine with the cooked celery, and pour the sauce over them. Follow these directions when combining cooked celery with any cooked vegetable.

EGG FOO YONG

1 cup onions
1 cup sliced celery
peanut oil
6 water chestnuts, peeled and sliced
6 eggs, beaten

salt
a few drops soy sauce
a handful of soy-bean sprouts (if available)

Sauté the onions and celery in oil until they are almost tender. The Chinese like their vegetables tender but crisp and not overcooked. Mix all the ingredients together and fry in cakes in oil to a golden brown on both sides. The cakes should be ½ inch thick. This is a fine luncheon dish for 4. Serve separately a cruet of soy sauce and Bahamian mustard.

CHOP SUEY

1 cup sliced onions
1½ cups sliced celery
¼ cup sliced green pepper
¼ cup peanut oil
SAUCE
1½ tablespoons cornstarch
1½ cups beef consommé
salt and pepper
1 tablespoon brown sugar

1 tablespoon soy sauce
6 water chestnuts, peeled and
  sliced
1 cup soy-bean sprouts
2 cups cooked chicken, beef, veal,
  pork, or shrimp
GARNISH
coarsely chopped browned almonds
  and chopped green onions

Sauté the onions, celery, and green pepper in the oil until they are almost tender. Then stir in the water chestnuts, bean sprouts, and the meat or shrimp. This is an excellent way to use leftover roast meats or chicken; duck or goose may also be used. Mix the cornstarch in the cold consommé, add the other sauce ingredients, and cook until it thickens. A tablespoon of minced preserved ginger may be used instead of the brown sugar. Pour the sauce over the hot meat and vegetables. Empty into a serving dish and garnish the top with almonds and green onions. Serve with hot brown rice. Chinese dishes may be made even more attractive with a garnish of julienne strips of ham or chicken. Serves 4, or more if served with many other dishes.

CELERY IN SALADS

One or two cups of chilled crisp tender celery may be added to Cabbage Slaw (page 147), Potato Salad (page 291), and turkey or chicken salads. Celery always improves shrimp, crab, or lobster salad. Julienne sticks of celeriac chilled and marinated in vinaigrette sauce and tossed with lettuce make an excellent salad. Vinaigrette sauce is French dressing with chopped chives, crumbled hard-boiled egg, capers, chopped parsley, and a little minced pickle added.

MASHED CELERIAC AND POTATOES

1 lb. celeriac
3 tablespoons butter
1 leek or 2 green onions, minced
salt and pepper
4 medium-sized potatoes, boiled

¾ cup cream
2 egg yolks, beaten
GARNISH
chopped parsley

Peel the celeriac and cut it in small cubes. Sauté the leek or onions in the butter a minute, add the celeriac, 3 tablespoons water, salt and pepper. Cover tight and cook slowly until tender. See that the vegetables do not cook dry; add a tablespoon or two of water if necessary. Do not drain. Skin the potatoes. Mash celeriac and potatoes together, bring the cream to a boil, pour over the beaten egg yolks, and add. Empty into a hot serving dish and sprinkle with chopped parsley. Serves 4.

CREAMED CELERIAC

2 lbs. celeriac
¼ cup diced onion
4 tablespoons butter
4 tablespoons chicken broth or
water

¾ cup light cream
2 teaspoons cornstarch
salt and pepper
GARNISH
¼ cup grated cheese

Peel the celeriac and slice it ½ inch thick, then cut in ½-inch strips. Sauté the onion in the butter a minute, add the celeriac, and water or broth. Cover tight and simmer gently until the celeriac is tender. Blend the cream with the cornstarch and add a little salt and pepper. (A dash of curry powder may be added if desired.) Mix the cream with the celeriac and cook until it thickens. Empty into a serving dish and sprinkle the top with cheese. Serves 4 to 6.

CREAMED CELERIAC WITH OTHER FOODS

1 lb. celeriac
½ cup chicken broth
creamed chicken or ham, mushrooms, seafood, peas, onions, etc.

GARNISH
chopped brown almonds or pistachio
nuts

Peel and cube the celeriac and simmer gently in the chicken broth until tender. This may be added to any creamed meats, vegetables, or seafood. Sprinkle the top with chopped almonds or pistachio nuts.

CHARD

Chard should have white or reddish fleshy, crisp stalks and bright green (not yellow) leaves without any trace of insect damage; old chard is stringy and coarse. Cook nothing but the best; it is better to have chard seldom than to run the risk of prejudicing your family against it. Large leaves of chard are among the best greens for making stuffed rolls. The stalks by themselves can be cooked in the same way as Braised Celery (page 171). Most rules for cooking spinach apply to chard.

CREAM OF CHARD SOUP

1 cup chopped or puréed cooked
chard
1 cup milk
1½ cups veal or chicken broth
1 cup light cream

1 teaspoon turmeric
GARNISH
⅓ cup chopped green onions
⅓ cup grated Parmesan cheese

Mix all the ingredients and heat or chill. Garnish the soup with the green onions and pass the cheese in a bowl. Refer to Cold Spinach Soup (page 297) for garnishes for cold chard soup. Leftover chard may be puréed with milk in the electric blender and served cold. Makes 4 cups.

BUTTERED CHARD

1½ lbs. chard
1 yellow onion or 6 green onions,
chopped
1 small green pepper, diced
3 tablespoons butter or olive oil

salt and pepper
1 teaspoon basil or ¼ teaspoon
nutmeg
2 tablespoons lemon juice

Wash and drain the chard as you would spinach. Separate the leaves and stalks and cut the latter in 2-inch lengths. Sauté the onion and pepper in the butter or olive oil in the bottom of a heavy pot or pressure cooker. When they have cooked a minute add the stalks of the chard, cover, and steam 1 minute. Then lay on the leaves—cut up, if they are large. Add all the seasonings, and lemon juice—no water because enough clings to the leaves—cover tight, and steam over a low flame until tender, about 15 minutes. In the pressure cooker it will take 1 full minute. Serve plain or sprinkle with buttered crumbs or a little grated cheese. Serves 4.

CHARD SOUFFLÉ

1¼ cups ground or puréed cooked
  chard
3 tablespoons butter
4 tablespoons flour
drained liquid from chard plus light
  cream to make 1¼ cups

salt and pepper
½ teaspoon thyme
3 egg yolks, beaten
3 egg whites, beaten until stiff

The virtue of using chard cooked as for Buttered Chard is that it is well flavored with onion and green pepper. It may be puréed in the electric blender. Make a cream sauce by melting the butter in a saucepan, blending in the flour, and adding the cream and chard liquid. Cook until it thickens. Season it, remove from heat, and add the egg yolks. Combine the sauce with the chard purée, then fold in the egg whites. Empty into a greased casserole or baking dish and bake about 30 minutes at 350°, or until set. It should be moist inside. Serves 4.

CHARD (OR OTHER GREENS)
WITH HAM AND ORANGE SAUCE

1 onion, chopped
3 tablespoons ham or bacon fat
1½ lbs. chard or spinach, or
  mustard, dandelion, or beet
  greens, washed and drained
1 cup smoked cooked ham, ground

1 teaspoon cornstarch
¼ cup orange juice
1 tablespoon lemon juice
salt, if necessary
        GARNISH
sieved hard-boiled egg

Sauté the onion in the fat in the bottom of a heavy pot or pressure cooker. Lightly mix the greens with the ham. Cover tight and steam 15 minutes or till tender. This will take 1 full minute in the pressure cooker. Blend the cornstarch with the fruit juices in a little bowl and drain the liquid from the greens into it. Empty the greens into a hot dish, pour the liquid into the pot, cook until thickened, and pour it over the greens. Go easy with the salt on account of the ham, but a dash may be needed. Sieve the egg over the top. This sauce is excellent over any greens. The egg may be omitted if desired. Serves 4.

CHARD WITH HAM CREAM SAUCE

recipe for Buttered Chard
3 teaspoons flour or cornstarch
liquid drained from chard plus light
   cream to make 1 cup
pepper and dash of salt

¼ teaspoon nutmeg or powdered
   cloves
½ cup ground ham
handful of chopped parsley

When preparing the chard cut it in 1-inch lengths to facilitate serving. Blend the flour or cornstarch with the liquid and cream and cook until it thickens. If it is too thick add a little more cream. Season and add the ham and parsley. Put the chard in a serving dish and pour the sauce over it. This sauce glorifies any cooked greens. Serves 4.

STUFFED CHARD ROLLS

8 large chard leaves, stemmed
boiling water
    CHOICE OF STUFFINGS
recipe for French Flageolet Green
   Beans (page 122)
cooked seasoned rice
chopped chicken, lamb, or ham with
   crumbs or sieved eggs

3 tablespoons olive oil
⅓ cup chopped onions
    SAUCE
⅓ cup sour cream
⅓ cup catsup
1 teaspoon basil or chervil

Choose perfect, untorn leaves and pour boiling water over them, cover the pot, and let stand exactly 5 minutes. Drain and gently lay them on a smooth surface. Add 2 or 3 tablespoons any of the stuffings. (Ground leftover meats should be well seasoned and moistened a little with gravy or cream. Crumbs may be added. Cold cooked beans [not string beans] or leftover pilau of brown rice make excellent stuffings.) Roll the leaves, tuck in the ends and roll again to protect the stuffing entirely. Put the olive oil, 3 tablespoons water, and onions in the bottom of a heavy pot, heat well, and lay the rolls on top. If you put them close together there is no danger of their falling apart. Cover tight and cook very gently for about 18 minutes. Lift carefully onto a serving platter or individual plates. Put the ingredients of the sauce onto the cooked onions in the pot, scrape the bottom, mix well, and pour over the rolls. This will serve 8 with a complete meal, or it will serve 4 as the main course for lunch or supper.

CHARD CASSEROLE

recipe for Buttered Chard
drained chard liquid plus light
   cream to make 1½ cups
2 tablespoons cornstarch

½ lb. mushrooms, sautéed
½ cup minced green onions
½ cup grated Swiss or Gruyère
cheese

Mix the liquid from the chard and the cream and cornstarch and heat until the sauce thickens. Put half the cooked chard in a greased baking dish, cover with the mushrooms and green onions, and add the rest of the chard. Pour the cream sauce over the top. Cover and bake 15 minutes in a 350° oven, uncover, sprinkle with the cheese, and bake 10 minutes more.

COLLARDS

When one considers that collards have been known since antiquity, are a valuable food, and are marketed like other greens and vegetables, it is remarkable that they are prepared and eaten almost exclusively in the South. They are used in the North almost entirely by transplanted Southerners. The usual way of cooking them is to boil them with good hickory-smoked bacon or salt pork. The juices, known as "pot likker," should be sopped up with hot corn bread or pone. For other ways of cooking them, consult the chapters on spinach and chard and their first cousins, kale and cabbage. Collards with corn pone and pot likker are one of the most popular everyday dishes of the South.

COLLARD SOUP

leftover cooked collards
salt and pepper
chicken broth or milk

GARNISH

green onions and cucumbers

Purée the leftover greens in the electric blender, or sieve them, and thin with either chicken broth or milk. Serve hot or cold and garnish with minced green onions and sliced cucumbers.

STEWED COLLARDS AND SALT PORK

1½ lbs. collards
1 thick slice smoked fat salt pork
 or 3 strips hickory-smoked bacon
2 onions, diced

1 green pepper, seeded and diced
salt and pepper
a few drops of lemon juice

Wash the collards well and trim off the stems unless they are very young. Do not drain them but let the water cling to the leaves. Cut the meat in 1-inch pieces and fry it until it is crisp in the bottom of a heavy pot. When the meat is brown, scoop it out and set aside. Remove about half the grease and fry the onions and green pepper until they begin to be tender. Add salt and pepper and the leaves and ½ cup water. Cover tight and cook gently until the greens are tender, about 15 or 18 minutes—or less than 5 minutes in the pressure cooker. Empty juices and collards into a serving dish, sprinkle a little lemon juice over them, and add the pieces of crisp pork to the top. Serve with corn pone. Serves 3 or 4.

CORN-MEAL PONE

1 cup water-ground corn meal
¾ teaspoon salt
½ teaspoon soda
½ teaspoon baking powder

3 tablespoons sour cream
buttermilk to make a batter
2 or 3 tablespoons butter or good
 fat

The quality of these delicious pones depends on the goodness of the meal used. Mix the dry ingredients and add the sour cream and buttermilk to make a light batter, one which will stand up when dropped from the spoon into a big iron skillet onto the melted fat. Cover with a tight lid and cook on top of the stove for about 25 minutes at the lowest heat. This amount makes 5 or 6 large pones. Serve hot with butter and pot likker.

FRIED COLLARDS

bacon pieces
collards, cut across in ½-inch strips
salt and pepper

lemon juice (optional)
minced green onions

Fry the bacon in a skillet until it is crisp, scoop it out, and fry the collards until tender, about 10 to 15 minutes. Salt and pepper them and add a few drops of lemon juice if desired. Empty into a serving dish and add the bacon pieces and green onions to the top.

CORN

If corn is kept after picking, the husks must not be removed until the corn is being prepared for cooking. Tests have shown that sweet yellow corn, unhusked, contains 160 calories per pound and carbohydrates 35.5 gm.; husked corn contains 297 calories per pound and carbohydrates 66.0 gm. The corn should be kept cold, as 50 per cent of its sugar becomes starch during a day's storage at 86°, but at 68° only 26 per cent of the sugar disappears.

There isn't much we can do about getting fresh corn unless we have our own cornfield or live near one. We can only be careful to buy the best-appearing corn with plump, tender kernels, still full of milk, and still unhusked.

To prepare corn for cooking (other than for serving on the cob), score the corn down the center of the kernels with a sharp-pointed knife, then cut and scrape them from the ears. This saves the trouble of chopping the kernels in a wooden bowl. The question of whether to cook the corn before it is put into fried or baked dishes is left to the cook's judgment. When corn is tender and full of milk, all it needs is to be well scored.

Three ears of corn, 7½ to 8 inches long, with well-packed kernels, make 2 cups corn cut from the ears.

CORN ON THE COB

There are three good ways of cooking corn on the cob. Put the husked ears in a big kettle of quite warm water with 1 tablespoon sugar, cover and bring to a boil, turn off the heat, and let the corn stand in the boiling water 2 minutes. Some cooks think 1 teaspoon lemon juice added to the water makes the ears tender.

Steaming corn is becoming more popular. Put the husked ears in a big steamer and cook over boiling water about 15 minutes.

To roast corn in the husks, turn back the husks to see that the corn is perfect, remove the silk, butter the corn, close the husks, and tie the ends with string. Put the corn in the oven, at least ½ inch apart, and roast 30 to 35 minutes at 350°. Serve with butter and salt. Never salt corn before it is cooked, as the salt tends to toughen it.

CREAM OF CORN SOUP

4, 5, or 6 ears of corn
milk
butter or diced bacon
½ cup diced onions
½ cup diced green pepper

salt and pepper
½ teaspoon turmeric
fresh dill or basil
1 cup light cream

Cook the corn in one of the ways described in the recipe for Corn on the Cob. To remove the kernels from the ears, score down the centers of the kernels with a sharp-pointed knife to release the milk and make the corn softer. Cut the kernels from the ears and scrape the ears; do this in a large bowl to prevent loss of milk. Grind the corn and press it through a sieve with some warmed milk—or, much better, purée the corn in an electric blender with milk, then sieve it to remove the sharp skins, which do not purée. Fry out diced bacon and remove the crisp bits. Sauté the onions and green peppers in the grease until tender and then purée with some milk. Butter may be used if preferred. Combine the vegetable purées and season well. Turmeric gives a rich yellow color to the soup. Squeeze a handful of stemmed dill and cut it fine with scissors—if dill is not available, 1 teaspoon basil may be used. Thin the purée to the consistency of heavy cream with milk and cream. The soup may be garnished with chopped green onions, chives, a little crisp popcorn, avocado slices, or chopped parsley. This is a delicious and nourishing soup, which may be served hot or cold. In the winter it may be made with canned niblets. Makes 4 to 6 cups.

CORN CHOWDER

4 strips bacon or 2 strips salt pork
1 cup thin onion slices
2 cups cubed raw potatoes
milk
2 cups cooked corn, cut from cob

salt and pepper
pinch of rosemary or savory
1 teaspoon sugar
paprika

Cut the bacon or salt pork into dice and fry until crisp; then remove and reserve the pieces. Sauté the onions and potatoes in the grease 3 minutes, cover, and cook until tender. Scald 3½ or 4 cups milk in a double boiler, add the corn, potatoes, and onions, and season well. Let the soup stand for 1 hour to ripen without cooking. When ready to serve, heat, and garnish with paprika. To make this a company dish, boil up ½ cup cream, pour it over 2 beaten egg yolks, and add just before serving. The pork or bacon bits may be added as a garnish. Makes 7 or 8 cups.

CORN IN OTHER SOUPS

1 to 1½ cups cooked corn, cut from cobs   4 or 6 cups clear or cream soup

Corn is a fine addition to chicken soup or to beef broth or vegetable soup. It may be leftover cooked corn, or it may be uncooked. Add it 2 minutes before soup is done.

SUCCOTASH

1 cup lima beans   1 green pepper, sliced thin
1 cup peas   ½ cup sliced onions
¼ cup butter   1½ cups heavy cream
salt and pepper   paprika
basil   *GARNISH*
2 cups cooked corn, scored and cut   chopped parsley or green onions or
from ears   red pimento strips

Cook the lima beans and peas in a little butter, salt, pepper, basil, and almost no water. Watch that they do not burn, and, when they are tender, add them to the corn with their liquid. Sauté the thinly sliced pepper and the onions in butter until tender and add them to the other vegetables. Salt and pepper them. All this may be done ahead of time. To serve, add the cream and heat. Empty into a serving dish, sprinkle with paprika, and add a garnish to the top. This will serve 6 or 8. It may be made with only corn and lima beans.

CORN AND STEWED TOMATOES

recipe for Stewed Tomatoes (page   1 cup raw corn
341)

Three or four minutes before the tomatoes are done add the corn. Some cooked okra may be added too if desired. Corn goes with a great many vegetables and is always a delicious addition.

SAUTÉED CORN, ONIONS, AND PEPPERS

2 big yellow onions or 1 Bermuda
   onion, sliced thin
1 big green pepper, sliced thin

¼ cup butter
2 cups raw corn
salt, pepper, and paprika

Sauté the thinly sliced onions and green pepper in a heavy skillet
or pot in the butter. When the vegetables are half tender add the corn
and stir around a minute, then cover and cook slowly 10 minutes,
stirring once or twice. It must not burn. When the vegetables are
tender, add seasonings. This is good with any meat or poultry.
Serves 4.

CORN AND POTATO CAKES

1 cup corn
1 to 1½ cups mashed potatoes
2 tablespoons grated onion
salt and pepper

butter
2 tablespoons grated cheese
cream
fat for frying

Ground raw corn or corn boiled up a minute, scored, cut and
scraped from the ears, may be used. The potatoes may be leftover
or cooked fresh and mashed, seasoned with onion, salt, pepper, butter, cheese, and cream. Mix in the corn, form into cakes, and fry
until a crusty brown on both sides. Makes 6 cakes.

BAKED CREAMED CORN AND ONIONS

Bermuda onions
sprinkling of ground cloves
salt and pepper
cooked corn
    CREAM SAUCE
4½ teaspoons cornstarch

onion water plus cream to make
   1½ cups
salt and pepper
1 teaspoon turmeric
grated Parmesan cheese

Cut thick slices of peeled Bermuda onions, 1 slice per serving.
Steam them tender with very little water. When they are done—but
not overcooked, for they must hold their shape—put them in a greased
baking pan. Season with a light sprinkle of cloves, salt, and pepper.
Cover with a good layer of cooked corn, cut from the cob. For the
sauce, blend the cornstarch smooth with the cream and onion liquid,

season, and cook until it thickens. Cover the corn with 2 or 3 table-spoonfuls, per onion slice, and sprinkle with grated cheese. Heat in the oven until the cheese browns.

MEXICAN CORN

1 Bermuda onion
1 green pepper
olive oil
½ lb. zucchini
½ lb. okra

salt and pepper
1 bud crushed garlic
2 cups raw corn
1 cup tomato sauce
1 teaspoon chili powder

Slice the onion and green pepper and sauté them in olive oil until half tender. Cut the zucchini in thin slices without peeling. Cut the tips (both ends) from the okra, boil it up in salted water, drain, and add to the other vegetables. Heat the garlic in a little oil, add the corn, and mix well. Combine all the vegetables, tomato sauce, and seasoning and put them in a baking dish and bake 20 to 25 minutes at 350°. Grated cheese may be added to the top if desired. Skinned, seeded, chopped fresh tomatoes may be used instead of tomato sauce if desired. Serves 5 or 6.

CREAMED CORN AND SHRIMP OR CRABMEAT

1 lb. fresh shrimp or cooked crabmeat
1 bay leaf
1 slice onion
salt and pepper
2 cups cooked corn

¼ teaspoon nutmeg
cream
4½ teaspoons cornstarch
patty shells or crisp toast
chopped parsley

Wash the shrimp but do not peel them. Cook them about 6 minutes with the bay leaf, onion, salt, pepper, and ½ cup water. Let them cool in the liquid, and reserve it for the sauce. Peel the shrimp and mix with the cooked corn. Strain the shrimp broth, add the nutmeg and enough cream to make 1½ cups. Mix the cornstarch to a smooth paste with a little water and add to the broth. Cook until it thickens, then add to the corn and shrimp. This may be served in patty shells or on crisp toast. It also is delicious with brown rice. If it is used with rice, more sauce may be made with more cream and cornstarch. It takes 3 teaspoons of cornstarch to thicken 1 cup of liquid. Garnish with chopped parsley. Serves 5 or 6.

PIMENTO CUPS STUFFED WITH CORN

canned whole pimentos
cooked corn, cut from ears
beaten eggs

melted butter
salt and pepper
parsley

Little fluted tin molds are necessary. Grease them and line with the whole red pimentos. To every cup of corn add 2 beaten eggs, a little melted butter, and salt and pepper. Fill the pimentos and bake in a 350° oven for 15 minutes. When done turn the molds out upside down and put a sprig of parsley on top of each.

CORN OMELET

2 tablespoons minced green pepper
3 scallions, minced
3 tablespoons butter
1 cup fresh cooked corn

¼ cup hot cream
salt and pepper
grated cheese or chopped parsley
4- to 6-egg omelet

Sauté the green pepper and onion 1 minute in the butter and add to the corn with the hot cream. Salt and pepper the corn mixture. This will fill a 4- to 6-egg omelet. When the omelet is cooked, pour the corn over the top, fold once, and slide it off onto a hot platter. Garnish with grated cheese or chopped parsley or some of both.

CORN FRITTERS

1 cup flour
½ teaspoon salt
2 egg yolks, beaten
1 tablespoon sugar
2 tablespoons melted butter

¼ to ⅔ cup milk
1 cup scored, cut corn
2 egg whites, beaten stiff
deep fat

Mix the flour and salt and add the egg yolks, sugar, butter, and milk to make a firm batter. Add the corn and fold in the whites. Drop the batter by spoonfuls into deep fat or oil and fry at 375° until a golden brown. Serve with syrup and crisp bacon or with chicken and gravy. Makes 6 to 8 fritters.

CORN BATTER CAKES

½ cup flour
1 teaspoon baking powder
1 teaspoon salt
2 cups corn, scored and scraped
   from ears

1 cup milk and 2 tablespoons
   melted butter, or ½ cup milk
   and ½ cup sour cream
2 egg yolks, beaten
2 egg whites, beaten until stiff

Sift the dry ingredients together and mix with the corn, add the milk and egg yolks, and fold in the stiffly beaten whites last. Drop batter from a spoon onto a hot griddle and fry as you would pancakes. Makes 6 or 8 cakes.

FRESH CORN AND CORN-MEAL BATTER CAKES

1 cup corn meal
½ teaspoon soda
¾ teaspoon salt
1 tablespoon sugar
¼ cup sour cream

¾ cup buttermilk
1 tablespoon melted butter
2 eggs, beaten
1 cup cooked corn, scored and cut
   from ears

Sift the dry ingredients together, add the sour cream, liquids, beaten eggs, and corn. If the batter is too thick for pancakes, add a little milk. Drop it from a spoon onto a hot griddle and fry. Honey and sour cream are excellent dressings. Serves 4.

FRIED CORN CAKES

3 ears corn (2 cups grated corn)
⅓ cup corn meal or ½ cup flour
½ cup cream, sweet or sour
1 teaspoon salt

½ teaspoon baking powder
1 teaspoon sugar
3 eggs, beaten

Bring the corn to a boil, drain immediately, then score the kernels down through the centers of the rows, cut and scrape from the ears. Add the rest of the ingredients, mix well, form into cakes, and fry in plenty of good hot fat on a griddle. If the eggs are beaten separately and the whites folded in last, these, like all cakes, will be a little lighter. Serve with syrup or with chicken gravy. Serves 2 to 4.

GREEN CORN CAKES

2 cups fresh uncooked corn, scored
  and scraped from ears
1 tablespoon fresh onion juice
1 tablespoon melted butter

⅓ cup cream
3 egg yolks, beaten
salt and pepper
3 egg whites, beaten until stiff

Mix all the ingredients, folding in the stiffly beaten egg whites last. Drop the batter from a spoon onto a well-buttered griddle and fry to a delicate brown on both sides. These are delicious with any meats or poultry, or they may be served with syrup or honey for a lunch dish. Makes 6 to 8 cakes.

CORN MUFFINS

1 cup corn meal
¾ cup white flour
1 teaspoon soda
1½ teaspoons cream of tartar
1 teaspoon salt
2 tablespoons sugar

¼ cup milk
2 tablespoons melted butter
1 egg, beaten
1 cup heavy sour cream
1 cup scored, cut corn

Sift all the dry ingredients together. Mix the milk, butter, egg, and sour cream. Add to the dry ingredients and stir in the corn. Do not beat muffin batter, just mix it and pour into greased muffin tins. Bake 5 minutes at 375°, then turn to 350° for another 10 to 12 minutes. Large muffins take about 7 more minutes to bake than little ones. This may be baked in a large pan as corn bread if desired. Serve hot with butter. Makes 9 big muffins or 15 small ones.

CORN PUDDING

1 green pepper, diced
½ cup finely diced onion
4 tablespoons butter
4 cups uncooked corn, scored and
  cut from ears

salt and pepper
¼ teaspoon nutmeg
2 tablespoons sugar
1½ cups milk
3 eggs, beaten

Sauté the pepper and onion in the butter until tender, and add them and the butter to the corn. Add seasonings and sugar, then the milk and beaten eggs. Empty into a greased baking dish and bake until set, but moist inside—about 25 minutes at 350°. Grated cheese may be sprinkled over the top 3 or 4 minutes before it is done. Serves 6.

CORN CREAM PUDDING

¼ cup finely diced onion	freshly ground pepper
¼ cup finely diced green pepper	1 cup light cream
3 tablespoons butter	3 egg yolks, beaten
2 cups scored, cut raw corn	3 egg whites, beaten until stiff
1 teaspoon salt	

Sauté the onion and pepper in the butter until they begin to be tender. Pour into mixing bowl and add all the other ingredients, folding in the stiffly beaten whites last. Pour into a greased baking dish and bake at 350° about 15 to 18 minutes or until set but moist inside. Serve with meats or poultry. Serves 4 to 6.

CORN SOUFFLÉ

1½ cups uncooked corn	3 tablespoons grated Cheddar
1 small green pepper, sliced	cheese
1 small onion, sliced	½ cup cream
1 teaspoon salt	4 egg yolks, beaten
1 tablespoon flour	3 egg whites, beaten until stiff
¼ teaspoon nutmeg	

Put the corn, the sliced pepper, and the onion through the meat grinder. Blend the salt, flour, nutmeg, cheese, and cream together, and bring to a boil, then pour over the beaten egg yolks. Add this mixture to the corn mixture and fold in the stiffly beaten egg whites. Bake in a greased soufflé dish 20 to 25 minutes at 350°. Serves 5 or 6.

CUCUMBERS

There is much more to the cucumber than just being "cool." It has survived three thousand years and has a place among the first twenty important vegetables of the garden. We think of cucumbers principally as an accompaniment to fish, as a garnish, as one of the principal additions to salads, or as various kinds of pickles. There are good ways of cooking cucumbers, too, and since it takes three of good size to make 100 calories, they can be eaten with the utmost abandon. Their greatest food value lies in the skin, so we should cook them, when possible, without peeling. Many people used to believe that cucumbers were hard to digest; they stopped thinking so when they stopped soaking cucumber slices to a state of limpness in cold salted water. If you must have cucumbers super-chilled, pack them in cracked ice a few minutes before you slice them, or remove them from one part of the refrigerator to the coldest spot for 15 minutes before slicing—just don't let them freeze.

Cucumbers are used in many dishes and in wonderful soups throughout Central Europe. I urge cooks to make some of these European soups. They are beautiful to see and delicious to eat.

CUCUMBER CANAPÉS

sliced cucumbers   soft cheese or sardine spread or chopped egg

Cucumber slices may be used instead of crackers or bread as the foundations of canapés. Spread the cucumber rounds with cheese, a paste of mashed sardines and mayonnaise, or a spread of seasoned, mashed hard-boiled eggs mixed with curry powder and mayonnaise.

CUCUMBER SANDWICHES

sliced chilled cucumbers   lemon juice
rounds of rye or whole-wheat bread   parsley butter

There isn't a sandwich more refreshing than a crisp slice of cucumber laid on a round of bread spread with chopped parsley mixed with a few drops of lemon juice and soft butter. A few leaves of watercress may be used instead of parsley. These are open sandwiches and should be prepared not long before serving.

RASSOLNIK
(Russian Cucumber Soup)

5 tablespoons minced dill pickle
3 cups veal or chicken stock
1 bunch beets
salt and pepper
1 tablespoon brown sugar or honey

lemon juice (if necessary)
1½ cups heavy sour cream
1 cucumber, peeled and sliced
2 hard-boiled eggs, sliced
handful of fresh dill, chopped

Let the finely minced dill pickle stand in the stock while the rest of the soup is being made. Cut the stems to within an inch of the beets and scrub the beets well. Cook them 20 minutes in 2 cups water, covered, or until they are tender. Peel them and mash them, with the water in the pan, through a sieve, or purée them in the electric blender. Season the purée with salt, pepper, and sweetening. Mix it with the pickle and stock and add some lemon juice if it needs it. The pickle may flavor it enough. Chill, and have the rest of the ingredients very cold. When ready to serve put ¼ cup sour cream in each of 6 soup plates, add the soup, mix a very little, then garnish with the sliced cucumber, sliced egg, and chopped dill.

GAZPACHO
(Spanish)

1 tablespoon cornstarch
4 cups veal or chicken broth
1 bud garlic, crushed
1 big sweet onion, diced
salt and pepper
dash of cayenne

1 pepper, roasted and diced
1 large tomato, skinned, seeded, and diced
3 tablespoons olive oil
1 cucumber, sliced thin

Blend the cornstarch with the broth and boil it with the garlic and onion for 10 minutes, gently. Season to taste and chill. Marinate the pepper and tomato in the olive oil and mix with the soup when it is cold. Put in 4 wide soup plates and garnish with the cucumber. Serve very cold.

CUCUMBER AND POTATO SOUP

4 potatoes
1 large onion
¼ cup butter
⅔ cup water in which potatoes cooked
salt and pepper

1 teaspoon turmeric
milk

GARNISH

1 large cucumber, coarsely shredded or diced
chopped chives or mint

Boil the potatoes in as little water as possible, drain, and save the water. Skin the potatoes. Peel and dice the onion and sauté it in the butter until tender; then mash it and the potatoes, with ⅔ cup potato water, through a sieve, or purée in the electric blender, seasoning with salt, pepper, and turmeric. Thin the purée to the consistency of cream with milk, then chill. The turmeric gives the soup a rich yellow color which looks handsome when the garnishes are added to each soup plate. Young cucumbers do not need peeling when they are shredded. Makes 6 or 7 cups of soup.

COLD CUCUMBER AND YOGURT SOUP
(Near East)

2 buds garlic, crushed
3 tablespoons olive oil
2 green peppers, roasted in the oven and diced
2 tomatoes, skinned, seeded, and diced

6 green onions, minced
salt and pepper
dash of cayenne
2 cucumbers, peeled and sliced
5 cups thick yogurt
chopped mint

Let the garlic, olive oil, peppers, tomatoes, and green onions marinate several hours together in a covered dish in the refrigerator. Add salt, pepper, and cayenne when ready to serve. The cucumber may be diced if you prefer. Divide the yogurt in 6 wide soup plates, and add the mixed vegetables, stirring them in a little. Sprinkle the top with a little finely chopped mint. Serve very cold. This is quite filling and is satisfying as the main dish for lunch or supper.

STUFFED BAKED CUCUMBERS

large cucumbers	cream
STUFFING	chopped hard-boiled eggs
sausage or ground ham or leftover meat	salt and pepper
cooked rice or breadcrumbs	*TOP*
½ cup minced green onions	crumbs and grated Parmesan cheese or sour cream

Select large, firm cucumbers, do not peel them, but cut them in half lengthwise. Boil them for 7 minutes in salted water. Drain and with a sharp knife cut along the sides of the seeds and scoop out the seeds. The resulting furrow should be large enough to fill with ½ to ⅔ cup stuffing. Mix the stuffing ingredients, seasoning well and moistening with cream. Stuff the cucumbers and top the stuffing with a mixture of crumbs and cheese or pour a good supply of sour cream over them and bake at 350° for 25 minutes or until cucumbers are tender. Cheddar cheese may be added to the stuffing if desired. These may be served with tomato sauce.

CREAMED CUCUMBERS WITH DILL

2 slices hickory-smoked bacon	1½ teaspoons cornstarch
1 unpeeled cucumber	½ cup light cream
salt and pepper	handful of fresh dill, skinned, squeezed, and cut fine
1 teaspoon turmeric	

Cut the bacon in 1-inch pieces, put it in a skillet, and let it fry out and begin to brown. Cut the unpeeled cucumber in scant ½-inch slices and lay them on top of the bacon. Fry and turn until they brown on both sides. Season with salt and pepper and a good sprinkle of turmeric. Put the bacon, grease, and cucumbers in a saucepan, add 2 tablespoons water, cover, and steam tender. This will take about 2 minutes over low heat. Blend the cornstarch with the cream and add the dill. Add this to the cucumber and cook until it thickens. This is a wonderful dish. The sauce may also be used for a variety of vegetables: creamed onions, cauliflower, zucchini, summer squash. This will serve 4, one serving each. If dill is not available, the sauce may be seasoned with 1 teaspoon curry powder, or with ⅓ cup Gruyère or Cheddar cheese.

CUCUMBERS AND SOUR CREAM

1½ cups heavy sour cream
salt and pepper
2 tablespoons lemon juice
½ teaspoon sugar
    ADDITIONS
handful of finely cut dill

½ cup minced green onions
canned red pimento strips
⅓ cup chopped chives
sliced tomatoes and green onions

2 cucumbers, peeled and sliced

An hour before serving, mix your choice of the additions (except the tomatoes) with the sour cream, salt, pepper, lemon juice, and sugar, and store in the refrigerator. The onions are always a good addition with any of the others. Fifteen minutes before serving mix with the cucumbers. If you use sliced tomatoes, add them to the cucumbers and sauce just before serving or the tomatoes will dilute the dressing. This dish is excellent with fish. Serves 5 or 6.

CUCUMBER JELLY

4 medium-sized cucumbers
1 white onion
1 teaspoon salt
3 cups boiling water
1 cup grapefruit juice
2 tablespoons gelatin
3 tablespoons lemon juice
2 tablespoons honey

dash of cayenne
3 drops green vegetable coloring
    GARNISH
1 cup sour cream
1 cucumber, sliced
¼ cup minced chives
salt and pepper
1 tablespoon lemon juice

Peel and slice 3½ cucumbers and put them and the onion through the meat grinder. Cover with the salt and boiling water and let stand until the water is cold. Strain it through a sieve. To the juice add the grapefruit juice. Soak the gelatin in the lemon juice and melt it over hot water. Add it and the honey, cayenne, and vegetable coloring to the cucumber-and-grapefruit liquid. Grease a ring mold, pour this mixture in it, and let it chill in the refrigerator until it is set. Unmold when ready to serve and fill the center with the garnish, combined according to directions for Cucumbers and Sour Cream. Decorate with the remaining ½ cucumber, sliced. Serves 8.

CUCUMBER AND SEAFOOD SALAD

3 small crisp cucumbers, peeled
  and sliced
½ lb. fresh shrimp, boiled and
  chilled, or ½ lb. fresh lobster or crabmeat

2 tablespoons minced green onions
crisp salad greens
⅓ cup French dressing
⅓ cup mayonnaise
2 tablespoons grated horseradish

Toss the cucumbers with the cold prepared seafood, the onions, and the greens. Mix the mayonnaise with the French dressing and add the horseradish to taste. The mayonnaise must be unsweetened oil mayonnaise. Just before serving, mix with the salad. Use enough greens to serve 6 or 8.

CUCUMBER AND WHITE WINE SALAD

2 or 3 small cucumbers
4 or 5 spring onions, minced
⅓ cup sauterne or chablis
1 tablespoon lemon juice
crisp salad greens, cut up

salt and pepper
1 teaspoon simple syrup
chervil or tarragon
¼ cup olive oil

Peel and slice the cucumbers ½ inch thick and marinate them 1 hour with the onions, wine, and lemon juice. When ready to serve put the cut-up greens in a salad bowl, mix with salt, pepper, syrup, herb, and oil. Add the cucumbers and marinade.

CUCUMBER MOUSSE

1 tablespoon gelatin
2 tablespoons lemon juice
1 cup grapefruit juice
2 cucumbers, peeled, seeded, and
  ground
¾ cup sour cream
¼ cup mayonnaise

2 drops Worcestershire Sauce
2 or 3 drops green vegetable
  coloring
            GARNISH
salad greens, sliced cucumbers, or
  tomatoes

Soak the gelatin in the lemon juice and melt it over hot water in a little grapefruit juice. Mix all the ingredients. Pour into a greased fancy mold or in small molds. Chill until set. Garnish with greens and sliced cucumbers, or with sliced tomatoes. Serves 6 to 8.

CUCUMBER SALAD WITH SOUR CREAM

2 cucumbers
⅓ cup minced green onions
watercress or field salad
whites of 2 hard-boiled eggs,
   chopped

SAUCE
1¼ cups sour cream

½ teaspoon mustard
½ teaspoon sugar
2 tablespoons lemon juice
salt and pepper
2 tablespoons olive oil

TOP
sieved yolks of 2 hard-boiled eggs

Peel and slice the cucumbers and mix them with the onions, greens, and chopped egg whites. Chill until ready to serve. Mix all the ingredients for the sauce and chill. When ready to serve put the cucumbers and greens in a salad bowl, add the sauce, mix a little, and sieve the yolks over the top. Use enough greens to serve 6 or 8.

CUCUMBER ASPIC SALAD

1 3-oz. package lime gelatin
¾ cup boiling water
¼ cup lemon juice, strained
1 white onion, grated
½ cup thick sour cream

½ cup mayonnaise
1 cup shredded unpeeled cucumber

GARNISH
sliced tomatoes or sliced cucumbers

Dissolve the gelatin in the water, add the strained juice and grated onion and let cool and partially set. Add the cream, mayonnaise, and cucumber. Pour into 6 greased small molds or 1 large mold. Chill until set. Unmold on a plate and garnish. The mold doesn't need additional dressing, but a little French dressing may be added to the greens.

CUCUMBER OIL PICKLES

16 small cucumbers
1 qt. onions, thinly sliced
salt
½ cup black mustard seed

1 cup white mustard seed
2 tablespoons celery seed
1¼ cups olive oil
cold cider vinegar

Slice the unpeeled cucumbers and put them and the onions in layers in a large bowl, salting each layer. Let this stand 3 hours, then drain well. Mix the seeds and put the cucumbers and onions in layers in quart Mason jars, adding seeds to each layer. Divide the olive oil and add it to the jars, then fill the jars with good vinegar and seal.

CASSIA PICKLES

75 2- to 3-inch cucumbers or
    1-inch slices of larger ones
1 gallon boiling water
2 cups coarse salt
more boiling water
1 teaspoon powdered alum

SYRUP

6 cups vinegar
5 cups light brown sugar
1 oz. celery seed
1 oz. cassia buds
3 additional cups brown sugar

The small cucumbers are prettier than the chunks, but either may be used. Mix the salt with the gallon of boiling water and when it has cooled pour it over the cucumbers and let them stand 1 week. Drain and cover with boiling water and let them stand 24 hours. Drain and cover with boiling water mixed with the alum and let stand 24 hours. Drain and cover with boiling syrup made with the vinegar, 5 cups sugar, and the seeds and buds. For 2 successive days drain off the syrup, add 1 cup light brown sugar, and pour over the cucumbers. The third day drain off the syrup, add the third cup of sugar, pack the cucumbers in jars, bring the syrup to a boil, and fill the jars and seal. This may seem like a long operation, but pickling cucumbers so that they stay crisp takes a little patience. If you have a corner to keep the pickles, each day's operation takes little time.

PEELED CUCUMBER PICKLES

8 or 9 large ripe cucumbers,
    peeled and sliced
½ cup non-iodized salt
1¾ cups light brown sugar

2 tablespoons mustard seed
5 whole cloves
2 sticks cinnamon
3½ cups vinegar

Remove the seeds from the cucumbers, sprinkle with the salt, and let stand 24 hours. Drain the cucumbers in a colander or sieve 1 hour or more. Make a syrup of the sugar, seed, spices, and vinegar by boiling them 5 minutes; add the cucumbers and simmer gently until they are clear—about 25 minutes. Pack in hot sterilized jars and seal.

TWELVE-DAY PICKLES

1 cup salt
25 4- or 5-inch cucumbers
vinegar

SYRUP

2 sticks cinnamon
1 teaspoon whole cloves
1 teaspoon whole allspice

2 tablespoons mustard seed
3 lbs. light brown sugar
3 cups fresh vinegar
1 tablespoon mustard

pea-sized piece of alum

Dissolve the salt in 1 gallon water, cover the cucumbers with it, and let them stand for 3 days. Drain them, cover with fresh water, and let them stand for 3 days, changing the water every day. The seventh day, drain and cover with weak vinegar, heat almost to a boil, remove from heat, and let stand 3 days. Drain and discard the vinegar. Put all the spices in a bag and boil it up with the sugar, vinegar, and mustard. Pour the boiling syrup over the pickles and repeat this 2 more successive mornings, draining it and letting it come to a boil each time. The third morning add the alum to the syrup and seal.

DILL PICKLES

grape leaves
fresh dill
½ cup grated horseradish (optional)
1 cup celery leaves
1 onion, sliced

50 medium-sized cucumbers
½ cup mustard seed (optional)
1 cup salt
1 pt. vinegar

Line a wooden bucket or stone jar with grape leaves, then add a bed of dill, horseradish—if you like—celery leaves, and sliced onion. Pack the cucumbers on this bed, standing them up close together. (Mustard seed may be added if desired—about ½ cup will add flavor.) Boil 4½ quarts water, add the salt, and let it cool. Put the vinegar on the cucumbers and add the water. Cover with grape leaves and a plate with a weight so that all the cucumbers stay below the surface of the water. Skim any scum that arises. Fermentation will take place in a couple of weeks. After it is completed the pickles will be ready to eat.

EGGPLANT

Most of our exotic recipes for this handsome plum-colored, shiny, melon-shaped vegetable come from the East, where it was first grown. Many people are familiar only with fried eggplant, but there are many other excellent ways to cook it. Those who have eaten eggplant cooked with lamb by the Turks or Armenians appreciate it as one of our best vegetables. The French have a dish called *ratatouille,* a mixture of onion, tomatoes, and eggplant; some cook it less than an hour, while others prefer a dish cooked twice as long to an unctuous fragrant mass. Cubes of eggplant may join onion, mushrooms, and lamb on skewers for shish kebab, one of the favorite dishes for outdoor cooking. Eggplant is excellent braised with meats, served as an appetizer, and in numerous casserole dishes.

Besides the small-to-large purple variety there are attractive little pure white eggplants which resemble elongated puffballs. These may be left unpeeled and cooked the same way as other varieties; they are perhaps a little more delicate in flavor.

EGGPLANT CAVIAR

2 buds garlic, crushed
¼ cup olive oil
1 medium-sized eggplant
¼ cup minced green onions
salt and pepper

1 teaspoon each cardamom and coriander powder

GARNISH
black olives, lettuce, or tomatoes

Marinate the garlic in the oil. Bake a whole unpeeled eggplant from 40 to 60 minutes in a 350° oven or until it is tender when tested with a cake tester. When it is cool enough peel and mash it. Add the other ingredients. Serve as a first course with the garnishes or as a spread for an appetizer.

FRIED EGGPLANT FINGERS

4 ½-inch slices eggplant   salt
⅓ cup olive oil   vinegar and water
3 buds garlic, crushed

Peel the eggplant and cut each slice in 4 or 5 strips. Put the oil and garlic in a heavy pan and heat it. Fry the eggplant fingers in the oil and keep turning them until they are brown and tender. They will absorb all the oil before they begin to cook, but keep turning them. They will release some of the oil by the time they are done. Salt them, put them on a platter, and marinate them 10 minutes in a little vinegar diluted with water, half and half. Drain, chill, and serve as an appetizer. These may be served on Ry-king, a good cracker for hors d'oeuvre.

FRENCH-FRIED EGGPLANT

1 eggplant   2 tablespoons melted butter
          BATTER   2 eggs, beaten
1⅛ cups flour   ⅔ cup milk
¼ teaspoon baking powder
¾ teaspoon salt   deep oil

It is not necessary to salt eggplant and press it under a weight. Peel it and slice it ¼ inch thick or peel and cut it in fingers. Mix all the ingredients for the batter, dip the eggplant in it, and fry at 360° until golden brown. Drain on brown paper.

FRIED AND BAKED EGGPLANT WITH HERBS

1 eggplant, sliced ½ inch thick   crushed garlic (optional)
salt and pepper   *GARNISH*
orégano, thyme, tarragon, or basil   crumbs and herbs
olive oil or butter

Eggplant absorbs a lot of oil. One of the best ways of preparing fried eggplant without the use of a great quantity of oil is to season the slices, sprinkle with herbs, and quickly brown them (with the garlic, if desired) on each side over a brisk fire in oil or butter. As they are browned lay them on a big cooky sheet, and then bake them in the oven at 375° until they are tender. They will not be greasy and will be full of flavor. The baking will take about 12 to 15 minutes. If you like, a few buttered browned crumbs mixed with a little herb may be sprinkled on the slices when they are ready to serve.

BAKED WHOLE EGGPLANT

2 medium-sized eggplants	bacon snips
basil or orégano	olive oil
salt and pepper	

Wash the eggplants and cut a thin slice from each end. On one side of each eggplant make 4 lengthwise slits and fill with an herb, salt, pepper, some bacon, and oil. Lay them in a baking dish, slit side up, and pour some oil on them. Cover tight and bake at 350° 30 minutes. Open and pour a little oil in the slits, cover, and bake until tender. Large ones take 1 hour and smaller ones 35 to 45 minutes. This is an excellent way to cook eggplants. Break them open to serve at the table. A large one will serve 4.

EGGPLANT, TOMATOES, AND CREAM

½ cup diced onion	salt and pepper
butter	⅔ cup cream
3 tomatoes, skinned and sliced	1 tablespoon cornstarch
1 medium-sized eggplant	½ cup grated cheese

Sauté the onion in the butter until tender, then add the sliced tomatoes and brown on both sides quickly with the onion. Peel and slice the eggplant, sauté it lightly, and finish cooking it in the oven (see recipe for Fried and Baked Eggplant with Herbs). Put alternate layers of the tomato-onion mixture and eggplant in a baking dish, seeing that it is all well seasoned with pepper and salt. Blend the cream and cornstarch and pour it over the vegetables. Add the cheese to the top and bake 10 minutes at 375°.

A variation of this may have a sautéed green pepper added and a sauce made of ⅔ cup tomato sauce, ⅔ cup light cream, 2 eggs, beaten, and ¼ cup corn meal. Add a little of the sauce to each layer of vegetables and pour the rest over the top and bake 25 minutes. Five minutes before it is done add grated cheese to the top. Eggplant is better if it is cooked almost tender before baking with other vegetables in a casserole. Serves 4 to 6.

MOUSSAKA

1 large eggplant or 2 of medium
    size
olive oil

STUFFING

3 cups ground cooked lamb
1 cup cooked brown rice
1 cup sliced mushrooms, sautéed
salt and pepper

2 teaspoons orégano
2 buds garlic, crushed
⅔ cup diced onions, sautéed
1 egg, beaten
chopped eggplant pulp

½ cup cream
⅓ cup grated cheese

Cut the unpeeled eggplant lengthwise in quarters, or, if it is very large, in sixths. Steam, cut side down, until it is half tender, or fry in olive oil until the skins, with a little of the flesh, may be removed intact. Grease a round baking dish and put the skins in the dish, lining it with points together in the center of the bottom, skins next to the dish. They ought to hang over the sides of the dish. Mix the ingredients of the stuffing and pack lightly. Fold the skins over to cover the top. Heat the cream with the cheese until the cheese melts, and pour it over the top. Bake 25 minutes at 350°. Turn down to 300° and bake 20 minutes more. Turn out on a serving dish upside down and serve with a light tomato or mushroom sauce. Serves 6 to 8, according to the amount of eggplant.

STUFFED EGGPLANT

1 large eggplant or 2 of medium size

LIGHT STUFFING

chopped eggplant pulp
1 to 1½ cups light toasted bread-
    crumbs
2 tablespoons brown sugar
4 tablespoons hot cream
salt and pepper
1 teaspoon tarragon

MEAT STUFFING

2 cups cooked ground ham, lamb,
    or chicken

1 cup mushrooms, sautéed
⅔ cup diced onions, sautéed
½ cup pine nuts
1 teaspoon curry powder
1 cup cooked brown rice
chopped eggplant pulp
¼ cup currants, marinated
    in ¼ cup sherry

TOP

browned sesame seeds

Bake the eggplants in the oven at 350° for 20 minutes or until they begin to become tender. Cut them in half and remove the pulp to within ½ inch of the skin, being careful not to cut the skin. Chop the pulp and mix with ingredients of either stuffing. If the stuffing seems a bit dry, add a little melted butter, milk, or cream. Put the eggplant shells in a greased baking dish close together so they will hold their shape. Stuff them lightly and bake 30 to 35 minutes at 350°. Browned sesame seeds sprinkled on top are very good and may be used on any baked or casserole dish—a change from breadcrumbs. Serves 6 to 8.

EGGPLANT AND HAM CASSEROLE

1 eggplant
olive oil
1 ½-inch slice ham, ground
salt and pepper
2 teaspoons thyme or orégano

1 large Bermuda onion, sliced and sautéed
1 green pepper, sliced and sautéed
1 cup sliced skinned tomatoes
1 cup shredded Cheddar cheese

Slice the eggplant and cut it in fingers. Do not peel it. Sauté the eggplant in some olive oil 2 or 3 minutes, turning it often; then add 2 tablespoons water, cover, and cook slowly about 6 or 7 minutes until it is steamed tender. Alternate layers of all the ingredients in a greased casserole, finishing with cheese on the top. Cover and bake 12 minutes at 375°; uncover and bake 10 minutes more at 350°. This will serve 4 generously but may easily be increased to serve more.

EGGPLANT AND BANANA CASSEROLE

1 eggplant
salt and pepper
orégano or thyme
good fat or oil

3 bananas
nutmeg
2 or 3 tomatoes, skinned and sliced,
  or 1⅓ cups tomato purée

Peel and slice an eggplant of good size but not too large. Season the slices on both sides with salt, pepper, and an herb. Brown in fat or oil and cook until almost tender. Set aside. Put a little more oil in the pan. Slice the bananas lengthwise, sprinkle with nutmeg, and brown them a little. In a greased baking dish put alternate layers of eggplant, bananas, and tomatoes—or a little purée on each layer. Top with tomatoes or seasoned purée. Cover tight and bake 25 to 30 minutes, half the time at 375°, and the latter half at 350°. Serves 6.

EGGPLANT LUNCHEON DISH

1 medium-sized eggplant,
  unpeeled, cut in fingers
¼ cup olive oil
1 to 2 cups diced cooked tongue,
  ham, or lamb
1 green pepper, sliced and sautéed
3 onions, diced and sautéed

salt and pepper
1 teaspoon savory or thyme
1 teaspoon light brown sugar
¼ cup corn meal
1 cup sliced, skinned tomatoes
⅔ cup light cream, heated
shredded Cheddar cheese

Sauté the eggplant fingers in the olive oil 3 minutes, add 2 table-spoons water, cover, and steam 8 minutes until tender. In a greased casserole arrange alternate layers of all the ingredients and seasonings except the cream and cheese. Bake, covered, 15 or 18 minutes at 375°. Uncover, pour the heated cream over it, and cover with cheese. Bake 6 minutes more. For an Armenian variation add ⅓ cup sultanas and ⅓ cup pine nuts and omit the cream. Serve with steamed brown rice. Serves 4 to 6.

EGGPLANT PANCAKES

1 medium-sized eggplant
1 egg, beaten
¼ cup flour
⅓ teaspoon baking powder

¾ teaspoon salt
1 teaspoon orégano
¼ cup minced green onion
olive and vegetable oil for frying

These pancakes make one conscious that there is a botanical affinity between eggplant and potatoes. They remind one of grated-raw-potato pancakes. A medium-sized eggplant should provide 2 cups of mashed cooked eggplant, and for every cup 2 tablespoons of flour are required. Cut the eggplant in quarters or sixths and lay them, cut side down, in a steamer over actively boiling water. Cover the steamer and cook for 10 minutes. The eggplant should be very tender, both skin and pulp. Skin the eggplant and slice it over a sieve, pressing just a little. About ⅓ cup of juice will drain off and should be discarded. Mash the pulp coarsely with a fork, not to a mush. Mix all the other ingredients and seasonings (except the oil) before mixing with the pulp. Mix well and fry in a mixture of olive and vegetable oils on a very hot pancake griddle. The cakes should be crisp on both sides. Turn down a little and fry until cooked through —not more than about 3 minutes. This will make 8 good-sized cakes or 12 small ones.

RATATOUILLE

1 large eggplant
olive oil
1½ to 2 cups sliced onions
2 green peppers, sliced
3 pimentos (canned in oil)
juice of ½ lime or lemon

3 or 4 large tomatoes, skinned and
  sliced
salt and pepper
2 tablespoons brown sugar
  GARNISH
chopped parsley

Wash the eggplant, remove a thin slice from either end, and discard. Cut lengthwise in eighths and lay it, cut side down, in a skillet or heavy pot. Cover and steam in ⅓ cup olive oil for 6 or 8 minutes. Remove liquid and eggplant to a large greased casserole and sauté the onions and green peppers in a little more oil. Cut the pimentos in strips. Add all the ingredients to the eggplant. Add another ¼ cup olive oil, cover tight, and bake 35 minutes at 350°. Uncover and cook another 20 minutes or until the liquid has cooked away some. When the dish comes from the oven sprinkle liberally with chopped parsley. Serves 6 to 8.

CHINESE EGGPLANT

1 large eggplant
¼ cup sesame or peanut oil
salt and pepper
1 tablespoon cornstarch
1 tablespoon light brown sugar

1 tablespoon soy sauce
1½ tablespoons minced preserved
  ginger and a little syrup
chopped green onions

Peel the eggplant and discard a ½-inch slice from the hard ends. Slice the eggplant ¾ inch thick. Very lightly brown it in a little of the oil, then salt and pepper it very lightly, lay the slices on a cooky sheet, and bake in the oven about 15 minutes until it is tender. Meanwhile blend cornstarch in ⅓ cup cold water, put in the top of the double boiler, add the sugar and soy sauce, and cook until it thickens. Thin with some of the sesame or peanut oil. Season with more soy sauce if you like. When the eggplant is done put it on a hot platter and spoon the sauce over it and sprinkle with the ginger and chopped onions. This is very good to serve with curry dishes or Chinese spareribs. Serves 6 to 8 with a Chinese meal.

BRAISED LAMB WITH EGGPLANT AND PILAFF

2½ lbs. breast, shoulder, or neck
    of lamb
olive oil
1 bud garlic
salt and pepper
2 teaspoons orégano
1 cup diced onions

½ cup diced celery
½ cup diced carrots
½ cup broth
½ cup tomato juice or purée
1 cup mushrooms
1 unpeeled eggplant, cubed

Start this early in the day. Wash the lamb and wipe it very dry. It should be cut in servings. Crush garlic in ⅓ to ½ cup olive oil, season it with salt, pepper, and 1 teaspoon orégano. Put the lamb pieces in this oil and stir them until they are well covered and let them marinate in it all day, until you are ready to cook it. Lift the lamb out of the marinade and brown it quickly in a heavy iron skillet, adding the onions just before it is finished. Put the celery and carrots in the bottom of a casserole or roasting pan and put the lamb and onions on top. Put the broth and tomato juice or purée in the skillet, scraping it well, heat, and pour over the lamb. Roast the lamb and vegetables at 325° for 45 minutes and meanwhile marinate the eggplant and the mushrooms in the oil marinade you used for the lamb. Add another teaspoon of orégano. When the lamb has cooked 45 minutes add the eggplant and mushrooms with the marinade and bake at 300° for 45 minutes more. Serve with pilaff:

1½ cups brown rice
1 cup tomato juice
2 cups veal or chicken broth
salt and pepper

½ teaspoon cumin powder
1 teaspoon turmeric
⅓ cup finely diced onion

Put the washed rice in a pot with all the rest of the ingredients well mixed and bring to a boil. Cover tight, turn the heat as low as possible, and cook for 45 minutes without raising the lid. Leave covered, turn the flame off, and leave for 10 more minutes. Serve hot with the lamb and eggplant. Serves 5 or 6.

NOODLES BAKED WITH EGGPLANT

6 oz. egg-noodle shells
2 buds garlic, crushed
⅓ cup olive oil
1 small eggplant
salt and pepper

½ cup tomato sauce
1 teaspoon powdered fennel
TOP
¼ cup crumbs
¼ cup grated Parmesan cheese

Boil the noodles in salted boiling water 7 or 8 minutes. Drain. Heat the garlic with the olive oil and mix with the noodles. Peel and cube the eggplant and steam it over boiling water until it is tender. Mix with the noodles. Salt and pepper the tomato sauce and add the fennel. Put the eggplant and noodles in a baking dish, pour the sauce over them, mixing it in a little, and top with mixed crumbs and cheese. Bake 10 minutes in a 375° oven. Serves 5 or 6.

EGGPLANT SOUFFLÉ

2 medium-sized eggplants
1 cup ground ham
3 tablespoons butter, melted
¼ cup light cream
3 egg yolks, beaten

½ teaspoon nutmeg
salt and pepper
½ cup fresh toasted breadcrumbs
⅓ cup ground browned almonds
3 egg whites, beaten until stiff

Boil the whole eggplants in a big kettle of water until tender, about 18 minutes. When possible to handle, peel them, slice, and drain in a sieve while mixing the rest of the ingredients. Mix the ham with the butter, cream, and egg yolks beaten together, and add the seasonings. Mash the eggplant, add the crumbs, and mix with the ham mixture. Add half the almonds to the beaten egg whites. Fold the whites into the eggplant mixture and pour into a greased baking dish and sprinkle the rest of the almonds on top. Bake for 30 minutes at 375°, or until the soufflé is set but still moist in the center. Serves 6 to 8.

CREAMED MASHED EGGPLANT

1 large eggplant	⅓ cup grated Cheddar cheese
3 tablespoons butter	salt and pepper
⅓ cup flour	2 teaspoons orégano
1 cup light cream	

Bake the whole eggplant in the oven until it tests tender with a cake straw—about 1 hour or more. Have the sauce ready. Melt the butter, stir in the flour until smooth, and slowly add the cream. When smooth, melt the cheese in the sauce and add the seasonings. This will be very thick, but it should be, or the eggplant will thin it too much. Skin and mash the eggplant. Mix with the sauce and heat a few minutes in the oven if necessary. Cooked brown rice goes well with this dish and lamb, stewed, roasted, or braised. Serves 5 or 6.

AGATHA'S EGGPLANT

1 good-sized eggplant	salt and pepper
2 strips bacon, diced	6 black olives, sliced
1 onion, minced	4 anchovy fillets, sliced
½ cup chopped celery	1 cup breadcrumbs
½ cup tomatoes	½ cup grated cheese
1 egg, beaten	

Peel and cut the eggplant in good-sized cubes. Steam over boiling water for 5 minutes. Fry the bacon until crisp, add it and the grease. Mix lightly with the next seven ingredients and half the crumbs. Put in a greased baking dish and sprinkle the top with the rest of the crumbs mixed with the cheese. Bake at 325° 30 minutes. Serves 5 or 6 or more.

JERUSALEM ARTICHOKES

This knobby, delicate-skinned little vegetable resembles a potato and may be cooked in many of the same ways potatoes are cooked. Scrub Jerusalem artichokes before cooking and remove any dark blemish. They may be boiled in their skins, but these should be removed while they are hot or the flesh will come off with the skins. They may be boiled and mashed, creamed, French fried (after they are boiled), and made into pancakes. They are so good that they should be eaten much more often than they are.

Salsify, or oyster plant, does not belong to the same family as the Jerusalem artichoke, but it may be cooked in the same ways, as the two vegetables' textures resemble each other. When peeling salsify roots, drop them in mildly acidulated water to keep their whiteness. They may be steamed tender, fried, dressed with butter, salt, and pepper, or they may be scalloped or creamed with or without cheese and garnished with chopped parsley. They have an interesting flavor of oyster, hence the name.

JERUSALEM ARTICHOKES AU GRATIN

1½ lbs. Jerusalem artichokes
salt
2½ teaspoons cornstarch
¾ cup light cream

1 tablespoon butter
salt and pepper
¼ teaspoon nutmeg
⅔ cup grated cheese

Scrub the artichokes and put them on to boil with 1 cup water and a little salt. They will be tender in 20 to 25 minutes, or less than 5 minutes in the pressure cooker. Rub the skins off but retain ⅓ cup of the liquid they boiled in to mix with the sauce. Blend the cornstarch with the cream, add the artichoke liquid and the butter and seasonings. Cook until it thickens. Put the sauce and vegetable in a greased shallow baking dish, cover with the cheese, and run the dish under the flame until the cheese melts. Serves 6.

BOILED AND BUTTERED JERUSALEM ARTICHOKES

1½ lbs. Jerusalem artichokes
salt
melted butter

GARNISH
chopped parsley, minced green onions,
chervil or basil or grated cheese

Boil the artichokes in 1 cup water with salt, drain and skin them. Put them in a hot serving dish with melted butter and top with any garnish mentioned.

JERUSALEM ARTICHOKE PANCAKES

1 lb. Jerusalem artichokes
1 onion, grated
1 large egg, beaten

salt and pepper
¼ cup flour
butter or oil

Thinly peel the artichokes, grate them, and, if much juice forms, drain it a little. Have all the other ingredients (except the butter or oil) ready to add so they may be fried quickly before liquid forms. Mix and fry the cakes in the butter or oil on a hot griddle until well browned. They may stand in the oven to cook a little longer until all are fried.

KALE

Kale has become, through cultivation, one of the handsomest of garden vegetables. Its crinkly green leaves promise good eating, but they must be cooked with care. No vegetable should be cooked after it is tender, and this is particularly true of kale. Kale may be cooked in almost as many ways as spinach, but allow a few minutes longer because it is not quite so tender a leaf. A hint for the ladies: there are few vegetables richer in vitamin A than kale—A being the complexion vitamin. We should cook foods in this category often; others are carrots, beet and turnip greens, sweet potatoes, and spinach. To prepare kale for cooking, remove the leaves from the coarse stalks. Wash the leaves in several waters to remove all sand and grit.

KALE VEGETABLE CHOWDER

3 strips bacon	1 cup diced carrots
1 cup diced onions	1 cup peas
1 tablespoon flour	1 white turnip, diced
salt and pepper	1 cup diced celery and leaves
4 whole cloves	1 cup skinned tomatoes
1 teaspoon thyme	1 cup diced string beans
2 bay leaves	4 beets
2 qts. warm water	3 cups kale, cut in ribbons
1 lump chicken concentrate from Lipton's chicken noodle soup	1 tablespoon brown sugar

Cut the bacon in 2-inch lengths and fry it a little. Add the onions and fry until they are light yellow. Stir in the flour and add seasonings, cloves, thyme, bay leaves, warm water, and the lump of concentrate. Add all the vegetables but the beets and kale. Simmer 20 minutes. Scrub the beets and cook them separately in 2 cups water, covered, until they are tender. Drain this water into the soup with the kale cut in very fine ribbons, simmer 20 minutes longer, and add the sugar. Skin the beets and cut them into fine dice and when the soup is done add them. If the beets are cooked longer they may lose their brilliant color. This may be served plain or with 1 tablespoon sour cream in each soup plate. One cup diced potatoes may be added with the kale if desired. Makes about 2½ quarts.

STEAMED KALE WITH FRANKFURTERS

1½ to 2 lbs. kale
water from cooking ham or tongue,
   if available
¼ cup minced onion
salt and pepper
1 teaspoon tarragon

1 tablespoon lemon juice or vinegar
butter or olive oil or 2 strips
   bacon, diced and fried
GARNISH
boiled and browned frankfurters

Wash the kale thoroughly but do not let it stand in water. Drain
and discard the coarse stalks and stems. Cut in 1½- to 2-inch lengths.
Put it in the top part of a steamer over 2 cups of ham or tongue
water, or in a heavy pot. Kale steamed in a heavy pot may need no
water added. When it has steamed 10 minutes and seems a bit dry,
2 or 3 tablespoons hot water may be added. Put the onion over the
top. Steam, covered, 10 minutes. Add the seasonings and tarragon.
If it is not tender cook it 5 to 8 minutes more or until it is. It may be
dressed with vinegar or lemon juice, butter, olive oil, or bits of bacon
fried crisp and a little of the grease. If it is steamed over ham or
tongue water it may be served in a bowl with some of the liquid,
accompanied with hot corn bread, as it is served in the south. Boiled
and browned frankfurters served with the kale make it a main dish
for lunch or supper. One and one-half pounds kale serves 3 or 4.

CREAMED KALE AND CHEESE

1½ lbs. kale
½ cup minced onion
sausage drippings or bacon fat
salt and pepper
1 tablespoon lemon juice
SAUCE
1 tablespoon butter

3 tablespoons flour
½ cup light cream
2 tablespoons grated Cheddar
   cheese
TOP
⅓ cup grated Cheddar cheese

Wash and stem the kale, then drain it a little and cut in 2-inch
lengths. Sauté the onion in the fat or drippings 2 minutes, then add
the kale, salt, pepper, lemon juice, and 2 tablespoons water. Cover
tight and cook slowly until it is tender. It may be cooked 3 or 4
minutes in the pressure cooker; reduce the pressure immediately. For
the sauce, melt the butter, stir in the flour until smooth, then blend
in the cream and cook until it is thick. Add the cheese. Drain the kale
liquid into the cream sauce, which is very thick. Stir until it is blended
and smooth. Empty the kale and sauce into a greased baking dish,

cover the top with cheese, and put under the broiler flame until it browns. This may be made ahead of time and baked a few minutes at serving time until the cheese melts and browns. Serves 3 or 4.

Note: See the section on Spinach (page 296) for Spinach or Kale Cakes and for other dishes that may be made with kale—e.g., Spinach Soufflé, Cream of Spinach Soup.

LEEKS

The leek, a cylindrical bulb of the onion family with long flat leaves, is too often relegated to seasoning and garnish uses. But it may be cooked solo as a vegetable, and there isn't one more delicious served in the ways asparagus is served. It may be braised and served with various sauces: butter, Hollandaise, cheese, parsley, cream, etc. The addition of sliced leeks fried in butter marvelously improves dishes of meats, seafood, fish, vegetables, rice, soups, salads, and sauces. Leeks have been used and appreciated in cookery from times immemorial, and we should give them their rightful place among our treasured vegetables. They have been the badge of the Welshman since the day of King Arthur's Knights of the Round Table. The first dish described here is an old one from the British Isles.

COCKALEEKIE

1 cock, dressed and left whole	salt and pepper
1 bunch leeks	12 prunes, unpitted
⅓ cup barley	

The old recipes all specify an old cock, hence the name; but if you prefer a tenderer bird (we are softer than our ancestors), get a good hen. Grease a heavy pot and put in the bird. Trim the roots of the leeks but use as much of the green ends as possible; wash them to remove sand and grit and cut them in 1-inch lengths. Add to the pot with 3 quarts water and the barley. Cover and cook on a flame so low that it takes 25 minutes to come to a simmer. After 1 hour add salt and pepper. It will take from 2 to 3 hours for the meat to separate from the bones, depending on the age of the chicken. One-half hour before it is done, add the prunes. Before serving, the loosened carcass and bones may be removed. Serve in a big tureen. The broth should be rich and the chicken very tender. Makes over 2 quarts.

VICHYSSOISE

4 good-sized potatoes
1 large onion
4 tablespoons butter
6 good-sized leeks
¼ teaspoon nutmeg
salt and pepper

5 cups rich chicken broth
1 cup milk
1 cup cream

GARNISH
minced chives

Peel and dice fine the potatoes and onion, put them in a heavy pot with the butter, and simmer gently while you prepare the leeks. Trim the leeks, removing no more of the green ends than necessary. Separate the leaves and wash them well. Cut them in ¼-inch lengths, then add them, the seasonings, and ⅔ cup water to the potatoes and onions. Cover tight and cook until the vegetables are very tender. Press through a sieve or purée in the electric blender, then add the chicken broth, milk, and cream. The goodness of the soup depends a great deal on the quality of the broth. This is usually served cold. Garnish with chopped chives. The soup should not be too thick; if necessary, add more broth and cream. ˉ Iakes 2 quarts.

SAUTÉED LEEKS IN SOUPS AND SAUCES

One fat leek, minced, makes ½ cup. Fried in butter until they are tender, leeks make a delicious addition to creamed soups made with celery or cauliflower. Leeks may be used in the same way as chives. One-half cup leeks, fried in butter, may be added to cream sauces, egg sauce, butter sauce, and mayonnaise.

BUTTERED LEEKS

1 or 2 bunches leeks
3 or 6 tablespoons butter

paprika
salt and pepper

A good-sized bunch of leeks will serve 4. Trim and wash them well. Leave as much of the green ends on as possible. They may be cut in half lengthwise if they are very large. Put them in a very heavy pot with the butter and the water that clings to them, cover tight, and steam tender—if leeks are young, they will take but 10 minutes—or cook in the pressure cooker 2½ to 3 minutes. When they are tender remove from the fire. Too long cooking destroys their delicate flavor. Empty them into a hot serving dish, add paprika to the liquid, and pour it over them. Season with salt and pepper. If the leeks are dried after washing, 2 or 3 tablespoons water may be added so they will not burn.

BRAISED LEEKS IN BROTH

1 bunch leeks	2 teaspoons cornstarch
2 tablespoons butter	1 tablespoon lemon juice
salt and pepper	*GARNISH*
½ cup chicken or veal broth	chopped parsley

Trim and wash the leeks well to remove sand and grit. If they are large cut them in two lengthwise. Heat the leeks in the butter in a heavy pot and add the seasoning and broth. Cover tight and simmer until the leeks are tender—10 to 12 minutes. When they are done blend the cornstarch with the lemon juice and 1 tablespoon cold water and add. Cook until the liquid thickens to the consistency of cream. Remove the leeks and sauce to a hot serving dish and garnish the top with chopped parsley. If preferred, the leeks may be served on thin crisp toast on individual plates. Serves 4.

LEEKS AND BROWN RICE

1 cup brown rice	3 big leeks, minced
2 cups chicken consommé	¼ cup butter

Cook the rice in the consommé 45 minutes, covered, over the lowest flame. Meanwhile sauté the leeks in butter. Stir into the rice, re-cover, and let stand 10 minutes with the flame turned off. Serves 4 or 5.

LEEKS AND EGG-NOODLE SHELLS

4 large leeks, cut in ½-inch lengths	12 oz. little egg-noodle shells
⅓ cup butter	boiling water
salt and pepper	grated Parmesan cheese

Sauté the leeks in the butter and season with salt and pepper. Boil the little noodle shells in salted boiling water about 6 minutes or until they are tender, drain them, and toss with the leeks. Empty into a hot serving dish and add Parmesan cheese liberally to the top. Serves 5 or 6.

CREAMED LEEKS

1 bunch leeks
2 tablespoons butter
¼ cup broth
salt and pepper
½ cup light cream

2 to 2½ teaspoons cornstarch
¼ teaspoon nutmeg
GARNISH
⅓ cup grated Cheddar or
Parmesan cheese

Trim and wash the leeks, leaving as much green as possible. Cut them in half lengthwise; this facilitates cleaning them. Let them heat in the butter, add the broth, cover tight, and cook slowly until tender. Add a little salt and pepper to the cream, blend in the cornstarch, and add to the liquid with the leeks. Add the nutmeg and cook the sauce until it thickens. Empty the leeks and sauce into a serving dish and sprinkle the top with cheese. They may be served on thin crisp toast if desired. Serves 4.

LEEKS WITH LEMON SAUCE

1 bunch leeks
2 or 3 tablespoons butter
2 or 3 tablespoons lemon juice
salt and pepper
paprika

½ to ¾ teaspoon cornstarch
crisp buttered toast
GARNISH
2 hard-boiled eggs, sieved

Heat the leeks in the butter, add 2 or 3 tablespoons water and the juice and seasoning. Cover and steam until tender. Blend the cornstarch with 1 tablespoon cold water and add. Cook until the sauce thickens, lay the leeks on the toast, spoon over the sauce, and sprinkle with the egg. Serves 4.

BAKED LEEKS AND TOMATOES

4 or 6 leeks
¼ cup butter
4 good-sized tomatoes
salt and pepper

basil
1½ teaspoons cornstarch
½ cup heavy cream

Trim and wash the leeks and cut them in 1-inch lengths. Put them with the butter in a shallow baking dish and bake them at 375° for 5 minutes while you skin the tomatoes. Cut the tomatoes in half across, sprinkle them with salt and pepper and basil, and lay them on the leeks. Bake them 5 minutes, then turn them over and bake 5 or 6 minutes on the other side. Blend the cornstarch in the cream. Lay the tomatoes on a hot platter and add the cream to the leeks in the pan. Let it thicken, see that it is well seasoned, then scrape all the sauce over the tomatoes. If the tomatoes are thick and large, ½ tomato will be sufficient for each serving—depending on whether the meal is simple or elaborate.

LEEK TART

2 large potatoes	fine browned crumbs
1 small onion	2 cups minced leeks (4 fat leeks)
salt and pepper	1 cup sour cream
¼ cup cream	1 egg, beaten
butter	

Peel and dice the potatoes and onion quite fine. Put them in a heavy pot to cook, covered, with ¼ cup water, salt, and pepper. When they are soft, do not drain; mash them, adding cream and butter. They should be creamy and light. Grease a pie plate and line it, sides and bottom, with the crumbs. Cover the crumbs with the potato, spreading it so it is like a pie crust. Sauté the minced leeks in butter until they are tender—about 3 or 4 minutes over a slow fire. Season with salt and pepper. Do not burn them. Spread them over the potato. Season the sour cream, mix with the egg, and spread over the leeks. Bake in a 375° oven until the cream is ivory color and the pie is hot. Serve immediately. Serves 4 to 6.

LEEKS AND CHICKEN LIVERS

1 lb. chicken livers	butter
2 teaspoons sugar	1¼ cups minced leeks
2 tablespoons flour	¼ cup cream
dash of mace or nutmeg	2 tablespoons sherry
salt and pepper	

If chicken livers are lightly sprinkled with 2 teaspoons sugar mixed with seasoning, mace or nutmeg, and 2 tablespoons flour, they will sauté in butter to a rich brown without too hot a flame. Sauté the leeks separately in a little butter and add them to the chicken livers when they are cooked. Empty onto a hot platter, add the cream and sherry to the pan the livers cooked in, let the liquid boil up, and scrape it over the livers and leeks. Calf's liver may be prepared the same way.

STUFFED EGGS WITH LEEKS

5 or 6 hard-boiled eggs, halved
1 cup minced leeks, sautéed in butter
salt and pepper

dash of nutmeg
sour cream
mayonnaise

Peel the eggs and cut them in half across, then remove the yolks and mash them with a fork. Make a smooth fluffy paste with the egg yolks and the other ingredients, lightly mixing in the fried leeks. Refill the egg whites.

LEEK OMELET

1 cup minced leeks
butter
salt and pepper

4- or 5-egg omelet (see page 106)
GARNISH
grated Parmesan cheese

Sauté the leeks in butter until they are tender, then season with salt and pepper. When the omelet is cooked spread the leeks over it, fold, slide it off onto a hot platter, and sprinkle the top with grated cheese. Sautéed leeks may be added to scrambled eggs also. Serves 3 or 4.

LEEKS AS GARNISH

As leeks are more delicate than onions, they may be used with a liberal hand. Minced leeks sautéed in butter may be added to fried or creamed seafood and fish and to broiled fish or steak. They improve veal or lamb stews, and if they are young and tender they need not be sautéed before adding to salads. Add sautéed leeks to fried calf's brains and to broiled or creamed sweetbreads. Sautéed leeks may be added to asparagus, creamed or buttered, to cauliflower, and to practically any vegetable that is improved by a delicate onion flavor. Add 1 cup minced sautéed leeks to hot potato salad.

LETTUCE

To most people lettuce means salad, and to make good salads it is important to know the different kinds of lettuce and how they may be combined with other greens, herbs, and a number of foods. There are five classes of lettuce, and each class contains more than one variety. The two most popular varieties of the *butterhead* class are Boston and Bibb lettuce. Boston lettuce is excellent in tossed green salads and for garnishing; it is too soft and becomes moist if combined with fruits and vegetables. Bibb is a delicious, tender, meaty, and attractive lettuce in small heads the shape of a rosette. It is a favorite lettuce to serve with French dressing, with or without Roquefort cheese. The best-known of the *Cos* class is romaine, much used by the Italians; it retains its crispness when used for tossed green salads or for garnishing salads of seafood, fruit, or mixed vegetables. The *leaf* (bunching) class includes Simpson and Slobolt lettuce—fine, crisp, loose heads, suitable for all salads. Many soft-leaf garden lettuces belong to this class and anyone growing them knows how fine a salad is when made with the young tender leaves mixed with a light French dressing and some fresh crushed herbs. *Stem* lettuce or celtuce has no heads, but the stems grow long and may be eaten raw or cooked. The *crisphead* class includes iceberg lettuce—very firm, closely packed heads which make good lettuce cups for seafood and other moist salad fillings; but it lacks the qualities of color and flavor so important in mixed green salads.

The best tossed salads are mixtures of lettuces with other greens which increases interest of texture, color, and flavor. These greens include chopped parsley, stemmed watercress, land cress, Belgian endive, chicory, sorrel, escarole, spinach, cabbage, celery cabbage, field and corn salad, celery leaves, very young and tender mustard greens, turnip and beet tops, chard, dandelion, raab, nasturtium leaves, and arracuolo, a tender, meaty leaf.

Besides greens, the most important ingredients of salads are all the members of the onion family: minced onion, scallions, leeks, shallots, chives, and garlic. Cooks are becoming less timid in their use of garlic, to the great improvement of their salads. As many as six buds may be crushed or sliced, fried a moment in olive oil or bacon fat, and mixed with a green salad. Garlic is especially fine with tender spinach leaves. Other vegetables most often used with lettuce are tomatoes, cucumbers, radishes, celery, beans, peppers, celeriac sticks, artichoke hearts, carrots, cauliflower, peas, and asparagus. Avocado is a great favorite, and fruits of all kinds make excellent main-course salads for lunch or supper. Other excellent salads for main dishes may be made with seafood, chicken, turkey, tongue, ham, eggs, and cheese.

Herbs give variety and fascinating, subtle flavors to salads. The most widely used are tarragon, basil, fennel, summer savory, chervil, mint, anise, thyme, dill, and marjoram. There are others, and experiment with combinations of herbs will reward anyone who loves salads. Mayonnaise is never used on green tossed salads, only French dressings and their variations. Mayonnaise may be used on meat, egg, fruit, and vegetable-filled salads.

There are some soups and a few cooked dishes of lettuce. But the best way to use lettuce is to eat it raw, because of its delicate texture and flavor.

LETTUCE SOUP

1 large head Boston lettuce
1 bunch green onions
3 tablespoons bacon or ham fat
salt and pepper
1 teaspoon curry powder
1 teaspoon basil or tarragon
½ teaspoon paprika

½ teaspoon turmeric
1 cup milk
1 cup light cream
                GARNISH
2 or 3 hard-boiled eggs
grated Parmesan cheese

Wash, drain, and shred the lettuce quite fine. Mince the onions, using as much of the green ends as are fresh and in good condition. Sauté the onions 2 minutes in the fat, then add the lettuce, seasonings (including curry powder, herb, paprika, and turmeric), and ⅓ cup water. Cover and steam until tender, or cook in the pressure cooker 1½ minutes. Reserve 3 tablespoons of the lettuce and purée the rest, using an electric blender if available. Thin the purée with the milk and cream and add more seasonings if necessary. Add the reserved lettuce. Garnish each soup cup or plate with 2 or 3 slices of egg and Parmesan cheese. This may be served hot or cold and is a very fine spring or summer soup. Serves 4 to 6.

LETTUCE AND ALMOND SOUP

1 head Boston lettuce	salt and pepper
1 head romaine lettuce	1 cup milk
1 bunch green onions, minced	1 cup light cream
¼ cup ham or bacon fat	1 cup chicken broth
1 teaspoon curry powder or	*GARNISH*
turmeric	⅓ cup chopped browned almonds

Wash and shred the heads of lettuce very fine. Sauté the minced onion in the ham or bacon fat for 2 minutes, using as much of the green ends as you can. Combine the onion, lettuce, and seasonings, add ⅓ cup water, and steam tender, covered, or cook 1½ to 2 minutes in the pressure cooker. Reserve 3 or 4 tablespoons of the lettuce and purée the rest, through a sieve or in the electric blender; then add the reserved shredded lettuce. Thin with the milk, cream, and chicken broth. One-half cup of cream and more broth may be used if desired. Serve hot or cold, garnished with the almonds. Serves 6 to 8.

LETTUCE AND PEA SOUP

1 head Boston or Simpson lettuce	1 teaspoon basil or tarragon
2 lbs. fresh peas	¼ teaspoon nutmeg
1 bunch green onions, minced	milk
¼ cup butter	1 cup light cream
salt and pepper	chicken broth (optional)
1 teaspoon simple syrup	

Wash and shred a medium-sized head of lettuce. Shell the peas. Sauté the minced onions (using the green part also) in the butter about 2 minutes and add the lettuce and peas. Season and add syrup, herb, nutmeg, and ⅓ cup water, and steam tender, tightly covered— or cook 2 minutes in the pressure cooker. Reserve 3 tablespoons of lettuce and peas and purée the rest through a sieve or in the electric blender. Return the peas and lettuce to the soup and thin with milk, cream, and broth if desired. The consistency should be like heavy cream. This may be served hot or cold. Serves 6 to 8.

BRAISED LETTUCE

SAUCE

6 mushrooms or chicken livers, sliced
2 tablespoons butter
salt and pepper
¼ teaspoon nutmeg
⅔ cup light cream

3 teaspoons cornstarch
⅓ cup chicken broth
2 tablespoons sherry

2 or 3 heads Boston lettuce
3 tablespoons melted butter
⅓ cup minced green onions

Sauté the mushrooms or livers in the butter 3 or 4 minutes and add the seasonings. (If livers are used, mash them.) Blend the cream with the cornstarch and add. Add the broth and stir until it thickens. Add the sherry. Clean and trim the lettuce. It may be left whole if the heads aren't too large, or it may be cut in wide ribbons. Drain it well and put it in a heavy pot on top of the melted butter. Stir it over a gentle fire until it is slightly tender, but do not cook it until it is a limp mass. The sauce must be ready to pour over it. Transfer to a serving dish. Sprinkle the onions over the top.

STUFFED LETTUCE ROLLS

large outside leaves or small heads of lettuce
boiling water
3 strips bacon
3 or 4 tablespoons cream
FILLING
1 cup ground meat: chicken, veal, turkey, or lamb
3 chicken livers, sautéed and mashed

½ cup minced mushrooms, sautéed
½ cup breadcrumbs
½ cup cooked brown rice
2 pork sausages, sautéed, or ⅓ cup ground ham
salt and pepper
1 egg, beaten
3 tablespoons sherry

Blanch the lettuce leaves for 2 minutes in boiling water then drain well. If small individual lettuces are used, just core them. Half-fry the bacon and lay it on the bottom of a baking pan or heavy pot. Add the cream. Mix all the filling ingredients and place a portion on each lettuce leaf. Roll the leaves like packages, with the ends folded under so they will stay intact. (Or fill the cores of small lettuces and tie them with string.) Lay the rolls on the bacon, close together. Bake in the oven or braise in a covered heavy pot very slowly for 25 minutes. When they are tender, lift carefully onto a hot platter and pour the pan liquid over the top. Makes 8 to 12 small rolls.

WILTED LETTUCE 1

salad bowl of lettuce
other greens, if desired
3 strips bacon
¾ cup sliced onions
2 teaspoons basil or tarragon
2 or 3 teaspoons light brown sugar

salt and pepper
3 tablespoons lemon juice, vinegar,
   or sweet Italian vermouth
GARNISH
2 hard-boiled eggs

Use Simpson or tender romaine lettuce torn into good-sized pieces. Any tender greens such as spinach or turnip tops or beet tops may be added to the lettuce. This amount of dressing will be sufficient for a bowl of greens to serve 5 or 6. Cut the bacon in 1-inch lengths and fry it until it is crisp. Reserve the bits of bacon and fry the onions in the fat until tender, then add the herb, sugar, and seasonings to taste. Instead of the sugar, half as much honey may be used. Add the lemon juice. Let the dressing heat, pour it over the greens, add the bits of bacon, mix well. Sieve the egg over the top. Serve immediately.

WILTED LETTUCE 2

salad bowl of lettuce
3 strips bacon
2½ teaspoons cornstarch
1 cup light cream
3 teaspoons light brown sugar
salt and pepper

1 teaspoon basil
¼ teaspoon dry mustard or ½
   teaspoon curry powder
1 egg, beaten
2 tablespoons lemon juice
2 tablespoons weak vinegar

Prepare a large bowl of salad greens torn into pieces. Cut the bacon into 1-inch pieces and fry it. When it is crisp remove the pieces and add them to the greens. One-half cup minced green onions may be added if desired. Mix the cornstarch with the cream, add, sugar, seasoning, herb, and mustard. Cook until the cream thickens, remove from stove, add the beaten egg, and cook a few seconds more, stirring continuously. Add the juice and vinegar and pour over the greens. Serve immediately.

BIBB LETTUCE WITH HOLLANDAISE SAUCE

1 small head Bibb lettuce per   **Hollandaise Sauce (page 137)**
person

Trim and wash the lettuces very well and drain. Put the heads in a steamer, tops down, and steam over boiling water for 2 minutes. Shake them to remove excess moisture. Put them on salad plates and add 2 or 3 tablespoons Hollandaise sauce to the top of each. Serve after the entrée as a separate course in place of a green vegetable or salad.

TOSSED GREEN SALAD

salad bowl of crisp lettuce
handful of stemmed watercress
few leaves of stemmed torn sorrel
4 anchovy fillets or crumbled
   Roquefort cheese
½ cup minced green onions

FRENCH DRESSING

3 tablespoons lemon juice, weak
   tarragon vinegar, or lime juice
dash of simple syrup
salt and freshly ground pepper
1 teaspoon powdered fennel
7 or 8 tablespoons olive oil

Use any fresh, cleaned, drained greens you wish; the watercress and sorrel are suggested additions. Cut the fillets into ½-inch lengths and toss them (or the crumbled cheese) and the onions with the greens. Just before serving, mix each ingredient for the dressing with the greens, one at a time. Dressed salad should never stand. The dressing may be mixed ahead of time, but for everyday salads one gets in the habit of mixing the salad just before serving, according to one's own taste.

A salad bowl of greens for two should have about one-third as much acid in the dressing. One teaspoon syrup in a good-sized bowl of greens doesn't make it sweet, it merely emphasizes the flavors. Use other herbs instead of fennel if you prefer.

SALAD WITH ROQUEFORT SOUR-CREAM DRESSING

¼ cup Roquefort cheese	½ teaspoon paprika
⅓ cup sour cream	6 or 7 tablespoons olive oil
3 tablespoons lime or lemon juice	2 minced green onions
salt and pepper	salad bowl of crisp greens

Mash the cheese and blend it with the sour cream until it is smooth. Mix the rest of the ingredients in slowly, adding the onions last. Mix with the salad greens.

CHINESE MUSHROOM AND LETTUCE SALAD

finely shredded lettuce	⅓ cup chopped chives or green
1 lb. fresh mushrooms	onions
broth	2 tablespoons sherry
2 tablespoons olive oil	

Make a good-sized bed of shredded lettuce in the salad bowl. Select small mushrooms of uniform size, clean, and leave them whole. Steam them tender in a little chicken or light meat broth, adding a little at a time as needed. When the mushrooms are done add them and not more than ¼ cup liquid to the lettuce and toss with the olive oil, chives or onions, and sherry. The Chinese use their dried mushrooms for this dish but the fresh are as good. This may be served as a vegetable.

SPRING GARDEN SALAD

salad bowl of tender leaf lettuce	salt and pepper
3 hard-boiled eggs	1 tablespoon tarragon vinegar
2 or 3 teaspoons honey (to taste)	bruised tarragon leaves
2 tablespoons lime or lemon juice	7 tablespoons olive oil

Wash the lettuce and dry it thoroughly, then break it into pieces into the salad bowl. Separate the yolks and whites of the eggs. Mash the yolks to a cream with the honey and add the rest of the ingredients. Mix with the lettuce and sieve the egg whites over the top of the salad.

RUSSIAN CHICORY SALAD

salad bowl of curly chicory
½ cup oil mayonnaise
¼ cup tomato sauce

⅓ cup sour cream
1 tablespoon horseradish

Use bitter, very crisp chicory for this dressing. Mix the ingredients together and toss lightly with the greens. Use plenty of greens for this amount.

Note: See page 166 for oil mayonnaise.

CHICKEN-LIVER SALAD

3 or 4 chicken livers, boiled or
   fried
French dressing

salad bowl of crisp (preferably
   Bibb) lettuce
2 hard-boiled eggs

This is one of the finest salads, especially with Bibb lettuce. Mash the livers and mix them with the French dressing. Toss the dressing with the lettuce and after it is mixed sieve the eggs over the top.

LETTUCE SANDWICHES

crisp lettuce leaves or shredded
   lettuce
whole-wheat or rye bread
butter
mayonnaise or mayonnaise and
   mustard

ADDITIONS
sliced turkey, duck, or chicken
sliced or ground ham
sliced or mashed hard-boiled eggs
sliced tomatoes and bacon
grated cheese
sliced cucumber and minced fresh dill

Sandwiches with lettuce must always be made fresh, or the lettuce will become wilted and limp. Slice the bread thin and toast it if you wish. Butter it before adding mayonnaise or mayonnaise mixed with mustard; the latter is good with ham.

Peanut-butter sandwiches are good with minced pickle added, and lettuce is necessary for freshness. A book could easily be written about the part lettuce plays in salads and sandwiches, but the hints at the beginning and the end of this section must suffice.

OKRA

As the first part of this book points out, those who have okra in their gardens can appreciate its delicate flavor at its best. In recent years it has become available in Northern markets, but for generations in the South it has been served as a vegetable and has gone into the making of gumbos, soups, and salads. Indeed it is possible that the gumbo or soup-like stew took its name from the Congo word for okra, a corruption of *quingombo*.

The addition of okra in ½-inch lengths to chicken, meat, or vegetable soups makes the dishes especially attractive. Okra may also be added to many vegetables: peas, tomatoes, onions, peppers, corn, squash, and eggplant. Pilaus of rice and okra are familiar Creole dishes. Anyone loving the cuisine of the South enjoys cooking with this vegetable.

OKRA SOUP

1 cracked shinbone of beef	1 cup finely diced carrots
salt and pepper	4 tomatoes, skinned, seeded, and
1 bay leaf	sliced
1 large onion, sliced	1 cup diced onions
1 pt. okra, sliced	1 green pepper, diced
1 teaspoon thyme	1 tablespoon lemon juice
1 teaspoon brown sugar	

Get a bone with some meat on it. Put it in a big soup kettle with 2½ quarts water, salt, pepper, bay leaf, and onion. Cook gently 2¼ hours. Cool and skim all fat off. The okra should be well washed, with ends removed, and cut in ½-inch slices. Strain the soup, add all the rest of the ingredients, and cook 1 hour. Makes over 2 quarts.

CREOLE CHICKEN GUMBO

4 strips bacon
1 5-lb. roasting chicken, disjointed
1 cup diced smoked ham
1 cup diced onions
1 teaspoon thyme
salt and pepper
1 tablespoon brown sugar

½ teaspoon ginger
1 lb. tomatoes, skinned and sliced
3 qts. warm (not boiling) water
1 lb. young okra
2 to 4 teaspoons gumbo filé
(optional)

Cut the bacon in pieces and fry it a little in the bottom of a large soup kettle, then add the chicken, ham, and onions. Cook gently for 20 minutes until everything is nice and brown. Add the thyme, seasonings, sugar, ginger, and tomatoes and cook another 10 minutes. Add the warm water, cover, and simmer very gently for 2 hours. Remove the bones from the chicken and return the meat in large pieces to the kettle. Wash the okra well, tip it, and cut in ½-inch slices. Add it to the soup and cook gently for ½ hour longer. For a real Creole flavor, add the filé and stir it in after the soup is done and ready to serve; do not cook it. Filé contains sassafras, and unless stirred vigorously the soup will become stringy. At first use only 2 teaspoons of filé to learn whether or not you like the flavor. Gumbos are always accompanied by rice.

Gumbos may be made with meat and carcasses of chicken or turkey, and they are also excellent ways of using leftover roasts and ham bones. Serves 10 to 12.

OYSTER GUMBO

1 3½- to 4-lb. chicken, disjointed
3 tablespoons flour
salt and pepper
fat, oil, or butter
1 cup diced smoked ham
1 green pepper, diced
1½ cups diced onions
½ cup diced celery
2 bay leaves

1 cup skinned sliced tomatoes
⅛ teaspoon cayenne pepper
1 tablespoon brown sugar
2 teaspoons curry powder
2 qts. warm water
1 lb. fresh okra
2 tablespoons butter
2 cups oysters and liquor

Toss the chicken in the flour seasoned with salt and pepper and brown it in some fat, oil, or butter in the bottom of a soup kettle.

Add the ham, green pepper, and onions, and cook them together for 15 minutes over a low flame. Then add the celery, bay leaves, tomatoes, cayenne, sugar, curry powder, and warm (not boiling) water. Cover and simmer very gently for 1¾ hours. Scoop out the chicken, remove the meat from the bones, and return it to the soup. Clean the okra, stem it, and brown it lightly in the butter and add it to the gumbo and cook 20 minutes longer at just a simmer. See that the mixture is well seasoned, adding more salt, pepper, and curry powder if desired. Gumbo filé may be added if desired, as directed in the recipe for Creole Chicken Gumbo. Just before serving, heat the soup, add the oysters and their liquor, and serve immediately. This will serve 10 or 12. The accompaniment should be boiled brown rice. Serve in soup plates with rice on the side. This improves every time it is reheated, and may be extended by adding a can of flaked crabmeat or a pound of freshly cooked shrimp and their broth.

CRAB OR SHRIMP GUMBO

recipe for Oyster Gumbo, omitting   6 large crabs or 1 lb. shrimp
oysters

Follow the preceding directions for Oyster Gumbo. Wash the crabs and put them in boiling water and cook them 15 minutes. Use no more water than is necessary and add it to the gumbo with the okra. Pick the crabmeat from the shells and add 10 minutes before the gumbo is done. If shrimp is used, simmer the washed shrimp in 1 cup water for 5 minutes. Let them cool in the liquid, shell them, and add them and the broth to the gumbo 10 minutes before it is done. A rich seafood gumbo may be made using all three: oysters, crab, and shrimp. If it becomes too thick, more broth or water may be added. Always serve with hot boiled brown rice. This may serve 12.

OKRA WITH TOMATO AND SOUR CREAM

1 lb. okra   ½ cup thick sour cream
salt and pepper   *GARNISH*
½ cup thick tomato sauce   grated cheese or chopped parsley

Wash and tip the okra and cook in ⅓ cup seasoned water, covered, for 5 to 7 minutes or until it is tender and the water absorbed. Mix the sauce and sour cream, add, and heat. When it is hot, pour into a serving dish and sprinkle the top with cheese or parsley. A good canned tomato sauce may be used. Serves 4 or 5.

OKRA WITH CORN AND GREEN PEPPERS

2 green peppers, diced
½ cup minced green onions
4 tablespoons butter
2 cups corn, cooked and cut from
    ears

½ lb. okra, sliced
salt and pepper

Sauté the green peppers and onions in the butter until they are tender. Add the corn. Wash and tip the okra and cook it 7 minutes in very little water. Watch it carefully so that it does not burn, for it will absorb the water. Season, toss all the vegetables together, and add more butter or a little hot cream if necessary. Serve with any meat or poultry. Serves 4 to 6.

FRIED OKRA

3 cups okra
salt and pepper
fine corn meal

olive oil
GARNISH
chopped parsley or green onions

Wash the okra and cut off the ends. Cut it in half, or leave whole if the pods are quite small. Let them cook 3 or 4 minutes in a little salted water. If the water is not absorbed, drain them. Roll them in seasoned fine corn meal and brown them in olive oil. Empty into a serving dish and garnish with parsley or minced green onions. Cooked whole okra may be dipped in egg and flour batter and French-fried in oil. Drain on brown paper and serve with fried chicken. Serves 4 or 5.

CREAMED FRIED OKRA

1 lb. okra
3 strips hickory-smoked bacon
2 teaspoons cornstarch
1 cup light cream

⅓ cup grated Cheddar cheese
salt and pepper
¾ teaspoon turmeric

Wash the okra and remove the ends. Add ⅓ cup water and cook slowly, covered, 5 to 7 minutes or until it is tender and the water evaporated. Cut the bacon in 1-inch pieces and fry in a skillet until crisp, then remove the pieces. Put the okra in the fat and fry it briskly for 2 minutes. Blend the cornstarch with the cream (milk may be used if a leaner dish is desired). Add the cheese and seasonings, pour over the okra, and cook very gently until the sauce is thick and the cheese melted. Pour into a serving dish and add the pieces of bacon to the top. Serves 4 or 5.

OKRA PILAU

1 cup brown rice	2 cups okra
1 cup tomato juice	2 tablespoons butter
salt and pepper	GARNISH
½ teaspoon curry powder or turmeric	½ cup minced green onions

Wash the rice and put it in a heavy pot with 1 cup water, tomato juice, a little salt, pepper, and curry powder or turmeric. Let it come to a boil, cover, and turn down to the lowest possible flame. Cook for 45 minutes without raising the lid. Turn off the flame and let it stand another 7 or 8 minutes. Wash the okra well, cut off the ends, and slice it in ½-inch lengths. Add ⅓ cup water and cook it slowly, covered, 7 or 8 minutes or until it is tender. Watch that it does not burn. Add the butter to the rice and lightly toss it with the okra. Empty into a serving dish and add the onions to the top. This pink rice is attractive tossed with crab or shrimp. Serves 4 or 5.

OKRA PILAU WITH SHRIMP OR CRAB

½ lb. fresh shrimp or crabmeat	salt
1 bay leaf	recipe for Okra Pilau

Wash the shrimp and cook them in 1 cup water, with the bay leaf and a little salt added, for 7 or 8 minutes. Let them cool in the liquid, then strain and reserve the liquid for cooking the rice. (If crabmeat is used, warm it in a little butter.) Peel the shrimp. Measure the shrimp broth and add enough tomato juice and water to make 2 cups. Chicken broth may be used instead of water and tomato juice if desired. Cook the rice and okra as for Okra Pilau (preceding recipe). When the rice is done add the seafood, cooked okra, and butter. Empty into a hot serving dish and sprinkle onions over the top. This recipe may be doubled to serve 8 or 10. These pilaus are wonderful ways of cooking brown rice to serve with game, poultry, fish dinners, or curries. They also may be served as a main supper dish preceded by a soup and accompanied by a green salad.

LAMB OR VEAL STEW WITH OKRA

1½ lbs. lamb or veal for stew	2 tablespoons fat
2 tablespoons flour	2 tomatoes, skinned
1 tablespoon brown sugar	3 tablespoons white wine
2 teaspoons orégano	2 cups okra
salt and pepper	*GARNISH*
⅔ cup diced onions	chopped parsley

Have the meat cut in 1½-inch cubes. Mix the flour, sugar, 1 tea-spoon orégano, and seasoning, and toss with the meat. Brown the meat with the onion in the fat in a heavy pot, then add the tomatoes, 1 cup water, and wine. Cover and braise for 50 minutes. Wash and tip the okra and slice in ½-inch slices. Add it to the stew and cook 15 minutes more. See that it is well seasoned and sprinkle another teaspoon of orégano into the stew. Garnish the top with parsley. Serve with boiled brown rice. Serves 4.

OKRA SALAD

very tender young okra	salad greens
tomatoes, skinned, chilled, and sliced	oil mayonnaise

Wash the okra in soda water so it is bright green. Rinse very well, then cook for 7 minutes in salted water. Use ⅓ cup water to 1 pound okra, cover tight, and let the water be absorbed. Chill the okra. Lay the tomatoes on a bed of greens, put 3 or 4 okra pods on top of each tomato, and dress each with 2 tablespoons oil mayonnaise. Chilled cooked okra may be tossed in a green salad. Only young and tender pods should be used in salads.

ONIONS

One might say the onion is the universal vegetable. At least in the vegetable kingdom it is of prime importance, as it may be prepared by itself and also may be cooked and prepared with every other vegetable. It "perfumes" the canapé and sandwich; it is necessary to nearly every soup and stew; it seasons fish, meats, poultry, casseroles, egg and cheese dishes, salads, breads, and sauces. It is made into tarts and soufflés. It is canned and pickled, alone and with other vegetables. The onion and its cousins, the shallot, garlic, leek, and chive are used by every good cook in every land. The green onion, the yellow, white, red Italian sweet, and the big Bermuda are the garden's most important vegetables.

ONION SOUP

4 large sweet Italian onions or 2   8 cups hot beef consommé
  large Bermuda onions   2 tablespoons Marsala or Madeira
5 tablespoons butter   *GARNISH*
¼ teaspoon powdered cloves   Italian or French bread, toasted
salt and pepper   with Gruyère cheese
1 teaspoon honey

Peel and slice the onions very thin, put them in a heavy pot or skillet with the butter, cloves, salt, pepper, and honey, and cook gently until tender, about 20 minutes, over a very low flame. Add the boiling consommé and cook, covered, for another 20 minutes over an equally low flame. The soup is better if it is made several hours before serving. When ready to serve, heat, add the wine, and put into soup bowls or plates. Put a piece of cheese toast on top of each serving. If more body is desired, blend 1½ teaspoons cornstarch with 2 tablespoons cold water and add to the soup just before it is done. Makes about 8 cups.

CREAM OF ONION SOUP

5 medium-sized onions   1 cup cream, scalded
3 tablespoons butter   2 egg yolks, beaten
6 or 7 cups hot chicken consommé   dash of nutmeg or mace
1 tablespoon cornstarch   *GARNISH*
salt and pepper   grated Parmesan cheese
2 tablespoons cold water

Peel and slice the onions very thin and put them in a heavy pot or skillet with the butter over a low fire. Cook them 20 minutes but watch that they do not burn. Stir them occasionally. Add the boiling consommé and cook another 20 minutes, covered. Blend the cornstarch with the water, add 2 minutes before the soup is done, and cook until it thickens a little. Mix the cream with the egg yolk and nutmeg, add a little of the soup to it, and then mix it all in. Do not boil after the cream is added. Serve and pass a bowl of cheese to add to the top. Makes about 7 cups.

BRAISED BEEF WITH RED WINE AND ONIONS

1 onion, diced
1 bay leaf
½ cup red wine
¼ cup rum
2½ lbs. round or chuck

honey and oil
salt and pepper
12 small white onions
3 teaspoons cornstarch
2 tablespoons wine

Make a marinade of the diced onion, bay leaf, wine, and rum. Put the beef in it for 12 or more hours and turn it at least six times. When ready to braise it, remove the meat from the marinade and brown it quickly in a tablespoon or more of honey and a little fat or oil. See that it is glazed on all sides. Put it in a heavy roaster, season, rinse the glazing pan out with the marinade and pour it over the meat. Braise at 325° for 30 minutes, then another 30 minutes at 300°. Boil up the white onions so they are hot, drain, and put them with the meat. Cover and cook another ½ hour or until the onions and the meat are done. Blend the cornstarch with 2 tablespoons cold water and add to the liquid. Cook until it thickens. Add the fresh wine just before serving. Put the meat on a hot platter surrounded with the sauce and onions. Knoedel or hot brown rice would be a good accompaniment. Serves 6.

BROWN RICE WITH GREEN ONIONS

1½ cups brown rice
3 cups chicken broth
1 teaspoon turmeric
¼ cup currants
¼ cup sherry

⅓ cup pine nuts (pignolias)
⅓ cup minced green onions
1 tablespoon minced preserved
    ginger or sweet pickles

Cook the rice, covered, with the broth and turmeric. For complete success with brown rice the measurements must be exact, as well as the cooking time, which is 45 minutes, with the fire at pilot-light strength, immediately after it comes to a boil. Turn the fire off after 45 minutes and keep covered for 10 minutes more. The pot must have a tight lid and be heavy. Marinate the currants in the sherry while the rice is cooking. Mix them and the rest of the ingredients in when the rice is done. This amount will serve 7 or 8 and is so good that any left over is always welcome. It is easy to reheat: sprinkle it with a little water and steam it, covered, until it is hot.

CHICKEN STUFFED WITH GREEN ONIONS

1 2-lb. broiler
oil and tarragon
1 cup chopped green onions
salt and pepper
1 teaspoon summer savory
butter or bacon fat

BROTH
chicken neck, wing tips, gizzard,
    and feet

1 carrot, minced
1 onion, minced
1 teaspoon beef extract
1 teaspoon tarragon or basil
salt and pepper

½ cup white wine
½ cup light cream
3 tablespoons cornstarch

If possible, get fresh-killed chicken. Have it left whole and keep it in the refrigerator 2 days at least before cooking. Rub it with oil and sprinkle it with tarragon. In the morning before you cook it mix the onion, salt, pepper, savory, and a little melted butter or bacon fat, and stuff into the chicken. Do not sew it up; if a few onions mix with the sauce that is good. Simmer all the ingredients for the broth with 2 cups water, over 1 hour (or 20 minutes in the pressure cooker). Let it stand until cool and strain it, mashing some of the vegetables through the sieve. Put the chicken in a pot with 2 cups of this broth, cover, and simmer very gently for 50 minutes, turning it over two or three times. Fifteen minutes before it is done add half the wine. Blend the cornstarch with the cream, add it slowly, and cook until it thickens; then add the rest of the wine. Serve the whole chicken with all the sauce in the big shallow dish accompanied by hot brown rice. This will serve 4.

ONIONS MADÈRE

1½ lbs. white onions
brown sugar or honey
butter
dash of powdered cloves or mace

salt and pepper
⅓ cup Madeira
¼ cup seedless raisins
2 tablespoons currants

Peel the onions and glaze them in the sugar or honey and butter until they are syrupy and brown all over. Put them in a shallow baking dish and add the spice, a light sprinkle of salt and pepper, the wine, and raisins and currants. Cover tight and bake about 40 minutes or until they are just tender. If there is a quantity of liquid after 20 minutes, uncover for the last half of the cooking. These are excellent with game or beef.

ONION PIE

FILLING	*DOUGH*
2¼ cups thinly sliced onions	1 cup flour
3 tablespoons butter	1½ teaspoons baking powder
salt and pepper	½ teaspoon salt
⅛ teaspoon powdered cloves	¼ cup lard
2 large eggs	milk
1 tablespoon flour	1 tablespoon soft butter
1 cup heavy sour cream	

Cook the onions with the butter, salt, pepper, and cloves in a heavy skillet until they are tender, about 20 minutes. Meanwhile make the dough. Sift the dry ingredients, cut in the lard, and add just enough milk to make a dough you can handle. Roll it out, handling as little as possible, spread with the butter, fold once, and roll it out to fit an 8- or 9-inch pie plate. Spread the onions evenly over the dough. Beat the eggs with the flour, add a little salt, and mix with the sour cream. Spread this over the filling and put the pie in a 375° oven for 15 minutes; then turn it down to 325° for another 5 to 7 minutes, or until set. This may be served as a lunch or supper dish with a salad, or with a roast-pork or ham dinner. It is served hot. A cup of sliced sautéed mushrooms may replace ¾ cup of the onions. Serves 6 to 8.

VEGETABLE MEAT LOAF

1 thick slice beef liver, ground	1 teaspoon each, basil, tarragon,
1½ lbs. top round of beef, ground	thyme
1 cup shredded raw potato	½ cup tomato sauce or catsup
1 cup shredded raw carrot	1 teaspoon Worcestershire sauce
1 cup finely diced onion	2 tablespoons lemon juice
½ lb. mushrooms, sliced	⅓ cup milk
¼ cup butter	½ teaspoon powdered cloves
2 egg yolks	2 egg whites, beaten until stiff
salt and pepper	6 strips lean bacon

If the butcher won't put the liver through the grinder for you, sear it and grind it. Mix it with the ground beef, shredded potato, and carrot (use a fine disk shredder). Sauté the onion and mushrooms separately in a little butter. Mix all the ingredients (except the bacon) together, folding in the stiffly beaten egg whites last. Line a large baking dish with the bacon strips. If the mixture seems a bit dry, a little sherry or tomato juice may be added. Fill the baking dish with the mixture and cover. Bake very slowly for 2 hours at 300°. Any liquid may be drained off and thickened with a little cornstarch mixed with cold tomato juice or water. If a quantity of sauce is desired, use a little more broth or tomato juice added to the liquid. Empty onto a chop plate or platter. If the bacon needs browning, remove it, brown, and replace on the top of the loaf. Serves 10 or 12. This is as fine as a pâté.

ONION SOUFFLÉ

8 white onions
salt and pepper
¼ teaspoon powdered cloves
2 tablespoons butter
4½ tablespoons flour

½ cup cream
5 egg yolks, beaten
3 egg whites, beaten until stiff
tomato or cheese sauce

Peel and slice the onions very thin and cook with ⅓ cup water, salt, pepper, and cloves. When very tender, mash the whole mixture through a sieve or purée in the electric blender. There should be about 2 cups of purée. Make a sauce by melting the butter, blending in the flour, and adding the cream. Cook until it is thick and add the egg yolks and the purée. Fold in the egg whites. Pour into a well-greased baking dish and bake at 350° 25 or 30 minutes or until set. Serve with a light tomato or cheese sauce. A quick and easy tomato sauce may be made by using a small tin of tomato sauce mixed with an equal amount of sour cream. Heat the tomato sauce and then mix with the sour cream. Serves 6.

ONIONS COOKED IN BROTH

1½ lbs. white onions
2 cups beef or chicken broth
¼ teaspoon powdered cloves
2 tablespoons red wine
1 teaspoon honey

salt and pepper
cornstarch
more wine
GARNISH
chopped parsley

Peel the onions and cook them in a heavy pot with the broth, clove, wine, honey, salt, and pepper until just tender. Blend the cornstarch (1 tablespoon to every cup of liquid) with 2 or 3 tablespoons wine or cold water. Add it to the liquid with the onions and cook until it thickens. Empty into a serving dish and sprinkle with chopped parsley.

ONION AND APPLE CASSEROLE

2 or 3 large Bermuda onions
butter
salt and pepper
5 tart apples

brown sugar
cinnamon
⅓ cup onion liquid

Peel and slice the onions quite thin, cook them in as little water as possible with a little butter, salt, and pepper. They should be only half tender. Peel and slice the apples thin. Put alternate layers of onions and apples in a greased baking dish, sprinkling each layer of apples with a little sugar and cinnamon, and each layer of onions with salt and pepper. Bits of butter may be added to every layer. Add the onion liquid to the top, cover tight, and bake 45 minutes, half the time at 350° and the latter half at 325°. Fifteen minutes before they are done, if they are too liquid, take the lid off. They should be firm and moist. Serve with pork. Serves 6 to 8.

CREAMED ONIONS

1½ lbs. white onions
3 tablespoons butter
salt and pepper
choice of other vegetables
  (optional):
  1 bunch new carrots
  2 cups corn
  3 green peppers, roasted and
    sliced
  1 qt. Brussels sprouts

1 lb. fresh okra
1 lb. little new white turnips
1 cauliflower
2 lbs. fresh peas
1½ lbs. little new potatoes
2½ tablespoons cornstarch
onion liquid and cream to make 2
  cups
dash of nutmeg
grated cheese or chopped parsley

If you are cooking onions alone, 2 cups of sauce may be too much, but with another vegetable as well that amount will be necessary. Always use all the water from cooking vegetables (except potatoes) to make the sauce. Peel the onions and cook with butter, salt, pepper, and ½ cup water. Cook any other vegetables you wish. Prepare carrots, turnips, cauliflower, or potatoes as nearly the same size as the onions as possible. Little new potatoes are best if baked or boiled in their jackets. Blend the cornstarch with some cream, measure it with the drained vegetable liquid, add more cream to make 2 cups, add nutmeg, and cook until it thickens. Combine with the onions and other vegetable, empty into a greased baking dish, and cover liberally with grated cheese or chopped parsley. Heat in a hot oven until the cheese melts, or put under the broiler. As much or as little of either vegetable may be prepared as required. A large casserole of mixed creamed vegetables may be made ahead of time and is an excellent dish to serve a number of people.

BAKED CREAMED BERMUDA OR ITALIAN ONIONS

4 large Bermuda onions or 8 sweet red Italian onions	½ cup onion water
	1 cup cream
salt and pepper	2 tablespoons butter
powdered cloves	salt and pepper
light brown sugar	
SAUCE	TOP
3 tablespoons flour	chopped parsley or grated cheese

The sauce quantities are sufficient to serve 8 persons. Cut the onions in half. (Half a Bermuda onion is sufficient for each person. Two smaller Italian onion halves may be required for each person.) Cook them in very little water until they are three-quarters done and still firm. Lay them in a large greased baking pan, cut side up, and sprinkle each half with salt, pepper, clove, and light brown sugar. Melt the butter in a saucepan, blend the flour with it, and when smooth add the onion water and cream. Cook until the sauce thickens and season with salt and pepper. Spoon over the onions and bake 35 to 40 minutes in a 325° oven. Five minutes before they are done add grated cheese to the top; or after they come from the oven sprinkle with chopped parsley. Lift onions and sauce onto a hot platter with a pancake turner.

STUFFED BERMUDA ONIONS

½ Bermuda onion per person	cream sauce
pork sausage	grated cheese
fresh dry breadcrumbs	

Follow the recipe for Baked Creamed Bermuda or Italian Onions, but when the onions have cooked almost done carefully remove the centers, chop them, and mix with pork sausage and crumbs. Stuff the onions, add the cream sauce, and bake as directed. (Omit the brown sugar and clove.) Five minutes before they are done, sprinkle with grated cheese.

BUTTERED ONIONS

small white onions or very large   paprika
  green onions   cornstarch (optional)
3 or 4 tablespoons butter   1 bouillon cube (optional)
salt and pepper   grated Parmesan cheese (optional)

Peel as many onions as required, usually 3 or 4 to a person. If large new green onions are available they should be cooked with 4 or 5 inches of their green stems left on. They are excellent buttered or creamed. Bring to a boil in ⅓ cup water, cover, and cook slowly 15 to 18 minutes. Watch them to see that they do not burn. Some of the butter and the seasoning may be added while they are cooking. (The pressure cooker takes from 4 to 7 minutes, depending on the size of the onions. They should not be cooked to a mush, so open the pot after they have cooked 4 minutes to test whether they are done.) Empty the onions into a hot serving dish, dress with more butter, and sprinkle with paprika. The liquid in the pot is fine thickened with a very little cornstarch, if there is more than ¼ cup. A little more butter may be added and a bouillon cube melted in it. This makes an excellent sauce for the onions, and the top may be sprinkled with a little grated cheese.

FRENCH-FRIED ONIONS

Bermuda onions or sweet Italian onions   salt and pepper
cold milk   beaten egg
flour   deep fat or oil

Peel the onions, slice them ¼ inch thick, and separate into rings. Soak them in cold milk for ½ hour. Drain well and then dust with flour seasoned with salt and pepper. Dip in beaten egg and dust again with flour. Put a few at a time in a wire basket so they do not stick together, and fry at 375° to 380° in deep oil. Drain on brown paper and keep in a warm oven with the door open until all are fried. These are excellent with broiled meats and fish. Onion rings may also be dusted with seasoned flour and fried without egg. Or they may be soaked in cold milk, drained, and fried crisp in plenty of very hot oil in a skillet. Drain on brown paper and lightly dust with salt.

CURRIED ONIONS

¼ cup dried currants
3 tablespoons sherry
1 to 1½ lbs. white onions
4 or 5 tablespoons butter
salt and pepper

1 to 2 teaspoons curry powder
cream
3 teaspoons cornstarch
1 tablespoon lemon juice
1 teaspoon honey

Marinate the currants in the sherry 1 hour. Peel the onions and cook 15 to 18 minutes with 2 or 3 tablespoons butter, salt, pepper, and ½ cup water. Meanwhile put the curry powder (according to taste) in the top of a double boiler and cook it in 2 tablespoons butter over hot water 10 minutes. When the onions are done, drain the onion liquid into a cup and add enough cream to make 1¼ cups. Blend in the cornstarch. Add the lemon juice and honey to the curry mixture and then add the cream and cook until it thickens. Add the onions and currants with the sherry. These are excellent with fish, seafood, or poultry.

SWEET PICKLED ONIONS

3 qts. small white onions
boiling water
⅔ cup salt
3 sticks cinnamon

1 tablespoon whole cloves
1 tablespoon whole allspice
1¾ cups sugar
6 cups vinegar

Cover the onions with boiling water for 2 minutes and then drain. Cover with cold water and peel—the skins come off easily when they are scalded. Mix the salt in cold water to cover the onions and let stand overnight, then rinse in cold water and drain. Put the spices in a double cheesecloth bag and boil gently ten minutes with the sugar and vinegar. Remove the spice bag, add the onions to the syrup, bring to a boil, and pack while hot in sterilized Mason jars and seal. The syrup from all pickles is fine, after the pickles are eaten, for seasoning strong vinegar for salads and for adding to ham.

ONIONS IN SALADS

Bermuda onions or sweet red onions, thinly sliced in rings, may be marinated in a jar with French dressing. They keep well several days, and as many as are required may be mixed through green salads or laid on top of sliced tomatoes and cucumbers.

Slice Bermuda onions or sweet red onions very thin and mix them with sour cream. Add salt and pepper, 1 teaspoon curry powder or Bahamian mustard, and serve very cold. Sliced cucumbers and strips of red pimento may be added.

All tossed green salads are better if several sliced green onions are added.

A very good orange salad may be made with paper-thin rings of Bermuda onion, sliced oranges, and sliced black Italian olives. This should be dressed with French dressing and garnished with watercress or lettuce.

ONIONS IN CANAPÉS AND SANDWICHES

Grated onions or onions chopped very fine, added to ground ham or chicken for sandwiches, improve the spread infinitely. Grated onions added to cream cheese, caviar, all sorts of fish spreads, chopped liver, or mashed boiled eggs, make excellent canapés and sandwiches.

Put slices of sweet onion on rounds of rye bread, top with grated cheese and put under the broiler until the cheese is melted.

Season mayonnaise with grated onion before spreading on sandwiches of all kinds.

No hamburger should be without a slice of sweet Italian or Bermuda onion.

PARSNIPS

It seems ridiculous to have to try to "sell" one of the most delicious vegetables of the garden, but all too many people feel, at best, apathetic about parsnips. They are missing a great deal of pleasure, for parsnips are delicate and sweet of flavor, and of a creamy texture which lends itself to many fine dishes.

The best way to prepare parsnips is to steam them in their jackets and then skin them as you do potatoes. They may also be boiled in very little water or scraped while raw. They should not be cooked too long or some of the flesh will come off with the skin. Like many other vegetables, parsnips are best when young and not too large. Large ones may be used in soups and stews, as large carrots are. Small, young parsnips are tender all through; large parsnips should be cut lengthwise after cooking and may reveal a core, which should be cut out and discarded. Parsnips are among the best additions to stews, meat pies, and soups, for they lend a sweetness like that of a dash of sugar. Every experienced cook knows that a bit of sweetening of some kind rescues many a dish from dullness. The parsnip was a favorite vegetable in Roman times, and its rediscovery is long overdue.

PARSNIP AND TURNIP SOUP

1 lb. parsnips	salt and pepper
1 lb. little white turnips	chicken broth or tomato juice
¼ cup diced onions	GARNISH
¼ cup butter	chopped parsley

Scrape the parsnips and peel the turnips, then slice them. Sauté the onion a minute or two in the butter, then add the vegetables, salt, pepper, and ¾ cup water. Cover tight and cook 12 to 15 minutes until very soft—or cook in the pressure cooker for 2½ minutes. Then mash (without draining, of course) through a sieve, or purée in the electric blender. Thin with either chicken broth or tomato juice. The combination of these two vegetables is very pleasant. Served cold, this makes a good summer soup, and it is equally good served hot in winter. Garnish with chopped parsley. Use enough liquid to make 6 cups.

CHICKEN PIE WITH PARSNIPS

1 4-lb. chicken, disjointed
beef bone or 1 teaspoon meat
    extract
1 carrot, diced
1 cup diced onions
salt and pepper
1 bay leaf
⅔ cup white wine

FILLING

meat of chicken
8 small white onions, peeled and
    boiled
1 lb. parsnips, skinned and boiled

3½ tablespoons cornstarch
½ cup cream
2½ cups broth
1 egg yolk
½ teaspoon nutmeg
3 tablespoons sherry

CRUST

1¼ cups flour
1 teaspoon salt
1 teaspoon baking powder
⅓ cup butter and lard mixed
ice water
2 tablespoons soft butter

Choose a young chicken that will simmer tender in a little over 1 hour. Put it on to cook with the beef bone, diced carrot and onions, seasonings, bay leaf, 2½ cups water, and the wine. Cover and simmer as gently as possible until the meat may easily be separated from the bones. If desired, the peeled onions and parsnips may be put in with the chicken 20 minutes before it is done. Scoop them out and reserve for the filling. Bone the chicken and strain the broth. Arrange the boned chicken, the onions, and the parsnips in a big baking dish. Blend the cornstarch with the cream and stir in the broth. Let it cook until it thickens, stir a little into the egg yolk, add to all the broth, add the nutmeg and sherry, and pour over the chicken and vegetables. For the crust, sift the dry ingredients and cut in the cold shortening with a wire pastry-cutter. Add just enough ice water so the dough may be handled. Roll it out and spread with the soft butter, fold once, and roll it out to fit the top of the dish. Lay it on and pinch the edge, making a thick rim around the edge. Make five or six incisions in the top for the steam to escape. Bake 15 minutes at 375°, then another 10 or 12 minutes at 325°. Serves 6.

JELLIED TONGUE WITH PARSNIPS
AND OTHER VEGETABLES

1 4-lb. pickled beef tongue
1½ tablespoons baking soda
1 celery root, diced
1 large onion, diced
4 parsnips, skinned and sliced
2 carrots, diced
4 whole cloves
2 tablespoons honey
juice of 1 lemon

2 teaspoons basil
2 teaspoons thyme or marjoram
salt and pepper
½ cup white wine
gelatin
1 egg white, half beaten

GARNISH

greens

It is best to use tender, juicy, pickled tongue for this, not fresh or smoked tongue. Wash it well with baking soda in lukewarm water, for the broth is to be used for the jelly. Rinse it well, almost cover it with lukewarm water, and add the vegetables, cloves, honey, lemon juice, and herbs. Cover and let it come very slowly to a simmer, and after it has cooked 2 hours add the salt and pepper. Let the tongue simmer another hour. Turn it over three or four times during the cooking. It is done when it may be easily pierced with a fork. Lift it from the kettle and strain the broth without pressing the vegetables through. Measure the broth. Allowing for the wine (do not add it yet), for every cup of liquid soak 1 teaspoon gelatin in 3 tablespoons cold water and add it to the broth with the half-beaten egg white. Let the broth come to a boil and simmer for 2 minutes to clarify it. Dampen and wring out a cloth, line a sieve with it, and strain the broth. Add the wine after the broth has cooled a little. Put 1 cup broth into a large greased mold and let it set in the refrigerator. Skin and nicely trim the tongue, and when it is perfectly cool lay it on the set jelly and add the rest of the broth. When ready to serve, unmold on a platter and garnish with salad greens. If the tongue is to be served hot first, the jelly may be molded and chilled separately. Cold sliced tongue may be served with a garnish of chopped jelly around it. Tongue, hot or cold, may be served with mustard or horseradish sauce. Serves 6 to 8.

INDIAN VEGETABLE CURRY

¼ cup butter
2 buds garlic, crushed
1 large Bermuda onion, grated
   (not chopped)
1 tablespoon turmeric
1 tablespoon coriander
1 teaspoon crushed cardamom
1 teaspoon ginger
½ teaspoon chili powder
1 teaspoon cumin powder
1 teaspoon caraway powder
½ teaspoon powdered cloves
3 tablespoons dried currants
½ teaspoon dry mustard
1 tablespoon honey

3 tablespoons minced chutney
salt and pepper
½ cup powdered coconut (or
   grated fresh coconut with milk)
1¼ cups beef consommé
½ cup tomato purée or juice
2 tablespoons lemon or lime juice

COOKED VEGETABLES
cauliflower, steamed
tomatoes, grilled
parsnips, steamed
white onions, steamed

ACCOMPANIMENTS
hot boiled rice and India chutney

Melt the butter in the top of the double boiler and add the garlic and onion. Add all the dry ingredients and let it cook over simmering water for 10 minutes, then add the other sauce ingredients. Stir well, cover, and let cook 45 more minutes. If all the condiments are not available, use 3 tablespoons good curry powder. The Indians cook their vegetables in the curry sauce. I prefer putting the cooked vegetables in a serving dish and pouring the sauce over them. The vegetables keep their flavors better this way, but either is permissible. The vegetables and sauce may be added to rice on each person's place. This is not a very powerful curry and should please most people. Indians usually make curry with condiments, not with commercial curry powder. This curry is also fine to serve with lamb, mutton, veal, or poultry. White turnips, eggplant, potatoes, lima beans, carrots, celery, and green beans may also be curried and served without meat for a supper dish. White wine is very welcome with curry. This will curry 2 pounds of vegetables.

ROAST FILLET OF BEEF RICHELIEU

1 3½- to 4-lb. fillet of beef
butter or oil
salt and pepper
1 teaspoon cornstarch
⅓ cup consommé, cold
2 tablespoons tomato sauce or
  purée
¼ cup sherry
   COOKED VEGETABLES
cauliflowerets

cooked green beans
grilled sliced tomatoes with basil
  and tarragon
peas
potato balls, rolled in butter and
  parsley
artichoke hearts
sliced parsnips, glazed
lima beans
little white onions, glazed

Trim the fillet, rub it with butter or oil, salt, and pepper. Roast it 30 to 40 minutes at 350°. It should be rare. Baste with butter two or three times. When it is done remove it to a large hot platter. Mix the cornstarch with the cold consommé and add it with the tomato sauce or purée and sherry to the roasting pan, let it boil up well, and then pour it over the meat. Garnish the platter with cooked vegetables heaped in mounds so that their colors alternate. Not all the vegetables are required; choose as many as are needed. This dish will serve 8.

GLAZED PARSNIPS

6 parsnips
salt and pepper
3 tablespoons butter

3 tablespoons orange juice or other
  fruit juice
4 tablespoons brown sugar or honey

Steam or boil the parsnips in very little water. When they are tender skin them and cut them in half lengthwise. Put them in a skillet, season them and glaze to a light brown and until they are syrupy all over in the butter, fruit juice (or some of the liquid they cooked in), and sweetening. More butter and sugar may be added. Serves 4 or 5.

PARSNIPS IN FRUIT SAUCE

6 or 8 parsnips
salt and pepper
3 tablespoons butter
½ teaspoon turmeric
¼ teaspoon mace

2 teaspoons cornstarch
⅓ cup orange juice
1 to 2 tablespoons lemon juice
GARNISH
chopped parsley

Steam or boil the parsnips or cook them 3 or 4 minutes in the pressure cooker. If they are cooked in very little water about 3 tablespoons of it may go into the sauce. When they are done, skin them and cut in half lengthwise. Season, add mace and turmeric, heat them in the butter, blend the other ingredients, and add. Cook until the sauce thickens. Serves 4 or 5. This is an attractive yellow sauce. Sprinkle chopped parsley over the top. Grapefruit juice may be used instead of orange and lemon juice.

MASHED PARSNIPS

1½ lbs. parsnips
salt and pepper
nutmeg, mace, or allspice
1 tablespoon brown sugar
butter

½ cup hot cream
GARNISH
minced green onions
chopped parsley

Steam or boil the parsnips, skin and mash them, seasoning to taste and adding spice and sugar. Melt the butter in the hot cream, and mix in. The top may be garnished with minced green onions or chopped parsley. For a variation, mix with mashed white or sweet potatoes or turnips. Serves 4.

PARSNIP CAKES

6 parsnips
3 tablespoons butter, melted
salt and pepper
dash of mace, nutmeg, or allspice
4 tablespoons rice flour
¼ cup light cream

1 large egg, beaten
2 tablespoons grated onions
chopped nuts, grated Parmesan
  cheese, or fine crumbs
fat for frying

Steam or boil the parsnips, skin, and mash them with the butter, seasoning, flour, cream, egg, and onions. Form into 10 or 12 cakes and roll them in the nuts, cheese, or crumbs. Fry a good brown on both sides in butter, oil, or good fat.

PARSNIP PIE

1 lb. parsnips
1 lb. peas
1 cup cubed potatoes
2 tablespoons cornstarch
1 cup light cream
3 tablespoons grated onion

¼ teaspoon nutmeg
⅓ cup vegetable water
salt and pepper
1 prebaked pie shell
GARNISH
grated Parmesan cheese

Cook the vegetables separately in very little water so that from both peas and parsnips there is no more than ⅓ cup liquid to drain for the sauce (do not use the potato water). Skin the parsnips. Blend the cornstarch with the cream, add the onion, nutmeg, vegetable water, salt, and pepper. Cook until the sauce thickens. Follow the directions for the piecrust in the recipe for Chicken Pie with Parsnips, line a 9-inch pie plate, and bake the crust, 15 to 18 minutes at 375°, or until it is done and a rich brown. Arrange the vegetables in the crust, pour the hot sauce over them, cover with cheese, and brown in a hot oven. Serve immediately. Serves 6.

PARSNIP PUDDING

2½ to 3 cups hot mashed parsnips
2 teaspoons grated lemon rind
¼ cup orange juice
¼ cup light cream
salt and pepper

¼ teaspoon powdered cloves
¼ teaspoon nutmeg
3 egg yolks, beaten
3 egg whites, beaten until stiff
3 tablespoons brown sugar

Mix the parsnips with the rind and juice, cream, seasoning, spices, and egg yolks. The mixture must be creamy and light. Add more juice and cream if necessary. Beat the whites until stiff, add the sugar, and beat to a meringue. Fold in last. Bake in a greased baking dish 25 minutes at 350°. It must be moist inside. This is a fine dish to go with the Thanksgiving turkey. Serves 5 or 6.

CREAMED PARSNIPS

6 parsnips
3 tablespoons butter
dash of mace or nutmeg
salt and pepper
3 teaspoons cornstarch
¾ cup light cream

¼ cup parsnip liquid
½ teaspoon turmeric
GARNISH
chopped parsley or grated
Parmesan cheese

Scrape the parsnips and cut them in half lengthwise. Put them in a pot with the butter, nutmeg, salt and pepper, and 3 tablespoons water. Cover tight and steam them tender—or cook them in the pressure cooker for 3 or 4 minutes. If cooked in a pot be careful that they do not burn; add 2 tablespoons water at a time, when necessary. Blend the cornstarch with the cold cream, add the parsnip liquid, and cook until it thickens. Add the turmeric for a delicate fragrance and color. Heat the parsnips in the sauce, empty into a serving dish, and sprinkle with parsley or cheese. Serves 5.

CANDIED PARSNIPS

6 or 8 parsnips
3 tablespoons butter
1 tablespoon grated orange rind

⅓ cup molasses
⅓ cup corn syrup or honey

Cook the parsnips until tender, skin, and cut in half lengthwise— or cut them before they are cooked. Melt the butter in a heavy skillet and stir in the grated rind, molasses, and corn syrup or honey. Add the parsnips and cook until they are syrupy and brown all over, adding more molasses or syrup if needed. The molasses may be omitted, and corn syrup and honey used. This is a change from candied sweet potatoes and is good with chicken or pork. Serves 4 to 6.

SALADE DE PANAIS

4 young parsnips, cooked   olive oil mayonnaise
½ cup cooked peas   lettuce
½ cup sliced celery hearts

Chill the vegetables. Cut the parsnips in ½-inch rounds, making sure to cut out the inside core, if any. Toss the vegetables together, moistening well with mayonnaise. Serve on a bed of crisp lettuce.

PEAS

Young green peas, picked fresh from the garden before the pods grow too full, are among the choicest vegetables. They are always gratefully accepted by the family, and are first choice for serving at the most elaborate dinners and banquets. When one listens to such preposterous statements as "I like canned peas better than fresh," or "I like frozen peas better than fresh," one can only realize that peas have been a greatly abused vegetable. Their flavor and texture are delicate, and they must be carefully selected and cooked. They may have been picked too old, or they may have been cooked too long and perhaps drained, the latter being one of the major crimes in culinary practice. It is too bad that when peas become over-plentiful they are allowed to become old and sold as fresh. They are much better dried for winter use. Dried peas make wonderful and nourishing dishes when fresh peas are too expensive or not in the market.

Young, tender pods right out of the garden are good to cook. Those in the markets are usually not in perfect enough condition to cook. Chinese snow peas are always cooked in the pods. If the pods of new peas are washed before shelling, the peas will not have to be washed and will be the better for it. Plain buttered peas are always cooked with a minimum of water added, no more than 2 or 3 spoonfuls. The water is absorbed or served with the peas. They should be covered and cooked at low heat; watch to see that they do not burn.

They may be pressure-cooked less than 1 minute; the pressure should be reduced immediately. Perfectly cooked peas will hold their shape and retain maximum flavor.

FRESH PEA SOUP

¼ cup butter
⅓ cup minced green onions or
   chopped white onions
1 small green pepper, diced
2 to 2½ lbs. peas
salt and pepper
¼ teaspoon nutmeg

1 teaspoon sugar
1 teaspoon basil or chervil
milk and cream

GARNISH
whole cooked peas or chopped
   parsley

Melt the butter in a heavy pot or pressure cooker and sauté the onion and green pepper until half tender, 3 or 4 minutes. Add the peas, seasonings, nutmeg, sugar, and herbs, and ½ cup water. Cover tight and cook until the peas are tender or 1½ minutes in the pressure cooker. Add 1 cup milk to this mixture and mash through a sieve or purée in the electric blender. If desired, a few whole peas may be reserved before puréeing, for a garnish. Add enough milk to make the soup like heavy cream. This may be rich enough, but thin cream may be added with the milk. This will make 7 or 8 cups of soup. It may be served hot or cold.

PEA AND TURTLE SOUP

recipe for Fresh Pea Soup
1 large can green turtle consommé

2 tablespoons sherry

Make the recipe for Fresh Pea Soup, using 1 cup light cream to thin it when mashing through a sieve or puréeing it in the electric blender. Combine with the turtle soup and then thin it more with milk if necessary. Add the sherry and serve. This may be served hot or cold. The peas may be puréed with chicken broth instead of cream or milk. Or the peas may be puréed with the turtle consommé. The soup, when it is in the plates, may have a spoonful of whipped cream with a dash of mace or nutmeg added. If it is puréed without cream or milk, it may be flavored with ¼ to ⅓ cup of sherry—imported preferred.

PEA AND AVOCADO SOUP

recipe for Fresh Pea Soup   **1 avocado**

Mash three-quarters of the avocado and mix with the soup—or purée with the peas. Cut the rest of the pear in thin slices to garnish the top of the soup in the plates. A little curry powder may be added to the soup.

PEA AND LETTUCE SOUP

recipe for Fresh Pea Soup   **1 small head loose lettuce, shredded**

When cooking the onions and peppers, stir in the lettuce just after they have cooked a little. Before puréeing, reserve a little of the peas and lettuce for garnishing the soup plates.

SPRING SOUP

COOKED VEGETABLES	1 cup okra rings
12 asparagus tips	6 or 8 cups chicken broth
1 cup peas with basil	1 tomato, skinned, chopped, and
1 cup julienne carrot sticks	seeded
1 cup corn	GARNISH
½ cup minced leeks or green	chopped parsley
onions, sautéed	

There is nothing quite as fresh and delicious as these freshly cooked (all separately) spring and summer vegetables added to a rich clear chicken broth. The liquors they cooked or steamed in should be added to the soup. Use no more raw tomato than specified, as it is to give color and freshness, not to dominate the flavor. Add no more than 2 or 3 tablespoons of asparagus liquor. If the rules for cooking the vegetables are followed there won't be much liquid left after cooking. Sprinkle a little chopped parsley over it after it is put in the plates.

FRENCH HABITANT PEA SOUP

1 lb. dried yellow peas
½ lb. salt pork
1½ cups finely diced onions
1 cup diced carrots
1 cup diced white turnips

½ cup minced celery leaves
1 teaspoon each thyme and basil
salt and pepper
GARNISH
chopped parsley

Wash the peas well so they will need no changing of water. Cover them with 3 quarts of water and soak 6 hours or overnight. Wash the pork in hot water, slice, and add it to the peas and water. Bring to a simmer very slowly and skim, then add the vegetables and herbs. Simmer, covered, very gently for 3 hours, add salt and pepper, and simmer 1 hour longer. Remove the pork and ⅔ cup peas, and mash the soup through a sieve. Add the peas to the soup, fry the pork crisp, and add it. Garnish with chopped parsley. Makes 2½ quarts.

SPLIT-PEA SOUP WITH FRESH PEAS

2½ cups dried green peas
ham bone with some meat on it
3 whole cloves
salt and pepper
handful celery leaves
¾ cup diced onions
½ cup diced carrots

1 bay leaf
1 teaspoon each thyme and basil
milk or chicken broth
GARNISH
1 cup cooked fresh peas and
    chopped parsley

Wash the peas and put them to soak in 10 cups water. Soak 6 hours or overnight, then add the ham bone, cloves, a little salt, pepper, vegetables, and herbs. Simmer, covered, for 2 hours or until the peas are almost a liquid. This may be done in the pressure cooker with 2 cups less water; cook about 25 minutes. Remove the ham and bone and mash the peas through a sieve or purée in the electric blender. The soup may be thinned with either broth or milk. Add the cooked fresh peas and garnish each plate with a little chopped parsley. Dried-pea soup may have a dash of nutmeg added, and it may have crisp bacon added as a garnish. Makes 2 quarts.

PURÉE OF FRESH PEAS

4 spring onions, minced
2 tablespoons olive oil
2 lbs. fresh peas
1 teaspoon basil

salt and pepper
GARNISH
3 tablespoons sesame oil or olive oil
4 tablespoons chopped chives

Sauté the onions in the olive oil ½ minute, add the peas, basil, and seasonings. Cook with 2 or 3 tablespoons water until tender (in the pressure cooker, 40 seconds). Remove ½ cup whole peas for garnish, then mash the rest through a sieve or purée in the electric blender. Empty into a serving dish and add the oil to the top. Chill. When cool and ready to serve add the whole peas and chives to the top. This may be served as an appetizer, spread on little pieces of toast, or it may be served as an accompaniment to a cold meat platter for a buffet supper. Serves 4 to 6, or 6 to 8 as an appetizer.

BUTTERED PEAS

3 or 4 tablespoons butter
4 shallots or green onions, minced
1 or 2 lbs. peas
1 teaspoon honey or light brown sugar

salt and pepper
¼ teaspoon nutmeg (optional)
1 teaspoon basil, tarragon, or chervil

Melt the butter in a heavy pot or pressure cooker and add the shallots or green onions. Let them cook a little, then add the shelled peas and all the ingredients except the herb. Add 2 or 3 tablespoons water, cover tight, and cook gently until tender, 10 or 12 minutes, watching that they do not burn. The pressure cooker will take 40 seconds or so after the pressure comes up. Let the pressure come down immediately by putting the cooker in cold water, or the peas will become too soft. Add the herb and serve hot. There is approximately 1 cup peas to a pound.

CREAMED BUTTERED PEAS WITH MINT

2 or 3 tablespoons minced mint   recipe for Buttered Peas (omit the
⅓ to ⅔ cup heavy cream   herb)

The quantity of butter, cream, and mint depends on the quantity of peas cooked. One pound will serve 2 or 3 people, depending on how abundant the meal is. Stem the fresh mint, crush the leaves together, and cut them fine with kitchen scissors into the cream. Let this stand at room temperature at least ½ hour before cooking the peas, so the mint will perfume the cream. When the peas are cooked mix in the minted cream, heat, and serve. Fresh mint may be added to peas cooked without cream.

PEAS WITH PARMESAN CHEESE

¼ to ⅓ cup olive oil   salt and pepper
4 green onions, minced   ¼ teaspoon nutmeg (optional)
1 or 2 buds garlic, crushed   1 teaspoon basil, tarragon, or
1 or 2 lbs. peas   chervil
1 teaspoon honey or light brown   ⅓ cup grated Parmesan cheese
  sugar

Put the olive oil in the pot and sauté the garlic and minced onion. Cook a few seconds, then add the peas, sugar, seasonings, nutmeg, and 2 or 3 tablespoons water. Cover and cook slowly until tender. Add the herb. The Italians use basil a lot, and it is a good herb for this dish. When the peas are in the serving dish sprinkle the top with the cheese. Serves 2 to 4.

PEAS WITH HAM OR PROSCIUTTO

¼ cup diced onions   1 cup ground cooked ham or 4 or
3 tablespoons butter   5 slices prosciutto
2 lbs. peas   salt and pepper
1 cup shredded lettuce   1 teaspoon basil

Sauté the onion in the butter 1 minute, add the peas, mix the lettuce with the ground ham, and add it. If the prosciutto is used, do not cook it with the peas but frizzle it in a little butter and add it when the peas are done. Add salt sparingly on account of the ham, and add the pepper and basil. Add 2 or 3 tablespoons water, cover tight, and cook until the peas are tender over a low flame. If desired, sprinkle a little grated Parmesan cheese over it when it is in the serving dish. Serves 5 or 6.

OMELET WITH PEAS

recipe for Buttered Peas
4- to 6-egg omelet (page 106)

GARNISH
grated Parmesan cheese

Use 1 pound peas for this size omelet, which will serve 3 or 4 persons. When the omelet is cooked add the peas, fold once, slide off onto a hot platter, and sprinkle cheese over the top. To serve 4, use 6 eggs.

PEAS WITH FRANKFURTERS OR KNACKWURST

½ cup minced green onions
3 tablespoons butter
1 big knackwurst, or 2 or 3 skinless
    frankfurters, sliced
more butter

1 tablespoon brown sugar
2 lbs. peas
salt and pepper
dash of nutmeg

Sauté the onions in 3 tablespoons butter 1 minute. In a skillet glaze the sliced knackwurst or frankfurters in a little butter and the sugar until a crusty brown. Mix them with the peas and to the onions with 2 or 3 tablespoons water, and seasonings. Cover with a tight lid and cook until the peas are tender. Serves 4 to 6.

PEAS WITH NOODLE SHELLS

recipe for Buttered Peas
2 buds garlic
⅓ cup olive oil
12 oz. tiny noodle shells

salt
butter

GARNISH
grated Parmesan cheese

Cook the peas. Crush the garlic in a big skillet and add the olive oil. Cook the noodle shells in plenty of salted boiling water for about 8 minutes, and when they are tender drain and add them to the garlic and olive oil over a low heat. Stir until all the shells glisten with oil and if necessary add a little butter. Stir in the hot peas and when mixed pour into a hot serving dish and add cheese liberally to the top. Serves 8.

NOODLE SOUFFLÉ WITH PEAS

1 cup tiny egg noodles
salt
1½ lbs. fresh peas, cooked as for
　Buttered Peas

SAUCE

1 tablespoon cornstarch
½ cup milk

½ cup light cream
salt and pepper
¼ cup grated Parmesan cheese
3 egg yolks
3 egg whites, beaten until stiff

GARNISH

grated Parmesan cheese

Boil the noodles in salted water for 7 minutes and drain them. Mix the cooked peas with the noodles. Make the sauce by blending the cornstarch with the cold milk and cream. Cook until it thickens, remove from the heat, and add the seasoning, cheese, and egg yolks. Return to the fire long enough to melt the cheese and thicken the sauce. Combine the sauce with the peas and noodles, then fold in the stiffly beaten egg whites. Empty into a greased baking dish, sprinkle the top with cheese, and bake at 350° until it sets but is still moist inside, about 20 to 25 minutes. Serves 6.

PASTA WITH PEAS AND BASIL OR PARSLEY SAUCE

¼ cup minced green onions
¼ cup olive oil or butter
1 teaspoon thyme
1 teaspoon basil
salt and pepper
2 lbs. peas

SAUCE

3 buds garlic
2 or 3 tablespoons dried or fresh
　(preferably) basil or big handful
　parsley

⅓ cup pine nuts (pignolias)
⅓ cup grated Parmesan or
　Romano cheese
olive oil
salt and pepper

10 oz. fine egg noodles
¼ cup butter

GARNISH

grated Parmesan cheese

Sauté the onions in oil or butter, add the herbs, seasonings, and peas, and simmer gently until tender with only 2 or 3 tablespoons water. For the sauce crush the garlic and mix with the basil (preferred) or parsley, nuts, and cheese. Put this through the grinder two or three times with some oil so that it is like a smooth purée. The electric blender is ideal for this. Add salt and pepper. Boil the noodles 10 minutes in plenty of salted water, drain, and mix with ¼ cup butter. Mix the hot peas with the hot pasta and stir in the sauce. Serve immediately with a bowl of Parmesan cheese to sprinkle over it. This is an altogether remarkable sauce. It is particularly attractive if fine green noodles are used. They should be the finest egg noodles. If pine nuts are not available, walnuts may be used. Serves 8.

CASSEROLE OF FRESH GREEN PEAS

1 head Boston lettuce, shredded
1 bunch green onions, minced
4 cups fresh peas
1¼ cups fluffy ground ham
2 teaspoons basil
1 teaspoon tarragon
salt and pepper

½ teaspoon nutmeg
1 tablespoon honey
½ cup chicken consommé
TOP
½ cup heavy cream
handful finely chopped parsley

Grease a casserole and in the bottom make a bed of the shredded lettuce and minced green onions. Mix the peas and ham with the herbs, seasoning, nutmeg, and honey, and add to the lettuce. Pour the consommé over, cover very tight, and bake 30 minutes in a 350° oven. While the vegetables are cooking marinate the finely chopped parsley in the cream. When ready to serve, boil up the cream and pour it over the top. Serves 8 or 9.

PEA SOUFFLÉ AMANDINE

recipe for Buttered Peas (omit herb
and onion)
¼ cup milk
2 tablespoons flour
¼ cup browned ground almonds

½ cup cream
2 drops almond extract
3 egg yolks, beaten
3 egg whites, beaten until stiff

Use 3 pounds fresh peas, cook them as directed, and when done mash them through a sieve with the milk, or purée in the electric blender, and add the flour. There should be over 2 cups of purée. If cooked with the specified amount of water, the peas will not have to be drained; there will be very little left. Bring the ground almonds and cream to a boil and add to the purée with the extract and egg yolks. Fold in the stiffly beaten egg whites last and pour into a greased soufflé dish. Bake at 350° about 25 minutes. Remove from the oven when still a little moist in the center. Serve immediately. Serves 6.

PETITS POIS À LA FRANÇAISE

¼ cup butter
2 bunches green onions
1 small head lettuce (Boston or
  Bibb)
2 or 3 cups shelled peas (2 or 3 lbs.)
salt and pepper

¼ teaspoon nutmeg
1 teaspoon honey
tarragon, thyme, chervil, or basil
                    GARNISH
chopped parsley

Melt the butter in a heavy pot, mince the scallions or green onions with the lettuce and make a bed on the butter and add the peas to the top of the lettuce. Add the seasonings and dribble the honey and any two of the herbs over the peas. If only dried herbs are available add 2 teaspoons, but if fresh herb leaves are at hand use 2 or 3 tablespoons of them, minced, and you will have a fragrant dish. Add not more than 4 tablespoons water, cover tight, and cook over a gentle flame until the peas are tender, or about 10 or 12 minutes. Empty into a hot serving dish and add a little chopped parsley. Two pounds of peas will serve 4.

PETITS POIS À LA CRÈME

recipe for Petits Pois à la Française
½ cup heavy cream, whipped

pinch of turmeric
dash of salt

When the peas are done have ready the cream, seasoned with the turmeric and salt. Heat it a moment in the double boiler just so it is warmed a little, being careful not to melt it. Put the peas in a serving dish and add the cream to the top. The turmeric will give a rich color and add a little to the flavor.

PEAS BOILED IN A JAR

peas
salt and pepper
butter

honey
mint or parsley

Put the peas in a jar or little baking dish with a tight lid and add salt, pepper, 2 tablespoons butter to 1 pound peas, 1 tablespoon light brown sugar or 1 teaspoon honey per pound, and a few mint leaves or parsley. Add no water, put on the cover, and set the jar or pot in a big kettle with boiling water coming within 2 or 3 inches below the lid of the peas. Cover the kettle and boil for ½ hour. Lift the pot of peas from the water and serve them. Lacking a tight lid, aluminum foil may be tied around the top of a dish you wish to serve the peas in. Only the youngest, freshest peas can be cooked this way. Old peas will not cook tender.

PEAS AND POTATOES

½ cup diced onions	salt and pepper
¼ cup butter	handful chopped fresh dill
2 lbs. peas	¼ cup cream (optional)
2 cups diced potatoes	

Sauté the onions in the butter 1 minute, add the peas and the potatoes, which should be as finely diced as the size of the peas so that they will cook in the same time. Add salt, pepper, and 2 or 3 tablespoons water. Cover tight and cook gently for 10 minutes. Stem and squeeze the dill, cut it as fine as possible, and add it to the peas and potatoes. Cover and cook until the vegetables are tender. They should be done in 2 or 3 more minutes. Add a little more butter or the cream. If dill is not available, another herb may be used, but dill is particularly good with this combination. More cream or cream sauce may be added if desired. Serves 6.

CHINESE SNOW PEAS

⅓ cup diced onions	⅓ cup hot water
2 tablespoons butter	*DRESSING (OPTIONAL)*
½ lb. snow peas	⅓ cup cream
salt and pepper	scant teaspoon cornstarch
1 teaspoon basil	2 tablespoons chopped dill or
drop of honey	parsley

Sauté the onions in the butter 1 minute. Bermuda onions, green onions, or white onions are better than strong ones. Tip and string the peas, which should always be cooked in the pods. Add the peas to the onions, cover, and cook slowly 5 minutes. Add seasonings, basil, honey, and water; cover and cook another 5 minutes. Serve plain or with the cream mixed with the cornstarch and dill or parsley. Let the sauce boil up with the peas and serve. Serves 4.

PURÉE OF PEAS OR LIMA BEANS

3 tablespoons butter
⅓ cup minced green onions or ¼
    cup minced white or yellow
    onions
3 cups fresh peas (2½ to 3 lbs.)
1 teaspoon honey or sugar

salt and pepper
¼ teaspoon nutmeg
2 teaspoons basil
½ cup cream
2 tablespoons flour (optional)

Sauté the onion in the butter a minute, add the peas, 3 tablespoons water, honey, seasoning, nutmeg, and basil. Cook, covered, until the peas are very tender. The pressure cooker will take 60 to 80 seconds. Mash the peas and the liquid through a sieve with the aid of a little of the cream—or purée in the electric blender. Add as much cream as is necessary—the purée must be thick to serve as a vegetable. It may be served in sauce dishes accompanying meat or fish, or the flour may be added and the purée baked 5 to 7 minutes in a greased baking dish. Then it will be solid enough to be served on the plate with the entrée. It is extremely delicate and delicious without the flour, but either way is very good. Any leftover purée may be formed into little cakes, dipped in crumbs, and fried in butter—or it may be thinned with broth or cream and milk for soups. Serves 6.

PEAS AND LIMA BEANS WITH CHEESE SAUCE

recipe for Buttered Peas (page 255)
recipe for Buttered Lima Beans
    (page 116)

SAUCE
2 tablespoons butter
3 tablespoons flour
1 cup light cream

liquid from peas and beans plus
    milk to make 1 cup
dash of nutmeg
½ cup grated Cheddar cheese
GARNISH
½ cup grated Parmesan cheese

Cook 2 pounds of each vegetable separately, following the directions given in the recipes. Drain off any liquid into a cup and fill with milk. Mix the vegetables together in a serving casserole. Melt the butter and blend in the flour and when smooth add the cream and the milk mixture. Cook gently until it thickens, add nutmeg and cheese, and cook until the cheese melts. Pour over the vegetable and cover with Parmesan cheese. If this is too cheesy for your taste, use less on top. Brown a few minutes in the oven, just until it heats and the cheese melts. Serves 8 to 10. This dish may also be made with the following combinations:

Buttered Peas and Buttered Onions. Use 2 pounds peas and 1 to 1½ pounds onions.

Buttered Peas and Buttered Carrots. Use 2 pounds peas and 1 bunch new carrots. One and a half cups of cheese sauce is sufficient.

Buttered Peas and 2 cups diced boiled buttered beets. This is an unusual but good combination. Some of the beet water may be used in making the cream sauce.

Buttered Peas and Buttered Cauliflowerets.

Buttered Peas and Corn. 2 cups corn, cooked and cut from the ears, and ½ pound cooked, buttered okra (optional).

Peas may also be combined with buttered celery, white turnips, or parsnips.

MASHED SPLIT PEAS

2 cups dried peas	1 tablespoon lemon juice
⅔ cup diced onions	2 tablespoons butter
½ cup diced carrots	1 tablespoon brown sugar or honey
⅓ cup diced celery (and leaves)	⅓ cup light cream
1 bay leaf	*GARNISH*
½ teaspoon thyme	fried onions, crisp bacon, or
salt and pepper	browned chopped almonds

Wash the peas and soak them 5 or 6 hours in 3 cups water. When ready to cook measure the water and add enough to make 2½ cups, add it to the peas with the vegetables, bay leaf, thyme, salt, and pepper. Cover tight and cook to a mush, being careful that it does not burn; add a little more boiling water if necessary. Remove the bay leaf and mash the vegetables through a coarse sieve. Add the lemon juice, butter, sweetening, and enough cream so the purée is the consistency of fluffy mashed potatoes. If it must be reheated add plenty of cream or it will become too thick. If onions are used to garnish, heat minced green onions in a little butter. Crisp bacon pieces or brown almonds are both very good. This dish should be added more frequently to our menus, especially in winter, for it is delicious with any meat, fish, or poultry. Lentil purée may be made the same way. Either may be used to fill red pimentos, tomatoes, or green peppers for baking. (See Sweet Potatoes and Red Pimentos, page 317.) Serves 6 or more.

VEGETABLE LOAF

2 cups dried split peas or lentils
1 bay leaf
1 cup diced onions
salt and pepper
2 teaspoons orégano or thyme
juice of 1 lemon
½ cup light cream

⅓ cup olive oil
⅓ cup diced green pepper
½ cup mixed nuts, browned oil or butter
⅓ cup whole-wheat flour
GARNISH
tomato sauce

Wash the split peas or lentils and soak them in 3 cups water for 4 hours. Drain them, measure the water, and add enough to make 2 cups. Split peas may take a little more water. Combine the water, split peas, bay leaf, ½ cup onions, salt, pepper, and orégano or thyme. Cook in a heavy pot with a tight lid 1 hour or until the liquid is absorbed and the peas are very tender. Mash through a sieve or purée in the electric blender with the lemon juice, light cream, and olive oil. Sauté the other ½ cup onions and green pepper in a little oil or butter until they are almost tender. Chop the nuts fine and combine all the ingredients. Put the mixture in a greased bread pan or baking dish and bake 40 minutes, half the time at 350° and half at 325°. This may be served from the dish or turned out onto a platter. It may be served with any poultry or meat gravy or a simple tomato sauce. A canned tomato sauce may be used, mixed with some sour cream and chopped parsley. Heat it and serve in a sauce boat. This makes an excellent supper dish without meat. Serves 6.

COLD PEA SALAD WITH SOUR CREAM

3 lbs. peas, cooked as for Buttered Peas
¾ cup minced green onions
¼ cup mayonnaise

salt and pepper
1¼ cups thick sour cream
1 tablespoon lemon juice
chopped chives, mint, or dill

Cool the peas, and when they are cold and ready to serve mix with all the other ingredients. Finely minced chives, mint, or dill to taste may be mixed with the sour cream. This is a fine accompaniment for a cold supper of salmon or other fish or for a buffet. A cup of julienne celery hearts may be added. Serves 6. Four pounds of peas will serve 10.

COLD RICE AND PEA SALAD

1 cup brown rice or wild rice
2 cups chicken consommé
1 teaspoon turmeric
recipe for Buttered Peas (2½ lbs.)

1 lb. fresh shrimp
¼ cup olive oil
GARNISH
chopped chives or parsley

If wild rice is used, wash it in many waters until the water is clear. Cook the rice in the consommé with the turmeric, covered, over a flame of pilot-light strength 45 minutes. Leave covered for an extra 15 minutes with the fire turned off. The turmeric cooked with the rice gives it a yellow color. Do not remove the cover while the rice is cooking. Toss the rice with a fork and let it cool in a large bowl. Cook the peas as directed. Cook the shrimp and peel them. When all the ingredients are perfectly cooled, toss them lightly together with the olive oil. This does not have to be chilled more than 15 minutes in the refrigerator. If each part of the dish is well made it is one of the finest dishes and good to serve as a first course. It does not require salad dressing. Serves 7 or 8.

GREEN SALAD AND PEAS

Bibb lettuce
handful chopped stemmed mint
½ cup chopped scallions
1 small cucumber

1 cup peas cooked with olive oil
and basil
French dressing

Use 2 or 3 heads of Bibb lettuce. Tear the leaves apart but do not cut them up, for they are small and tender. Try to get a small, crisp cucumber. Peel and slice it. Cool the cooked peas. When they are cold toss everything together and moisten with a little French dressing. Always serve tossed salads immediately after adding the dressing.

PEPPERS

Peppers, like tomatoes, are native to the Americas and were first appreciated in Europe. They appear in our markets at all seasons of the year, and from Italy and Spain we can learn some new uses for them to add to our daily fare. Peppers for general use in cookery are the mild, sweet green, yellow, or red bell peppers. Hot peppers, or chilis, are used sparingly in sauces and in dishes usually from Mexico, other tropical countries, and the Orient. The sweet pepper is used in appetizers and soups, with fish, meat, poultry, eggs, rice, in salads, as a vegetable, in sauces, and in canning and pickling. In this country canned red peppers are called pimentos. They are excellent for garnishings, in salads, and for stuffing and baking in the same way as fresh peppers. For some dishes it is necessary to skin peppers. To do this, roast them in a hot oven until the skin blisters and blackens a little; while they are hot put them in a paper bag or a pot with a tight lid to steam a few minutes, and their skins will come off easily. To prepare peppers for stuffing, boil them 3 or 4 minutes and drain. Remove the fibers and seeds either before or after they are boiled. Cut them in half or remove the tops for stuffing whole.

ROASTED PEPPERS

4 large sweet peppers	½ cup olive oil
4 buds garlic, crushed	salt

Wash the peppers and roast them in a 350° oven from 15 to 25 minutes, depending on the thickness of the flesh. When they blister and the skin blackens and they may be pierced easily with a sharp-pointed knife they are done. Heat the garlic in the olive oil and add a little salt. Skin the peppers, remove the pith and seeds, and cut in 1-inch strips. Put them in a glass jar, add the oil, and when cool store in the refrigerator. They are excellent for appetizers, to add to rice dishes, and to toss in green salads. Roasted, sliced, and chilled green peppers are much better to my taste than the raw hard peppers one finds in some salads. Uncooked, they give the impression of hardness, not crispness. The oil in which the roasted peppers are marinated may be used to fry fish and to season cooked vegetables.

PEPPERS STUFFED WITH CHEESE AND NUTS

6 small, long sweet peppers
salt and pepper
4 oz. cream cheese
1 teaspoon lemon juice

¼ cup sour cream
⅔ cup coarsely chopped browned
   pecans or walnuts

Cut the peppers lengthwise to make little boats. Steam them 2 or 3 minutes, then chill them. Small peppers usually have thin flesh and do not require skinning. Make a firm, smooth paste of the rest of the ingredients and stuff the cold peppers. These may be served as an appetizer or may accompany a salad.

CANNED PIMENTOS

2 qts. sliced sweet red peppers
boiling water
ice water

1 cup vinegar
1 cup olive oil

Seed the peppers and cut in strips or seed and leave whole. Cover with boiling water and let stand a few seconds. Drain and cover with ice water. Drain them and put them in sterilized jars. Bring the vinegar to a boil for 2 minutes, add the oil, and when it boils pour over the peppers and seal.

PIMENTO-CHEESE PASTE

1 canned red pimento
¼ cup soft Roquefort or
   Gorgonzola cheese
1 tablespoon soft butter

2 tablespoons sour cream
2 tablespoons fresh onion juice
paprika or chopped parsley

Mash the pimento until it is almost a purée. Mix the cheese with the butter, sour cream, and onion juice, and mix with the pimento. This may be spread on rounds of hot buttered toast or rye bread. Sprinkle the top lightly with paprika or chopped parsley.

PEPPERS AND FISH PASTE

sweet peppers
1 small can sardines or tuna fish in
  olive oil
1 tablespoon lemon juice

2 tablespoons minced green onions
2 tablespoons sour cream
1 teaspoon anchovy paste

Cut peppers in half, boil them until tender—about 3 minutes—and then drain them. Cut them in 1½-inch-thick strips and chill them. Mash the fish in the oil, add all the other ingredients, and spread on the peppers.

PEPPER AND TOMATO SOUP

2 large peppers
1 qt. tomatoes, skinned and chopped
2 tablespoons fresh grated onion

salt and pepper
⅓ cup olive oil
¼ cup chopped parsley

Roast the peppers for 25 minutes. Simmer the tomatoes, onion, salt, and pepper for 15 minutes. Skin the peppers if necessary, stem and seed them. Cut in strips and marinate them in the olive oil 1 hour. Add the oil and peppers to the tomatoes and mash through a sieve or purée in the electric blender. Add the parsley and serve hot or iced. This may be made of tomato juice puréed with a can of red pimentos. First cook the tomato juice with the onion 15 minutes. The peppers give the tomato fine flavor. Pimento may also be added to a tomato-vegetable soup and puréed. Serves 4.

SAUTÉED PEPPERS AND ONIONS

olive oil and butter
1 Bermuda onion or 2 or 3 yellow
  onions, sliced

2 or 3 big sweet peppers, sliced
salt and pepper

Put half butter and half oil in a heavy skillet and sauté the sliced vegetables 2 or 3 minutes, then cover and cook for 10 minutes, uncover, and cook until just tender. They must be still firm and not limp. Salt and pepper them. Serve with grilled steak or fish.

FRENCH-FRIED PEPPER RINGS

sweet peppers   flour
salt and pepper   deep oil

Scoop out the seeds and pith from the peppers after removing the
stem end. Cut in ¼-inch rings. Shake them in a bag of flour mixed
with salt and pepper. Put the rings, 6 or 8 at a time, in a wire frying
basket and fry them as you would onion rings, in deep oil at 370°,
to a golden brown. Drain on brown paper and serve with grilled
chops or steak.

BAKED PEPPERS

large red, yellow, or green peppers   olive oil
salt and pepper

Wash and bake the peppers whole at 375° for 25 to 30 minutes
or until they are tender. Serve one to a person on small plates as a
vegetable, with salt, pepper, and a cruet of olive oil. These are very
good and a change from more ordinary vegetables. Serve with any
kind of meat.

PEPPERS, TOMATOES, AND EGGS

2 cups finely diced onions   pinch of cumin powder
⅓ cup olive oil or bacon fat   3 large tomatoes, skinned and
4 large peppers, diced fine   chopped
salt and pepper   1 tablespoon brown sugar
1½ teaspoons summer savory or   5 eggs, beaten
  orégano

Cook the very finely diced onions in the olive oil until half tender,
then add the green peppers and cook until they are tender. Add
seasonings, herb, cumin, and tomatoes and brown sugar. Cover and
cook until very soft, about 30 minutes. Uncover after 20 minutes if
the sauce is very thin. When done add the beaten eggs, stir until they
set, and serve. Serves 4.

STUFFED GREEN PEPPERS

Select perfect peppers of good size. They may be stuffed whole if you remove a piece from the top and scoop out the seeds and pith, but it is easier to cut them across to make cups or lengthwise for boats. After they are prepared boil them for 3 or 4 minutes, drain them upside down, and fill them while they are still warm if they are to be baked. Let them cool before filling them if they are to be served cold. When baking, put them close together in a pan with 2 or 3 tablespoons butter and the same of water in the bottom of the pan to prevent burning. Allow ⅓ to ½ cup stuffing for each pepper half. Because the stuffings are all precooked it is not necessary to bake the stuffed peppers more than 15 to 18 minutes at 350° unless otherwise directed. Boiling them first makes them almost tender enough before they go into the oven. A minute or two more boiling may be necessary if they are to be cooled and stuffed.

RICE AND SEAFOOD STUFFING

1 cup cooked brown rice
½ lb. cooked fresh shrimp, lobster, or crabmeat
1 cup sliced mushrooms, sautéed

¼ cup minced green onions
salt and pepper
                    TOP
grated cheese or chopped parsley

Bake 15 minutes at 350°.

CRABMEAT STUFFING

1 small pepper, diced and boiled 6 minutes
1 red pimento, diced
salt and pepper
1 teaspoon curry powder
1½ to 2 cups lump crabmeat

1 hard-boiled egg, mashed
½ cup sour cream
⅓ cup oil mayonnaise
                    TOP
chopped chives or parsley or grated cheese

Bake 15 minutes at 350° or use cooked crab and serve cold.

CREAMED CHICKEN STUFFING

creamed chicken

TOP

buttered crumbs and grated cheese

Bake 15 minutes at 350°.

SWEETBREAD STUFFING

creamed sweetbreads

TOP

buttered crumbs and grated cheese

Bake 15 minutes at 350°.

CALF'S BRAINS STUFFING

1 pair sautéed calf's brains, cubed
½ cup cooked rice
½ cup chopped browned almonds
2 tablespoons catsup

½ teaspoon curry powder
2 hard-boiled eggs, mashed
TOP
grated cheese

Bake 20 minutes at 350°.

SPLIT-PEA OR LENTIL STUFFING

puréed split peas or lentils
chopped green onions
crisp bacon bits

TOP
grated cheese before baking or
chopped parsley after baking

Bake 20 minutes at 350°.

SAUSAGE AND SPLIT-PEA STUFFING

puréed split peas or lentils
small pork sausages, browned

TOP
grated cheese or crumbs

Bury 1 sausage in the purée in each pepper half.

CORNED-BEEF OR HAM STUFFING

corned-beef hash or ground ham
cubed potatoes, sautéed, or cooked
   rice

cream to moisten
TOP
crumbs or grated cheese

Bake 15 minutes at 350°.

CORN STUFFING

cooked corn, grated from ears
minced green onions, sautéed in
   butter

TOP
chopped parsley

Bake 10 or 15 minutes at 350°.

LIMA-BEAN AND MUSHROOM STUFFING

cooked lima beans
sautéed mushrooms and green
   onions

TOP
chopped parsley

Bake 10 or 15 minutes at 350°.

ITALIAN STUFFING

tiny bread cubes sautéed with garlic
   crushed in olive oil
sliced black olives in oil

anchovy fillets, cut in half
TOP
chopped parsley

Bake ½ hour at 350° and baste with olive oil.

ORIENTAL STUFFING

cooked minced lamb
cooked brown rice
dried currants or seedless raisins,
   soaked in sherry 30 minutes
pine nuts or chopped almonds

curry powder
crushed garlic in olive oil to moisten
TOP
chopped parsley

Bake 18 minutes at 350°.

BROWN RICE SALAD WITH PEPPERS

1 cup brown rice
2 cups chicken consommé
recipe for Roasted Peppers (marinated with garlic and olive oil)

1 cup mushrooms, sautéed
2 anchovy fillets, chopped
4 black Italian olives, sliced

Wash the rice, bring it to a boil with the consommé, cover tight, and let it cook 45 minutes over the lowest flame. Remove from heat, leave the rice covered, and let it stand 10 more minutes. Mix with 6 or 8 strips of peppers roasted and marinated in garlic and olive oil, the mushrooms, anchovy fillets, and olives. This may be served hot with veal scaloppine or cold with cold meats or as a first course. Serves 6.

ROASTED PEPPERS AND POTATO SALAD

recipe for Roasted Peppers, marinated
3 or 4 large potatoes, boiled and skinned

¼ cup white wine
½ cup minced green onions
oil mayonnaise
salt and pepper

Cut 6 or 8 strips of the marinated roasted peppers in ½-inch lengths. Cube the skinned potatoes and while they are still warm add the wine. Toss all the ingredients lightly together. This may be served either warm or cold. Garnish with crisp greens. Serves 6.

PEPPER RELISH

12 sweet red peppers
12 sweet green peppers
15 white onions
boiling water

1½ cups sugar
1 qt. best vinegar
¼ cup salt

Remove stem ends, pulp, and seeds from peppers, peel the onions, chop the vegetables fine, cover with boiling water for 3 minutes, and drain. Cover again with boiling water, let stand 10 minutes, and drain. Boil the sugar, vinegar, and salt slowly 4 minutes, add the vegetables, and boil 15 minutes. Seal in sterilized jars.

PEPPER AND CORN RELISH

1 head cabbage, chopped fine   4 cups best vinegar
salt   ½ cup sugar
24 large green peppers   1 tablespoon turmeric
3 dozen ears of corn   2 teaspoons salt

Salt the cabbage in layers and let it stand 2 hours, then drain and squeeze all the water out. Remove stem ends and seeds from peppers and chop fine. Cut the kernels from the corn and add it and the chopped peppers to the cabbage. Boil up the rest of the ingredients, add the vegetables, and boil 5 minutes. Seal in sterilized jars. This is excellent with meat.

POTATOES

Whenever possible, potatoes should be cooked in their skins. Boiled potatoes should be cooked in very little water—½ to 1 cup—which may be saved for soup, sauces, gravies, or bread. Potatoes should be kept in a cool (not cold) dark place, never in closed containers but in bags or bins where air can get to them. New potatoes cook more quickly than old potatoes. Test for doneness with a sharp pointed knife. Boiled potatoes must be drained immediately. Little new potatoes are delicious when baked. Little new thin-skinned potatoes may be scrubbed with a coarse vegetable brush and may not need skinning after they are cooked, no matter how they are dressed or prepared. A medium-sized white potato has the same number of calories as a large orange, and should be considered just as important a part of our regular diet because of its nourishing qualities.

POTATO AND LEEK SOUP

4 leeks, minced   1 qt. milk
1 large onion, minced   ½ cup light cream
4 tablespoons butter   GARNISH
4 good-sized potatoes   minced green onions and chopped
salt and pepper   parsley

Trim the leeks, separate them, and wash them well to remove the sand. Mince them and the onion and sauté 2 minutes in the butter.

Peel and dice the potatoes and add them to the leeks. Salt and pepper the vegetables and cook a minute, then add 1½ cups water, cover, and cook until very tender. Purée them through a sieve or in the electric blender and thin with the milk and cream. This may be served hot or cold. Garnish each soup plate with minced green onions and parsley. This makes about 8 cups of soup. It should be the consistency of cream.

POTATO AND WATERCRESS SOUP

Follow the directions for Leek and Potato Soup and when the soup is done add 1 bunch watercress, washed, stemmed, and ground. This soup may be served hot or cold. The leeks may be omitted if desired but they improve without interfering with the flavor of the cress.

POTATO AND FISH CHOWDER

2½ lbs. striped or sea bass	4 oz. salt pork or bacon, diced
FISH STOCK	2 cups diced raw potatoes
fish trimmings	2 cups diced onions
1 onion, sliced	⅔ cup diced celery
1 carrot, sliced	½ cup cracker crumbs
½ teaspoon thyme	salt and pepper
salt and pepper	1 cup dry white wine
	1 cup heavy cream, scalded

Have the fish filleted, reserving head, skin, and bones for stock. Cover the fish trimmings with 3 cups water, add the sliced onion and carrot with the thyme and seasonings and simmer for 20 minutes. Strain the broth for the chowder. Cut the fish in 4-inch pieces. Fry out the diced pork in the bottom of a soup kettle and on top of it lay alternate layers of the fish, the diced vegetables, and crumbs. Over each layer sprinkle salt and freshly ground pepper very lightly. Add the wine and the fish broth, which should come just to the top of the food. Cover tightly and simmer very gently for 40 minutes. Cooked slowly, the fish does not break up. When ready to serve, add the cream. Enough crumbs should be used to give the soup a little body. This chowder may be made with other firm-fleshed sea or fresh-water fish. Serves 6 or 7.

POTATO SOUP WITH DILL AND CHEESE TOAST

1 lb. potatoes
1 large onion, minced
3 tablespoons butter
handful of fresh dill
½ cup light cream
milk

salt and pepper
                        TOAST
Italian or French bread
butter
Brie or Cheddar cheese

Peel and dice the potatoes. Sauté the onions in butter 1 minute, add the potatoes and ½ cup water, and simmer, covered, until tender. A minute before they are done stem the washed dill, squeeze it, cut it fine with scissors, and add it. Purée with cream and milk in a blender, or put through a sieve and add cream and milk. Season. Cut the bread 1 inch thick, butter it, and cover with a thick slice of soft cheese. Bake it in the oven until the cheese melts. If the bread is very soft, toast it on one side first. Pour the hot soup in the plates and add a slice of cheese toast to the top of each. Makes about 1½ quarts.

POTATO AND SHRIMP SOUP

1 lb. potatoes
1 large onion, minced
3 tablespoons butter
milk
½ cup light cream

salt and pepper
1 lb. fresh shrimp
1 teaspoon thyme
                        GARNISH
chopped parsley

Peel the potatoes and dice them. Sauté the onion in the butter 1 minute, add the potatoes and ½ cup water, and simmer, covered, until the vegetables are tender. Purée them with a little milk and the cream through a sieve or in the electric blender. Season with salt and pepper. Wash the shrimp but do not peel them. Cook them 5 or 6 minutes in 1 cup water with salt, pepper, and the thyme. Let them cool in the liquid. Peel the shrimp and add them and the shrimp broth to the potato soup. Serve hot with chopped green onions or parsley sprinkled over the top of each soup plate. Makes over 2 quarts.

BAKED AND PAN-BAKED POTATOES

Small new potatoes, as well as large old potatoes, are very good baked. Scrub potatoes and let them boil up to heat through. Drain, and put in a hot oven. Old potatoes take from 40 to 60 minutes. Start them at 375° and reduce heat after 30 minutes. Small new potatoes take half as long to bake as old potatoes. Serve them with freshly ground aromatic pepper, salt, plain or smoked, and butter. If soft instead of crisp skin is desired, wrap them in a napkin for 2 minutes after they come from the oven. Make a habit of eating the skins, which many people consider the best part of the potato. Medium-sized potatoes may be pan-baked with roasts. Peel them, boil up to heat through, drain, and put them in the pan with the meat 40 minutes before the meat is done. After 20 minutes, turn them so they brown on both sides.

STUFFED BAKED POTATOES

Cut baked potatoes in half lengthwise, or split the skin open. Scoop out the insides and mix with the ingredients for any of the following stuffings. Replace the stuffing in the skins and put in the oven to heat and brown. These amounts will fill 6 large baked potatoes.

HAM STUFFING

1½ cups ground cooked ham
½ cup hot cream
freshly ground pepper
a little salt
2 tablespoons butter

2 eggs, beaten

TOP

2 tablespoons grated cheese per potato half

Bake 12 minutes.

LEEK STUFFING

¾ cup minced leeks, sautéed in ¼ cup butter

½ cup light cream, heated
salt and pepper

Put in a hot oven until browned a little.

NUT STUFFING

⅓ cup peanut butter or ¾ cup
   ground browned nuts (almonds,
   pecans, or walnuts)
salt and pepper

½ cup hot light cream
¼ cup butter
1 egg, beaten

Bake 5 minutes.

HERB STUFFING

6 tablespoons minced fresh herbs
   (chervil, basil, tarragon, or parsley, and green onions)
3 tablespoons butter

½ cup hot cream
salt and pepper
TOP
paprika

Bake until hot.

CHEESE STUFFING

1 cup grated Gruyère cheese
1 teaspoon thyme or ½ teaspoon
   nutmeg
½ cup hot cream

salt and pepper
3 tablespoons butter
TOP
chopped parsley

Bake until hot.

MUSHROOM STUFFING

¾ cup sliced mushrooms, sautéed
¾ cup minced green onions
salt and pepper

½ cup hot cream
½ teaspoon thyme or tarragon
3 tablespoons butter

Bake 5 minutes in hot oven.

ANCHOVY OR CAVIAR STUFFING

3 or 4 tablespoons anchovy paste
  or 4 tablespoons caviar
1 bud garlic, crushed
salt and pepper
¼ cup chopped green onions

⅔ cup sour cream
1 egg, beaten
     TOP
chopped parsley

Bake 5 minutes in a hot oven. Serve these with baked fish or creamed seafood.

MASHED POTATOES

4 to 6 potatoes
½ to ¾ cup cream
¼ to ⅓ cup butter
milk
salt and pepper
paprika
lumps of butter

ADDITIONS

3 or 4 tablespoons ground nuts or nut
  butter
chopped green onions or chives
chopped parsley
½ cup grated cheese
minced fresh chervil, tarragon, or basil
½ cup chopped sautéed mushrooms

Peel and boil the potatoes, or boil them in their jackets; in the latter case they may have to be reheated after they are skinned and mashed. Mash or rice the hot potatoes, boil up the cream, with any of the additions, if desired, butter, and a little milk, and add with seasonings. Mix until creamy and light, pile into a hot serving dish, sprinkle with paprika and little lumps of butter. Any of the additions are delicious with these. Allow one good-sized potato per person.

CHAMP OR IRISH MASHED POTATOES

1½ lbs. potatoes
salt and pepper
½ cup milk

½ cup cream
1 cup minced green onions
melted butter

Peel, boil, and mash the potatoes. Season with salt and pepper. Boil up the milk and cream with the onions and mash them into the mashed potatoes. When they are served, each person may make a depression in his potatoes and add melted butter. Serves 4.

MASHED POTATOES AND EGGS

Mashed Potatoes   chopped parsley
eggs   grated cheese

Grease a large shallow baking dish or individual ramekins and fill
with the seasoned hot mashed potatoes. Make a depression for each
of the required number of eggs. Drop an egg in each depression and
cover with parsley and cheese. Bake in a hot oven until the eggs set.
This is a good luncheon or supper dish.

POTATO PIE

CRUST	FILLING
1¼ cups flour	4 or 5 potatoes
¾ teaspoon salt	salt and pepper
2 teaspoons baking powder	1 cup creamed cottage cheese
⅓ cup butter and lard, mixed	¼ cup sour cream
about ½ cup milk	1 medium onion, grated
2 tablespoons soft butter	1 egg, beaten

Sift the dry ingredients for the crust and cut in the butter and lard
with a pastry-cutter. Add just enough milk so the dough may be
handled, roll it out, spread with the 2 tablespoons soft butter, fold
once, roll the dough again, and line an 8-inch pie plate. Any trimmed
edges may serve as strips across the filling. Four or five potatoes the
size of very large eggs should make 2¼ cups mashed potatoes. Boil
them in their jackets, skin, and mash them. Mix lightly with all the
other ingredients. Fill the crust and bake for 10 minutes at 400°,
then turn down the heat to 325° and bake another 15 to 17 minutes.
This will serve 4 to 6. By increasing the ingredients this pie may be
made any size. It may be served with practically any meat or fish.

MASHED-POTATO TART

CRUST

crumbs
4 or 5 potatoes
1 teaspoon baking powder
2 tablespoons flour
1 egg, beaten
2 tablespoons melted butter
2 tablespoons light cream
salt and pepper

FILLING NO. 1

1 cup sour cream

2 eggs, beaten
½ cup grated Gruyère cheese
¼ teaspoon nutmeg
salt and pepper
more cheese for top

FILLING NO. 2

1 cup sour cream
2 eggs, beaten
½ cup ground ham or sausage
salt and pepper
cheese or crumbs for top

Grease a 9-inch pie plate and sprinkle it with fine crumbs. Boil 4 or 5 potatoes in their jackets, skin, and mash them through a coarse sieve or rice them to make 2 to 2½ cups. Sift the dry ingredients into them and lightly mix in the other ingredients. Line the pie shell, making a depression in the center to receive the filling, as though the potato mixture were piecrust dough. It may be rolled out if preferred, but it will be fluffier if patted into the shell. Mix either filling, spread over the potato crust, and sprinkle cheese or crumbs over the top. Bake 20 minutes at 350°. Serves 4 to 6.

ALMOND (OR CHEESE OR ONION) POTATO SOUFFLÉ

2½ cups riced hot potatoes
½ cup hot light cream
salt and pepper
½ cup ground browned almonds
¼ teaspoon mace or nutmeg

4 egg yolks, beaten
4 egg whites, beaten until stiff

TOP

2 or 3 tablespoons ground almonds

Mix all the ingredients very lightly with the riced potatoes, folding in the stiffly beaten whites last, and sprinkle the top with ground almonds. Bake in a greased baking dish about 15 minutes at 375°. The soufflé must be puffy but not dried out. A good soufflé may be made with ¼ cup grated onion instead of the almonds. For a cheese soufflé add ½ cup grated Cheddar or Gruyère cheese and sprinkle grated cheese on top. Other mashed vegetables, such as yellow or white turnips or parsnips, may be mixed with the potatoes for a soufflé. This is an excellent way to use leftover vegetables. Serves 4 to 6.

MASHED-POTATO CROQUETTES

There are several ways of making mashed-potato croquettes. Seasoned mashed potatoes may be cooled until they stiffen, then rolled into fingers, dipped in beaten egg, rolled in Parmesan cheese, and fried in deep oil at 370°. They may be laid on brown paper in a warm oven with the door open for a short time. They may also be browned on a greased baking sheet in a 375° oven. Or 2 egg yolks may be added to 2 cups seasoned mashed potatoes, and 2 stiffly beaten egg whites may be added last. These may be dropped on a greased cooky sheet and baked at 375° or dropped by spoonfuls in 375° hot oil. Grated cheese or ground nuts may be added, or the croquettes may be rolled in either the cheese or nuts.

POMMES LORETTE

1 lb. potatoes	**PUFF BATTER**
cream	**1 cup boiling water**
deep fat	**½ cup butter**
	1 teaspoon salt
	1 cup flour
	4 eggs

Peel the potatoes, boil them in salted water until tender, drain, and let them dry out a moment in a warm oven with the door open. Rice them and mix until fluffy with a little cream. Make the puff batter by boiling 1 cup water, the butter, and salt together. When the butter is melted remove it from the fire and stir in the flour, beating until it is smooth. Return the saucepan to a very low fire and stir until the mixture shrinks from the sides of the pan. Remove from the fire and stir in 1 whole egg at a time, beating well until they are all added. Then add the potatoes. Drop the puffs by soupspoonfuls into deep fat and fry at 360° until they are a nice light brown. Serve immediately. Serves 8.

FRENCH-FRIED AND OTHER DEEP-FRIED POTATOES

French-fried potatoes should be cut the size of one's little finger. Julienne potatoes are cut the size of matchsticks. Gaufrettes are cut on a special cutter for that purpose. Potato or Saratoga chips are cut paper-thin on a cutter. All are wiped dry before frying, or are chilled and wiped dry. Fry them, a few at a time, in a wire basket in clear hot fat from 375° to 390°, depending on their thickness. French-fried potatoes should be fried at 390° and take the longest to cook through and become a light rich brown. Dry them on brown paper, salt, and serve immediately. Never cover them or they will become limp. Never fry too many at once or they will stick together, especially the chips. They are the only ones that may be stored when cool. When served they may be reheated in the oven.

POMMES SOUFFLÉES

Idaho potatoes   salt
beef suet (preferred) or lard or
  vegetable shortening

Peel long potatoes, remove a thick slice from each end and from each narrow side, and continue slicing them a good ⅛ inch thick. The slices must be cut along the long grain of the potato, or they won't puff up. They should be ovals of uniform size. Rinse them in cold water and quickly dry them between towels. Have two kettles of fat ready, one at 275°, and one at 400°. Drop 8 or 10 slices at a time into the kettle of fat at 275°. This first cooking takes about 4 minutes, and the fat must not be too hot. Shake the kettle so that the slices do not stick together. Use a large wire scoop and remove about 4 slices at a time to the second kettle of fat, at 400°. This second cooking takes a few seconds, until the slices puff and become a light brown. Remove them to a towel and discard any that do not puff. Puffed slices will deflate, and should be kept between towels in the refrigerator. When ready to serve, heat a kettle of fat to 400° and put in the potatoes, which will brown and crisp immediately. They should be hollow and inflated. Remove from the kettle immediately, lightly salt them, and serve with grilled meats. They will not deflate again. Allow 6 puffs to a person. This recipe was taught me by M. Pierre Rogalle in the kitchen of the Brussels Restaurant, New York.

POTATOES ANNA

5 or 6 large potatoes
salt and freshly ground pepper
½ cup very soft butter

GARNISH

chopped parsley or minced green
onions

Peel and slice the potatoes paper-thin. A slicer is best for this purpose. Grease a mold and put in layers of the potatoes, adding a very slight sifting of salt and pepper to each layer and 1 tablespoon soft butter. Cover the mold with a tight lid or tie with aluminum foil. Bake the potatoes at 375° for 20 minutes, then turn the heat to 325° and bake 20 or 30 minutes more. Too long baking makes the potatoes brown and sticky. Remove the lid or foil, empty the form onto a hot plate or platter upside down, and decorate the top with a little chopped parsley or minced green onions. Serves 6 to 8.

SCALLOPED POTATOES WITH HERBS

4 large potatoes
fresh dill or chervil, or dried
  marjoram, thyme, or basil

2 onions, grated
salt and pepper
⅓ to ½ cup melted butter

Prepare potatoes as for Potatoes Anna, sprinkling each layer of potatoes with 2 tablespoons minced fresh herbs or 1 teaspoonful dried crushed herbs. (Skimp the dried thyme or marjoram. Two or three handfuls of fresh dill may be used. Stem, squeeze it, and cut fine with scissors.) Add 1 tablespoon grated onion to each layer of potatoes, salt, pepper, and melted butter. Bake in a greased mold with a tight cover for 40 or 50 minutes at 375° half the time and at 325° the second half. Serves 6.

SUSANNE'S POTATO CASSEROLE
(Hungarian)

4 large potatoes
1 cup diced onions
3 tablespoons butter

salt and pepper
4 hard-boiled eggs, sliced
2 cups sour cream

Boil the potatoes in their jackets, skin, and slice them. Sauté the onions until tender in the butter. Put alternate layers of all the ingredients in a greased casserole, reserving enough sour cream for a

1-inch layer on the top. Bake about 12 minutes in a hot oven, or until it is very hot and the top is browned a little. Serves 7 or 8.

POTATO, HAM, AND EGG CASSEROLE

5 medium-sized potatoes, boiled, skinned, and sliced
5 hard-boiled eggs, sliced
1½ cups ground cooked ham
1 cup minced green onions

salt and pepper
1 canned pimento, sliced
2 cups thin cream sauce
TOP
buttered crumbs

Put all the ingredients in layers in a greased casserole, spreading the top with a ½-inch layer of the cream sauce. Sprinkle the top with the crumbs. Bake 25 minutes at 350°. These potato casserole dishes may be greatly increased in size to serve many people and are good to take on picnics. Serves 8 to 10.

CREAMED POTATOES GRUYÈRE

diced cooked potatoes
salt and pepper
¼ teaspoon nutmeg

⅔ cup grated imported Gruyère cheese
1 cup cream

The required number of potatoes may be boiled and diced, or little new potatoes may be scrubbed and baked. Keep them hot. Add seasonings and cheese to the cream, bring to a boil, put the potatoes in a warm serving dish, and pour the sauce over them. This is a most delicious dish with this cheese, but other cheeses may be used. It is not necessary that the cheese be completely melted. It is left to the cook's conscience whether light or heavy cream is used.

POTATOES CHANTILLY

4 good-sized potatoes
1 cup cream, whipped
salt and pepper

½ teaspoon nutmeg
TOP
½ cup Parmesan cheese

Boil, skin, and rice the potatoes into a greased shallow baking dish. Whip the cream and add the seasonings. Spread the cream over the potatoes, sprinkle the top with cheese, and bake in a 375° oven for 7 minutes or until lightly browned. Serves 7 or 8.

CREAMED BAKED NEW POTATOES

little new potatoes
1 cup heavy cream
salt and pepper
1 teaspoon turmeric

1 cup chopped green onions
TOP
3 tablespoons chopped parsley

Scrub the required number of thin-skinned new potatoes, let them come to a boil, drain, and bake in a 350° oven until tender. Quarter them but do not skin them. Put them in a hot serving dish. Mix the cream with the seasonings and onions, let it come to a boil, and pour it over them. Sprinkle the top with the parsley.

DOUBLE-BOILER CREAMED POTATOES

3 good-sized potatoes
salt and pepper

2 tablespoons grated onion
1 cup light cream

Peel the potatoes and shred them quite fine on a disk grater. Add salt, pepper, and the onion. Put them in the top of a double boiler with the cream, cover tight, and cook over boiling water until thick and tender. Serves 4.

BAKED CREAMED SHREDDED POTATOES

2 lbs. potatoes
2 eggs, beaten
½ cup cream

2 teaspoons salt
2 cups milk
freshly ground pepper

Peel the potatoes and grate them on a disk shredder. Put them in a well-greased casserole. Beat the rest of the ingredients together and pour over the potatoes. Bake them, uncovered, 50 minutes at 350°. They should be set but moist. This is one of the finest potato dishes. Serves 5 or 6.

SHREDDED POTATOES BAKED IN BUTTER

4 large potatoes
¾ cup melted butter

salt and pepper
grated cheese

Peel the potatoes and shred quite fine on a disk. Put the potatoes in a well-greased baking dish, mix the butter with salt and pepper, and add. If the butter doesn't seem enough, add some more. Cover tight and bake at 350° 30 minutes. Uncover and bake 15 minutes more. Sprinkle the top with grated cheese 5 minutes before the end of this time. These are good with or without cheese. They may also be spread with ¾ cup sour cream mixed with chopped chives 4 minutes before they come from the oven. Serves 4 to 6.

POTATO AND HAM CASSEROLE

1-inch slice of ham	freshly ground pepper
1 large onion, chopped	1 small can evaporated milk
3 cups sliced raw potatoes	1 cup milk

If the ham is very salty, freshen it by pouring boiling water over it, then drain. Make a bed of half the onions and half the potatoes in the bottom of a casserole, lay the ham on it, and add the rest of the vegetables. Mix some pepper with all the milk and pour it over the top. Cover and bake slowly 1 hour. Serves 3 or 4.

CREAMED POTATOES AND HAM

2 lbs. new potatoes, baked	3 tablespoons chopped parsley
2 thin slices ham, sautéed and cut in strips or cubes	3 tablespoons chopped green onions or chives
2 cups medium-rich hot cream sauce	

When the potatoes are baked cut them in halves or quarters and mix them with the ham. Put the potatoes and ham in a hot serving dish and pour the hot cream sauce over them. Add the parsley and chives or onions to the top. This is a fine lunch or supper dish.

WHOLE POTATOES FRIED IN BUTTER

1 lb. small new potatoes, or potatoes cut in olive shapes	⅓ cup butter salt and pepper

Peel and wipe the potatoes and put them in the bottom of a big pan with a tight-fitting lid. Add the butter (no substitute), cover, and cook until they are brown and tender. Shake them a few times so they will brown all over. This will take about 25 minutes or less time if the potatoes are cut in small olive shapes. Serves 4.

HASHED BROWN POTATOES

potatoes   ham or bacon fat
salt and pepper   chopped parsley (optional)

Chop raw potatoes very fine or dice cold, boiled potatoes. Salt and
pepper them and put them in a frying pan with plenty of sizzling hot
fat. If the potatoes are raw, turn the flame low after a minute and
stir once or twice while they cook tender; then turn the flame high,
pat them into a cake, and brown. Turn them over, brown the other
side, and add more fat when necessary to keep them from burning.
When they are a deep brown, slide the cake onto a hot plate or platter. Chopped parsley may be added to the top. Precooked potatoes
are browned the same way, except that they do not have to cook
through and need not be stirred at all.

FRIED POTATOES WITH CHIVES OR CHEESE

4 or 5 potatoes, peeled and diced   ½ cup chopped chives or 1 cup
salt and freshly ground pepper   grated Cheddar or Gruyère
bacon, ham, or other good fat   cheese

Chill the potatoes. Salt and pepper them and put them in a big
skillet with plenty of hot fat. Brown them and then put them in the
oven for 10 minutes to cook through. If cheese is used, add it to the
top of the potatoes before they go into the oven. Empty into a serving
dish and sprinkle with the chives, if you use them. Serves 4 or 5.

POTATO OMELET

1 cup fried potatoes   4 tablespoons butter
6 eggs   TOP
3 tablespoons cream   chopped chives
salt and pepper

The potatoes may be leftover fried potatoes warmed up, or newly
fried. Make the omelet by beating the eggs, adding the cream, salt,
and pepper, and frying it in the butter. Add the potatoes to the top,
fold once and empty onto a hot platter. Add the chives to the top.
Serves 4 or 5.

POTATOES COOKED IN CONSOMMÉ

new potatoes
consommé
1 bud garlic, crushed

bacon or ham fat
chopped parsley

Scrub small new potatoes and, if the skin is not thin, scrape them. Put them in a heavy pot with 1 cup consommé and the garlic. Cook gently until the consommé is absorbed, and add more if necessary, until the potatoes are done. They may then be browned in fat. Or enough consommé may be used to make a sauce; thicken it a little with cornstarch so it is like cream. Sprinkle chopped parsley over the potatoes.

POTATO STUFFING FOR ROAST GOOSE

6 good-sized potatoes
1 strip salt pork, diced
1 cup chopped onions
goose fat
2 eggs, beaten
1/3 cup diced celery
salt and pepper

1/3 cup sliced Brazil nuts, browned
1 teaspoon thyme
1 teaspoon basil
2 tablespoons chopped parsley
1 cup cubed rye or whole-wheat
    bread, toasted

Cook the potatoes, skin, and mash them. Fry out the salt pork and use only the crisp pieces of pork. Sauté the onions in some goose fat. Mix all together lightly and stuff the goose.

POTATO CAKES

2 large potatoes
1 small onion, grated
3/4 cup flour
1 1/2 teaspoons salt

1/4 teaspoon pepper
3/4 teaspoon baking soda
buttermilk
4 or 5 tablespoons hot oil or butter

Peel the potatoes, boil one, drain, and mash it. Grate the other into the hot potato and add the grated onion. Sift the dry ingredients and add them with just enough buttermilk to enable the mixture to be dropped from a spoon. Fry in cakes on a hot griddle in the oil or butter. When they are browned on both sides they may finish cooking in the oven for 3 or 4 minutes. Makes 8 cakes.

POTATO PANCAKES

4 potatoes, peeled	salt and pepper
1 onion	2 eggs, beaten
3 tablespoons flour	hot fat or butter

Grate the peeled potatoes and onion quickly so water doesn't form. Add the flour, salt, pepper, and beaten eggs. Fry on a well-greased griddle until crisp and brown, then put them in the oven to cook 2 or 3 minutes while the rest of the pancakes fry. The oven will cook them through, and they do not have to be fried for very long. These are good with pot roast or grilled meats. Serves 4.

MASHED-POTATO PANCAKES

2 cups riced or mashed potatoes	2 tablespoons butter
2 tablespoons chopped parsley	½ cup milk
1 cup soft breadcrumbs	salt and pepper
1 onion, grated	*COATING*
2 eggs, beaten	crumbs or corn meal

Mix all the ingredients. Form into cakes and roll them in crumbs or corn meal. Brown on both sides in hot fat or butter. They may be kept warm on a greased cooky sheet in a warm oven 3 or 4 minutes until ready to serve. Makes 12 cakes.

HOT POTATO SALAD

5 or 6 large potatoes	1 cup sliced onions
6 strips bacon, cut in 1-inch lengths	4 tablespoons red wine
	salt and pepper

Boil the potatoes in their jackets until tender. Meanwhile fry out the bacon. Scoop out the bacon bits and sauté the onions in the bacon fat. Skin the potatoes, slice or cube them, and mix with the red wine while they are hot. Add the onions, bacon bits, salt, and pepper, and serve warm. Serves 5 or 6.

COLD POTATO SALADS

When making potato salads, mix while the potatoes are still warm and let stand several hours so the potatoes will absorb the flavors. Add wine, truffles, or dill while the potatoes are hot. These salads must be liberally moistened with dressing so they won't taste like the proverbial "cold potato." The exact quantities of sour cream, French dressing, and mayonnaise may be left to the cook; the perfection of the salad depends on the additions and seasonings. Chill them in a bowl several hours, unmold them on a chop plate, cover with a layer of mixed mayonnaise and sour cream, and sprinkle with grated cheese, sieved egg yolks, or finely chopped nuts. Red pimento strips and sliced olives also may be used. Other cooked vegetables may garnish the salad, as may sliced tomatoes, watercress, and cucumbers. Potato salad is most useful to serve a large crowd and is one of the great dishes, if properly made. Allow one good-sized potato per person.

DILL POTATO SALAD

5 or 6 potatoes, boiled and cubed
2 tablespoons lemon juice
2 handfuls fresh dill, stemmed, squeezed, and cut with scissors

salt and pepper
1 large onion, grated
½ cup oil mayonnaise
sour cream

HAM AND POTATO SALAD

5 or 6 potatoes, boiled and cubed
⅓ cup red wine
1½ cups ground or cubed ham
3 tablespoons chopped parsley
½ cup chopped green onions or chives

2 hard-boiled eggs, sliced
salt and pepper
1 tablespoon chopped pickles
1 tablespoon capers
⅔ cup oil mayonnaise
1 cup sour cream

ONION POTATO SALAD

5 or 6 potatoes, boiled and sliced
4 sweet red onions, sliced paper-thin
salt and pepper
12 stuffed olives, sliced

3 tablespoons chopped parsley
layers of cut fresh chervil or other herbs
½ cup French dressing with sour cream and mayonnaise

POTATO AND VEGETABLE SALAD

5 or 6 potatoes, boiled and cubed
½ lb. Jerusalem artichokes, boiled
  and sliced
1 cup peas, cooked with basil
2 or 3 soft-boiled eggs, mixed with
  the vegetables

½ cup minced green onions
salt and pepper
2 tablespoons vinegar
4 tablespoons olive oil
sour cream and mayonnaise to
  moisten

WHITE-WINE POTATO SALAD

5 or 6 potatoes, boiled and cubed
½ cup white wine
2 tablespoons parsley
handful of fresh tarragon leaves,
  cut with scissors

½ cup French dressing mixed with
  oil mayonnaise
TOP
mayonnaise, sliced hard-boiled
  eggs, and pimento strips

CELERY POTATO SALAD

5 or 6 potatoes, boiled and sliced
⅓ cup white wine
1 cup celeriac or celery hearts, in
  julienne sticks
6 or 8 artichoke bottoms
½ cup minced green onions

1 teaspoon Bahamian mustard
French dressing mixed with sour
  cream or mayonnaise
TOP
chopped pistachio nuts or almonds

POTATO ROLLS

1 envelope or cake of yeast
⅓ cup lukewarm water
2 tablespoons brown sugar or
  honey
½ cup potato water and milk
1½ cups hot mashed potatoes
3 cups graham flour

2 teaspoons salt
3 eggs at room temperature
½ cup light brown sugar
½ cup melted butter
more milk
TOP
melted butter

Mix the yeast, warm water, and sugar or honey, and let it stand in a warm place until it becomes foamy. Mix the potato water and milk with the potatoes. When this mixture is lukewarm combine with the foamy yeast and let it stand in a warm place ½ hour. Then stir in 1 cup of the flour and the salt. Beat the eggs until thick with the brown sugar, stir them in, and add the melted butter. Beat hard, then add the rest of the flour and a little lukewarm milk—about ¼ to ⅓ cup, just enough so the dough is light. Beat very hard, set the bowl in a dishpan of warm (not hot) water, cover with a tea towel, and let stand 1½ hours. Punch down and beat for 1 minute with a wooden spoon. The dough may be rolled out, cut in rounds, and brushed with melted butter; or pieces may be pinched off and put in greased muffin tins. Let rise 30 minutes. If desired, 9 muffin tins and 1 small loaf pan may be filled. The rolls take 15 minutes to bake at 375°, and the small loaf 40 minutes. Turn the temperature down to 325° for the latter half of the baking of the bread. These are extremely light and delicious rolls.

One-third of the flour may be rye, in which case use a little less liquid.

POTATO DOUGHNUTS

1 cup hot mashed potatoes	2 teaspoons baking powder
1 cup light brown sugar	½ teaspoon salt
1 cup evaporated milk	⅛ teaspoon powdered cloves
2 eggs, beaten	deep fat
about 3⅓ cups flour	

Add the sugar to the potatoes, and when it is melted add the milk and beaten eggs. Sift the dry ingredients, using only 3 cups flour. Combine the mixtures and if the dough is not firm enough to roll add the rest of the flour; it must be as soft as possible. Roll out about ⅓ inch thick, cut with a doughnut-cutter, and fry in deep fat at 370° until brown on both sides, turning once. Drain on brown paper. When cool shake in a bag containing powdered sugar and store in an earthenware jar with a top. Makes about 24 doughnuts.

POTATO CUSTARD

¾ cup hot mashed potatoes	½ cup light cream
2 tablespoons butter	1 teaspoon grated lemon rind
½ cup light brown sugar	3 tablespoons lemon juice
2 egg yolks, beaten	2 egg whites, beaten until stiff

Stir the butter into the hot potatoes, add the sugar, egg yolks, and cream. Add the grated rind and juice to the stiffly beaten egg whites and fold in last. Bake in greased custard cups at 350° about 18 minutes or until set, or bake 25 minutes in a piecrust. Serves 4.

POTATO CHOCOLATE CAKE

1 cup butter
1½ cups light brown sugar
4 egg yolks, beaten
½ cup milk
2 squares chocolate, grated
1 cup hot mashed potatoes
2 cups pastry flour

2 teaspoons baking powder
1 teaspoon each powdered cloves, cinnamon, and nutmeg
1 cup raisins
1 cup sliced nuts
¼ cup light brown sugar
4 egg whites

Cream the butter and 1½ cups sugar until fluffy and smooth. Add the well-beaten egg yolks and milk. Melt the grated chocolate in the hot mashed potatoes and stir it into the batter. Sift all the dry ingredients, mix the raisins and nuts through them, and add. Beat the egg whites until stiff, add ¼ cup sugar, beat to a thick meringue, and fold it in last. This cake may be baked in a long pan or in layers. It is very good with caramel frosting. Bake about 30 minutes at 325°. It is done when the cake shrinks from the pan.

RADISHES

Radishes, which appear in almost every garden, are an attractive and welcome accompaniment to cold suppers when served raw, and also make a crisp addition to antipasto, hors d'oeuvre, and curries. They belong to the same family as the turnip and, when cooked, have a very delicate turnip flavor. Besides the little round red radishes, there are long smooth white radishes and very large radishes, white inside and dark brown or black outside, called by the Chinese "white beets."

RADISHES AS HORS D'OEUVRE

white radishes   red radish roses

Shred white radishes on a disk shredder so that they look like coconut. Heap the shreds in the center of a fancy dish. Surround the white mound with radish roses. Leave an inch of stem on perfect radishes and cut petals, starting at the root end and going almost to the stem. If scored through the skin first, the petals are easier to cut. Put the radishes in ice water until the petals curl back.

BUTTERED RADISHES

1 bunch red radishes
⅓ cup finely diced Bermuda or
   green onions

3 tablespoons butter
salt and pepper

Wash and trim the radishes, leaving on ½ inch of stem. The onions must be very finely diced. Sauté them a little in a heavy pot with the butter, add ⅓ cup water and radishes, cover, and cook 8 or 10 minutes or until the radishes are tender. Season after they are done so the salt won't reduce the color. They become pink and are attractive served plain, or they may be creamed a little or heaped on top of a stew after it is in the serving dish. They should be cooked separately from the stew.

CREAMED BLACK RADISHES

4 black radishes
¼ cup minced green or white
   onions
2 tablespoons butter
salt and pepper

¼ cup hot water
2 teaspoons cornstarch
½ cup light cream
½ teaspoon turmeric or curry
   powder

Scrape or peel the radishes and cut them in eighths lengthwise if they arc large. Sauté the onions in the butter a minute, then add the radishes, salt, pepper, and water. Cover and steam tender or cook in the pressure cooker 2½ minutes. Mix the cornstarch with the cream and add the turmeric or curry powder. When the radishes are done add the cream and heat until it thickens. This is very good. Serves 4.

CHINESE RADISH CAKES

2 cups shredded large black radishes
¼ cup minced white or green onions
1 egg, beaten

¼ cup rice flour
salt and pepper
butter for frying

The large radishes should be 8 inches long and 2 inches thick. These cakes are made in Chinatown and are not usually served to Americans unless a Chinese friend orders them. They are very good and resemble potato pancakes. Combine the first five ingredients and fry till brown on both sides, then put them, still in the skillet, in the oven for 15 minutes to complete the cooking. Makes 6 cakes.

SPINACH

Those who have labored in gardens know how to care for their produce when it is prepared for the table. Others who depend on the markets may like to know that preparing fresh spinach is little trouble if, when the root is cut away, it is first washed in warm water in a large dishpan. The warm water quickly sends the soil on the leaves to the bottom of the pan. Wash twice more, with cold water, and the leaves will be perfectly free from grit. Do not let spinach soak in the water more than 2 minutes. Drain it in a wire basket before storing in the refrigerator for salad or cooking. One of the finest salads is made with the raw, tender leaves of fresh spinach; packaged spinach will not do for this.

CREAM OF SPINACH SOUP

1½ lbs. spinach
1 good-sized onion, chopped
1 small green pepper, minced
¼ cup butter
1 teaspoon sugar
salt and pepper

1 teaspoon basil or tarragon
½ cup light cream
milk

GARNISH
3 tablespoons minced green onions

Remove the roots from the spinach, wash in three waters, and drain a little. Put the onion, green pepper, and butter in the bottom of a heavy pot and sauté gently 3 minutes, then add the spinach, sugar, seasonings, and herb. Add no water, cover tight, and steam until the spinach is tender. In a pressure cooker this takes less than 1 minute. Mash through a sieve or purée the vegetables in an electric blender. Add the cream and enough milk to thin to the right consistency—as thick as cream. This improves if allowed to stand a few hours before it is heated to serve. Sprinkle the top with the onions. Serves 6.

SPINACH AND PEA SOUP

recipe for Cream of Spinach Soup   2 tablespoons butter
1½ cups, shelled fresh peas (1½ lbs.)   pinch of rosemary or tarragon

Make the soup with 1 pound spinach. Cook the peas separately in very little water, the butter, and herb. Leave half of them whole and purée half and add both to the spinach soup. Serves 8.

SPINACH AND MUSHROOM SOUP

recipe for Cream of Spinach Soup   dash of nutmeg
½ lb. fresh mushrooms   salt and pepper
3 tablespoons butter

Make the spinach soup with 1 pound spinach. Try to obtain small white mushrooms. Grind half of them and leave the smallest ones whole. Sauté them in the butter very gently for 5 or 6 minutes. Season and add them to the spinach soup. This gives the soup a delicious flavor. I have tried adding broth to spinach soup but I think it changes the character of the vegetable too much.

COLD SPINACH SOUP

recipe for Cream of Spinach Soup   sliced cucumbers
GARNISH   watercress sprigs
minced green onions   yogurt
minced fresh dill   diced dill pickles

After the soup has thoroughly cooled, chill it several hours in the refrigerator. Put in wide soup plates, pile 1 tablespoon of each of the garnishes on the soup in each plate. Add a heaping big kitchen spoonful of yogurt. This is a meal and one of the finest dishes to serve for lunch or supper in hot weather. These garnishes also make soup of puréed chard, kale, or other leftover greens into very fine dishes.

BUTTERED SPINACH

1 lb. fresh spinach	3 tablespoons butter
⅓ cup diced onions	salt and pepper
1 green pepper, diced	pinch of rosemary or 1 teaspoon basil

Cut off the spinach roots and discard any imperfect leaves. Wash three times. Let it drain a little. Sauté the onions and green pepper in the butter in the bottom of a heavy pot for 2 or 3 minutes, then add the spinach, seasoning, and herb without any water. Cover tight and steam until tender, 4 or 5 minutes. The pressure cooker is ideal for this and takes but a few seconds. Cooking spinach this way, with the onion and green pepper, enhances its flavor and is my favorite way to prepare this vegetable whether it is to be served with a sauce, in soup, in a soufflé, or just buttered. Serves 4.

SPINACH WITH BROTH SAUCE

recipe for Buttered Spinach	1 teaspoon simple syrup
chicken consommé or beef broth	GARNISH
2 or 3 teaspoons cornstarch	buttered croutons
2 teaspoons lemon juice	

There is always some liquid to drain from Buttered Spinach. Add enough consommé or broth to make 1 cup and mix with the cornstarch, lemon juice, and syrup. Add this to the drained spinach and heat it until the sauce thickens. Empty into a hot serving dish and add buttered croutons to the top. A pound and a half of spinach may be cooked to serve from 4 to 6. This sauce is a good alternative to a cream sauce.

SPINACH WITH MUSHROOM SAUCE

recipe for Buttered Spinach	1 tablespoon sherry or lemon juice
light cream	dash of nutmeg
2 or 3 teaspoons cornstarch	1 cup fresh mushrooms, sautéed

Drain the spinach well after it has cooked and add to the liquid enough cream to make 1 cup. Dissolve the cornstarch in the liquid and cook it in a small saucepan until it thickens; then add the sherry, nutmeg, and mushrooms. Mix the sauce lightly with the spinach and serve hot.

SPINACH WITH EGG AND CHEESE SAUCE
(Or with Curry or Hollandaise Sauce)

recipe for Buttered Spinach
cream
2 teaspoons cornstarch

⅓ cup grated cheese
2 hard-boiled eggs
1 tablespoon curry powder (optional)

Drain the liquid from the boiled spinach and add enough cream to make 1 cup. Blend in the cornstarch, add the cheese, and cook the sauce until it thickens. Peel the eggs, chop the whites, add them to the sauce, and mix it with the spinach. Empty into a serving bowl and sieve the yolks over the top. The cheese may or may not be omitted, and 1 tablespoon curry powder may be added to the sauce. Spinach may also be served with Hollandaise Sauce (page 137); when doing so, drain the spinach liquid and reserve it for use in a soup.

FRITTATA AL VERDE

½ cup cooked chopped spinach
2 tablespoons chopped parsley
2 tablespoons chopped chervil or tarragon
salt and pepper
4 eggs, beaten

1 tablespoon cream
1 tablespoon spinach liquid
1 tablespoon grated Parmesan cheese
4 tablespoons butter

Mix the spinach and herbs and seasonings. Use fresh herbs if you have them, as they make this a wonderful dish. Beat the eggs until light with the cream and liquid you have drained from the spinach. Add the tablespoon of cheese and lightly mix with the greens. Melt the butter in a frying pan, making sure that the bottom and sides are coated with butter. Cook the egg-and-spinach mixture in the pan over a brisk fire, lifting the sides a little so that the uncooked egg runs into the pan. When it is just cooked through (not dry) empty it onto a round warmed serving plate without folding it. The Italians serve this omelet in a big round cake. Pass more grated Parmesan cheese to sprinkle over the top. Serves 2.

CASSEROLE OF SPINACH

recipe for Buttered Spinach (2 lbs.)
milk and cream
2 tablespoons butter
4 tablespoons flour
salt and pepper

½ teaspoon rosemary
4 hard-boiled eggs, sliced
TOP
buttered crumbs
⅓ cup grated cheese

Coarsely chop the spinach before cooking the recipe for Buttered Spinach. Drain the liquid after it is cooked and add enough cream and milk to make 1½ cups. Make a cream sauce by melting the butter, blending in the flour, seasonings, and liquid. Alternate layers of spinach, cream sauce, and sliced eggs in a greased baking dish, top with crumbs and cheese, and heat in a hot oven until it browns— about 7 or 8 minutes.

EGGS FLORENTINE

recipe for Buttered Spinach
poached eggs

Hollandaise Sauce (page 137)

Cook the spinach and drain it a little. Have the required number of poached eggs ready. Empty the spinach into a hot serving dish and put the eggs on top. Add a big tablespoon of Hollandaise sauce to the top of each egg. Or cooked spinach may be put in ramekins and a raw egg may be added to each. Bake them in a hot oven 10 or 12 minutes until the eggs are set, then top with sauce.

SPINACH ROULADE

1 cup ground raw spinach
        CREAM SAUCE
2 tablespoons butter
4 tablespoons flour
1 cup milk
salt and pepper
½ teaspoon nutmeg or 1 teaspoon
        basil
3 egg yolks

3 egg whites, beaten until stiff
crumbs or corn meal
        FILLING
1 cup sour cream
1 cup ground ham or 1 cup sautéed
        sliced mushrooms
        TOP
⅓ cup melted butter
Parmesan cheese

Tightly pack 1 cup ground spinach so that the juice is squeezed out. Melt the butter, blend in the flour, and stir in the milk slowly over a low fire. When it thickens add the seasonings and egg yolks. Mix in the spinach and fold in the stiffly beaten egg whites. Put well-greased heavy paper on a cooky sheet and sprinkle it with crumbs or a little corn meal. Spread the mixture over a 12-by-16-inch area and bake 15 to 18 minutes at 375°. Mix the sour cream with the ham or mushrooms, heat, spread it over the spinach, and roll it up, lifting the edges with the paper. Put the roll on a hot platter, pour the melted butter over it, and sprinkle the top with cheese. Serve immediately. This is a fine luncheon or supper dish. Serves 4.

SPINACH WITH ANCHOVIES

recipe for Buttered Spinach
1 bud garlic, crushed
2 tablespoons olive oil

3 or 4 anchovy fillets or 2 or 3 tablespoons anchovy paste

GARNISH

grated Parmesan cheese

After the spinach is cooked it may be drained somewhat so as not to dilute the sauce too much. Warm the garlic in the olive oil, add the anchovy fillets cut in 1-inch lengths, or melt the paste in the oil. Mix it well with the spinach and empty into a hot serving dish. Sprinkle the top with grated Parmesan cheese. (Crumbled Roquefort cheese is also very good tossed with cooked spinach when the anchovy is omitted.)

SPINACH CHEESE BALLS

½ cup ground raw spinach
½ cup ricotta or cottage cheese
1 tablespoon grated Parmesan cheese
salt and pepper
½ teaspoon nutmeg

1½ teaspoons grated lemon rind
1 large egg yolk
¼ cup flour
chicken consommé or salted water
melted butter and grated Parmesan cheese

Press the ground spinach to extract the juice. The result will be about ⅓ cup. Use ricotta or not-too-moist creamed cottage cheese. If it is not smooth, first sieve it. Mix with the spinach seasonings, rind, egg yolk, and flour. Form into about 20 little balls. Test one in boiling consommé or salted water to see if it holds together. The less flour used, the better they are. Poach 2 or 3 minutes, then take out with a perforated spoon. These are delicious to serve in soup or as an entrée with melted butter and Parmesan cheese.

SPINACH-STUFFED EGGS

2 large handfuls spinach (or sorrel,   ¼ teaspoon nutmeg
   parsley, or watercress), stemmed   salt and pepper
¼ cup cream cheese   8 to 12 hard-boiled eggs
2 tablespoons sour cream

Put the raw greens through the grinder, soften the cheese with the sour cream, and mix. Add the seasonings. Cut the peeled eggs in half lengthwise and mash the yolks with the spinach mixture. Fill the white shells with the mixture. These eggs may be put in a shallow bowl and garnished with sprigs of watercress or used for garnishing cold salad or meat platters; or they are excellent for picnic lunches.

RISOVERDE

1 cup brown rice   2 buds garlic, crushed
2 cups consommé   ¼ cup olive oil
1 lb. fresh spinach (1½ cups)   GARNISH
2 green onions   grated Parmesan cheese

Wash the rice, boil it up in the consommé, cover tight, and steam 45 minutes over the gentlest possible flame. Grind the spinach and onions. Warm the crushed garlic and olive oil a few seconds over a gentle flame and mix it with the spinach and onions. When the rice is done mix it with the spinach and put it back in the pot, covered, until it heats thoroughly—about 5 minutes over a low flame. Empty into a warmed serving dish and pass Parmesan cheese to serve over it. Leftover spinach soufflé mixed with fresh cooked rice is also delicious. Serves 4 or 5.

SPINACH-RICE CROQUETTES

½ recipe for Risoverde   grated Parmesan cheese
1 egg, beaten   butter

Half the recipe for Risoverde may be made into delicious croquettes. Blend the spinach-and-rice mixture with the beaten egg, form into 12 or 14 balls the size of pullet eggs, and roll them in Parmesan cheese. Lay them on the bottom of a well-buttered shallow baking dish and bake them in a hot oven just long enough to brown them lightly. This will serve 6 or 7 as an accompaniment to meat or chicken. A little foresight in the perparation of Risoverde will provide two excellent dishes for two separate meals.

SPINACH SOUFFLÉ 1

recipe for Buttered Spinach (use 1½ lbs.)
½ cup spinach liquid
3 tablespoons flour
⅓ cup cream
1 teaspoon basil or ½ teaspoon rosemary
3 egg yolks
3 egg whites

When increasing the amount of spinach in the Buttered Spinach recipe, it is not necessary to increase the other ingredients. Drain the cooked spinach and use ½ cup of the liquid. Mash the spinach through a sieve or purée in the electric blender. Add all the ingredients except the egg whites—the ingredients may be added in the blender. More salt and pepper may be needed. The blender does not beat egg whites. Beat them stiff in a bowl and add the puréed spinach. Bake in a greased baking dish 25 or 30 minutes at 350°, or until the soufflé is set but still creamy inside. This will serve 6 to 8.

SPINACH SOUFFLÉ 2

2 cups raw spinach
1 small or 2 green onions
4 large egg yolks
¼ cup cornstarch
⅓ cup light cream
1 teaspoon basil
1 teaspoon tarragon
½ teaspoon salt
¼ teaspoon pepper
4 egg whites, beaten until stiff
GARNISH
grated Parmesan cheese

Wash and drain the spinach. Put the stems and leaves through the grinder with a small onion or 2 green onions. Blend the cornstarch smooth with the egg yolks or cream. Mix all the ingredients, folding in the stiffly beaten egg whites last, and put the mixture in a well-greased baking dish. Bake 35 to 40 minutes at 350°. I like the inside rather moist so that, when serving, I can spoon it over the well-set crust; 35 minutes will be sufficient for this. Pass Parmesan cheese to sprinkle over the top. A soufflé made of uncooked spinach has a very fresh flavor. This will serve 4 to 6, depending on whether it is a very simple meal or with a full course dinner. Any leftover soufflé may be sieved or puréed in the electric blender with milk and makes a fine soup.

SPINACH OR KALE CAKES

1 cup ground spinach or kale (⅔ lb.)

⅓ cup sieved cottage cheese

½ teaspoon salt

1 teaspoon basil

1 teaspoon fennel

2 tablespoons rice flour

2 tablespoons grated Parmesan cheese

1 egg, beaten

butter

SAUCE

1 teaspoon cornstarch

vegetable juice and light cream to make ½ cup

salt and pepper

1 teaspoon tarragon

1 green onion, minced

Grind the spinach or kale, press it to extract the juice, and reserve the juice for the sauce. Add the rest of the ingredients for the cakes, drop them from a spoon in hot butter, and fry a nice brown on both sides. These must be turned carefully; do not use margarine, as it sticks. Blend the cornstarch with the vegetable juice and cream. Add the seasonings and tarragon and cook until it thickens. Add the onion and serve over the cakes. This makes 8 cakes and will serve 4. It is suggested for a separate vegetable course; they are delicious and very attractive with the green sauce.

SPINACH SALAD

tender raw spinach leaves, stemmed

3 strips bacon

3 or 4 buds garlic, sliced thin

1 teaspoon powdered fennel

tart French dressing

2 hard-boiled eggs

Only the most perfect young leaves should go into spinach salad. Have the leaves washed and well drained, and store all day in the refrigerator, covered. When the salad is to be made fill the bowl with them. Cut the bacon in 1-inch lengths and put it in a skillet with the garlic. Fry gently until the bacon is crisp and the garlic is light brown. Empty the bacon, garlic, and the grease over the leaves and mix well with an herb—fennel, if available. Add a little quite tart French dressing—not as much as usual, on account of the bacon grease. After it is well mixed sieve the eggs over the top and do not disturb it again. The leaves must be fluffy and not moistened too much with dressing. This is one of the finest salads.

SQUASH

There are, of course, many varieties of squash, but for cooking purposes we may divide them into two classes: the first group, the Hubbard and acorn (Fordhook) squashes, has richer and meatier flesh than the second group, called summer squash, which has many variations. Perhaps the most popular squash of the latter group is zucchini because it has more flavor than the white or yellow vegetable marrow or summer squash. It is a great favorite of Italians, here and abroad. The banana squash belongs somewhere in between these two groups but is not so commonly known. It has a deep orange flesh which, when cooked, is not as rich as that of either the Hubbard or acorn. Mashed cooked Hubbard squash, although a little more moist than the sweet potato, may be seasoned and served in many of the same ways. Squash pie is every bit as good as pumpkin pie, and some prefer it.

Summer squashes of all types are best when cooked while they are young. The small ones do not require peeling, and the seeds are either unnoticeable or perfectly tender when cooked. Because of their high water content it is much better to fry, bake, or steam them than to cook them in water.

SQUASH SOUP

2 cups peeled, cubed Hubbard or acorn squash
¼ teaspoon ginger or mace
2 or 3 tablespoons honey or brown sugar (to taste)
salt and pepper
3 cups chicken broth
⅔ cup light cream
2 or 3 tablespoons rum or sherry

Steam the squash tender over boiling water. Mash the squash and blend it, until smooth and creamy, with all the other ingredients. If it is to be reheated add the rum or sherry just before serving. Serves 6.

BAKED HUBBARD OR ACORN SQUASH

1 Hubbard squash or 3 or 4 acorn   salt and pepper
  squashes   brown sugar or honey
nutmeg, mace, or ginger   butter

Cut the squash in half, remove fibers and seeds. Cut Hubbard squash in 4-inch squares; acorn squash is served half to a person. Sprinkle the squash with the seasonings, sugar, and bits of butter. Bake at 325°. If the Hubbard is thick it will take almost an hour; the acorn squash will take 30 to 45 minutes. Small acorn squashes are very good baked whole; they may be tested for tenderness with a cake straw and will take about an hour in a slow oven. Pass spices, honey, and butter and let each person prepare his own. Cantaloupe and honeyballs cut in half, dribbled with honey, a piece of butter, and a dash of nutmeg are delicious baked—those not sweet enough to eat fresh.

STUFFED ACORN SQUASH

3 or 4 acorn squashes   *STUFFING*
butter   corned-beef hash or chopped ham,
salt and pepper   chicken, or sautéed sausage meat
     diced sautéed onion (optional)
     buttered crumbs or cooked rice
     cream sauce

Stuffed squash may be served as the main dish for luncheon or supper. The squash is easier to fill if you cut it in half, remove fibers and seeds, season, and dot with butter before it is baked. Bake about 30 minutes or until just tender. Make a stuffing of two-thirds meat to one-third cooked rice or crumbs moistened with a little cream sauce. Diced sautéed onion may be added. Lightly add the stuffing to the baked squash and bake 8 or 10 more minutes until the stuffing is well heated and browned a little.

MASHED HUBBARD SQUASH WITH ORANGE

4 cups peeled, cubed Hubbard
squash
1 tablespoon grated orange rind
⅓ cup orange juice
2 tablespoons butter

3 tablespoons cream
1 or 2 tablespoons honey or brown
sugar
salt and pepper
dash of nutmeg, mace, or ginger

The squash may be baked (see page 306) or it may be steamed over boiling water about 15 minutes or until tender. Mash the squash. Mix all the other ingredients together and bring to a boil. Mix with the squash. Some squashes contain more water than others, so these quantities may have to be increased or decreased to make a mixture like fluffy mashed potatoes. Cold mashed squash may be made into small cakes and fried in butter. Serves 4 to 6.

HUBBARD SQUASH SOUFFLÉ

recipe for Mashed Hubbard Squash
with Orange
1 tablespoon cornstarch

3 egg yolks, beaten
3 egg whites, beaten until stiff

Add the cornstarch and egg yolks to the mashed squash; then fold in the stiffly beaten whites. Empty into a greased baking dish and bake 25 minutes at 350°, or until the soufflé is set. If desired, the orange may be omitted and more spices and cream added with a little rum or sherry. This is a fine dish to serve with roast turkey. Serves 5 or 6.

SQUASH CORN BREAD

1 teaspoon soda
¾ cup mashed Hubbard squash
1 cup buttermilk
1 cup sour cream
2 tablespoons brown sugar

1 tablespoon butter
2 cups corn meal
1½ teaspoons salt
2 egg yolks
2 egg whites, beaten until stiff

Mix the soda with 1 tablespoon cold water. Mix all the ingredients, folding in the stiffly beaten egg whites last. Bake in a greased pan 30 minutes at 350°. Serve hot with butter.

Note: One-half cup of mashed squash may be added to the yeast and flour mixture for hot rolls.

SQUASH PUDDING

2½ tablespoons cornstarch
1⅔ cups milk
2½ cups mashed Hubbard squash
⅓ cup light molasses or honey
salt and pepper

¼ teaspoon powdered cloves
¼ teaspoon cinnamon
3 eggs, beaten
TOP
browned chopped almonds

Mix the cornstarch with the milk and cook until it thickens. Mix all the ingredients together, put in a greased baking dish, sprinkle the top with almonds, and bake 50 minutes at 300°. Serve as a vegetable. Serves 4 to 6.

HUBBARD SQUASH PUDDING OR FILLING FOR PIE

1⅓ cups strained mashed squash
4 egg yolks, beaten
¾ cup cream
3 tablespoons Jamaica rum
¾ cup brown sugar
1 teaspoon lemon juice
¼ teaspoon ginger

½ teaspoon ground cloves
1 teaspoon cinnamon
½ teaspoon nutmeg
few grains salt
4 egg whites, beaten until stiff
halved brown pecans

Mix all the ingredients (except the pecans); fold in the stiffly beaten egg whites last. Put the mixture into a greased pudding dish and bake at 350° 40 or 45 minutes until set. The pudding should be moist inside. The pecans may be put over the top when it is done. This is suitable for pie filling for 1 unbaked pie shell. It will fill 2 small shells and will take less time to bake as it will be in a shallower dish.

Note: Pumpkin may be substituted for squash in this recipe and in the recipes for pudding and soufflé.

SQUASH MERINGUE

3 or 4 cups mashed Hubbard
  squash
butter
cream
nutmeg or ground cloves

honey or brown sugar
3 egg yolks, beaten
2 or 3 egg whites
3 or 4 tablespoons light brown
  sugar

Season the squash with butter, cream, spices, and honey to taste.
Add the egg yolks. The mixture must be quite thick and not watery.
Beat the egg whites with the sugar until stiff. Put the squash in a
shallow baking dish and cover with the egg whites. Bake in a 350°
oven 10 or 12 minutes, until the meringue is puffy and light brown.
Serve immediately. Serves 5 or 6.

GLAZED SQUASH WITH ORANGE OR GRAPEFRUIT SAUCE

summer, crookneck, Hubbard, or
  butternut squash
2 or 3 tablespoons corn syrup
2 or 3 tablespoons butter
salt and pepper

mace or nutmeg
1 teaspoon cornstarch
⅓ cup orange or grapefruit juice
GARNISH
minced green onions

Peel and seed the squash if necessary, and cut it into 1-inch cubes.
One and one-half to 2 cups of cubed squash will serve 2 persons.
Prepare the required quantity and increase the ingredients propor-
tionately. Those specified are for 2 cups. Put the corn syrup and
butter in a heavy pot, add the squash and glaze it over a brisk fire,
and add the seasoning. Put in 2 tablespoons water, cover tight, and
cook for 10 minutes slowly, or until the squash is tender. Blend 1
teaspoon cornstarch with ⅓ cup juice, add it to the vegetable, and
cook a moment until it thickens. Empty into a serving dish and cover
with a little minced green onion.

FRIED SQUASH WITH CARAMEL SAUCE

2 butternut or crookneck squashes
3 tablespoons light corn syrup
bacon fat and butter
salt and pepper

⅓ to ½ cup cream
GARNISH
grated cheese

This is a delicious sauce for squash of summer varieties that may be sliced. If the skin seems a little coarse, scrape off a thin layer with a sharp knife, leaving the green inner skin. Young squash need not be peeled or seeded. Slice the squash ¾ inch thick and glaze it a deep brown on both sides, almost burning it, in the syrup and fat and butter. Use more syrup if necessary. Corn syrup makes a good glaze and is not sweet. Salt and pepper the slices and cook uncovered until they are just tender; the whole cooking will take about 8 minutes. Empty the squash into a serving dish and add the cream to the pan. Let it come to a boil and dissolve all the dark crumbs in the pan. The cream will instantly turn a rich light brown. Empty the sauce over the squash and top with the cheese. If the squash is slightly bitter, this only gives an added interest to the dish. One-inch cubes of peeled Hubbard squash are very good cooked this way. Serves 4 to 6.

CASSEROLE OF SUMMER SQUASH

4 tablespoons butter
2½ lbs. squash—bush scallop,
    crookneck, or butternut
1 cup minced green onions
salt and pepper
3 teaspoons cornstarch

1 teaspoon curry powder
1 tablespoon brown sugar
1 tablespoon lemon juice
1 cup light cream
GARNISH
½ cup grated cheese

Grease a baking dish, leaving bits of butter on the bottom of the dish. If very young squash is used, it generally need not be peeled or seeded. Cut it in ½-inch slices and alternate layers of squash and green onions in the dish. Add bits of butter to the top. Cover and bake (or cook in a heavy pot on top of the stove) until it is tender. Mix all the other ingredients with the cream. When the squash is done, if there is a quantity of moisture, add another teaspoon of cornstarch to the cream. Let the cream thicken a little over low heat; then pour it over the squash and cook until it thickens more. Season the sauce well with salt, as the squash is not salted before it bakes because it sweats too much. Sprinkle the top with the cheese. This squash is very good combined in casserole dishes with other vegetables such as eggplant, tomatoes, corn, okra, peas, and lima beans. Serves 4 or 5.

SUMMER SQUASH WITH DILL OR CHEESE SAUCE

2 or 3 summer squashes
¼ cup diced onions
⅓ cup diced green pepper
olive oil or butter
salt and pepper
½ teaspoon nutmeg

DILL SAUCE
1 handful of fresh dill, stemmed

½ cup light cream
2 teaspoons cornstarch
salt and pepper

CHEESE SAUCE
⅔ cup light cream
1 teaspoon cornstarch
½ cup grated Cheddar cheese
salt and pepper

If the skin on young squash seems too tough to cook, scrape a little layer off with a sharp knife, leaving the green inner skin. Slice the squash in ¾-inch lengths. Sauté the onion and green pepper in the oil or butter until it is half tender. Then add the squash and seasonings, cover, and cook until the squash is tender. This will take 10 or 12 minutes for young squash. Squeeze the stemmed dill and cut it fine into the cream. Let it marinate 1 hour, if possible, before using. Blend with the cornstarch, season, and cook until the sauce thickens; then mix with the cooked squash. Empty into a serving dish and add chopped parsley or chopped green onions to the top. If the cheese sauce is to be used blend the cornstarch with the cream, add the cheese and seasonings, and cook until it thickens. Proceed as with dill sauce. Serves 2 to 4.

SQUASH AND SOUR CREAM

1 cup sour cream
handful of fresh dill, stemmed and
  minced
salt and pepper

recipe for Summer Squash with Dill
  Sauce
1 teaspoon cornstarch

Season the sour cream with dill, salt, and pepper, and let stand 1 hour. When the squash has been cooked according to directions, blend 1 teaspoon cornstarch with the sauce on the squash and, when it has thickened, add the sour cream. Heat and serve.

BRAISED PORK SHOULDER OR LAMB WITH
SUMMER SQUASH

1½ lbs. meat
2 tablespoons brown sugar or
   honey
fat or oil
salt and pepper
2 teaspoons orégano
2 teaspoons flour

½ cup diced onions
⅔ cup tomato purée
2 8-inch summer squashes
syrup and butter
salt and pepper
          GARNISH
chopped parsley or mint

Cut the meat in 1½-inch cubes. Heat the sweetening with good bacon fat or oil. Mix the seasonings and flour and toss the meat in them, then brown it on all sides in the melted fat until well glazed. Add the onions and fry a little; then add the tomato purée, cover, and braise until the meat is tender. Before the meat is quite done, cut the young unpeeled squash in 1-inch-thick slices and glaze in a little corn syrup and butter or bacon fat; add salt and pepper and a fresh sprinkle of orégano if you like. Lay the pieces of squash on top of the meat and cook until it is tender, about 10 minutes. Garnish the top with a good quantity of chopped fresh parsley or mint. Mint goes particularly well if you are cooking lamb. This stew may be cooked in the pressure cooker. The meat will take 12 minutes. Then open the cooker and lay the squash on top and cook 5 minutes. It is very good served with cooked brown rice. Serves 4.

SUMMER SQUASH BAKED WITH PINEAPPLE

8-inch summer squashes
fresh pineapple, finely sliced
salt and pepper
green onions, minced

oil

          SAUCE
½ cup cream
1 cup grated Cheddar cheese

Boil the whole squashes in a big kettle of water for 10 minutes. Remove them and cut them in half lengthwise; then scoop out the seeds and discard them. Fill the cavities with fresh pineapple and sprinkle with salt, pepper, and minced green onions. Place the squashes in the bottom of a heavy pot, or, if quite a number are being cooked, put them in a baking pan with a little oil in the pan. They may be baked in the oven for 20 minutes, or covered and cooked on top of the stove. When they are tender, put them on a platter or on individual serving plates and add the cheese sauce to the top. For the sauce, heat the cream with the cheese. When grating Cheddar cheese, pack it solid to measure it. If the sauce is made ahead of time it will become solid and may be thinned with the oil the squash cooked in. This amount of sauce will cover 6 to 8 squash halves. One half should be served to each person.

ZUCCHINI ITALIAN STYLE

⅓ cup olive oil
2 or 3 buds garlic, crushed
small zucchini, sliced thin

salt and pepper
GARNISH
grated Parmesan cheese

Use the specified amount of oil for 2 pounds of zucchini. Put the oil and garlic in a heavy skillet and heat. Add the unpeeled, very thinly sliced zucchini. Let it cook gently for 4 or 5 minutes, uncovered, turning often so it is well covered with the oil. Salt and pepper it, and when it is tender empty it into a serving dish and sprinkle liberally with grated Parmesan cheese. This squash is tender before it is cooked, so it does not have to be cooked long. Use plenty of oil and garlic. Serves 4 or 5.

STUFFED ZUCCHINI

1 to 1½ lbs. zucchini
STUFFING
1 cup ground ham or cooked
  sausage meat
½ cup soft breadcrumbs
½ cup grated Parmesan cheese
2 tablespoons grated onion

SAUCE
5 tablespoons olive oil
1 bud garlic, crushed
1 teaspoon cornstarch
⅓ cup tomato sauce or purée

Cut unpeeled zucchini in 2½-inch lengths. Scoop out the centers with an apple corer, making space enough to hold a good quantity of stuffing. The zucchini must be thick enough to make good-sized tubes. Mix the stuffing and fill the zucchini. Lay them on the bottom of a baking dish with the olive oil mixed with the crushed garlic. Use 2 buds if you like it. Cover and bake 20 to 25 minutes at 350°, turning the squash once. Lift the zucchini out of the dish. Mix the tomato sauce with the cornstarch and add to the oil and garlic in the baking dish. When the sauce thickens, pour it over the squash. Young summer squash and cucumbers may be stuffed this way. The cucumbers may need peeling.

ZUCCHINI STUFFED WITH LITTLE SAUSAGES

5-inch-long zucchini
small pork sausages, sautéed

light cheese cream sauce or tomato
sauce

The zucchini must be fat enough in shape so that, when they are cut in half and scooped out, a small fried sausage will fit in each half. It may be steadied with a toothpick put through the sausage and the squash. First boil the zucchini whole for 10 minutes, remove from the water, and cut them in half. Scoop out the centers the size of the sausage, then fill and put them close together in a well-oiled baking dish. Bake them 10 minutes and cover with sauce.

ZUCCHINI SALAD

small zucchini
2 buds garlic, crushed
¼ cup olive oil
tossed green salad

French dressing
GARNISH
minced green onions
¼ cup grated Parmesan cheese

Cut the ends from washed zucchini and cut it in 1-inch lengths. Steam 2 or 3 minutes over boiling water. Lay the pieces on a platter, do not pile them. Separated, they do not become limp when chilled. When they are cool put them in the refrigerator. Mix the oil and garlic, and 15 minutes before mixing the salad marinate the zucchini in the garlicked oil. Toss the zucchini with green salad mixed with not very much French dressing. When it is well mixed, sprinkle with cheese and green onions over the top.

SWEET POTATOES

Sweet potatoes are the garden's gift to feast days, and on any day they are a welcome addition to game, roast goose, duck, chicken, and pork of all kinds, both fresh and smoked. They are rarely served with beef, and never—at least in the North—with fish.

We think of sweet potatoes as a great culinary contribution of the South because they have long been used there and because they grow best in warm climates. The sweet potato is truly a versatile vegetable and can be used in dishes from soup to dessert. It is one of the all-round richest vegetables and has been known to sustain people who lacked any other food for long periods of time—and it kept them healthy and strong too. Sweet potatoes should be served frequently to growing children and to the undernourished. There are dozens of delicious ways of cooking them: baked, boiled, roasted with meats, fried, mashed, candied, combined with various fruits in casseroles, in rolls, pies, puddings, soufflés, and Creole pones.

BOILED AND BAKED SWEET POTATOES

When preparing sweet potatoes for any use it is much easier to boil them first and then skin them. Otherwise they are difficult to peel, some of the potato is wasted, and they turn black. If they are to be served plain, cover them with cold water and cook 20 minutes, or until they are just tender and not falling apart. Skin them and reheat, if necessary, in melted butter, and serve them with salt and freshly ground pepper. One of the best ways of serving sweet potatoes or the orange-colored, moist-fleshed yam is to bake them. Scrub them, let them come to a boil, and drain. Put them in a hot oven, and they will continue cooking quickly. Bake 40 to 60 minutes. When they are tender, wrap them 2 or 3 minutes in a tea towel to steam and loosen the skin, which can then be easily removed. Serve with meat gravy or butter.

BAKED SWEET POTATOES WITH ROAST MEATS

Boil the potatoes 10 or 12 minutes, long enough so they may be skinned but not until they become tender. Skin them and put them with the meat ½ hour before the roast is done. Turn them several times in the drippings. They will become syrupy and brown.

SWEET-POTATO BISQUE

1 lb. sweet potatoes   salt
3 cups chicken broth
¼ cup honey   *GARNISH*
dash of nutmeg   sherry or light rum
½ cup heavy cream   sliced roasted chestnuts or browned
                                       almonds or pecans

Boil, skin, and mash the potatoes. Mix to a creamlike consistency with the broth and honey. Add the nutmeg and cream. Add salt if the broth is not seasoned sufficiently. Put a tablespoon of sherry or rum in each soup plate, add the hot soup, and top with 3 slices of roasted chestnuts or a few slivered almonds or pecans. This makes 6 cups of soup.

MASHED SWEET POTATOES

½ cup light cream   1 tablespoon grated lemon rind
¼ to ⅓ cup butter   (optional)
salt and freshly ground pepper   juice of ½ lemon (optional)
4 or 5 boiled and skinned sweet
   potatoes

Plain mashed sweet potatoes without sweetening may be as much of a treat as anything else infrequently served. Heat the cream with butter, salt, and pepper. Mash the potatoes with the mixture until creamy and light, adding more hot cream if necessary. For a variation, add the lemon rind and juice. Pile into a hot serving dish and serve immediately. Many people prefer mashing potatoes by hand to using the electric mixer because the potatoes become cold in the mixer and must be reheated in the oven. Unless carefully done, they dry out too much in the oven and lose their creamy texture. Allow one good-sized sweet potato per person.

MASHED SWEET POTATOES WITH CREAM, SHERRY, AND HONEY

5 or 6 sweet potatoes	salt and pepper
⅓ cup butter	½ teaspoon nutmeg or mace
½ to ⅔ cup cream	¼ to ⅓ cup sherry
⅓ cup brown sugar or honey	juice and rind of 1 orange (optional)

Boil, skin, and mash the potatoes. The amounts of cream and butter depend on the size of the potatoes, but enough is required to make the potatoes light and creamy. Heat the sweetening, cream, and butter before adding to keep the potatoes hot. Season and add the sherry to taste. If desired, 2 or 3 tablespoons rum may be used. Part of the liquid may be orange juice and grated rind. The following recipes suggest further additions to this dish. Serves 6 to 8.

SWEET-POTATO CAKES

recipe for Mashed Sweet Potatoes with Cream, Sherry, and Honey	¼ cup brown sugar
1 egg, beaten	½ cup fine crumbs
BREADING	butter
½ teaspoon allspice	

The mashed potatoes should not be too soft; allow for the beaten egg and mix it with them. Let the mixture cool, and form into cakes. Cover with the mixed breading and fry a golden brown in butter. Leftover mashed potatoes may be used.

SWEET POTATOES AND RED PIMENTOS

whole red canned pimentos	sprigs of parsley
recipe for Mashed Sweet Potatoes with Cream, Sherry, and Honey	

Grease individual fluted tin molds and line them with drained pimentos. Carefully fill the pimentos with the well-seasoned mashed sweet potatoes; these may be prepared ahead of time. Put each cup in a muffin tin to steady it. Fifteen minutes before serving, heat in a moderate oven. Turn the molds out and stick a sprig of parsley in the top of each. These are bright red and handsome to serve as a garnish around a platter of other vegetables or a roast.

SWEET-POTATO SOUFFLÉ

recipe for Mashed Sweet Potatoes
  with Cream, Sherry, and Honey
3 egg yolks, beaten
3 egg whites, beaten until stiff

TOP

⅓ cup mixed ground nuts, sugar,
  and cinnamon

Mix the potatoes with the egg yolks, and fold in the stiffly beaten whites. Pour into a greased baking dish, sprinkle with mixed nuts, sugar, and cinnamon and bake 25 minutes at 350°, or until set. It should be moist inside. Serve immediately. If 12 persons are to be served use 6 potatoes, more seasonings, and 5 or 6 eggs. This is a fine dish for a holiday dinner with goose or turkey. It should bake in a large baking dish for 45 minutes.

SWEET-POTATO AND BANANA SOUFFLÉ

recipe for Mashed Sweet Potatoes
  with Cream, Sherry, and Honey
3 bananas, sieved

3 egg yolks, beaten
2 egg whites
¼ cup brown sugar

Make the seasoned mashed potatoes with 4 or 5 potatoes and sieve the bananas into the hot potato so they will not darken. Add the egg yolks. Beat the whites stiff and add the brown sugar and beat to a meringue. Combine the two mixtures and bake in a greased casserole 25 minutes at 350°.

SWEET POTATOES AND CHESTNUTS

recipe for Mashed Sweet Potatoes
  with Cream, Sherry, and Honey

1 small jar chestnuts in syrup
3 tablespoons Jamaica rum

When mashing the potatoes omit the sugar or honey and sweeten them with the syrup drained from the chestnuts. Pile the mashed potatoes in a greased baking dish and cover the top with the chestnuts. Put in the oven until they are hot, bring to the table, pour over the rum, and blaze. Honey and dark rum seem to have an affinity for tropical or Southern dishes, especially when combined with fruits.

SWEET POTATOES AND APRICOTS

recipe for Mashed Sweet Potatoes   1 to 1½ cups stewed dried
   with Cream, Sherry, and Honey   apricots, mashed
1 tablespoon grated orange rind   *TOP*
juice of 1 Sunkist orange   12 apricots, brown sugar, and rum

Add the rind, juice, and mashed apricots to the potato mixture and empty into a greased baking dish. Arrange halved stewed apricots over the top, smooth side up, and sprinkle with brown sugar. Heat in the oven until glazed on the top, bring to the table, add 2 or 3 tablespoons dark rum, and blaze.

SWEET POTATOES AND APPLES

recipe for Mashed Sweet Potatoes   cinnamon and brown sugar
   with Cream, Sherry, and Honcy   butter
4 tart apples, peeled and sliced   corn syrup

Mash the sweet potatoes and season according to directions. Sprinkle the apples with sugar and cinnamon and brown them in the butter. Dribble a little syrup over them, cover, and steam until almost tender. Lightly mix or put in alternate layers with the sweet-potato mixture in a greased baking dish and heat in the oven. A little brown sugar may be sprinkled over the top before heating.

SWEET-POTATO AND CRANBERRY PUDDING

recipe for Mashed Sweet Potatoes   ½ cup orange juice
   with Cream, Sherry, and Honey   ½ cup light brown sugar or ⅓ cup
2 cups cranberries   honey

Mash and season the potatoes according to directions. Wash the cranberries, stew them 10 minutes or until very soft in the juice and sweetening, and purée through a sieve. Combine the thick purée with the potatoes, empty into a greased baking dish, and put in the oven for 7 or 8 minutes until very hot. Serve with poultry or pork.

SWEET POTATOES AND COCONUT

recipe for Mashed Sweet Potatoes   1¼ cups grated dry or 1½ cups
with Cream, Sherry, and Honey   grated fresh coconut

When mashing the potatoes use honey and rum. Put half of them
in a greased baking dish, spread with half the coconut, then cover
with the rest of the potatoes and sprinkle the rest of the coconut over
the top. Brown a little in a hot oven. The potato mixture must be
moist, fluffy, and smooth.

SWEET-POTATO ALMOND CROQUETTES

2½ cups mashed sweet potatoes   nutmeg
sherry   ½ cup chopped almonds
honey or brown sugar   half-beaten egg white
salt and pepper   fine crumbs and sugar
butter   oil for frying
cream

Mix the first eight ingredients. The mixture should be stiff enough
to form into little cakes, balls, or rolls. Chill them and when ready to
fry roll them first in the egg white and then in crumbs mixed with
sugar. Fry at 365° in deep fat until a golden brown. Drain on brown
paper. Serves 6.

SWEET-POTATO AND PEACH CASSEROLE

5 or 6 sweet potatoes   1 tablespoon grated orange rind
¼ cup honey   juice of 1 Sunkist orange
½ cup cream   1½ cups sliced peaches
½ teaspoon nutmeg   *BLAZE*
2 tablespoons Jamaica rum   3 tablespoons Jamaica rum
salt and pepper   brown sugar
¼ cup butter

Boil, skin, and mash the potatoes and add the other ingredients,
lightly mixing in the peaches. The peaches may first be marinated in
a few drops of rum and honey if desired. Put the mixture in a greased
baking dish, sprinkle with brown sugar, and heat in the oven. Bring to
the table, pour over the rum, and blaze. Serves 7 or 8.

FRIED SWEET POTATOES

sweet potatoes
corn meal
light brown sugar

salt
butter or oil

Allow 1 potato for each serving. Choose long narrow potatoes of uniform size. Boil them about three-fourths done, skin them, and slice them in ⅜-inch disks. Mix a breading of half corn meal and half brown sugar and salt it a little. Completely cover the potato slices in this mixture and fry until tender and a golden brown in the butter. They may also be deep-fried in oil for 30 seconds at 365°. These are delicious with any poultry or pork.

CARAMEL SWEET POTATOES

4 sweet potatoes
½ cup white sugar

⅓ cup boiling water
⅓ cup heavy cream

Boil the potatoes until tender, skin, and cut them in half lengthwise. Put the sugar in a heavy iron skillet and brown it until it is very dark. Turn off the heat and add the boiling water. Stir over a low flame until the sugar is melted and becomes a thick syrup. More water may be added if the sugar doesn't melt. When the syrup is thick, glaze the potatoes in it, a few at a time. When they are thickly glazed remove them to a serving dish. Add the cream to the pan, boil it up, and empty over the potatoes. When perfectly done, this is a superb dish. Serves 4.

CANDIED SWEET POTATOES

4 or 5 sweet potatoes
bits of butter
grated orange rind

1 cup light corn syrup
1 cup Sunkist orange juice
⅓ cup light brown sugar

Boil the potatoes until tender, skin, and cut in 3 slices the long way. Lay them in a well-greased-shallow baking dish or pan, put bits of butter over each slice, and sprinkle with grated orange rind. Pour the syrup and juice over the potatoes, sprinkle with the brown sugar, and bake 1 to 1½ hours very slowly, uncovered. Add more corn syrup if desired. They should be syrupy and rather translucent. Serves 4 or 5.

MAPLE CANDIED SWEET POTATOES

5 or 6 sweet potatoes
¼ cup butter
½ cup orange juice

¾ cup maple syrup
corn syrup
maple sugar (optional)

Boil the potatoes until tender, then skin them. Cut them in 3 slices lengthwise and lay them on the bottom of a greased baking pan or dish, adding bits of butter to the top. Pour the juice and the maple syrup over them. Add enough light corn syrup to cover, and bake them very slowly for 1 to 1½ hours, uncovered. Fifteen minutes before they are done sprinkle the top with crumbled maple sugar if you have it.

SWEET-POTATO AND HAM OR SAUSAGE CASSEROLE

4 sweet potatoes or yams
sugar
hot cream
butter

salt and pepper
mace or nutmeg
8 slices Canadian bacon, thin ham, or pork sausages

Boil and skin the potatoes. They may be sliced, or mashed with a dash of sugar, hot cream, butter, salt, pepper, and a little mace or nutmeg. Sauté the ham or Canadian bacon or pork sausages until brown. Alternate layers of sliced or mashed potatoes with the pork, ending with a layer of meat on top. Put in the oven just long enough to heat. This is a lunch or supper dish and may be served with a green salad or cabbage slaw. Serves 4.

SWEET-POTATO ROLLS

2 cups mashed cooked sweet potatoes (1 lb.)
3 tablespoons light brown sugar
¼ cup butter
1 yeast cake, or 1 envelope granular yeast
¼ cup lukewarm water

2 tablespoons sugar
¾ cup milk
1 teaspoon salt
1 egg, beaten
2 cups flour or 1¾ cups whole-wheat flour
½ teaspoon nutmeg

While the potatoes are still hot mix them with the brown sugar and butter. Let cool to lukewarm. Mix the yeast with the lukewarm water and 2 tablespoons sugar until it is foamy. Scald the milk with the salt and when it is lukewarm mix it with the yeast, beaten egg, and the potatoes. Add the flour and nutmeg and beat until very smooth. Set the bowl in a dishpan of water somewhat warmer than tepid. Cover with a tea towel and let rise until very light—1¼ to 1½ hours. Beat down for about 3 minutes, then roll the dough on a floured board and cut into any desired shapes. Dough may be rolled a little less than ½ inch thick and cut in small rounds; half of them may be brushed with butter, the other rounds may be placed on top. Put in greased pans and let rise until light, about 30 to 45 minutes. They must be put to rise in a warm place, covered with a tea towel. All light rolls must be baked as soon as they have risen, or they will spread. They may also be baked in muffin tins. Bake 18 to 20 minutes at 375°. Serve hot. Makes 2 dozen rolls. These are very delicate and moist.

CREOLE SWEET-POTATO PONE

½ cup butter
⅓ cup brown sugar
2 eggs, beaten
⅓ cup molasses
⅓ cup light corn syrup
¾ cup milk

juice of 1 Sunkist orange
1 teaspoon grated orange rind
1 teaspoon cinnamon
½ teaspoon clove
1 teaspoon ginger
3 cups grated raw sweet potatoes

Cream the butter and sugar, add the beaten eggs and all the other ingredients, and mix well with the grated potatoes. Pour into a greased pan and bake slowly 1 hour. Serve hot or cold, for dessert.

SWEET-POTATO PIECRUST
(For Meat Pies)

1 cup flour
¼ teaspoon nutmeg or mace
1 teaspoon baking powder
½ teaspoon salt

1 cup cold mashed sweet potatoes
⅓ cup butter, melted
1 egg, beaten

Sift all the dry ingredients together and work in the sweet potatoes, then add the melted butter and beaten egg. Roll the dough out like biscuit dough, handling as little as possible. Fit over top of a baking dish filled for meat or chicken pie.

Note: Pumpkin may be substituted for sweet potatoes in the recipes for bisque, pie, pudding, and soufflé.

SWEET-POTATO PIE

1 lb. (2 medium-sized) sweet potatoes
½ cup butter
⅔ cup brown sugar
2 teaspoons cinnamon
1 teaspoon nutmeg
4 egg yolks, beaten

juice and rind of 1 lemon
1 cup light cream
1 jigger brandy
4 egg whites
⅓ cup brown sugar
1 unbaked single piecrust

Boil, peel, and mash the potatoes, cream the butter and sugar, and add. Then add the spices, egg yolk, juice, rind, cream, and brandy. Beat the whites stiff, add the sugar, beat to a meringue, and fold in last. Make a rich piecrust, add the filling, and bake 10 minutes at 400°; then turn the heat to 325° and bake about 30 minutes or until the filling is set but soft. If desired, the filling may be poured into a greased baking dish and baked and served as a pudding with heavy cream. For holiday serving, pour 2 tablespoons dark rum over the top and blaze.

TOMATOES

The tomato may be technically a fruit, but for purposes of cookery it is used as a vegetable. It is perhaps as widely used as the onion, for it flavors and seasons nearly every kind of food and is the principal ingredient of innumerable dishes. Tomatoes are used in canapés and sandwiches; with meats, fish, eggs, cheese, rice, vegetables; in sauces, salads, and soups. In canning they make fine relishes, pickles, preserves, sauces, soups, and juice. Because tomatoes are likely to dominate the flavor of other foods, when they are required only to season it is best to skin and seed them. Unless otherwise directed, it is always better to skin them. Two simple ways are: hold them over a fire with a fork until the skin blackens and cracks; or scald them a minute in boiling water, then put them in cold water, and the skin can be easily removed. All Latin countries use tomatoes in great quantities. In Italy they are not served overripe, but when they are firm and tinged with a little green. Very ripe tomatoes become more acid and are used in sauces and soups. Green tomatoes are excellent fried or grilled. They must be mature, however, and not underdeveloped. Every well-stocked garden has its rows of tomato vines.

When thickly sliced tomatoes are specified in a recipe, it is well just to cut the tomatoes in half. In recipes calling for tomato purée, this may be made by sieving skinned tomatoes, or putting them through the blender and sieving out the seeds.

TOMATO FRAPPÉ

3 cups tomato juice or fresh tomatoes
1 tablespoon fresh onion juice
1 teaspoon salt
1 teaspoon Worcestershire Sauce
1 teaspoon basil
1 teaspoon sugar
1 cup cream (optional)

If fresh tomatoes are used, skin, purée, and strain out the seeds. It is well to have every ingredient chilled first so ice will not have to be added. Blend all the ingredients in the electric blender. This is a most delicious drink to serve at the beginning of a meal. It may be made without cream. It may be shaken in a cocktail shaker with a little ice.

TOMATO SHERBET

3 cups tomato juice or puréed,   salt and pepper
  seeded tomatoes   ½ teaspoon fenne^l
2 tablespoons honey or syrup   *GARNISH*
1 tablespoon fresh onion juice   avocado halves
¼ cup white wine or 3 tablespoons   mint, basil, or tarragon
  lemon juice

Mix all the ingredients, pour into a freezing tray, and freeze until quite firm. This may be served in parfait glasses, topped with a sprig of mint, or as filling for small avocado halves, and is a good accompaniment for cold fish or meat. Any fresh minced herb such as basil or tarragon leaves may garnish the top. Serves 4 to 6.

TOMATOES WITH AVOCADO DRESSING

large tomatoes, halved and skinned   ½ cup oil mayonnaise
watercress   3 drops Worcestershire sauce
          DRESSING   2 tablespoons fresh onion juice
1 avocado, sieved

Put 1 thick tomato half on each plate on a bed of watercress, mix avocado dressing, and garnish with it. This may be a first course or a salad.

TOMATOES WITH SEAFOOD DRESSINGS

tomatoes, skinned and halved   ½ cup oil mayonnaise
watercress or lettuce   1 teaspoon curry powder
          DRESSING   1 tablespoon fresh onion juice
1 cup diced fresh shrimp or flaked
  lobster or fresh crabmeat

Put the tomatoes, 1 to a person, on a bed of greens and add a thick layer of the lightly mixed seafood dressing. Another excellent dressing is made with a can of mashed sardines mixed with mayonnaise and onion juice. Always use unsweetened mayonnaise with fish.

TOMATOES WITH EGG DRESSING

tomatoes, skinned and halved
lettuce or watercress
DRESSING
2 hard-boiled eggs, mashed

⅓ cup oil mayonnaise
2 tablespoons anchovy paste

Put 1 skinned tomato half on each plate, on a bed of greens. Dress with a thick layer of the lightly mixed dressing.

BAKED TOMATO SANDWICH

buttered rye or whole-wheat bread
sliced Cheddar cheese

sliced thin ham
sliced tomatoes

Put a layer each of cheese, ham, and tomato between 2 slices of buttered bread and put the sandwiches in a hot oven for 10 minutes or until the cheese melts. These are excellent for a quick snack with beer.

SMALL TOMATO SANDWICHES

rounds of buttered rye or whole-
wheat bread
soft cheese
crisp bacon, minced

skinned, thinly sliced tomatoes
GARNISH
sieved hard-boiled egg

When making sandwiches that include tomatoes, always have all the ingredients ready and put them together just before serving. The tomatoes will moisten the bread too much if they stand any length of time. Spread the buttered bread with soft cheese and minced bacon. Top with a skinned, thinly sliced tomato the same size as the bread, and garnish the top with sieved egg. This is an open sandwich. Tomatoes may be added to egg, chicken, turkey, or ham sandwiches.

GRILLED TOMATO SANDWICH

buttered rye or whole-wheat bread
sliced skinned tomatoes

salt and pepper
Cheddar cheese, sliced or grated

Cover the bread or toast with a thick slice of tomato, season, top with cheese, and put under the broiler until the cheese browns and bubbles.

TOMATO SANDWICH WITH ROQUEFORT CHEESE OR CAVIAR

buttered rounds of rye or whole-
   wheat bread
sliced skinned tomatoes
3 oz. Roquefort or blue cheese, or
   caviar

⅓ cup sour cream
1 tablespoon fresh onion juice
       GARNISH
chopped parsley

Cover each round of bread with a slice of tomato. Mash the cheese with the sour cream to make a light fluffy dressing and add the onion juice. If caviar is used instead of cheese, be careful not to mash the caviar, but mix very lightly. Spread the dressing on the tomato and sprinkle the top with finely chopped parsley.

CLEAR TOMATO BOUILLON

2 qts. veal or chicken stock
2 beef bones
1½ lbs. cubed beef
1 qt. tomato purée
1 cup diced carrots
1 stalk celery, sliced
salt and pepper

1 cup diced onions
2 bay leaves
1 teaspoon thyme and basil
2 tablespoons lemon juice
     TO CLARIFY
2 half-beaten egg whites

Put all the ingredients together (except the egg whites) and bring to a very slow simmer, covered. Skim and continue cooking at the lowest bubble for 2½ hours. Strain without mashing any of the vegetables through. Add the egg white and boil for 1 minute. Wet a clean cloth, line a sieve, and pour the soup through. This will make it clear. Cool and keep in Mason jars in the refrigerator until used.

TOMATO AND ORANGE CONSOMMÉ

tomato purée or juice
orange juice

     GARNISH
chopped mint or green onions

Use half tomato and half orange juice, mix, and serve either hot or cold. This combination is very refreshing. Sprinkle a little garnish over the top of each cup of soup.

TOMATO AND BEET SOUP

1 qt. fresh tomatoes
2 bunches beets (8 beets)
salt and pepper
¼ teaspoon powdered cloves
juice of 1 lemon

3 tablespoons brown sugar
3 tablespoons fresh onion juice
GARNISH
chopped green onions and sour
cream

Skin the tomatoes and mash them through a sieve or purée them in the electric blender, then sieve the seeds out. Scrub the beets and cut the stems to within 1 inch of the beets. Add 2 cups water, cover, and cook them until they are tender. Skin them, then sieve with the water they cooked in or purée them in the blender. Mix with the tomato purée and the other ingredients to taste. This may be served hot or cold and garnished with the green onions and a blob of sour cream. If the soup is too thick it may be thinned with more tomato juice. Makes almost 2 quarts.

TOMATO AND SEAFOOD SOUP

2 pts. mussels or clams or 1 lb. shrimp
  or 2 cans clams in broth
2 cups diced onions
2 buds garlic, crushed
4 large tomatoes, skinned and sliced

⅔ cup olive oil
1 bay leaf
1 teaspoon thyme
chopped parsley
salt and pepper

If fresh seafood is used, wash it well. To cook mussels or clams, scrub them and let them steam until they open over 2 cups boiling water. Let the juice drip into the water as you remove the fish from the shells. This liquid must be strained through a cloth to remove the grit, and used in the soup. Shrimp should be left unpeeled and cooked in water for 5 minutes and let cool in the broth. Peel the shrimp and use the strained broth in the soup. A mixture of shell fish may be used. After it is cooked set it aside. Cook the onions, garlic, and tomatoes in the olive oil until they become somewhat tender; then add the fish liquid plus enough water to make 6 cups. Add the bay leaf and thyme and let simmer ¼ hour, strain through a coarse sieve, then add the reserved fish and 2 or 3 tablespoonfuls chopped parsley. Taste before adding salt and pepper.

ITALIAN VEGETABLE SOUP

4 large tomatoes, skinned and
  chopped
1 green pepper, diced
1 cup diced onions
2 potatoes, finely diced
1 carrot, diced
salt and pepper

2 buds garlic, crushed
½ cup olive oil
2 teaspoons basil
1 bay leaf
1 cup little egg-noodle shells
       GARNISH
grated Gruyère cheese

Put all the vegetables, seasoning, garlic, and olive oil in a heavy pot and cook for 10 minutes, stirring a few times. Add the herbs and 6 cups water and simmer gently for 25 minutes. Ten minutes before the soup is done add the tiny noodles. Serve the soup and pass a bowl of cheese to sprinkle over the top. A cup of green beans, cut in ½-inch lengths, may be added with the other vegetables. Makes about 2 quarts.

TOMATO SOUP WITH DILL

¾ cup diced onions
½ cup diced carrots
¼ cup butter
5 cups skinned, chopped tomatoes,
  puréed
salt and pepper

1 tablespoon brown sugar or honey
3 tablespoons lemon juice
large handful chopped dill
       GARNISH
chopped parsley and sour cream

Sauté the onions and carrots in the butter for 3 minutes over a gentle fire, then add the tomatoes, salt, and pepper. Simmer gently for 15 minutes, then mash through a sieve or purée in the blender. Add the sweetening, lemon juice, and the fresh dill which you have stemmed and minced. Let the soup simmer 5 minutes. Garnish each soup plate with a little chopped parsley and a spoonful of sour cream. This is good hot or cold. Makes about 6 cups.

CREAM OF TOMATO SOUP

recipe for Tomato Soup with Dill
1 cup cream

2 tablespoons cornstarch

Prepare the soup and when it is done blend the cream with the cornstarch, bring to a boil, and add. The dill is excellent with the cream and may be boiled up with the cream and let stand before the tomato part of the soup is done. The dill may be omitted and 4 whole cloves cooked with the tomato soup.

TOMATO SOUP WITH ORANGE JUICE

recipe for Tomato Soup with Dill
  (omitting the dill)
1½ to 2 cups strained orange juice

GARNISH
sliced avocado or cucumbers

Make the tomato soup as directed but omit the dill. When it is done, add the orange juice and garnish each plate with a few slices of avocado or cucumber. This is excellent hot or cold.

Note: Good tomato soup may be made with 2 cups beef or chicken stock added. A regular beef, bones, and vegetable soup is vastly improved if 1 quart tomato purée is added to a large kettle of soup.

SHRIMP CREOLE

1½ lbs. fresh shrimp
1 bay leaf
1 small onion, diced
salt and pepper
2 tablespoons butter
⅔ cup diced onion
1 green pepper, diced
4 stalks tender celery, diced
1 tablespoon flour
2 cups skinned, chopped tomatoes

2 cups peas
8 stuffed green olives, sliced
2 tablespoons chili powder
1 tablespoon vinegar
1 teaspoon brown sugar
½ teaspoon thyme
    GARNISH
1½ cups brown rice
3 cups chicken broth
chopped parsley or green onions

Wash the shrimp and cook them 5 minutes with the bay leaf, 1 diced onion, salt, pepper, and 1 cup water. Let them cool in the broth, then peel them. This broth is used in the sauce. Sauté in the butter the ⅔ cup diced onion and the green pepper and celery until tender. Then blend the flour with the shrimp broth until smooth, and mix all the ingredients except the shrimp and the garnish. Simmer this sauce for 15 minutes. Wash the rice and cook it in the chicken broth, covered, for 45 minutes at the lowest possible heat, without lifting the lid. Empty the rice into a greased mold or ring and then onto a hot platter or chop plate. Add the shrimp to the sauce and see that it is seasoned well. Surround the rice with the sauce. The rice looks attractive if it is sprinkled with chopped parsley or green onions. Serves 6.

LOBSTER WITH TOMATO CREAM

SAUCE

¾ cup heavy cream
1½ tablespoons cornstarch
salt and pepper
½ teaspoon curry powder

⅔ cup tomato sauce

3 tablespoons butter
1 lb. cooked fresh lobster, flaked
1 jigger brandy

To make the sauce blend the cornstarch with the cream, season-ings, and tomato sauce and cook it until it is a little thickened. Melt the butter in a pan, add the flaked lobster, and stir it until it is covered with the butter. Add the brandy and blaze. Extinguish the blaze be-fore it is all burned out. Put the lobster in the hot sauce and serve. This may be made in a chafing dish if desired. This will serve 4, but the recipe may easily be increased to serve 6 or 8. A green-pea or spinach soufflé is a good accompaniment.

FISH BAKED WITH CHILI SAUCE AND SOUR CREAM

1 slice salmon, or boned, skinned fillets
⅓ cup Chili Sauce (page 347) or tomato sauce (page 334)

½ cup heavy sour cream
grated Parmesan cheese

Fish cooked in this sauce should be boned and skinned. Whitefish or sole cooked this way is very good. If preparing salmon, boil it first, 8 or 10 minutes, skin and bone it carefully so it remains whole. Cover with the mixed tomato or chili sauce and sour cream and bake slowly until the fish is done. Sprinkle with Parmesan cheese.

POT ROAST WITH TOMATOES AND RED WINE

5-lb. round of beef
8 or 10 fat pork strips for larding
2 buds garlic, sliced
2 tablespoons brown sugar
2 tablespoons flour
diced pork fat

1 cup diced onions
½ cup diced carrots
2 cups skinned, diced tomatoes
salt and pepper
2 cups red wine

Make incisions in the beef and press in slivers of garlic and pork lardings. Rub in the sugar and the flour on both sides, and brown all over in a little diced pork fat. Make a bed of half the vegetables in a heavy pot, seasoning them and the meat. Put the beef on the vegetables, and cover with the rest of them. Add the wine and braise as slowly as possible for 3 hours or until the meat is tender. Remove the meat and keep it hot. Purée or press through a sieve all the sauce. This makes the gravy smooth and rich. If it is too thin, blend 1 or 2 tablespoons cornstarch in 3 or 4 tablespoons cold water and thicken the sauce gradually. It should be like heavy cream. Put the meat on a hot platter, cover with a little of the sauce, serve the rest in a gravy boat. Chopped parsley sprinkled over the top improves the appearance and flavor.

SWISS STEAK WITH TOMATOES

4 lbs. top round of beef, 3 inches thick
4 tablespoons brown sugar
½ cup flour
oil or butter
2½ cups diced onions
salt and pepper
2 teaspoons thyme or savory
⅓ cup red wine

⅓ cup water
1 teaspoon Worcestershire sauce
3 or 4 large tomatoes, skinned
1 cup mushrooms, sautéed
  (optional)

SAUCE

puréed liquid and 2 tablespoons
  cornstarch

With a meat hammer pound half the sugar and flour into each side of the meat and brown it on both sides in a little oil or butter. Make a bed of half the onions in the roaster, lay the meat on them, add thyme, salt, and pepper, and cover with the rest of the onions. Add the wine, ⅓ cup water, and Worcestershire sauce. Cover tight and roast at 300° for 1½ hours. Turn the meat. Cut the tomatoes in half and lay them over the meat after you turn it over. Cover and roast another hour or until the meat is tender. It may be turned down a little so that it cooks very slowly. The slower it cooks, the less it shrinks. When it is done lift it from the pan, keep it warm, and strain the sauce, which may be puréed in the electric blender with the cornstarch. Heat it until thick in a saucepan, add some to the top of the meat, and cover with mushrooms or chopped parsley. Serve the rest of the sauce in a gravy boat. Baked new potatoes go well with this. More herbs may be added to the top of the tomatoes when they are put on the steak. A smaller piece of meat will take less time to cook. This meat will serve 8, but if left over is excellent cold or warmed in the gravy.

DILL DUMPLINGS WITH TOMATO SAUCE

TOMATO SAUCE
2 tablespoons butter
⅓ cup diced onion
2 cups tomato juice
salt and pepper

DUMPLINGS
1 cup flour
¾ teaspoon salt

2 teaspoons baking powder
1 teaspoon butter
1 teaspoon lard
¼ cup minced fresh dill
½ cup milk or more

GARNISH
chopped parsley

Sauté the onion in the butter until it is a little tender, add the juice, salt, and pepper, and bring to a boil. For the dumplings, sift the dry ingredients and cut in the butter and lard with a pastry-cutter, add the dill, and lightly mix. Add just enough milk so the dough may be nipped off and rolled into balls. This makes 9 dumplings. Roll them in flour and chill them 15 minutes in the refrigerator. Bring the sauce to a boil, drop in the dumplings, cover tight, and cook for 12 minutes at a gentle boil. The sauce and dumplings may surround a piece of boiled salmon, or they may be served in side dishes with any meat or poultry. Sprinkle the dumplings with a little chopped parsley.

SPANISH OMELET

SAUCE
⅓ cup diced onions
1 small green pepper, diced
3 mushrooms, sliced
3 tablespoons olive oil
3 black olives, sliced
1 tablespoon lemon juice
salt and pepper

1 large tomato, skinned, seeded, and chopped

4 to 6 eggs
salt and pepper
3 tablespoons butter

GARNISH
chopped parsley

Sauté the onion, green pepper, and mushrooms in the oil until they are tender. Stir in the rest of the sauce ingredients and cook gently for 5 minutes. To make the omelet, beat the eggs with 2 or 3 tablespoons water, salt, and pepper. Melt the butter in an omelet pan and cook the eggs so they have a delicate skin on the outside and are almost set but creamy in the inside. Fold and slip onto a hot platter, cover with chopped parsley, and surround it with the sauce. Serves 2 or 3.

SCRAMBLED EGGS AND TOMATOES

2 tablespoons grated onion
3 tablespoons butter
2 tomatoes, skinned, seeded, and
chopped

salt and pepper
4 or 5 eggs, half beaten
GARNISH
chopped chives

Sauté the onion 1 minute in the butter, then add the tomatoes and salt and pepper. Stir in the eggs and when they are set but still moist empty onto plates or on a hot platter and sprinkle with chives. Allow 2 eggs per person or 3 large eggs for every 2 persons.

HERBED TOMATOES WITH POACHED EGGS

basil, thyme, or rosemary
salt and pepper
flour
skinned tomatoes, sliced thick

oil or butter
poached eggs
hot toast (optional)
grated cheese

Mix an herb with salt, pepper and a little flour. Dip both sides of the tomatoes in the mixture and fry a crusty brown in the oil or butter over a brisk fire. Top each tomato slice with a poached egg and sprinkle with cheese and put under the broiler a minute. Cheese cream sauce may be used. The tomatoes may be put on crisp toast or cooked and served on fireproof plates.

TOMATOES FILLED WITH EGGS

whole tomatoes, skinned
buttered crumbs
1 egg per tomato
cream

salt and pepper
grated cheese
toast

Cut good-sized holes in the tops of the tomatoes and carefully scoop out the inside flesh. Put 2 tablespoons crumbs in each tomato, then drop in a raw egg and 1 tablespoon cream. Add salt and pepper to the outside and fill with grated cheese. Put the tomatoes in a buttered dish, close together, and bake in a 350° oven for 15 minutes. If the tomatoes are very ripe, do not skin them or they may crack and open.

EGGS BAKED IN TOMATO SOUP

eggs
butter
crumbs
hot tomato soup

GARNISH

grated cheese
chopped chives or parsley

The eggs may be baked in ramekins or in a shallow baking dish. Grease the dish, sprinkle with buttered crumbs, and break the required number of eggs over the crumbs. Add enough hot soup almost to cover and bake in the oven until the eggs are set, or about 10 or 12 minutes. Two minutes before they are done, sprinkle with cheese, or after they come from the oven sprinkle with either of the other garnishes.

TOMATO-ORANGE SOUFFLÉ

¼ cup finely diced onion
2 tablespoons butter
1¼ cups tomato purée
salt and pepper
grated rind of 1 orange

1 cup orange juice
⅓ cup flour
4 egg yolks, beaten
4 egg whites, beaten until stiff

Sauté the onion in the butter until it is tender. Add the purée, salt, pepper, and orange rind. Simmer gently 5 minutes. Blend the orange juice smoothly with the flour and the beaten egg yolks, and add. Fold in the stiffly beaten whites last, pour the mixture into a greased baking dish, and bake 25 minutes at 350°. This may be served instead of a vegetable or with a light cheese cream sauce for a main luncheon dish. Serves 4 to 6.

BAKED TOMATOES WITH MUSHROOM CAPS

large tomatoes, skinned and thickly sliced
salt and pepper
fine crumbs
grated Parmesan cheese

large mushroom caps
olive oil

GARNISH

chopped parsley

Liberally grease a baking pan, lay the required number of thickly sliced tomatoes on it, salt and pepper them, and sprinkle with a mixture of crumbs and cheese. Dip big mushroom caps in salted olive oil and lay one on each slice of tomato. An improvement—if liked—is a crushed bud of garlic first added to the olive oil. Bake the tomatoes 10 minutes at 375°. Lift onto a serving platter and garnish the tops of the mushrooms with chopped parsley. Serve with grilled meats.

For plain grilled tomatoes, dip the thick slices in salted garlic olive oil and put them under the broiler flame until they cook a little. Sprinkle with Parmesan cheese and let them lightly brown. This will take 5 minutes, 5 inches from the flame.

TOMATO AND OKRA PILAU

1 cup brown rice	1 large green pepper, diced
2 cups water or broth	salt and pepper
4 strips bacon	1 teaspoon chili powder
½ lb. okra	1 tablespoon brown sugar
4 large tomatoes, skinned and sliced	TOP
2 large onions, diced	½ cup grated cheese

Wash the rice and cook it 45 minutes in the water—or, better, broth—covered, at the lowest possible heat. Cut the bacon in 1-inch lengths, fry it in a large heavy skillet, scoop out the pieces, and reserve. Cut off the tips and stem ends of the okra and blanch in boiling water for 1 minute. Drain, rinse, and cut it in small rounds. Fry all the vegetables in the bacon grease with seasonings, chili powder, and sugar. They should cook slowly about 20 minutes. When the rice is done, lightly toss it with the vegetables so it is well mixed. Put the bacon pieces on top and sprinkle with the cheese and put it in a hot oven until the cheese melts. Serves 6.

TOMATOES, RICE, AND SAUSAGE

ingredients for Tomato and Okra Pilau (omit the bacon and substitute ½ lb. pork sausages)	1 cup grated cheese

Fry the sausages until they are brown and remove from the grease. The use of okra is optional; blanch it and cut it up. Fry the onions and green peppers and okra in the sausage drippings until they are tender. Add the tomatoes and cook for 5 minutes. When the rice is cooked mix it with the vegetables and sausages, pile it in a greased baking dish, and cover with the cheese. Bake in a hot oven until the cheese melts.

TOMATOES WITH CHEESE FONDUE

FONDUE

2 tablespoons butter
2 tablespoons flour
1½ cups rich milk
¼ teaspoon nutmeg
⅛ teaspoon salt

3 drops Worcestershire sauce
½ lb. Swiss or Gruyère cheese, cubed

tomatoes, skinned and thickly sliced
toast

Melt the butter in the top of the double boiler and stir in the flour. When it is smooth add the milk and cook until it thickens, then add the seasonings, Worcestershire sauce, and the cheese. Stir until the cheese is melted. The tomatoes are not to be cooked but well heated in the oven. Put each slice on a piece of crisp buttered toast and add the fondue to the top of the tomatoes. Serve with a green salad for lunch or supper. Serves 5 or 6—one slice or ½ tomato per person.

TOMATO AND LENTIL PURÉE

1½ cups dried lentils
1 cup broth
1 small carrot, finely diced
1 onion, finely diced
salt and pepper
1 teaspoon thyme
2 strips bacon

½ cup diced onion
1 small green pepper, diced
2 tomatoes, skinned and chopped
2 tablespoons lemon juice
salt and pepper

GARNISH

crumbs and cheese

Wash the lentils and soak them in 2 cups water for 5 or 6 hours, then add the broth, carrot, 1 diced onion, salt, pepper, thyme. Cover and simmer 35 to 45 minutes to a thick mush and press through a sieve or purée in a blender. Cut the bacon in 1-inch lengths and fry it crisp, then scoop out the pieces and mix them with the lentil purée. Fry the ½ cup diced onion and green pepper in the bacon grease until tender, add the tomatoes, lemon juice, and seasonings. Mix with the lentil purée and put it into a greased baking dish. Sprinkle the top with crumbs and cheese and bake in a hot oven until it browns a little on top. Serves 6.

TOMATOES CREOLE

6 large tomatoes, skinned and
   sliced
salt and pepper
flour

3 tablespoons butter
1 large green pepper, minced
1 cup minced green onions
½ cup light molasses

Put in layers in a casserole the sliced tomatoes, seasonings, a light sifting of flour, bits of butter, very finely minced green pepper and onion. Pour the molasses over the top and bake 50 minutes in a 300° oven. Serves 6.

TOMATO, EGGPLANT, AND ZUCCHINI CASSEROLE

1½ lbs. tomatoes, skinned
2 teaspoons basil
2 teaspoons tarragon
2 tablespoons brown sugar
salt and pepper
⅓ cup olive oil

2 buds garlic, crushed
1 small eggplant, quartered and
   thinly sliced
½ lb. unpeeled zucchini, sliced
2 big onions, sliced
1 green pepper, sliced

Slice the skinned tomatoes, and press against a coarse sieve to extract a little of the juice, then cut them in pieces. Put half the tomatoes in the bottom of a greased casserole and sprinkle with half the herbs, sugar, salt, and pepper. Put the olive oil in a big pan with the garlic and quickly sauté the eggplant, zucchini, onions, and pepper one at a time, and put them over the tomatoes. Season the vegetables as you sauté them. Add the rest of the tomatoes, herbs, and sugar. Bake 30 to 35 minutes, half the time at 375° and half at 350°. Serves 6.

TOMATO AND CORN-MEAL CASSEROLE

3½ cups skinned, sliced tomatoes
½ cup minced green onions
2 eggs
½ cup corn meal

salt and pepper
½ cup sour cream
½ cup grated cheese

Put the tomatoes and onions in layers in a greased baking dish. Beat the eggs, add the corn meal, salt, pepper, and sour cream. Pour this over the vegetables and sprinkle the top with cheese. Bake 15 minutes at 375° and 15 minutes at 350°. Serves 6 or 8.

CURRIED OR CREAMED TOMATOES

tomatoes, skinned and sliced thick
salt and pepper
powdered fennel, basil, tarragon, rosemary, summer savory, or thyme
butter

CURRY SAUCE
2 tablespoons butter
1 tablespoon curry powder
2 tablespoons grated onion
1¼ cups orange juice
3 teaspoons cornstarch
salt and pepper
1 teaspoon grated orange rind
1 teaspoon brown sugar or honey

CREAM SAUCE
2 tablespoons butter
2 tablespoons flour
salt and pepper
¼ teaspoon nutmeg
½ cup light cream
⅔ cup milk
⅓ cup grated Cheddar or Swiss cheese

GARNISH
minced green onions or chopped parsley or chives

Place the slices or halves, 1 to a person, in a well-buttered baking pan, sprinkle with salt, pepper, and one of your favorite herbs. (Minced fresh herbs are always preferable, but they are not always available; dried ones will do.) Powdered fennel, a favorite of Italians, is one of the most fragrant herbs to use with tomatoes, whether baked or stewed.

For the cream sauce, melt the butter, stir in the flour until it is smooth, then add the seasonings and the liquids slowly and cook until it thickens. Add the cheese and let it melt. For the curry sauce, put the butter and curry powder in the top of the double boiler and let it cook over boiling water. After 8 minutes add the onion and let it cook 2 minutes. Blend the cornstarch with the cold orange juice and add with all the other ingredients. Cook until it thickens. If a creamy sauce is desired, add 2 tablespoons sour cream to the sauce.

Heat the tomatoes 5 minutes in a very hot oven after the sauce is ready. Spoon either sauce over them and serve, either on plates or on a platter. Cover with one of the garnishes.

STEWED TOMATOES AND SOUR CREAM

4 cups skinned and coarsely
chopped tomatoes
2 tablespoons grated onion

salt and pepper
2 tablespoons flour
1 cup thick sour cream

Stew the tomatoes 15 or 18 minutes with the onion, salt, and pepper. Blend the flour with the sour cream so that it is smooth, add it to the tomatoes, and simmer for 3 minutes. Serve in side dishes. Serves 4 or 5.

STEWED (OR BAKED) TOMATOES

½ cup finely diced onion
½ cup finely diced green pepper
3 tablespoons butter
salt and pepper
4 cups skinned and thickly sliced
tomatoes

1 tablespoon brown sugar
1 teaspoon thyme or powdered
fennel
2 tablespoons fine bread or cracker
crumbs

Whether stewed tomatoes are canned or fresh, they must be cooked at least 20 minutes to remove the raw taste. Sauté the onion and pepper in the butter gently 3 or 4 minutes, then add all the other ingredients and cook very gently, almost covered, for 20 or 25 minutes. This excellent way of cooking tomatoes may become a casserole dish if you double the quantities and bake for 2 hours at a very low heat until thick. Serves 4.

STEWED GREEN TOMATOES

6 large green tomatoes
3 tablespoons brown sugar
salt and pepper

½ cup tomato sauce
½ to 1 cup thick sour cream

Choose green tomatoes that have only the faintest blush on them; small, hard green tomatoes won't do for cooking. Remove a small slice from each end and cut them in half. Put them in a pot with ¼ cup water, sprinkle them with the sugar, and add all the ingredients except the cream. A smooth tomato sauce comes in small cans. Cover and cook gently for 40 minutes. When done stir in the sour cream and just heat through. Serve in side dishes. Serves 5 or 6.

FRIED GREEN TOMATOES

big green tomatoes, unskinned   salt and pepper
grated Parmesan cheese   hot oil
corn meal

Cut the tomatoes in ¾-inch slices. Mix grated Parmesan cheese
and cornmeal, half and half, add salt and pepper, and dip both sides
of the tomato slices in the mixture. Have a quantity of oil quite hot in
an iron skillet and brown tomatoes on both sides over a brisk fire.
Then place them on a baking sheet and bake them 10 minutes or
until tender in a 350° to 375° oven. Do not bake too long, for they
must be just tender. Serve immediately.

TOMATO AND PEACH CASSEROLE

4 or 5 big tomatoes, skinned   3½ tablespoons flour
4 or 5 large peaches, skinned   ¼ cup tomato sauce or catsup
salt and pepper   ¼ cup orange juice

Slice a tomato in the bottom of a greased casserole, sprinkle with
salt, pepper, and flour. Slice a peach on top of it and sprinkle with the
same. Repeat until all are added in layers. Mix the tomato sauce or
catsup with the orange juice and pour it over the top. Bake 30 to 35
minutes in a 350° oven. This may be served with curried chicken.
Serves 5 or 6.

TOMATOES STUFFED WITH BANANAS

good-sized tomatoes, skinned   4 to 6 tablespoons butter
1 small banana for each tomato   sour cream
nutmeg   mayonnaise (for serving cold)
honey

With a sharp knife cut off a thin slice from the top of the tomato,
loosen the pulp, scoop out with a spoon, and discard. Mash the bananas on a plate with a fork, dribble over them a little honey and a
dash of nutmeg, then fill the tomatoes to overflowing with the bananas. Melt the butter in the bottom of a heavy pot and put the tomatoes on the butter, close together. Cover tight and cook 8 minutes
or until the bananas are puffy. With 2 big spoons lift the tomatoes
onto serving plates and put a blob of sour cream with a dash of nut-

meg on top. If they are baked in the oven in a pan allow no more than 2 minutes' longer cooking, otherwise the tomatoes may crack. These may be served cold with mayonnaise on a bed of watercress for a tomato-fruit salad.

STUFFED TOMATOES

large tomatoes, skinned and pulp removed, or quartered to the base
mayonnaise (if served cold)
chopped parsley or mushroom caps (if served hot)

STUFFING NO. 1
cooked brown rice
flaked tuna fish in oil
capers
minced green onions

STUFFING NO. 2
cooked brown rice
ground ham or chicken
crushed garlic in olive oil
dried currants
orégano

STUFFING NO. 3
cooked crabmeat, lobster, or sliced shrimp
diced celery hearts
cooked fresh peas
curry powder
oil mayonnaise
capers

STUFFING NO. 4
cubed Gruyère cheese
tiny cubes toast
garlic crushed in olive oil
Bahamian mustard
sliced black olives

None of the stuffings needs baking except No. 4, and that is on account of the cheese, which must be cubed very small. Bake it 10 or 12 minutes and serve hot or cold. To be good the rice must never overbalance the fish or meat used but must be half or less of the filling. Fillings must be moist. The best brown rice may be cooked in double its amount in chicken or light meat consommé 45 minutes, covered, over the lowest possible flame. Turn off the fire, leave on the lid, and let it stand an additional 10 minutes. Every grain will be separate. If tomatoes are baked they must be left whole but if they are to be served cold they may be quartered down to the base, spread open a little, and the filling added. Cold stuffed tomatoes are usually served with a fine unsweetened olive-oil mayonnaise. The baked ones may have a light cheese cream sauce, a mushroom cap, or chopped parsley as a garnish. In Stuffing No. 1 anchovy fillets may replace tuna fish.

TOMATO MEAT SAUCE
(For Pastas)

6 cups skinned, chopped tomatoes
1 bay leaf
2 buds garlic, crushed
¼ cup olive oil
1 lb. chopped beef
1 teaspoon each fennel, basil, and
   orégano
½ cup sweet Italian vermouth
salt and pepper

6 mushrooms, sliced and sautéed
3 dried mushrooms, soaked 1 hour
1 can tomato paste
2 cups finely diced onions
⅓ cup butter

GARNISH
chopped parsley
grated Parmesan cheese

Put the tomatoes in a heavy pot with the bay leaf. In a skillet warm the garlic in the olive oil, add the beef, and let it brown quickly; then add it to the tomatoes with the herbs, wine, salt, pepper, and sautéed mushrooms. Drain and rinse the dried mushrooms and add them with the tomato paste. Sauté the onions in the skillet in the butter until they are tender and add them. Cover and simmer over the lowest flame for 2 hours. If the sauce becomes too thick add some more crushed tomatoes or tomato juice. This is better if made a day before using. When the sauce is done, if it seems watery instead of thick (there is a difference in the quantity of juice that tomatoes contain), add 2 tablespoons of flour blended smooth with a little of the juice. Cook it 10 minutes after adding the flour. Serves 8.

MUSSEL OR CLAM TOMATO SAUCE

recipe for Tomato Meat Sauce
   (omit the meat)

2 pts. fresh mussels or clams or 2
   cans mussels or clams

Make the sauce exactly the same way, except that the fresh mussels or clams should be steamed over 1 cup hot water until they open. Strain the liquor through cloth, add it to the sauce when it begins to cook. Reserve the mussels or clams to add after the sauce is done and ready to serve; they should not be cooked any more. Do the same with drained canned seafood. The sauce may be added to hot pasta and the seafood piled on top. This makes a most inviting dish. Pass Parmesan cheese in a bowl. Crabmeat or lobster may be heated in butter and used instead of the other seafood. Garnish the fish with chopped parsley.

TOMATO ASPIC

2¼ cups tomato purée or tomato juice
2 tablespoons grated onion
salt and pepper
1 teaspoon powdered fennel or basil

2 tablespoons gelatin
juice of ½ lemon
1 tablespoon sugar or honey
2 cups chicken consommé

Simmer the tomato purée or juice with the onion, salt, pepper, and herb for 5 minutes; then strain through a fine sieve. During this time soak the gelatin in the lemon juice, then add it to the strained hot juice so it will melt, and add the sugar or honey. Combine with the consommé, cool, and chill. This may be poured into small greased molds for garnishing or salad, or into a greased ring so that the center of the aspic can hold fruit salad, vegetable salad, or Waldorf salad. Tomato aspic may be made without consommé, using 4¼ cups tomato purée or juice.

TOMATOES WITH VEGETABLES, VINAIGRETTE

skinned tomatoes

VINAIGRETTE SAUCE
French dressing
sieved hard-boiled egg
capers
mustard

garlic

cooked and chilled green beans, cauliflower, peas, asparagus, celeriac sticks

Either remove the pulp from the whole tomatoes or quarter them to the base. Mix the sauce and marinate any one or two of the vegetables in it. Fill the tomatoes. The tops may be garnished with chopped parsley or mayonnaise. Set them on a bed of watercress or any other crisp green.

TOMATO AND ANCHOVY SALAD

quartered skinned tomatoes
anchovy fillets
sliced olives
French dressing
crisp lettuce

ADDITIONS

sliced cucumbers
sliced radishes
minced green onions

Tomatoes go well with any combination of salad vegetables in tossed green salads. Anchovy fillets, cut in half, make any green salad interesting. Quartered hard-boiled eggs are a very pleasant addition. Always add tomatoes just before serving so they will not moisten the greens too much.

TOMATO JUICE

18 or 20 lbs. ripe tomatoes
3 or 4 green peppers
4 large onions, sliced

1 bunch Pascal celery, sliced
2 tablespoons light brown sugar
1½ tablespoons salt

Skin and chop the tomatoes, cook them until they are tender, then strain. Seed the peppers and put them, the sliced onions, and sliced celery and leaves through the food mill or meat grinder. Put them in 3 cups water and boil until soft and tender, then mash through a sieve. Add the sieved mixture to the tomato juice with the sugar and salt and boil 5 minutes. Bottle hot. This delicious juice is a fine thing to have on hand for serving cold or making into soups.

TOMATO SOUP FOR CANNING

7 qts. tomatoes
4 large onions
1 big bunch Pascal celery
1 big green pepper, seeded
10 whole cloves
5 bay leaves

2½ tablespoons salt
2½ tablespoons light brown sugar
1 teaspoon pepper
¾ cup butter
½ cup flour

Chop all the vegetables, add 2 cups water and all the ingredients except the butter and flour and boil for 30 minutes. Put through a strainer. Melt the butter and blend in the flour until smooth, then mix with some of the strained tomato, and then combine all of it and simmer for 3 minutes. Seal hot in sterilized Mason jars.

CHILI SAUCE

12 large tomatoes
4 large sweet red peppers, seeded
4 large white onions
1½ cups vinegar
1 cup light brown sugar

1½ teaspoons cinnamon
¼ teaspoon powdered cloves
2 teaspoons salt
dash of red pepper

Grind the vegetables and drain off all the liquor or the sauce will be too thin. Combine with the rest of the ingredients, boil 15 minutes, and can.

LITTLE YELLOW TOMATO PRESERVES

8 lbs. little yellow tomatoes
3 lemons
8 lbs. sugar

ginger root the size of a walnut (or preserved ginger)

Wash the tomatoes, dry them, prick each one with a needle, and separate into 4 lots. Slice the lemons very thin, add them to 6 cups water, and boil 15 minutes, then add the sugar and ginger and boil to a thick syrup. Put ¼ of the tomatoes at a time in the syrup. The kettle must be large enough so they are not crowded. Cook until they may be pierced with a fine straw. Take out, drain, and put in sterilized jars. Cook each lot the same way in the syrup. When all are in jars, boil the syrup down, pour it over the tomatoes, and seal.

GREEN TOMATO PICKLE

4 qts. green tomatoes
1 pt. onions
2 green peppers
2 red peppers
½ cup salt
1 lb. brown sugar

3 cups vinegar
1 tablespoon mustard
½ teaspoon pepper
1 teaspoon mace
1 teaspoon powdered cloves
3 sticks cinnamon

Slice the tomatoes. Slice the onions and peppers very thin. Put all the vegetables in a large bowl in alternate layers, sprinkling each layer with salt. Let this stand overnight. Drain well in the morning; unless well drained it will be too thin. Add all the ingredients and boil 1 hour. Bottle when cold.

ORANGE AND TOMATO MARMALADE

4 Sunkist oranges
4 lbs. tomatoes, skinned and sliced

juice of 1 lemon
sugar

Cut the oranges as thin as possible, discard seeds, and mix with the tomatoes and lemon juice. Let stand 24 hours, mash a little, and simmer 2 hours. Let stand another 24 hours, then measure the number of cups. Boil the mixture 1 hour, add an equal number of cups of sugar, and boil until it reaches marmalade consistency. Boiling down before adding the sugar keeps the marmalade light. Don't boil marmalades until they are heavy and thick; they thicken as they cool. Seal hot.

TOMATO CATSUP

12 or 14 lbs. tomatoes, skinned and
  sliced
3 large onions, ground
2 tablespoons pepper
10 whole allspice
2 teaspoons powdered cloves
1 teaspoon cinnamon
1 teaspoon curry powder

1 teaspoon fennel
1 cup light brown sugar
2 cups vinegar
1 teaspoon ginger
3 dashes Tabasco sauce
3 teaspoons mustard
1 tablespoon paprika
2 tablespoons salt

Cook the tomatoes, mashing them some, until they are tender. Mash them through a sieve. Add all the rest of the ingredients, simmer 3 hours, strain, and bottle.

TURNIPS

The large cabbage family of loose-leaf varieties and the tight-leaf kinds that form heads also includes some root vegetables: the white and yellow turnip, the rutabaga, and the radish (see page 294). The light green kohlrabi also belongs to this group; it is a globe with little tubes running up the sides and ending in leaves. It is more delicate in flesh and flavor than the white turnip, and its leaves may be cooked as greens. Peeled kohlrabi cut in julienne sticks may be served marinated in French dressing or tossed raw in green salads. Young sweet white turnips may be served the same way. Either of these may be roasted with duck—the popular French dish *Canard aux Navets*—or with rack of lamb. The astringent quality of the turnip combines well with the richness of duck and lamb.

The rutabaga is a large darker-skinned vegetable with deep yellow flesh and a much stronger flavor than the white turnip. It is good mashed and seasoned with salt, pepper, butter, and cream. Some prefer to moderate its flavor by mashing it with equal amounts of white potato.

Turnips are a valuable food, but nearly all the vitamin A seems to go into the greens, which contain from 36,000 to 46,000 units per pound. The greens, like kale, spinach, and beet greens, are good steamed and dressed with hickory-smoked bacon and a dash of lemon juice or mild vinegar. Many vegetable soups and stews are improved by the addition of turnips.

TURNIP AND POTATO SOUP

1 lb. white turnips	salt and pepper
2 good-sized potatoes	dash of nutmeg
2 strips bacon	*GARNISH*
½ cup onion, diced	bacon pieces and green onions, or
milk	grated Parmesan cheese
light cream	

Peel and dice the turnips and potatoes. Cut the bacon in 1-inch lengths and fry it crisp; then scoop out the bits of bacon and reserve. Sauté the onion in the grease until it begins to color, and add the turnips and potatoes. Stir them around and cook gently 3 minutes, then add 2 or 3 tablespoons water, cover tight, and cook gently until the vegetables are soft enough to mash through a sieve or purée in the electric blender with milk. Thin with milk and cream until the right consistency to serve. Season well and garnish each soup plate with the pieces of bacon and minced green onions or grated Parmesan cheese. Serves 4.

TURNIP GREENS FOR SOUP OR VEGETABLE

1 lb. turnip greens
¼ cup minced green pepper
⅓ cup diced onion
salt pork or bacon, diced and fried
   until crisp
salt and pepper

dash of lemon juice
    FOR SOUP
broth or milk
    FOR VEGETABLE
sliced hard-boiled eggs

Wash the greens in two or three waters until they are free from grit. Trim any coarse stems. Sauté the green pepper with the onion in the grease from the fried pork fat or bacon. Reserve the pieces of pork or bacon to garnish either soup or vegetable. Cut the greens in 2-inch lengths, mix them with the vegetables, cover tight, and steam 8 to 12 minutes until tender. Season with salt, pepper, and a dash of lemon juice. For soup, purée the greens in the electric blender, thinning with milk or chicken broth; or simply add milk and cream or broth to the cooked greens. If the greens are not puréed they should be cut very fine before they are cooked—in ¼-inch ribbons. To serve as a vegetable, remove to a hot serving dish and garnish the top with slices of hard-boiled eggs. Serves 4.

RACK OF LAMB WITH TURNIPS

8-chop rack of lamb
summer savory
1 tablespoon Kitchen Bouquet
2 tablespoons honey
8 little white turnips or kohlrabi,
   peeled
8 little white onions, peeled
butter

salt and pepper
2 tablespoons lemon juice
1 teaspoon meat extract
¼ cup hot water
    SAUCE
broth or milk
cornstarch
crushed lemon balm

There is a layer of fat on the lamb, and some of this must be browned off or the dish will be too greasy. Rock it back and forth, pressing with a fork, over a very hot fire in an iron skillet until it is well burned. Pour off all this fat. Sprinkle with the herb, mix the Kitchen Bouquet and honey, and paint the rack all over Glaze the peeled vegetables in butter and some of this honey mixture. Put the lamb, fat side up, in a baking pan and surround with the vegetables and sprinkle with a little salt and pepper and the lemon juice. Dissolve the meat extract in the hot water and pour it over the lamb.

Bake 45 minutes, or until the vegetables are done, in a 325° oven. Lift meat and vegetables onto a hot platter and make a sauce in the baking pan. For every cup of milk or broth, blend 1 tablespoon cornstarch in a little cold liquid. Add it, with all the milk or broth, to the pan, cook until it thickens, and serve in a sauceboat. If you have lemon balm, crush a tablespoonful over the lamb after it is on the platter. Serves 4.

ROAST DUCK WITH TURNIPS
(Canard aux Navets)

1 5½- to 6-lb. duck
fat or butter
1 tablespoon Kitchen Bouquet
2 tablespoons honey
8 or 10 little white turnips or
    kohlrabi, peeled
8 or 10 little white onions, peeled

1 teaspoon thyme
brown sugar
salt and pepper
⅓ cup good red wine
SAUCE
½ cup light cream
1 tablespoon cornstarch

Wash and dry the duck and brown it in a heavy pan over a brisk fire in a very little fat or butter, or bake it at 375° for 25 minutes. Drain off all the grease that has collected in the pan. Mix the Kitchen Bouquet and honey and paint the duck all over with them. This will make a fine glaze when the duck is done. Brown the turnips and onions in butter in a hot pan with 2 or 3 tablespoons brown sugar. Add to the duck and sprinkle all with the thyme and a little salt and pepper. Add the red wine, cover tight, and cook in the oven at 325° for 1¼ to 1½ hours or until the duck is tender. Lift the duck and vegetables to a hot platter and reduce the sauce if there is more than 1 cup. Blend the cream with the cornstarch and add. Cook until it thickens. Serve in a separate tureen. A good accompaniment is Mashed Split Peas (page 263). Serves 4 to 6.

BEEF AND KIDNEY STEW WITH TURNIPS

1 lb. top or bottom round, cubed
1 beef or veal kidney, sliced
2 tablespoons flour
salt and pepper
1 teaspoon summer savory or
    thyme
2 to 4 tablespoons butter
3 tablespoons brown sugar

2 whole cloves
½ cup red wine
½ cup hot water
1 large onion, sliced
6 or 8 small white turnips, peeled
6 or 8 mushrooms or peeled
    chestnuts (optional)

Put the beef and the kidney in a paper bag with the flour, seasonings, and herb, and shake well so that the meat is covered. Sauté the
meat until a nice brown in 2 or 3 tablespoons butter or good fat and
2 tablespoons brown sugar. This should be done in the heavy pot the
stew is to cook in. Add the cloves, wine, hot water, and onion. Cover
tight and braise slowly for 45 minutes. Glaze the turnips in a little
fat and sugar and add them to the stew and cook 40 minutes or until
tender. To make this dish a little special add the mushrooms or chestnuts, or both, 15 minutes before the turnips are done. If the sauce
needs thickening, blend a little cornstarch with 3 tablespoons cold
water and add a little at a time. Serve with mashed potatoes. Serves 4.

BUTTERED TURNIPS

1½ lbs. white turnips or kohlrabi
salt and pepper
dash of nutmeg or mace
butter

GARNISH

chopped parsley or minced green
onions

Peel the turnips or kohlrabi and cut them in half. Put them in a
heavy pot with ⅓ cup water, salt, and pepper, and cover tight. Simmer, after they begin to boil, until they are tender. Watch that they
do not burn. Add nutmeg and butter and serve in a hot dish. If there
is water to drain, reserve it for soup; never throw vegetable water
away. In the pressure cooker this will take from 5 to 8 minutes if the
turnips are small and left whole; sliced turnips will take 3 to 5 minutes. The time depends somewhat on the age of the vegetable; they
take about the same time as potatoes. If the liquid is to be used,
blend in a little cornstarch, add butter, and cook until it thickens.
A little lemon juice may be added, and the vegetables may be sprin-

kled with chopped parsley or minced green onions. Rutabaga, sliced, may be cooked the same way. Serves 4.

TURNIPS COOKED IN CHICKEN BROTH

1½ lbs. white turnips
1 cup chicken broth
1 tablespoon lemon juice
2 teaspoons cornstarch

2 tablespoons butter
GARNISH
chopped parsley

Peel the turnips, choosing small ones if possible; if not, cut them in half or in ½-inch slices. Let them simmer, covered, in the broth and lemon juice until they are tender—15 to 22 minutes, depending on their age. When they are just done, thicken the sauce with the cornstarch blended in a little cold broth or water. Add the butter, empty into a hot serving dish, and garnish with parsley. Serves 4.

GLAZED TURNIPS

recipe for Buttered Turnips or Turnips Cooked in Chicken Broth

honey or brown sugar
butter

When the turnips are tender (they must not be cooked until they get too soft), put them in a heavy pan with 2 or 3 tablespoons of their liquid, 2 or 3 tablespoons sweetening, and the same of butter, and glaze on all sides.

TOMATO-CREAMED TURNIPS

2 lbs. white turnips or kohlrabi
⅓ cup diced onions
¼ cup butter
salt and pepper
1 teaspoon thyme or basil
3 teaspoons cornstarch

⅓ cup light cream
½ cup tomato purée
⅓ cup grated Cheddar cheese
GARNISH
chopped parsley

Peel the turnips and cube or slice thick. Sauté the onions in the butter 2 minutes, then add the turnips. Add ⅓ cup water, seasonings, and herb. Cover and cook until the turnips are just tender. Blend the cornstarch with the cream, add the tomato purée and cheese. Cook until thick. When the turnips are done, mix in the sauce, empty into a serving dish, and garnish with chopped parsley. Serves 5 or 6.

CREAMED TURNIPS WITH CHEESE

1½ lbs. white turnips or kohlrabi
⅓ cup diced onions
3 tablespoons butter
salt and pepper
1 teaspoon basil

½ cup light cream
1 tablespoon cornstarch
⅓ cup grated Cheddar cheese
GARNISH
chopped parsley

Peel and cut the turnips or kohlrabi in 1-inch cubes. Sauté the onion in the butter in a heavy pot for 2 minutes. Add the turnips, ¼ cup water, salt, pepper, and basil. Cover and cook until just tender. This may be done in the pressure cooker for 2½ to 3 minutes. Blend the cream with the cornstarch, add the cheese, and let it thicken over a slow fire. This will be very thick; mix it with the turnips, and their liquid will thin it. When well mixed empty into a hot serving dish and garnish with parsley. As many small white onions, cooked separately, may be combined with the turnips, put in a baking dish, and covered with more sauce. Use 1 cup light cream, twice as much cornstarch and cheese. Sprinkle grated cheese over the top and bake until browned. This may be made ahead of time and will serve 8. It is excellent with duck, goose, or roast pork.

MASHED TURNIPS

recipe for Buttered Turnips (diced)
1½ teaspoons cornstarch

½ cup cream
buttered browned crumbs

When the turnips are done mash them. Blend the cornstarch with the cream and heat until it thickens. Stir into the turnips. The cornstarch will correct the water which is contained in some turnips. Put the turnips in a baking dish and cover with the crumbs. Let heat in the oven 2 or 3 minutes. Cheese may be used instead of crumbs if preferred. Mashed rutabagas may be prepared the same way.

MASHED TURNIPS OR RUTABAGAS AND POTATOES

Mash and mix equal amounts of cooked turnips and white potatoes. Rutabagas are especially good this way, as it makes them creamier and less strong in flavor. This dish is usually served with duck or pork.

MASHED-TURNIP CAKES

2 eggs, beaten
⅓ cup buttermilk or sweet milk
1¼ to 1½ cups leftover mashed
   turnips or rutabagas

¼ cup corn meal
salt and pepper
¾ teaspoon baking powder
butter for frying

Beat the eggs and add the buttermilk or sweet milk, then blend into the mashed turnips. Mix the dry ingredients and then combine mixtures. Fry the cakes a golden brown in butter. This makes 8 or 9 puffy cakes.

BAKED TURNIPS OR RUTABAGAS

Turnips or small rutabagas may be baked in the oven the way white potatoes are and take from 1 to 1¼ hours. Serve with small sauceboat of melted butter mixed with chopped parsley, 1 tablespoon lemon juice, salt, and pepper.

TURNIP SOUFFLE

1½ cups mashed turnips
1 cup light cream
2 tablespoons cornstarch
¼ teaspoon mace
3 egg yolks, beaten

3 egg whites
1 tablespoon brown sugar
         TOP
3 tablespoons fine buttered crumbs
3 tablespoons grated Parmesan cheese

The turnips may be plain or mixed with potatoes. They may be freshly cooked or leftover. Blend the cream with the cornstarch. Cook until it thickens, add nutmeg, and stir in the yolks. Blend the sauce with the mashed turnip. Beat the egg whites until stiff and then add the brown sugar and beat again. Fold the egg whites into the turnip mixture, empty into a baking dish, and cover with mixed crumbs and Parmesan cheese. Bake 25 minutes in a 350° oven or until nicely browned. Serves 4.

FOOD VALUES OF VEGETABLES

[On the basis of one pound, edible portion]

Composition of Following Foods in Terms of 11 Nutrients and Caloric Value	Calories	Protein (Gm.)	Fat (Gm.)	Carbohydrate (Gm.)	Calcium (Mg.)	Phosphorus (Mg.)	Iron (Mg.)	Vitamin A (I.U.)	Thiamine (Mg.)	Riboflavin (Mg.)	Niacin (Mg.)	Ascorbic Acid (Mg.)
Artichokes	135	1.4	.2	5.7								
Asparagus	95	10.0	.9	17.7	95	282	4.1	4540	.73	.86	6.4	150
Beans, lima	580	34.1	3.6	106.7	286	718	10.4	1270	.95	.50	6.4	145
Beans, snap, green	159	10.9	.9	34.9	295	200	5.0	2860	.36	.50	2.3	86
Beans, snap, wax	159	10.9	.9	34.9	295	200	5.0	681	.36	.50	2.3	86
Beets	190	7.3	.5	43.5	123	195	4.5	91	.09	.23	1.8	45
Beet Greens	123	9.1	1.4	25.4	536[1]	204	14.5	30,418	.36	.82	1.8	154
Broccoli	132	15.0	.9	25.0	590	345	5.9	15,890	.45	.95	5.0	536
Brussels Sprouts	213	20.0	2.3	40.8	154	354	5.9	1816	.36	.73	3.2	431
Cabbage	109	6.4	.9	24.0	209	141	2.3	363	.27	.23	1.4	227
Carrots	191	5.5	1.4	42.2	177	168	3.6	54,480	.27	.27	2.7	27
Cauliflower	114	10.9	.9	22.3	100	327	5.0	409	.50	.45	2.7	313
Celery	82	5.9	.9	16.8	227	182	2.3	0	.23	.18	1.8	32
Chard	82	5.5	.8	17.2	410	140	9.8	10,920	.22	.28	1.7	148
Collards	182	17.7	2.7	32.7	130	263	7.3	31,190	.50	1.23	(9.1)[2]	454
Corn	418	16.8	5.5	93.1	41	549	2.3	1771[3]	.68	.55	7.7	55
Cucumbers	55	3.2	.5	12.3	45	95	1.4[4]	0[4]	.14	.18	.9	36
Dandelion Greens	200	12.3	3.2	40.0	849	318	14.1	61,970	.85	.65	3.8	163
Eggplant	111	4.3	.8	21.7	59	146	1.6	100	.27	.22	3.2	19
Endive, Escarole	91	7.3	.9	18.2	359	254	7.7	13,620	.32	.55	1.8	50

Vegetable												
Garlic	450	4.4	.2									
Kale	182	17.7	2.7	32.7	1022	281	10.0	34,232	.45	1.18	9.1	522
Kohlrabi	73	5.1	.2	16.4	113	122	1.5	Trace	.14	.12	.6	149
Leeks	204	10.0	1.4	46.8	236	227	5.0	182	.50	.30	2.3	77
Lettuce, headed	68	5.5	.9	13.2	100	114	2.3	2452	.18	.36	.9	36
Mustard Greens	74	7.6	1.0	13.2	728	126	9.6	21,370	.30	.68	2.8	338
Okra	130	7.2	.8	29.6	328	248	2.8	2950	.31	.30	4.2	121
Onions, green	204	4.5	.9	48.1	614	109	4.1	(227)	(.14)	(.18)	(.9)	109
Onions, mature	204	6.4	.9	46.7	145	200	2.3	227	.14	.18	.9	41
Parsley	225	16.8	4.5	49.9	876	381	19.5	37,360	.49	1.25	6.5	877
Parsnips	277	5.3	1.8	64.4	202	282	2.5	3087	.27	.42	.7	63
Peas	445	30.4	1.8	80.4	100	554	8.6	2860	1.54	.73	12.3	118
Peppers, green	114	5.5	.9	25.9	50	114	1.8	91	.18	.32	1.8	545
Potatoes	376	9.1	.5	86.8	50	254	3.2	136	.50	.18	5.5	77[4]
Radishes	91	5.4	.5	19.0	168	140	4.5	1280	.14	.09	1.36	109
Rutabagas	147	4.2	.4	34.4	212	250	1.5		.29	.30	3.6	140
Spinach	91	10.4	1.4	14.5	3671[1]	68	13.6	42,767	.50	.91	2.7	268
Squash, summer	73	2.7	.5	17.7	68	127	1.8	1170	.23	.41	3.6	77
Squash, winter	173	6.8	1.4	40.0	86	222	2.7	22,473	.23	.55	2.3	36
Sweet Potatoes	558	8.2	3.2	126.5	136	222	3.2	34,958	.41	.23	2.7	100
Tomatoes	91	4.5	1.4	18.2	50	123	2.7	4994	.27	.18	2.3	104
Turnips	145	5.0	.9	32.2	182	154	12.3	Trace	.23	.32	2.3	127
Turnip Greens	136	13.2	1.8	24.5	1176	227	10.9	43,312	.41	2.09	3.6	617
Watercress	84	7.7	1.4	15.0	885	209	9.1	21,450	.37	.71	3.6	350

1 Calcium may not be available because of presence of oxalic acid.   2 Figures in parentheses indicate imputed rather than measured values.

2 Vitamin A based on yellow corn; white corn contains only a trace.

3 Based on pared cucumbers; unpared contain about 5.5 mg. iron and 1180 I.U. Vitamin A.

4 Year-round average. Recently dug potatoes contain about 109 mg. of ascorbic acid per lb. The value is only half as high after three months of storage and about one-third as high when potatoes have been stored as long as six months.

INDEX TO RECIPES

INDEX TO RECIPES